ELECTING OUR MASTERS

ELECTING OUR MASTERS

THE HUSTINGS IN BRITISH POLITICS FROM HOGARTH TO BLAIR

JON LAWRENCE

OXFORD

UNIVERSITY PRESS

OXFORD
UNIVERSITY PRESS

Great Clarendon Street, Oxford OX2 6DP

Oxford University Press is a department of the University of Oxford.
It furthers the University's objective of excellence in research, scholarship,
and education by publishing worldwide in

Oxford New York

Auckland Cape Town Dar es Salaam Hong Kong Karachi
Kuala Lumpur Madrid Melbourne Mexico City Nairobi
New Delhi Shanghai Taipei Toronto

With offices in

Argentina Austria Brazil Chile Czech Republic France Greece
Guatemala Hungary Italy Japan Poland Portugal Singapore
South Korea Switzerland Thailand Turkey Ukraine Vietnam

Oxford is a registered trade mark of Oxford University Press
in the UK and in certain other countries

Published in the United States
by Oxford University Press Inc., New York

British Library Cataloguing in Publication Data

Data available

Library of Congress Cataloging in Publication Data

Lawrence, Jon.
Electing our masters: the hustings in British politics from Hogarth to Blair/Jon Lawrence.
p. cm.
Includes bibliographical references and index.
ISBN 978-0-19-955012-8
1. Elections—Great Britain—History. 2. Political campaigns—Great Britain—History. 3. Great
Britain—Politics and government—18th century. 4. Great Britain—Politics and government—19th
century. 5. Great Britain—Politics and government—20th century. I. Title.
JN955.L38 2009
324.941—dc22   2008050974

Typeset by Laserwords Private Ltd, Chennai, India
Printed in Great Britain
on acid-free paper by
the MPG Books Group

ISBN 978-0-19-955012-8

1 3 5 7 9 10 8 6 4 2

To Joe

Acknowledgements

THIS book has not been as long in the making as *Speaking for the People*, but it has taken quite long enough for me still to relish the moment when it is finally ready to be set free on the world. *Electing Our Masters* began life while I was visiting professor at Harvard University in 2002–3. If I recall correctly, I had intended to use the year to write a book on political violence in Britain during the first half of the twentieth century. But I quickly realized, firstly, that I had already said most of what I wanted to say on this subject, and, secondly, that there was a great deal I had left unsaid about political communication in modern Britain in *Speaking for the People*. That book, as its title suggests, was concerned primarily with deconstructing politicians' claims to 'represent' others. In addition, its chronological range, 1867–1914, was rather modest, as befits a project that started life as a Ph.D. Already alarmed that many historians seemed to have interpreted the call to 'take political language seriously' as meaning that only political language now mattered, I wanted to develop some of the non-linguistic themes central to *Speaking for the People*. The persistence of low-level violence in British politics was one such theme, hence the aborted project, but this was merely one facet of the issue that really interested me: namely the issue of political *interaction* (the history of how politicians and public have interacted). In *Electing Our Masters* this issue is explored primarily through the prism of electioneering, although attention is also paid to what politicians like to call 'peacetime' activities such as 'nursing', 'surgeries', and public relations. This, to my shame, is probably because I am old enough and sad enough still to find elections interesting, occasionally even exciting. Long since cured of hard-core politicking by fatherhood and the electoral necessities of the 'third way', there remains, nonetheless, a part of my soul that has been indelibly stamped by canvass cards, ward newsletters, and 'Sunday visiting' programmes. Critics might argue that these things have left me with an exaggerated sense both of the gulf between voters and political activists, and of the redeeming qualities of most politicians. Personally, I just hope that they help me to make the inherent paradoxes of politics more human and understandable.

Since my rather barbed comments about unsolicited manuscripts in *Speaking for the People*, no one has had the temerity to send me a whole typescript for comment, and so naturally I have not felt licensed to inflict *Electing Our Masters* on anyone in return. That said, I have nonetheless amassed many intellectual debts over the past six years, and it is a pleasure to be able to acknowledge them here. Once again, Jane Elliott has read more of the manuscript than anyone, and has also lived with it in many other ways—my debt to her is immeasurable, and is probably best repaid in deeds rather than words. My graduate students, past and present, have contributed much to the development of this project, both by reading specific chapters and, more generally, by arguing me out of some of my more pig-headed ideas. I owe a particular debt in this respect to Vee Barbary, Laura Beers, Chris Cotton, Kit Good, Gary Love, David Thackeray, and Geraint Thomas. I have naturally also learnt much from colleagues at my three institutional homes since 2002: Liverpool, Harvard, and now Cambridge. In each I was lucky enough to have colleagues prepared to give generously of their time and ideas—I hope they will forgive me for not listing them all by name. Many others have also influenced the development of this book, including Krista Cowman, Matthew Cragoe, Jim Cronin, Andy Davies, David Feldman, Steve Fielding, Chris Hilliard, Susan Kingsley Kent, Helen McCarthy, Susan Pedersen, Paul Readman, Matthew Roberts, Miles Taylor, James Thompson, and James Vernon. I thank them all, both for their friendship and for their sage advice. I would also like to thank Pauline Stafford, my head of department at Liverpool, for generously allowing me research leave to work on this book only to be repaid by my following my partner south before the RAE. It will doubtless be some consolation that the book missed the state's latest widget-counting exercise by some margin. Although I have not yet had leave from Cambridge, I would like to thank both the university authorities and the Master and Fellows of Emmanuel College for providing me with a stimulating and congenial intellectual home since 2004—invaluable privileges that I never take for granted.

I also owe a considerable debt to the Economic and Social Research Council which funded the project 'Electing John Bull: The changing face of British elections, 1895–1935' (ESRC RES-000-22-0345). The research findings from this project are used extensively in Chapters 3 and 4. Finally, I would like to thank the institutions and people whose professionalism has done so much to facilitate the research for this volume. Since coming to Cambridge I have made particularly heavy use of the holdings of the University Library and the Churchill Archives Centre, and I would like to thank them for their help, and for permission to quote from the rich archival material in their possession. I would also like to extend my thanks to Bristol University Library Special Collections, especially the ever-helpful Hannah Lowery, the Bristol Record Office, the British Library of Political and Economic Science (LSE), the British Library, Devon Record Office (Exeter), Harvard's Baker, Houghton, and Widener libraries, the Labour History Archive and Study Centre, Manchester (with special thanks to Darren Treadwell), Manchester Archives, the University of Nottingham Manuscripts and Special Collections, Oswestry Public Library, the Bodleian Library, Oxford, the Parliamentary Archives, Shropshire Archives (Shrewsbury), the Sydney Jones Library (Liverpool), and Westminster Public Library. I must also thank those people and institutions who have supplied me with copies of images in their possession. For permission to reproduce these images in the present volume I am grateful to the Rt. Hon. Tony Benn (Figure 15), the British Library (Figure 11), Getty Images (Figure 14), PA Photos (Figures 17, 18, and the jacket), and the Syndics of Cambridge University Library (for their kind permission to reproduce Figures 1 to 6, 9, 10, 12, and 13). Finally, I would like to thank Christopher Wheeler, Matthew Cotton, and Kate Hind at OUP for believing in this project, and Heather Watson, my painstaking copy-editor, for helping me to rediscover the semicolon.

But *Electing Our Masters* is dedicated to Joe, who once helped save me from politics, and who now stands on the brink of citizenship himself—indeed if Brown, like Wilson, seeks to save his skin by lowering the age of majority he might be a voter before this book is even published. Joe is probably the biggest reason why I have not produced more widgets over the past fifteen years, and I can't begin to tell him how rewarding and life-affirming that has been.

Cambridge
May 2008

Contents

List of Figures

Abbreviations

BBC	British Broadcasting Corporation
BL	British Library
BLPES	British Library of Political and Economic Science
BRO	Bristol Record Office
BSE	Bovine spongiform encephalopathy ('mad-cow disease')
CAC	Churchill Archives Centre, Cambridge
CAJ	*Conservative Agents' Journal*
CND	Campaign for Nuclear Disarmament
CUL	Cambridge University Library
DRO	Devon Record Office
ENG	Electronic news gathering
ESRC	Economic and Social Research Council
GKL	Goldsmiths'-Kress Library of Economic Literature
ILN	*Illustrated London News*
ILP	Independent Labour Party
IRA	Irish Republican Army (Provisional)
ITN	Independent Television News
ITV	Independent Television
LCC	London County Council
LO	*Labour Organiser*
MO	Mass Observation
MP	Member of Parliament
NHS	National Health Service
PA	Press Association
PR	Public relations
RHS	Royal Historical Society
SDP	Social Democratic Party

Introduction

The Spirit of the Hustings

When Winston Churchill tried to explain Lord Rosebery's failure to realize his full potential as a politician, despite having succeeded Gladstone as Prime Minister in 1894, he concluded that Rosebery's greatest handicap had been that he never adapted to the demands of democratic politics. Having inherited an Earldom and over 20,000 acres at the age of 20, Rosebery had never cut his teeth on electoral politics, unlike many young Victorian aristocrats. Here lay the Liberal grandee's fatal flaw: 'He would not stoop; he did not conquer.' Churchill himself professed to dislike elections, but he was adamant that by the 1890s no one could succeed in politics without 'practical experience of its rough and slatternly foundations'. According to Churchill, Rosebery had possessed the skills to succeed. We are told that he 'captivated great meetings', but he knew nothing of the very different atmosphere of an election 'with its disorderly gatherings, its organized oppositions, its hostile little meetings, its jeering throng, its stream of disagreeable and often silly questions'. It was here, Churchill argued, not in grand meetings for 'ardent supporters ... marshalled in overwhelming strength', that the modern politician proved his fitness to govern. As Churchill put it, in an election 'Dignity may suffer, the superfine gloss is soon worn away ... much has to be accepted with a shrug, a sigh or a smile; but at any rate in the end one knows a good deal about what happens and why.' By this reckoning, Rosebery's failure was that he 'would not go through the laborious, vexatious and at times humiliating processes' of modern democratic politics. At one level it was a harsh, even unfair, judgement—sitting in the House of Lords from 1868 Rosebery was effectively barred from meaningful experience of electoral politics. But

Churchill was making a larger point: that Rosebery lacked the will and the temperament to cope with the rough and tumble of electoral politics—with the 'spirit of the hustings'—and that, as such, he was bound to fail. It had not always been so. Few front-rank politicians had experienced genuine popular elections in the first half of the nineteenth century, and even in the 1890s the Marquess of Salisbury was able to lead the Conservatives, and the country, from the House of Lords. True, he had once sat in the Commons, but even there he never faced a contested election.[1]

But Salisbury was the last Prime Minister to lead Britain from the Lords. In the twentieth century Conservative leaders such as Curzon and Halifax found that membership of the upper chamber effectively barred them from the premiership and in 1963 the Earl of Home famously renounced his peerages and fought a Parliamentary by-election on succeeding Macmillan as Conservative leader and Prime Minister. But was Churchill right to argue that experience of electoral politics had become essential for the modern politician, and, more especially, was he right to stress that it was above all the chastening, even humbling, aspects of electoral politics that represented the vital right of passage to high office? *Electing Our Masters* sets out to answer these questions by exploring the shifting relationship between politicians and the public from that late eighteenth century to the present. Its principal focus is the changing character of electioneering across this period, and its central thesis is that elections offer us a unique window on the historical evolution of British democracy. The book seeks to answer three fundamental questions about British politics. First, has the 'spirit of the hustings', where rival candidates came face-to-face with an often irreverent public, been a defining and enduring feature of the British way of voting? Second, how has Britain's long and sometimes turbulent history of electioneering shaped the political system we know today both for good and for ill? Third, is there still a place for the 'spirit of the hustings' in modern, mediated politics, and in particular, can the broadcast media be expected to sustain a public sphere within which politicians and public continue to meet on more or less equal terms?

The aim is therefore to offer more than a technical history of election-eering since the late eighteenth century. Elections represent one of the few moments when politicians and public are brought into direct, face-to-face contact with each other. How (and how much) this happens has naturally changed dramatically since 1800, but even today politicians routinely meet members of the public in doorstep canvassing, on walkabouts, and in broadcasting studios (though for the most part they no longer meet them in that classic location that so appealed to Churchill: the open public meeting). This book seeks to chart and explain these processes of change. As such, it is, first and foremost, not a history of electioneering per se, but rather a history of the changing dynamics of political interaction in modern Britain. Political communication is thus a central concern throughout, but the focus is less on technical change, important though that undoubtedly was, than on what culture has done with technology. In other words, how new possibilities for political communication, from advances in print technology, through radio and television to the internet, have been reconciled with the custom and practice of British politics. At all stages the theme of political interaction—direct and mediated—is kept centre stage. More technical, back-stage aspects of electioneering practice, such as registration work and canvassing (or now candidates' blogs), are discussed only through this prism.

In classic historian's style, this is a story of continuity and change over the long term, but it is resolutely not a simple 'Whig' history of progress. Nor, perhaps more importantly, is it an 'anti-Whig' history dominated by narratives of loss or decline. For one thing, politics is so resolutely present-centred that one continuously finds its practitioners proclaiming the 'newness' of things that had been routine a generation earlier—the continual rediscovery of commercial advertising between the 1900s and 1980s is perhaps the most glaring example. But more fundamentally, direct, face-to-face political interaction has neither been wholly banished from the political system, nor was it ever an unequivocally benign phenomenon. It is all too easy to romanticize the old ways in politics—to celebrate a supposed golden age when politicians and public met face-to-face at the hustings. But we should not forget that such ritualized exchanges were often far from inclusive—there was always a strong premium on boorish masculinity, while even the wittiest, most decorous exchange between heckler and politician rarely managed to elevate debate much above the level of the modern sound bite. Nor should we assume that the 'hustings' were necessarily democratic in their effects. These dramas of symbolic social levelling were tightly scripted, and tended both to emphasize the gulf between politician and public, and, ultimately, to affirm the right of the political class to rule (hence their appeal to Churchill).

Nonetheless, the performative aspects of public politics still matter. Theatricality and performance lay at the heart both of classic, face-to-face exchanges between voter and politician on the 'stomp', and of most modern, mediated forms of campaigning, where communication is indirect and usually one-way. Until the inter-war period, and the advent of radio and cinema newsreels, it was face-to-face interaction that dominated British public politics, and all but monopolized electioneering. True, politicians could also reach the public through the medium of the press, with its near-verbatim reports of major speeches, but as Joseph Meisel reminds us, the *theatre* of the platform was always as important as the speech itself.[2] Hence the enormous space devoted by the provincial press to the 'incidentals' of political meetings—to processions, entertainments, and 'personalities,' but, most of all, to interactions between speaker and audience. The meeting represented a highly charged social situation that many politicians found taxing and distasteful. This partly reflected the sheer physical ordeal of the stomp, but it was also because many disliked the need to act a part—to show false humility before the masses, and to dress and speak in a stylized manner (election manuals were full of useful advice about avoiding evening wear, fancy language, and, most of all, condescension). On other hand, some undoubtedly relished the chance to 'play' the crowd—one thinks of Lloyd George, Churchill, or Aneurin Bevan—or simply to 'play a part'. For instance, northern industrialists such as the Blackburn cotton magnate 'Sir Harry' Hornby ('th' owd Gam' Cock') displaying his command of local dialect and folkore, or Newcastle's Joseph Cowen wearing workman's corduroy and fustian despite being a wealthy gentleman, fully integrated into county society. There are also plenty of well-known late twentieth-century equivalents of such role-playing. Success stories such as Macmillan's 'make-over' for television politics in the late 1950s, Wilson's cultivation of a 'solid' pipe rather than his habitual 'flashy' cigar, Thatcher's voice training under the influence of Gordon Reece; but also disasters like William Hague's baseball cap, Neil Kinnock's lapses into the role of boisterous rock-star, and just about anything to do with Sir Alec Douglas-Home as televisual icon.[3]

Politics as performance matters because interaction and mediation are at the heart of public politics. By focusing on political interaction, we focus on the key point at which two very separate worlds collide—the formal political world of 'representation' and the informal political world of everyday life. We can learn much about the dynamics of public politics from dissecting the highly charged social interactions that take place in this space, but we can also learn a good deal about social and cultural change in a broader sense. Throughout the nineteenth century electoral politics were as much about entertainment as they were about policy. Voters, and especially non-voters, went to meetings to 'have their say', but also to have some fun. As late as 1930, Patrick Donner recalled a burly Islington navvy whacking his tearful young son, as eggs, tomatoes, and insults began to fly at one of his meetings, and then shouting: 'What's the matter with you? Isn't this better than a cinema?' One suspects that the child thought not, but it was certainly cheaper—and that still mattered a good deal before the onset of post-war affluence.[4]

One thing is certain: from the eighteenth century until after the Second World War, British elections demanded that politicians, however mighty, should humble themselves before open and often decidedly irreverent meetings of their constituents. It was one of the great attractions of the so-called 'pocket boroughs' abolished by the 1832 Reform Act that such seats protected politicians from the indignities of a popular election. Down to 1872, the brutal rituals of the nomination hustings were central to British electioneering. Here politicians were obliged to attend an open-air public meeting of their constituents—including non-electors as well as electors—at which their nomination would be confirmed, they would address the gathered multitude, and then a vote by show of hands would be held. The losing candidate would invariably demand a formal election, confined solely to registered voters, but the nomination day hustings nonetheless provided an important ritual of political inclusion and democratic levelling. Indeed elections as a whole demanded that the high and the mighty should learn to cultivate the 'common touch'. As John Markham has observed, at a mid-nineteenth-century election, 'the young heir to a peerage had to face a barrage of abuse from the "lower orders" and the humble freeman voter was temporarily courted by his betters'.[5]

The overlap between social, economic, and political power was very close throughout the eighteenth and nineteenth centuries. Not all rich men chose to go into politics, but virtually all men involved in politics were rich, often very rich. This was mainly because politics was an expensive business. MPs remained unsalaried until 1911, and candidates were expected to meet the full administrative costs of an election until 1918. Moreover, the cost of actually fighting an election was higher still, even where a constituency was not manifestly corrupt. Electioneering itself was costly—massively so by late twentieth-century standards—but candidates were also expected to spend lavishly in other ways. Local party organization needed to be subsidized, full-time agents and their assistants had to be employed, and potentially most expensive of all, constituencies had to be 'nursed' through systematic donations to local charitable (and not so charitable) causes. Moreover, many wealthy candidates went much further, winning fame and goodwill in their constituency through extraordinary acts of generosity: endowing a hospital or university, laying out a public park, or building a library.

Hence at one level, nineteenth-century elections can be read as ritualized celebrations of Britain's unequal, hierarchical society: rich and powerful men spent lavishly on public goods, and in return were affirmed as leaders of their community through the elaborate theatre of a public election. By this reading, people did not so much elect their masters to power as confirm the legitimacy of their masters' existing power through election. But it was rarely quite so simple. For one thing, elections could be contested—although in practice most were not until well into the nineteenth century—so that the affirmation of one 'natural' leader necessarily meant the rejection of another. They could also be about more than a candidate's status as a good, beneficent patron: they could be about *issues* such as political reform, religious freedom, or agricultural protection. But perhaps most importantly, as the comments above suggest, if, for the most part, elections ultimately affirmed class hierarchies, they did so by temporarily denying the full, brutal power of those hierarchies. At the most basic level, candidates were expected humbly to canvass the 'independent voters' for their support even when open voting meant that many of those voters were far from 'independent' in practice. But perhaps most importantly, candidates were also expected to take part in the public rituals that surrounded the election—rituals such as the ceremonial entry to the constituency, the nomination hustings, the declaration and the chairing of victorious candidates, all of which brought them into direct contact with the general public.

True, election rituals hardly brought the powerful and powerless together as equals, but they were at least recognized as interconnected members of a supposedly healthy, functioning community. Even rituals which appeared to encapsulate unequal, hierarchical relationships, such as chairing the victor, still involved wealthy politicians placing their well-being in the hands of the populace. Moreover, election ceremonies were always as much about celebrating communal identities as about acknowledging loyalty to the great man. They also tended to place politicians in considerable peril. Raised precariously above the crowd, candidates made an easy target for malcontents and were almost wholly dependent on their supporters for their personal safety, as Hogarth's *Chairing the Members* underlined for comic effect (see Fig. 1). Similarly, whilst the nomination hustings might raise candidates physically above the crowd, they also underlined the strong obligation on them to make a good show of addressing their constituents (see Fig. 2). Protected from the hurly-burly of the crowd, if not necessarily from stray missiles, candidates were expected to put up with a good deal of derisive and boorish behaviour in the name of 'accountability' and letting the people 'have their say'. And since the hustings could usually be reached only by progressing through the same volatile crowd, candidates also frequently had to put up with a good deal of rough usage both before and after their nomination. In a rigidly class-bound and unequal society, the spirit of the hustings represented a rare opportunity for Markham's 'lower orders' to let off steam at their masters' expense.

But what has all this to do with modern electioneering—hasn't everything changed since the first half of the nineteenth century? Well, yes and no. By the 1870s the hustings and open voting had disappeared, but in other respects the class dynamics of British politics remained little altered. The candidate's election meetings now became the principal site for symbolic acts of social levelling, and politicians, such as Rosebery, who shunned this arena, struggled to establish themselves as credible democratic leaders. But by 1918, not only had the cost of fighting an election been drastically reduced,[6] Labour's emergence as a powerful independent force had ended any pretence that politics was still a gentlemen's closed shop. When Patrick Donner asked Sir Arthur Benn about securing a Conservative candidacy in 1930, Benn, who had recently lost his Plymouth seat after almost two decades in Parliament, asked if he was serious when 'Labour Members cut their toe-nails in the library' (and, he might have added, many seize every opportunity to mock and insult 'gentleman' MPs as mercilessly as any heckler).[7] The class dynamics of elections were similarly transformed. Elections could no longer be about the symbolic, if temporary, disavowal of class difference when almost every contest involved a Labour candidate. True, few Labour candidates were still at the work-bench by the time they entered politics, but even fewer had been to the manor born.[8] There had, of course, always been room for a few impecunious men of talent in British politics, but henceforth the professional politician became the norm. Initially, the distinctive class origins of many Labour leaders probably obscured this shift. But by the close of the twentieth century few Labour candidates remained plausibly plebeian. In many respects, the class gulf between candidates and voters had been restored—most politicians, unlike most voters, were now professionally qualified as well as professionally political. But it was probably their membership of 'the political class', rather than the upper class, that now most defined their 'otherness'.

Labour's emergence had itself been linked to broader political and social changes, not least the incremental shift to a fully democratic franchise between 1867 and 1928 (although it was only in 1948 that Labour finally ushered in a strict system of one-person-one-vote by abolishing business votes, university seats, and the few surviving double-member boroughs). Historians have long debated whether Labour's breakthrough after 1918 was mainly a consequence of that year's reform act, which finally ushered in universal male suffrage and broke the sex-bar on citizenship (enfranchising over eight million women, mainly wives over 30). It is now generally accepted that the transformation of the electorate in class terms was relatively minor, especially compared to the transformation in terms of gender and age.[9] From the 1880s male heads of household had found it relatively easy to qualify for the vote, almost regardless of their social class—unless, that is, they were very poor. Down to 1914, pauper disqualification and the vagaries of the tenement vote continued to work against the poorest, especially in the big cities, although some still made it onto the electoral register.[10] But the 1918 Act abolished pauper disqualification and eased the tough Victorian residency requirements—overnight the politics of poverty were transformed. Henceforth, British politics would be more about the largesse of governments rather than of candidates—a trend that had already begun to take shape before the war, notably with the 'New' Liberals' introduction of non-contributory state pensions and state-supported national insurance (Lloyd George famously sought to refute charges that National Insurance represented a new 'poll tax' by proclaiming that workers would get 'nine pence for four pence').

But this is a book more about the culture of politics than its content—throughout issues play a back-seat to questions about the broader social and cultural meaning of the interaction between politicians and public. Crucially, it starts from the assumption that the irreverent spirit of the hustings lived on long after the formal abolition of public nomination and open voting in 1872. Plebeian traditions of heckling, disruption, and mockery resurfaced in new contexts, most obviously in the election meeting, which grew massively in importance from the 1870s. Moreover, it was not simply that the spirit of the hustings persisted despite the best intentions of Britain's political elites. On the contrary, Britain's tempestuous election culture remained widely accepted as an inevitable, even legitimate, feature of a healthy political system. Heckling came to be seen as a cherished, rough-and-ready means of testing the mettle of would-be MPs, while more disorderly forms of popular intervention were also widely excused as examples of 'high spirited' enthusiasm. During the nineteenth century there developed a widespread belief that the public possessed the right, not only to see their would-be political masters in the flesh, but also to inter-rogate them on questions of policy and on their personal fitness to govern. What this meant was that elections obliged British politicians to submit themselves to intense and often deeply disrespectful public scrutiny not once, at the nomination-day hustings, but daily at open meetings across their constituency. Perhaps significantly, Victorian and Edwardian election manuals advised candidates that there was no personal indignity that should not be borne with grim forbearance, or better still, with cheery goodwill, during a campaign. But above all, politicians were not to become 'tainted' by the crowd—they must not abandon the gentlemanly virtues of restraint and self-control that marked them off from 'the mass' and defined their claim to be fit and proper leaders. Hence Rudyard Kipling's injunction: 'If you can talk with crowds and keep your virtue | Or walk with kings—nor lose the common touch' ('If—' (1895)). In his mammoth Victorian history of the political platform, Henry Jephson observed that in terms both of lan-guage and actions 'a special amount of latitude has always been allowed to the persons participating in [election meetings]'.[11] Hence Seymour Lloyd's advice, in 1909, that 'even gross discourtesy' was 'best met by unswerving good humour'.[12] But then 'heckle' was no gentle word—it derivation was from the 'hackle', a steel-pinned comb for splitting flax—and it often seemed as though the heckler's principal objective at a meeting was to try and raise the candidate's hackles, thereby undermining his efforts to come across as a man of 'hearty genial disposition, with a kindly ready word, and a warm shake of the hand for everybody', as one late Victorian advice manual described the candidate's ideal public persona.[13]

The age-old contest between heckler and speaker at British elections can therefore be read as a highly developed manifestation of class war. On one level, heckling simply underscored the forced egalitarianism of an election—even the most powerful politicians were expected to answer their assailants' questions, and to do so with civility. But it was also a tactic for testing the sincerity of a politician's self-presentation as a good sport, 'perfectly free of any tinge of condescension'.[14] Candidates were told that they must not be 'above entering the abode of the labourer and asking after the wife and children', and that they must never put on airs or demonstrate a sense of moral or social superiority.[15] Like Rosebery, those who failed to display this 'common touch' had limited prospects in British politics by the late nineteenth century. Writing just after the First World War, the liberal journalist C. E. Montague claimed that ex-servicemen had come to distrust Liberal politicians because they saw them as 'preaching the brotherhood of nations but not knowing how to speak without offence to a workman from their own village'.[16] And for every politician who relished the challenges of electioneering, with its constant battle of wits and will-power, there was another for whom it was a grim ordeal from start to finish. Facing his third General Election in 1923, Neville Chamberlain confessed that he hated 'this beastly election campaign', although he was quick to acknowledge that 'it has to be endured with all the indignities & humiliations which it involves'. The following year, after the sudden collapse of MacDonald's minority Labour government, he professed to feel sickened at the prospect of having to face another 'ordeal of humiliation' at the polls.[17] Similarly, in the aftermath of the 1951 election, the Conservative MP and diarist 'Chips' Channon recorded, 'I still feel as if I have been squeezed dry. Indeed an election is like a violent love affair; one must be charming all the time; one is keyed up and every ounce of vigour and vitality goes.'[18]

But if electioneering, and especially the rigours of the public meeting, represented an unwelcome ordeal for many politicians, such rituals none-theless remained a central aspect of British elections so long as constituents demanded them. After the First World War many politicians began to doubt the utility of meetings as means of mobilizing mass support. They also became fearful that the continuation of unruly electoral politics might simultaneously alienate the new female voters and encourage post-war mili-tants who were preaching doctrines of class war and revolution (or fascist counter-revolution). But whilst these years witnessed a concerted effort to reform the disorderly customs associated with the old 'masculinist' political system, there was no attempt to break with the tradition that the open meeting represented the centre-piece of electioneering. Despite claims to the contrary, the rapid growth of new communication media such as radio and cinema newsreels in the first half of the twentieth century did little to dent popular participation in electoral politics, especially for the many for whom the diversions of commercial leisure were simply too costly (such as Donner's Islington navvy). But things were very different with the rise of television from the 1950s. Even before the BBC ended its self-imposed moratorium on election news coverage in 1959, commentators had begun to bemoan lacklustre election meetings and poor attendances. Despite Aneurin Bevan's sterling efforts, platform oratory was at a discount in the 1950s—most meetings were sober, rational affairs shaped by a powerful ethos of civic duty rather than popular entertainment. With the advent of televised campaigning in 1959, audiences as well as speakers began to question the continued utility of sober, didactic political meetings. After Sir Alec Douglas-Home's disorderly televised meetings in 1964, politicians of all parties also became increasingly wary of the risks involved in holding traditional open meetings during an election. By the mid-1960s, electioneering was already being repackaged for the television age, and interaction with the electorate was increasingly confined to carefully choreographed photo-opportunities timed to catch the broadcast news bulletins. By the 1970s election meetings had become little more than private rallies of the faithful—staged partly to boost the morale of party workers, but mainly as news events for the press and broadcasting media. True, many politicians continued to undertake personal canvassing and public walkabouts during the campaign, but here they could generally rely on a strong entourage of party 'minders' to save them from any awkward interactions with real voters.

However, despite these dramatic changes, the television age did not liberate politicians from the trials of public interrogation. Just as many of the traditions associated with the hustings had been transferred to election meetings after 1872, so many of the traditions associated with election meetings reappeared in new forms in the late twentieth century. Perhaps most striking was the rise of the television interviewer to take over the mantle of the persistent heckler at public meetings. But the public proper has not been wholly excluded from modern, mediated politics—face-to-face interaction survives in many forms. Public meetings may have all but disappeared, but they have been replaced by new forms of public accountability which are in many respects more onerous for the politician. Well into the twentieth century, most politicians believed that 'accountability' required little more than ensuring that an agent replied to constituents' letters, holding an annual 'meeting of account' in the constituency, and maintaining a high public profile during the election. Today, most not only hold weekly local 'surgeries' (a fascinatingly pathological term which hints at the unequal, cliental relationship at the heart of these exchanges), but they also spend as much time as possible in local publicity stunts in the hope of gaining positive coverage in the local press and on regional broadcast media. Most also seize every opportunity to be involved in the plethora of radio phone-ins and studio discussion programmes which involve members of the general public. Such programmes are, as one aide to Tony Blair noted in 2005, the modern equivalent of Gladstone's public meetings.[19] In this sense electioneering has ceased to be something confined to elections. In what Americans would call our 24/7 media age, politicians are always campaigning, and well-timed interventions from the public can therefore always derail the politician's message—as farm worker Craig Evans and health protester Sharron Storer both dramatically demonstrated during the otherwise uneventful 2001 General Election.

In 2005, with Blair's political credentials greatly tarnished, the Prime Minister actively pursued bruising encounters with real voters in what came to be known as his 'masochism strategy', though his preferred venue was the relatively controlled environment of the TV studio, rather than the street. There was a strong parallel here with John Major's self-consciously anachronistic rediscovery of the soapbox in the 1992 General Election. In both cases beleaguered Prime Ministers sought to rebuild their credibility by demonstrating their willingness, not simply to listen to voters, but to do so in a context which emphasized both accountability and vulnerability. In such encounters the 'spirit of the hustings' appeared to be alive and well in the era of mass media politics. But we should not be complacent. For one thing, there is no strong obligation on politicians to take part in such bruising face-to-face encounters. Like Margaret Thatcher in 1987, a politician sitting comfortably in the polls could probably still afford to delegate such potentially difficult media encounters to an under-study (Norman Tebbit filled the bill for Thatcher in 1987, until the fall-out from 'Wobbly Thursday' smoked her out into the open for the last week). Additionally, we need to recognize that unlike the hustings or the election meeting, modern, televised forms of political interaction rely entirely on the mediating role of professional broadcasters. It is they who decide whose questions will be heard on a phone-in or studio discussion programme, whose impromptu intervention in the campaign will be covered in the news bulletins, and, of course, who actually gets to sit in a studio audience in the first place. Whereas once it was politicians themselves who helped sustain a public culture of face-to-face political interaction, it is now principally broadcasters who fulfil that role, and it is therefore to them that we must look if we wish to see the 'spirit of the hustings' nurtured and developed in modern British politics.

I

John Bull at the Hustings: Electoral Politics from the Ancien Regime to the Second Reform Act

The theatre of the hustings

O n the surface there would appear to be little in common between the disorderly excesses of an eighteenth- or early nineteenth-century election, and the much more sober electoral politics of modern times. Hanoverian elections were dominated by elaborate civic rituals, such as the candidates' procession into the constituency, the nomination 'hustings', and open voting, which made them intensely public affairs involving electors and non-electors alike. The public nomination ceremony, where rival candidates were expected to address their constituents from the hustings, has been seen as an important ritual symbolizing the inclusion of non-electors in the unreformed political system. Not only did the hustings allow non-electors to 'have their say' by demonstrating which candidates enjoyed their support (and opposition), but they also allowed for an open vote by show of hands. True, the defeated party could then simply call for a formal poll confined to the qualified electors, but this public demonstration of popular involvement has rightly been seen as vital to the perceived legitimacy of public politics in the era before the 1832 Great Reform Act. Moreover, public involvement did not necessarily stop with symbolic demonstrations of partisanship such as wearing party favours, shouting for and against the various candidates, voting by show of hands at the hustings, or chairing the victor after the poll. As O'Gorman has argued, election rituals were also ripe for irreverent displays of mimicry and mockery. Candidates' speeches might be drowned in a cacophony of 'rough music' or coarse plebeian wit, while public ceremonies intended to promote the candidate could be mercilessly parodied. Mock chairings featuring paupers, mill girls, or even animals were commonplace, as were similarly irreverent mock processions mimicking a candidate's entry into the constituency at the beginning of a campaign. One must also remember that voting itself remained an open, public act—the secret ballot was only introduced in 1872—and that this too gave ample opportunity for the politically excluded to 'have their say' at the expense of their supposed social superiors.[1]

The public rituals associated with electioneering represented moments of social levelling that were quite exceptional in a society that remained, in most other respects, intensely hierarchical and status bound. As *Blackwood's Magazine* recalled in 1883, early nineteenth-century elections had represented 'ten days' saturnalia of freedom and equality, of licence and lawyers, when the tenant and the landlord met on equal terms, and the small tradesman could shake his finger at Mr Magnum'. In fact until 1785, when polling was restricted to a maximum of fifteen days, the saturnalia of the election had been almost without limit—with the poll usually closing only when one side finally conceded the inevitability of defeat. The previous year, polling at the closely fought Bristol election had lasted continuously (bar Sundays and Easter) from 3 April to 8 May, a total of thirty-one days of 'licence and lawyers', while at Westminster the contest had lasted the full 40 days permitted under an Act of 1696. Throughout that time, beer would have flowed freely, and even the humblest freeman voter would have been conscious of holding the fate of his masters in his hand (always assuming he had not yet polled).[2]

By the early nineteenth century, national political issues were increasingly to be found forcing their way into constituency campaigns—particularly in relation to the politics of war, trade, and religion. Candidates' ritualized speeches from the hustings, and at the end of each day's polling, took on a more strongly political tone, while it also became increasingly common to inject national political issues into more informal meetings with constituents at local clubs or on market days. At the same time, outside pressure groups began to harness the inclusive rituals of electioneering to promote single-issue causes, especially after the 1832 Reform Act. Both the Ten Hours Movement, campaigning for the legislative restriction of the hours of labour for women and children, and later the Chartists, whose demand was for radical political reform including universal male suffrage, sought to mobilize the non-electors at the hustings. At the 1832 election, Richard Oastler's Ten Hours Movement implored electors and those '*not thought worthy* of that Privilege' to 'come and speak your minds' at nomination hustings across the west Yorkshire textile region. Their aim was simple: to ensure that '*Yorkshire* Slavery as well as *Black* Slavery be for ever abolished' by 'pledging the Candidates to a Ten Hour Bill'. The Chartists used similar tactics in 1841, calling on their supporters to expose the injustice of the 'reformed' franchise of 1832 by flocking to the hustings to ensure that Chartist candidates won the show of hands, even if the 'privileged' voters then refused to elect them at the formal poll.[3]

Always intensely partisan affairs, the hustings were frequently also distinctly disorderly. After their abolition (in 1872), *Blackwood's* recalled how candidates had been 'heckle[d] and occasionally pelt[ed] on the hustings', and public voting had taken place 'amid showers of cabbage stalks and rotten eggs'. At Leeds, in 1832, supporters of the radical tory (and Ten Hours campaigner) Michael Sadler clashed with their Orange (Whig) opponents, apparently because the latter had sought to destroy a Ten Hour flag depicting 'the horrors of *infant slavery*'. In a poster issued on the eve of the poll, Sadler attacked Edward Baines and his fellow Whig leaders for urging 'their obedient Dupes' to attack the tory Blues, knowing that they 'themselves [were] safe within the Hustings'. But though the Blues were portrayed as a 'Peaceable Party' attacked by a 'Band of Ruffians', their poster also celebrated 'the *dastardly flight* of the Orangemen' and regretted that Baines and the other Whig leaders had 'escaped their share of the Chastisement'. Opponents alleged that Sadler had himself been protected by an organized band of roughs, some armed with bludgeons, but in the poster it was the *spontaneous* violence of the crowd that was celebrated.[4]

It seems clear that at Leeds in 1832 both sides had gone to considerable lengths to surround themselves with bands of burly bodyguards, partly to ensure their personal safety, but also to intimidate their opponents. There was nothing unusual in this. At Bristol it was commonplace for candidates to hire 'bludgeon men', such as prize fighters or local shipwrights, to guard the steps to the city's Guildhall, where the poll was held. Their role was simple: to chase off the other side's hired muscle and then to assault any voter suspected of being opposed to their man. In 1830 the poll was moved to temporary hustings in the more open Queen's Square,

Fig. 1. William Hogarth's *Chairing the Members* (1758), reproduced with the kind permission of the Syndics of Cambridge University Library

where it was hoped that there would be less scope for such organized violence. This naturally raises questions about the role of 'the crowd' in the pre-reform system. Should the tumultuous scenes associated with Hanoverian elections, and captured in eighteenth-century prints such as Hogarth's famous *Chairing the Members* (Fig. 1), be dismissed as the artificial product of candidates' largesse and lavish treating—were they merely 'got up' crowds in thrall to their monied patrons? There can be little doubt that money did often represent a vital spur to eighteenth-century street politics. At Middlesex, in 1768, gangs of roughs, said to have been hired at a guinea a day, attacked Wilkite radicals at the poll, killing one man, and struck fear into the general populace by assaulting men and women indiscriminately in the street. Similarly, at Westminster in 1784 the Foxites alleged that 'banditti ... armed with bludgeons, staves and pistols' violently attacked their supporters, leaving many wounded and one dead. But if such organized disorder was all too commonplace, so too was *spontaneous* disorder and violence—indeed one begat the other. The very fact that wealthy politicians and their supporters were prepared to connive in disorderly behaviour gave licence to ordinary electors and non-electors to become the authors of their own electoral mayhem. For the most part this took a less sinister form—drunken rowdyism, cat-calls, perhaps casual stone-throwing and fist fights. But whilst the Victorian memoirist J. A. Bridges may have had a point when he described such scenes as the result of the poor's 'innate rowdyism, and a love of what they considered sport', in the right context such disorder could become overtly political. Indeed Bridges' own vignettes of mid-nineteenth-century electoral tumult reveal as much. For instance, we are told that in the 1860s, the Shropshire poor threw rabbit skins at supporters of Sir Baldwin Leighton because he had outraged local custom by prosecuting his keeper for selling game. In another constituency Conservatives apparently had chopped liver flicked at them during the election because a local tory dame had claimed that if the poor could not get enough good meat they should eat bullocks' liver instead. Patricia Lynch records a number of similar incidents from late nineteenth-century rural contests—at North Essex a barley cake was thrown onto the Conservative platform to symbolize the poor food that labourers had had to endure under protection, and at South Oxfordshire a dead cod was brandished at the meetings of a tory candidate alleged to have recommended cods' heads as suitable fare for the hungry poor (the class politics of food was clearly an emotive issue long before Edwardian Liberals sought to turn it to their advantage with their images of big and little loaves). But the sharp class overtones of the earlier episodes also remind us that the political crowd was never solely a creature of its wealthy would-be patrons.[5]

Given the volatility of the election crowd, the hustings were usually substantial structures capable of raising the candidates and their wealthy supporters high above the 'mob'. Indeed, after the 1832 Reform Act these structures appear to have become more and more elaborate, partly in order to house the growing number of press reporters and political hangers-on, partly to accommodate more individual polling booths (as required under the new act), but also to allow local tradesmen to extract even more cash from the candidates who had to bear the full cost of their construction (see Fig. 2). Of course even the hustings did not offer protection from missiles that were occasionally hurled from the crowd—missiles which could, quite literally, be animal, mineral, or vegetable (besides *Blackwood's* cabbage stalks and rotten eggs, overly zealous partisans were known to throw mud and stones, animal waste, and even dead animals—cats appear to have been a favoured weapon). Worse, candidates usually had to make a public procession to the hustings, forcing them to come face-to-face with the election crowd in all its irreverent high spirits. This could be a gruelling ordeal for any candidate, but it was one that it was wise not to evade. In 1837, at Totnes in Devon, Sir George Adams was mercilessly attacked as a closet tory who had 'run away on the eve of Battle' at the preceding election, rather than brave popular wrath at the hustings. This time he steeled himself to go to the poll, but was convincingly beaten by his two Whig opponents.[6]

Great weight was placed on a candidate's ability to display 'manly' courage and forbearance when faced by the indignities of a popular election. This meant displaying the stoical rather than the martial face of nineteenth-century 'masculinity'—candidates were expected to grin and bear it, and under no circumstances either to lose their temper or to descend, quite literally given the elevated nature of the hustings, to the level of the crowd. Ideas of 'manly' virtue were central to nineteenth-century electoral politics, not least through the near-ubiquitous rhetoric celebrating candidates' supposed 'manly independence'. In turn, elections themselves were often discussed as though they concerned only men, which, in terms of formal voting rights, was undoubtedly true. But just as vote-less men flocked to the hustings and the poll to join in the public

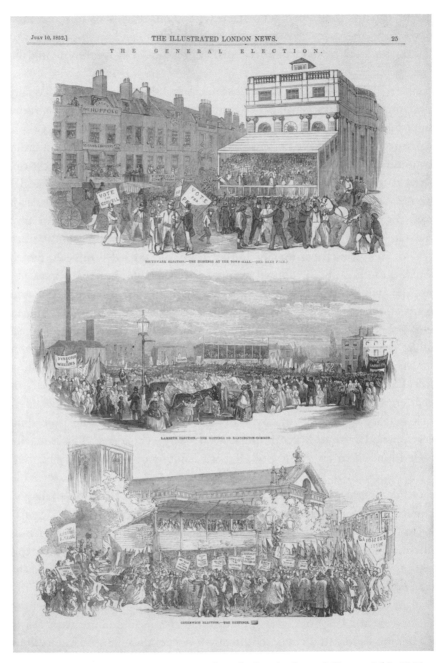

THE GENERAL ELECTION.

SOUTHWARK ELECTION.—THE HUSTINGS AT THE TOWN-HALL.—(SEE NEXT PAGE.)

LAMBETH ELECTION.—THE HUSTINGS ON KENNINGTON-COMMON.

GREENWICH ELECTION.—THE HUSTINGS.

Fig. 2. London hustings in 1852 (Southwark, Lambeth, and Greenwich), *ILN*, 10 July 1852, reproduced with the kind permission of the Syndics of Cambridge University Library

theatre of electioneering, so too did many women. Election literature
often emphasized their 'decorous' role in proceedings—as female relatives
supporting their menfolk on the hustings, or as genteel observers watching
proceedings from the safety of an upper-floor window. But such women
were still intensely partisan—as their propensity to bedeck themselves in
party favours proclaimed to all sides. Moreover, their less genteel sisters
often played a decidedly active part in election rituals. At Wakefield
in 1868, local mill-girls organized a mock chairing, with one of their
workmates dressed up in the Liberal colours. At Whitehaven in 1832,
female supporters of the tory 'Yellows' allegedly tore up the party flag of
a rival Whig 'blue' who was parading in their midst, and then severely
beat four apprentice carpenters who tried to steal a party favour from one
of their number. According to an admittedly partial source, 'in less than
two minutes, three of the carpenters were laid prostrate and made to kiss
their mother earth ... They were stripped of their colours.' Doubtless the
story was retold as a slur on the manliness of the Whitehaven 'blues', but
it nonetheless gives some insight into the licence that electioneering might
confer on female as well as male non-voters.[7]

As at Leeds, with its battles between Orange and Blue, or Whitehaven,
with its rowdy Yellows and Blues, eighteenth- and early nineteenth-
century electoral politics were everywhere strongly visual. During an
election vast sums would be spent distributing party favours such as flags,
ribbons, and neckties in the local colour of each party. Indeed, in many
constituencies the party was the colour—that is to say voters' primary
loyalties appeared to be to the cause of the 'Blues' or the 'Reds' against
their historic local enemies, rather than to national party factions at Westminster. When political symbolism was so highly charged, those keen to
promote single-issue causes such as anti-slavery, factory reform, or the
People's Charter often struggled to construct a public idiom that could
mobilize the customary visual language of politics without antagonizing
the partisan passions of one side or another. In the 1830s the Ten Hours
Movement, which sought to straddle the gulf between radical Toryism
and plebeian Radicalism, endeavoured to solve this problem by barring
the display of 'all Political banners, and party Colours of every Kind'
from its mass demonstrations. Instead, supporters were told to embrace
white as the (non-) colour for all flags, banners, and other regalia, supposedly to symbolize the purity of their cause. The Chartists chose a
different tack, embracing green as the movement's national colour, mindful

of its traditional associations with English radicalism. Radicals also had their own symbols to help mould a cohesive, solidaristic movement. Where the established parties often combined the visual symbolism of nation and locality (enmeshing family crests and emblems with powerful symbols of nation such as the Union flag), Radicals embraced a counter-iconography which valorized the symbols of honest labour and protest. Fergus O'Connor, controversial editor of the radical *Northern Star* and a leading Chartist, famously wore a rough fustian suit, while Richard Oastler was known to wear a torn coat—a battle honour from his struggles with the Leeds 'Bainesites' (significantly both were 'gentleman leaders' seeking ways of symbolizing their commitment to the workers' cause). They also embraced more overtly political symbols of dissent; the cap of liberty, with its connotations of republicanism, revolution, and liberation from slavery, the white hat associated with 'Orator' Hunt and the Peterloo massacre, and perhaps most provocatively, the Tricolour of revolutionary France.[8]

But this was an intensely verbal as well as visual political culture. Printed broadsheets, cartoons, and ballads played a prominent role in electioneering long before the Great Reform Act of 1832. Many were distinctly vulgar compared with the sober political pamphlets and leaflets that characterized the later nineteenth century. Charles Fox's contest at Westminster in 1784 generated much crude humour, not least because of the prominent part female Whig aristocrats such as Georgiana, Duchess of Devonshire played in the campaign. Tory election ballads sought to mock Fox for his dependence on this mobilization of female charms, although sexual innuendo often loomed larger than political critique in their ribald street literature. In one squib tories alleged that 'F-x has giv'n them many inches | Of his doodle do', while another appeared almost to be making excuses for their candidate's impending defeat,

> For if for the Man of the People you'll poll,
> You may tickle a Duchess's Tol de rol lol.
> When Devon's high Duchess the *thing* takes in hand,
> What man can refuse at her quarters to stand?

Such scurrilous versifying disappeared only slowly from British elections, despite the growing influence of a more puritan strand of Christian morality in the early nineteenth century. For instance, at Northumberland in 1826, opponents of the tory Henry Thomas Liddell distributed a four-line squib

'Breeches for Ever' which insinuated that Liddell's virility might be as unimpressive as his speeches.

> Liddell, your nether garments never doff;
> For if your sex is doubtful as your speeches,
> The girls would at your vain pretensions scoff,
> And scorn the empty promise of your breeches.

However, the growing influence of Evangelicalism on public life ensured that such vulgar humour was increasingly likely to meet severe censure. By the 1830s, not only sexual innuendo, but any immodest humour, was likely to be held up as proof that a candidate was unfit for public office. At Leeds, Edward Baines was attacked for publishing 'filthy allusions' to Jewish circumcision rites in his newspaper, the *Leeds Mercury*, and also for an election ballad which included the saucy refrain: 'I'll kiss in public if you please, | an operatives backside!' Baines's assailant, styling himself 'a hater of cant and indecency', argued that such language polluted the town with filth and threatened, if left unchecked, to 'disarm the female character of its best protection—Modesty'. Of course vulgarity did not disappear overnight, but together Evangelicalism, the new-found dominance of the 1832 Act's self-consciously 'respectable' £10 householder, and the desire to distinguish electoral politics from plebeian radicalism's increasingly assertive 'mass platform' did much to hasten the demise of the more vulgar excesses of eighteenth-century street politics. But we should not conclude, therefore, that electoral politics as a whole had somehow been 'tamed', or that the irreverent spirit which had run through Hanoverian electioneering suddenly disappeared. Rather it evolved in parallel with the growth of more formalized partisanship after 1832. But first, let us look more closely at methods of electioneering before the watershed of 1832.⁹

Electioneering before the Reform Act

It is important to recognize the diversity of election customs under the pre-Reform system. Electioneering was naturally very different in a so-called 'pocket' borough, with perhaps a handful of electors in thrall to a powerful landowner, compared with a large urban or county constituency with a mass electorate to be wooed, influenced, or bribed. Indeed, one of the great attractions of the pre-Reform 'pocket' boroughs was undoubtedly that a candidate was saved from many of the rigours and inconveniences of a genuinely popular election. These could prove quite a shock to the uninitiated politician. When Henry Brougham, a rising Whig star associated with the anti-slavery movement, fought George Canning at Liverpool in the 1812 General Election, having previously sat for the Duke of Bedford's 'pocket' borough of Camelford in Cornwall (total electorate 20), he was surprised to discover that his supporters expected him to 'speechify' in local clubs and benefit societies every evening till well past midnight, as well as to make a 'regular speech each day at the close of the poll'. In all Brougham estimated that he made over 160 speeches during his unsuccessful campaign in this bastion of toryism and the slave trade, and declared himself 'exhausted ... as I never saw a popular election before'. In fact, Brougham was attacked more as a pro-American than as an anti-slaver (Britain was on the brink of war with the United States), but he was also mocked for his woeful performances as a public speaker, which opponents claimed were characterized by strange 'twitching'.[10]

Although Brougham felt that such 'speechifying' was 'quite peculiar to the place', by the late eighteenth century there were a significant number of populous constituencies with large electorates where voters expected to be addressed at regular open meetings, and where even reluctant candidates felt obliged to comply with their wishes. Fox had spoken extensively at Westminster in his hard-fought campaigns of the 1780s, and by the 1800s it was an expected part of metropolitan campaigning. In 1804, Middlesex demanded daily public speeches of its candidates, and, as at Liverpool, these were often delivered to mass open-air audiences. Similarly, Canning addressed crowds of over 10,000 at both the 1812 and 1818 General Elections, albeit usually from the relative safety of hotel windows (in 1812, he delivered a close of poll speech from a window of John Gladstone's town house in Rodney Street—though since William Ewart was just a toddler at the time it must be doubtful whether the event proved a formative influence for the future colossus of the platform). But even in these 'popular' constituencies, where electors undoubtedly expected to be wooed by their would-be representatives, there were often other, less democratic, forces at work. Bribery and corruption were naturally rife, but so too were more subtle forms of political influence. At Liverpool the powerful Corporation exerted considerable control over the electorate. Until 1761 it had directly controlled both seats; thereafter it generally nominated one candidate—leaving others to squabble over the second seat. Significantly, the 1812 contest turned against Brougham when, on the sixth day of polling, the Canningites agreed to join forces with the Corporation party to dish the Whigs. By contrast in 1802, the dominant issue had been allegations from Joseph Birch, trailing in third at the poll, that the Corporation was plotting to capture both seats by secretly backing General Tarleton as well as General Gascoyne, their designated candidate (both were ultimately elected). But in such cases, influence and control was not absolute or unconditional. Rather it rested on widespread acceptance of the legitimacy of particular claims—in this case for the Liverpool Corporation to be directly represented at Westminster, though not, after 1761, to be the *only* city interest so represented. Hence the perceived advantage for Birch of alleging that the Corporation was seeking to exceed its legitimate claim on the borough.[11]

In small, 'pocket' boroughs one might imagine that popular politics would be of no account. At Hedon, a decayed medieval borough in Yorkshire, the local Corporation made lucrative use of its powers to create freemen voters. In 1820 the going rate was said to be 200 guineas, and 225 of the borough's 298 freemen voters were non-residents (many linked to the East India Company which maintained close ties to the Corporation). But even before the Reform Act the worm could turn, even in the smallest borough, if landlord influence was considered to be used 'illegitimately'. At Knaresborough, another small Yorkshire borough, Seymour tells us that the Duke of Devonshire's control over the burgage voters was so strong before the Reform Act that his chosen candidate had no need to set foot in the constituency, and locals had to be content with chairing an old pauper 'by way of proxy' for their absent representative. In truth, this absurd ceremony probably represented a conscious mocking of the Duke and his candidate in a town where there was considerable bitterness that most locals were denied access to the qualifying tenancies, and hence to the spoils, of electoral politics. The borough was marked by serious rioting against the Duke's influence in the 1800s, while in 1784 and twice in the 1800s, opponents sought to mount 'independent' challenges to the Duke's restrictive operation of the burgage franchise. At Boroughbridge, yet another decayed Yorkshire borough, Henry Pelham-Clinton, fourth Duke of Newcastle, normally controlled the return of both MPs (plus the two MPs for neighbouring Aldborough). However, in 1818 his influence was challenged by Marmaduke Lawson, the 25-year-old son of a local gentry family with claims to one of the four seats. According to Lawson,

Mundy and Murdoch, the borough's sitting MPs, had neglected both the town and Parliament, with neither having ever set foot in the constituency until it became known that they might be opposed at the poll. Lawson cleverly concentrated his attack on Murdoch, partly because the latter failed to attend the market-day hustings, but mainly because Mundy was the Duke's brother-in-law. Lawson declared that 'to have the shew of an election without a shew of those to be elected, is in itself a manifest contradiction, a mere mockery of words'. He attacked the Duke for having 'sent us such inefficient members', but tried to reassure voters who felt bound to support the Duke that they need cast only one vote in his interest. Lawson's aim was doubtless to reassert his family's claim to one of the four Aldborough/Boroughbridge seats under the Duke's control, but his chosen method—namely a direct challenge to the 'animated puppets put in motion by the grand ducal master of the show'—still represented an interesting attempt to exploit the politics of 'independence' and 'locality' to challenge supposedly 'legitimate' landowner influence. Lawson headed the poll—with thirty-seven votes—much to the anger both of the hapless Murdoch, and of the Duke, who duly sought to evict those tenants who had backed the Lawson family interest against his own.[12]

At Boroughbridge, a powerful 'outsider' aristocrat (the Duke's seat was at Clumber Park in Nottinghamshire) battled to retain control against a prominent local landowner who made much of the fact that unlike the Duke's 'foreign' imports he was a 'native growth' who had lived among the voters since infancy. County pride, resentment at dictation, support for higher taxes on the rich, and, according to the Duke's agents, a good dose of old-fashioned bribery, combined to bring victory to Lawson. Political 'influence' was certainly at work here, but it did not render the outcome of the contest predetermined, either for Lawson or for Newcastle. Eight years later, in 1826, the Duke's agent was warning that the position at Boroughbridge remained insecure, and that they might lose any contested election because the Lawsons, 'living on the spot', were able to court popularity by being 'liberal to the poor' whilst socializing with the well-to-do. Here one detects evidence that 'deference' may have played its part in Lawson's earlier triumph, but again we should be cautious. As O'Gorman has argued, 'deferential' political relationships were always negotiated and conditional—'the voters demanded, indeed anticipated, paternalist services of many kinds in return for their loyalty'. If those services were withheld 'loyalty' and 'deference' could easily evaporate, or else, as at Boroughbridge, be transferred to a rival claimant. Moreover, even the most dependent electors expected to be wooed for their votes, both publicly through rituals such as the market-day hustings, and privately through face-to-face canvassing in which their status as respectable, independent electors would be underscored. Candidates who neglected these customs, preferring to rely upon the brute reality of economic and social power, courted potential electoral disaster.[13]

Partly because most candidates and their patrons were mindful of these popular expectations, contested elections were relatively uncommon in the second half of the eighteenth century. Pre-election canvassing was widespread, and often resulted in one side or the other withdrawing from the contest before it had formally begun. But even so, there was a notable trend towards more frequent contests from the 1780s, particularly in populous borough constituencies. Between 1780 and 1831 there were contests in two-thirds of the boroughs with over 1,000 electors, whereas in the period between 1741 and 1774 barely half had seen contests. According to O'Gorman, across the boroughs as a whole, 27 per cent of seats were contested between 1741 and 1774 compared with 35 per cent in the five contests between 1818 and 1831. Nor was this trend confined to urban Britain, where the growth of a vibrant public culture of debate and contestation had developed during the eighteenth century around coffee houses, dissenting chapels, private clubs and societies, and through a burgeoning national and provincial press. In the counties, rival candidates contested only twenty-eight seats between 1774 and 1790, whereas between 1818 and 1832 there were fifty-three contests. True, the majority of county seats still went uncontested at any given General Election, but the trend was clear. As in the larger boroughs, it seems likely that one important factor here was the growing influence of the press, both national and county-based, which encouraged the further penetration of national issues into local politics, and made it easier for aspiring politicians to float a possible candidacy. At Yorkshire in 1807 the county's two largest landed families, one Whig the other tory, each spent almost £100,000 trying to secure the prestigious title of county MP for their man, but what is often forgotten is that they were effectively vying to take the second seat behind the great anti-slavery campaigner, William Wilberforce, whose more modest expenses were met entirely by public subscription.[14]

But if an emergent 'public opinion' was beginning to reshape electoral politics in the first decades of the nineteenth century, it was during the great reform crisis of 1831–2 that it became a transformative force. The sheer scale of the shift of opinion between the General Elections of November 1830 and April 1831, when Grey sought his mandate for reform, was staggering. At Bristol, the veteran tory MP Richard Davis had polled 1,634 votes more than his closest Whig rival in 1830, but in 1831 he withdrew from the contest after finding his initial canvass 'so unsatisfactory'. At Liverpool, the poll closed after just one day in 1830, with the two tories comfortably ahead, but in 1831 there was a Whig landslide, with General Isaac Gascoyne slipping to a crushing defeat despite having represented the city since 1796. In the larger boroughs (those with more than 600 voters), the tories were left with only a single seat after the 1831 election. Nor were the counties immune from this pro-reform electoral avalanche. In 1830 the tories held thirty-seven English county seats, but six months later they had been reduced to a rump of just seven. Only one county, Shropshire, returned two straight tories. In Northamptonshire, which had been a solidly tory county down to 1806, and where the representation had subsequently been shared between Whigs and tories by mutual agreement, reformers set their sights on securing a clean sweep in 1831. Moreover, to underscore their commitment to the cause, the county's reformers pledged to run their Whig champions, Lords Althorp and Milton, 'free of Expence' [sic]. Local tories complained bitterly of broken pledges, and of Whig aristocrats consorting with 'the dirty Radicals' of the towns, but their cause proved hopeless and they abandoned the poll after thirteen days. In this way, the election of 1831 intensified the politics of opinion, and gave a sharper national dimension to the division between opponents and supporters of political and constitutional change. But as we shall see, if Britain entered a new era of more sharply defined partisanship after 1832, this was not achieved at the expense of older electioneering customs. These survived in good heart for many decades.[15]

The impact of reform

Historians have long stressed the persistence of many of the techniques of eighteenth-century electioneering between the First and Second Reform Acts. In the early twentieth century, Charles Seymour argued that the Chandos clause, which introduced a £50 rental franchise to the counties, 'proved a mighty bulwark of agricultural strength in elections', because of the influence it gave landowners over their dependent tenants. Half a century later, D. C. Moore famously developed this argument into a full-blown account of how the Reform Act sought to preserve traditional forms of cliental rural politics, and hence landed power, in his study *The Politics of Deference*. In fact the Whig leadership fought hard to resist the Chandos clause fearing that it would erode independent opinion in the counties, and by ultimately allowing borough freemen to vote in county divisions, they also undermined their avowed goal of isolating the counties from the encroachment of urban influences. But the Whigs certainly saw themselves as champions of landed rather than commercial interests, and were keen to ensure that reform strengthened 'legitimate' forms of landowner influence. Even before Moore's intervention, Norman Gash and H. J. Hanham had already sketched a strong picture of continuity across the nineteenth century in terms both of electioneering techniques and the power of wealthy patrons to control political representation. Both pointed, not only to the continued influence of landowners in the counties, but to the survival of small boroughs on a massive scale. No longer 'pocket' boroughs in the mould of Aldborough and Boroughbridge, with just a few dozen dependent voters, but nonetheless constituencies where, given the survival of open voting, it was all too easy for the rich and powerful to dominate politics either through direct control or through covert bribery. The small boroughs returned approximately one-third of MPs between the First and Second Reform Acts, and by this reading most were either directly in thrall to a landed patron, or open to be bought by the highest bidder.[16]

But this picture of elite control can be overstated. For one thing, the old freeman vote, which had been particularly strongly linked to brazen bribery before 1832, was greatly curtailed by the 1832 Act. Many MPs resisted the outright abolition of these ancient rights, either on the radical grounds that they represented the most democratic elements of the franchise, or on the good tory grounds that ancient rights and privileges were sacrosanct. But Whig leaders distrusted the venal habits of the poor, and were determined to ensure that the new electorate would be dominated by voters with sufficient means to be capable of independent judgement. In the end the Whigs had to accept a compromise measure, curtailing the worst abuses of the old freeman franchise, but retaining not only the rights of existing freeman voters living within seven miles of a constituency, but also the power to confer *new* freeman voting rights by 'birth or servitude'. But whilst the Whigs did not secure the radical purge of potentially venal voters that they sought, the 1832 Act nonetheless effected a significant transformation in the social basis of the electorate. Before 1832, it has been suggested that over half the electorate would have been manual workers, afterwards this figure fell to about one-third (and probably fell further in subsequent years as the parties mobilized to increase the registration rate among the new £10 voters while at the same time assorted ancient right franchises died out with their owners). Therefore, one important consequence of the Reform Act was to draw a much sharper distinction between electors and non-electors—not least because, as Philip Salmon has argued, the new system of annual voter registration helped to increase the sense of being (or not being) 'a voter' (previously qualification to vote had been confirmed only during the contest itself, and had therefore been a major reason for the lengthy polls).[17]

There were, however, a few seats where plebeian voters remained in a clear majority after 1832 thanks to the sheer size of the local freeman vote. One such was Beverley in East Yorkshire, and it has to be acknowledged that it did much to bear out the Whigs' concerns about the venal instincts of poor voters. By all accounts bribery had long been endemic at Beverley, but things famously came to a head in 1868 when the novelist Anthony Trollope contested the seat in the Liberal interest. Trollope subsequently recalled the contest as 'the most wretched fortnight of my manhood' during which he was subjected to 'a bitter tyranny from grinding vulgar tyrants' managing his campaign, and came to realize that 'political cleanliness was odious to the citizens'. The novelist wrought his revenge on the town in his savage lampoon of the corrupt borough of Percycross in *Ralph the Heir* (1870–1), while the town itself was disenfranchised in 1870 after a Royal Commission inquiry into its endemic corruption. According to the Commission, in 1868, 800 of the 1,100 electors had been open to bribery, 250 from each party who expected to be paid before voting, and 300 of no party known locally as the 'rolling stock'. By eschewing bribery Trollope and his Liberal running mate had sealed their fate.[18]

Many of the tumultuous customs of electioneering also survived 1832 unchanged. Elections continued to be widely perceived as a time of licence and misrule of almost carnivalesque proportions. Asa Briggs comments that 'electioneering provided a favourable opportunity and a provocation for petty violence of every kind; it also provided a unique opportunity for making money or drinking free beer and eating free food'. In a similar vein, Gash argues that Dickens's infamous picture of Mr Pickwick's visit to 'Eatanswill' during an election was 'not so much an exaggerated as a pale and euphemistic version of the contemporary scene' (see Fig. 3). By this reading, violence and corruption remained endemic because they were not only tolerated but actively encouraged by all parties. The contest at Horsham in 1847 represents a good example of early Victorian excess. The small Sussex town was said to be awash with drink for the whole six weeks preceding the election—with the rival parties offering voters free evening entertainments known as 'Pink goes' and 'Blue goes', and free beer to all-comers (voters and non-voters alike). As the poll approached bribery and corruption became more brazen. At the same time, party money flowed freely into the hands of local tradesmen. The Blues alone spent £350 supplying party ribbons to festoon the town (approximately £200,000 at 2009 prices). Apparently, one reason that things got so out of hand was that the two candidates could claim only weak connections to the rival local camps of tory Pinks and Whig Blues, thereby blurring the traditional lines of partisanship in the town. Across the country, polling day itself was often particularly disorderly, with rival groups, resplendent in party colours, parading the streets in high spirits and mobbing supporters of the 'wrong' side. At Beverley in 1868 polling day was marked by continual fighting in the streets, the hustings were partly destroyed, and missiles hailed down on the dignitaries gathered for the declaration. The widespread custom for employers to grant a general holiday on election day—sometimes with pay—increased the numbers on the streets, and hence the potential volatility of elections. According to Richter, little had changed by the 1860s and 1870s. Elections continued to float on a sea of beer and violence, and even a good Liberal politician such as John Bright could view a disorderly and corrupt campaign, such as the Rochdale by-election of 1865, with complete 'nonchalance'.[19]

But we should be wary of accepting this picture of timeless election customs at face value. Firstly, as O'Gorman has acknowledged, customs did begin to change after 1832. Partly, this reflected the radical changes in who possessed the vote (both which people and which places). But it also reflected changes in the nature of elections. The introduction of the new system of voter registration allowed for much swifter polling. In 1832 polling was reduced to two consecutive days, and three years later voting in the boroughs was further reduced, to just eight hours on a single day (8 a.m. to 4 p.m.)—a far cry from the days when polling might last for

Fig. 3. 'The Election at Eatanswill' from Charles Dickens, *Pickwick Papers* (1836), reproduced with the kind permission of the Syndics of Cambridge University Library

many weeks. Finally, in the mid-1850s, county seats were also obliged to poll on a single day. From 1832, the authorities were obliged to provide multiple polling stations wherever there were more than 600 registered voters. Often these would be erected within enlarged central hustings, but they might also be scattered around the constituency, potentially reducing the central public focus of the election. At Bristol, the Queen's Square hustings were used for the last time in 1837; thereafter, temporary booths were erected in the city's various parishes, and the hustings became merely the site for enacting the nomination and declaration rituals. At Maidstone, the authorities provided twelve booths in 1835, three in each of the town's four wards, while at Great Yarmouth in 1837 there were sixteen—one for every hundred voters (far in excess of the requirements of the Reform Act). In the counties it was absolutely essential that booths should be scattered across the constituency once polling had been reduced to a single day.[20]

Secondly, however nonchalant Bright may have been about the fighting and drinking at Rochdale in 1865, by mid-century it had become more common for politicians and other commentators to condemn both disorderly behaviour and corruption. In 1857 another famous English novelist, William Makepeace Thackeray, contested Oxford as an independent Liberal, and was appalled by the violent behaviour of many of his own supporters. Joseph Grego tells how Thackeray saw a large gang of his supporters 'rough-handling' a small band of partisans for Cardwell, his Liberal rival for the seat. Immediately, he rushed out into the street and 'hurled himself into the thick of the fray'. At six foot two he apparently towered above the crowd, making it easier for him to lash out to right and left 'in defence of his opponent's partisans and in defiance of his own friends'. Here Thackeray is presented as a manly 'John Bull' figure determined to prevent foul play, despite the indifference of the 'more hardened electioneers' in his camp. Perhaps significantly, Grego chose to end his massive history of electioneering since the Stuart era with this account of Thackeray's heroics, perhaps suggesting his hope for the triumph of a more enlightened and humane approach to electoral politics. Grego's account conveys an image of an upper-class colossus, in both physical and moral terms, seeking to impose order on the unruly masses who are his 'inferiors' in every sense. It was an outlook strongly shaped by the legacy of 1867 and 1884—Britain's two-stage leap to full male householder democracy (Grego was writing in 1886), but the belief that upper-class men needed to restrain rather than encourage the unruly instincts of the masses was already well established by mid-century.[21]

Thirdly, and finally, one must recognize that partisanship and 'opinion' were much stronger forces in electoral politics after 1832 than before. In this sense, the great transformation of 1830–1 was never reversed. After the Great Reform Act, Britain entered a new electoral age where contests were both more frequent and more directly tied to the rhythm of party competition at Westminster. In a detailed study of voting at Shrewsbury between 1819 and 1841, Phillips and Wetherell conclude that reform itself 'converted voters into partisans'. In this double-member borough the candidates proved reluctant to break with tradition, declining to run joint party slates, or even to adopt common party colours, but even so partisanship increased dramatically at the election of 1831, and remained at high levels thereafter. Nationally, both unnecessary 'plumping' (choosing to cast only one vote when two candidates from one's preferred party were in the field) and 'splitting' (supporting candidates from rival parties) declined markedly after 1832. At the same time individual voters became more consistent in their voting habits over time. In a study of thirteen boroughs between 1761 and 1868, Phillips and Wetherell conclude that partisanship was close to random before 1832—that is, the chance that someone would vote the same way at consecutive elections was almost the same as the chance of voting differently. But after 1832, constituencies experienced 'extreme increases in consistency', with the chance of partisan voters shifting allegiance falling to 2 in 10. Salmon has done much to explain this intensification of partisanship after 1832. He suggests that more important than the politicizing effects of the crises of 1831–2, was the growth of party organization in the constituencies as political leaders sought to cope with the fact that, left to their own devices, many voters appeared remarkably reluctant either to claim or to defend their right to the franchise under the 1832 Act. Thus registration, more than reform, politicized the electorate after 1832 and thereby helped to inculcate unparalleled levels of partisan loyalty. Between the mid-1830s and the mid-1840s the Conservatives appear to have been the masters of the art of registration, proving more successful both in getting their own people onto the register, and in objecting to the registration of known opponents. Thereafter, the balance of forces was more even, and the sharpness of party divisions blunted by the Conservatives' split over the repeal of the Corn Laws, but even so the centrality of party activity to voter registration remained undiminished.[22]

Nor was this simply a story confined to the large, open boroughs that dominate Phillips and Wetherell's analysis of pollbooks. Even in the counties and small boroughs, 1832 ushered in an invigorated politics of opinion and partisan rivalry. In the counties, Whig power ebbed away after 1832 not because tory landowners began to exert greater control over dependent voters, but because the political defence of protectionism gave them a powerful issue around which to construct a strong anti-Whig coalition in the countryside. Indeed, when tory leaders appeared unreliable on such core issues, county seats proved quite capable of rebelling against the influence of powerful landowners in order to support independent tory-agriculturalist candidacies, as happened at South Nottinghamshire in both 1846 and 1851. Here, distant landowners found that they had much less direct control over county electors than is generally claimed—large-scale tenant farmers proved surprisingly immune to direction, while the bulk of the electorate was made up of small-scale yeoman farmers, tradesmen, and craftsmen, who were not directly dependent on the great landowners at all. If such groups normally accepted the leadership of the landed elite, this reflected the fact that, except in exceptional circumstances such as the fall-out from the Repeal of the Corn Laws, they were prepared to accept that they and the large landowners were bound by a common interest. But such support was both conditional and strongly issue-based. Moreover, issue politics impinged on the counties in other ways. In the mid-1840s, county seats that bordered large, rapidly expanding urban areas became the focus of a concerted campaign by the Anti-Corn Law League to manufacture 40-shilling freeholder votes in order to undermine Conservative electoral strength. Thousands of new votes were created in county constituencies such as South Lancashire, North Cheshire, the West Riding, and Middlesex, all of which returned two Free Traders in the General Election of 1847. It was a brief, but dramatic, invasion of 'town' influence which added further to the politicization of county politics after 1832.[23]

Partisanship could also burn bright even in the smallest, most apparently debased borough constituencies. At Knaresborough, where the Duke of Devonshire's iron control of the old burgage franchise had long caused resentment, the new wider franchise was seized upon as a chance to wrench the borough from the Duke's pocket. Overall, it is estimated that the number of patronage boroughs, where powerful landlords were normally able directly to control the representation, fell by two-thirds after 1832. Moreover, it was now rare for patronage to go uncontested in a small borough, so that wealthy patrons often found themselves embroiled in a constant struggle to maintain their 'influence'—potentially at great expense. According to Edwin Jaggard, 'after 1832 the majority of small towns were "open" and enjoyed a surprisingly vigorous political life'. As in the large boroughs, voters increasingly showed consistency in their party allegiance between elections, suggesting that their votes could not simply be bought by the highest bidder. They also displayed a strong propensity to avoid 'splitting' their votes between rival candidates—Jaggard found between 71 and 85 per cent of voters casting straight party votes ('doubles') in seven small boroughs between 1832 and 1880, with approximately half of all voters consistent partisans whose allegiance never wavered. Even in towns where bribery was endemic, such as Barnstaple in north Devon, almost a third of voters were consistent partisans across six elections. But then, even at Beverley the commissioners had found that approximately half the voters were consistent partisans who simply believed that they should be paid for their vote. Even here, the true 'rolling stock'—those willing to sell their vote to the highest bidder—represented less than a third of the electorate. Indeed, Phillips and Wetherell estimate that more than three-quarters of Beverley voters proved consistent partisans across three elections during the 1860s. Partisanship was still the key to victory for any candidate—bribery may have been endemic, much to Trollope's disgust, but it was, in effect, simply a means of taxing the candidate before latent partisanship could be translated into a concrete vote. Historians such as Gash, Hanham, and Hoppen may be right to emphasize strong continuities in popular politics across the nineteenth century, but they are wrong to portray the surviving aspects of eighteenth-century electioneering as mere anachronisms—to see them as hollow rituals devoid of political purpose, and fuelled only by the liberal supply of money and drink. On the contrary, such rituals remained part of a vibrant political culture in which politicians had to woo voters through both words and deeds.[24]

Rise of the platform

But if 1832 catapulted Britain into an era of more intense partisanship, it was by no means the only force for change in the second quarter of the nineteenth century. Mass communications, such as print and transport, grew at an unprecedented rate from the 1830s. Between 1665 and 1800,

85 newspaper titles had been launched across Britain. Down to 1830 there were another 126 new titles, but between 1830 and the repeal of the newspaper stamp duty in 1855, 415 new titles were launched. Thereafter, the rate of growth accelerated further. Between 1855 and 1861, when Gladstone announced the final abolition of the 'knowledge taxes' by repealing the paper duties, a further 492 titles were established, including the first newspaper in 123 English provincial towns. Some of these titles would certainly have been short-lived, but, as a measure of the explosion of the press between the First and Second Reform Acts, the figures are nonetheless impressive. Both local and national politics were brought direct to people's homes on an unprecedented scale, and politicians became increasingly aware of the potential value of the press as a means of directly addressing the wider public, and perhaps even of moulding that strange new creature 'public opinion'.[25]

No less important was the rapid development of a national rail network during the 1830s and 1840s. In the eighteenth century it had taken up to ten days to travel from London to Edinburgh by coach, and even with improved Macadamized roads the journey still took at least two days in the 1820s, but with the advent of the steam train that time was more than halved, and by the 1880s had fallen to just eight hours. Rapid and efficient rail transport made it much easier for politicians to address public meetings across provincial Britain. In the late 1830s and 1840s, Radical reform movements, such as the Anti-Corn Law League and the Chartists, made use of the new technology to coordinate elaborate national campaigns based around mass mobilization at public meetings—the so-called 'mass platform'. The tactic was not new of course, it had been central to the post-Napoleonic Radical politics of Henry Hunt and his followers, as the bloodshed at Manchester's St Peter's Field ('Peterloo') underscored in 1819, but the mass platform came into its own with these rapid improvements in the mobility of national leaders.[26]

Fearful of its associations with 'disreputable' radicalism, mainstream politicians initially proved reluctant to embrace the techniques of the mass platform. In theory, leading politicians could now tour the country during a General Election, using mass meetings both to establish direct contact with voters and to reach a wider public through the extensive reporting of their activities in the press, but there remained considerable cultural resistance to embracing the tactics of plebeian radical politics. True, Charles Fox had dabbled with the platform in the late eighteenth century, and by the

1800s large popular constituencies such as Liverpool, Bristol, and Middlesex had come to expect their candidates to 'speechify'. But for all that, most front-rank politicians remained strangers to the public meeting in the early nineteenth century. George Canning, the flamboyant tory foreign secretary, was unusual in representing a popular constituency (Liverpool) for more than a decade (1812–23). He was even more unusual in his eagerness to court public opinion from the platform. Traditional tories were appalled when Canning used public meetings, such as an address to the freemen of Plymouth in 1823, to outline the rationale of the government's approach to foreign policy. Such things were a matter for Parliamentary debate within the political elite, not 'speechifying' in the country. Indeed, reports of Parliamentary speeches themselves had only begun to be available to the public in the later eighteenth century as newspapers and private printers sought to evade legal restrictions on their dissemination, and it was not until 1909 that Hansard finally became an *official* record of Parliamentary debate.[27]

Elite disdain for the mass platform was often expressed in terms of disgust at the supposed rabble-rousing of 'gentleman leaders' such as Henry Hunt, the hero of Peterloo, or Chartist leaders such as Fergus O'Connor and Ernest Jones. But we should be wary of taking such arguments at face value. It was not just the vulgarity of the mass platform that politicians reviled; it was the fact that it represented a direct challenge to the existing social and political order. As Nicholas Rogers has argued, in the eighteenth-century radical protest had generally been articulated through a customary repertoire of actions which acknowledged the legitimacy of the existing order even when they appeared to mock or challenge its values. Protest was episodic, poorly organized, and largely parasitic on the established rituals of civic and national life. By contrast, in the wake of the Napoleonic wars, plebeian radicals and their 'gentlemen' allies mobilized large-scale demonstrations that were not only wholly autonomous from the official political culture, but also demanded the radical reconstruction of that culture along democratic lines. In a large-scale, quantitative study of popular protest, Charles Tilly has drawn similar conclusions. New, more orderly and autonomous, forms of protest such as the march and demonstration emerged through which a wide variety of subaltern groups sought to articulate their grievances and claims to redress. Eventually the legitimacy of such gatherings would be widely accepted, but in the early nineteenth century they were perceived, not inaccurately, as revolutionary challenges to the existing order. Hence the authorities' concerted efforts to crush radical organizations, to restabilize the social and economic system, and, crucially from our perspective, to distance the supposedly respectable world of conventional politics from the methods and ethos of the democratic mass platform.[28]

The embrace of the mass platform by nineteenth-century politicians was thus a slow and uneven process. Apart from William Huskisson, Canning's protégé and his successor as MP for Liverpool, few politicians were prepared to follow in Canning's footsteps in the first half of the nineteenth century. Peel, in particular, was notoriously suspicious of popular politics and of what he saw as craven attempts to court public opinion. But by the 1850s, with radical mass politics in retreat, it became more usual for government ministers to address public meetings in the provinces. Both Palmerston and Russell gave speeches which followed in Canning's footsteps by explaining government policy on both domestic and foreign affairs. However, neither saw this new ministerial platform as central to their political activity, and unlike later politicians they did not believe that it should play a part in the *development* of policy—this remained the distinct preserve of Parliamentary debate. Ironically, at this point, Gladstone, who would go on to revolutionize the ministerial platform, viewed Palmerston's open courting of public opinion with disdain. According to David Steele, by the later 1850s Palmerston was 'concerned to counter the parliamentarians by bringing public opinion to bear'—a strategy that was still deeply distasteful to Gladstone as a former Conservative strongly influenced by Peel. But Palmerston's was, for all that, a distinctly cautious engagement with popular politics. His principal concern was to influence public opinion via the press, with which he maintained close social and financial ties, and his ventures into public speaking were generally tame affairs. For one thing, unlike Gladstone or Bright, he was said to be a weak orator, frequently padding out his speeches with redundancies such as 'you know what I mean', and rarely raising the content of his discourse above 'local flattery and homilies to civic pride'. When he famously visited the provinces to address public meetings of working men, his audiences were 'carefully selected' to ensure a good reception, and hence good 'copy' in the daily press. There was powerful symbolism in these early examples of the politics of public relations, but, for all that, they hardly represented a full-blooded engagement with the world of popular politics. But all was about to change.[29]

Steele may be right that Gladstone 'followed where Palmerston led' when it came to embracing the platform, but once he had made the leap,

Gladstone quickly made the platform his own. True, when, in May 1864, he made his famous speech on the need to bring more working men within 'the pale of the Constitution' it was to Parliament, not to a mass meeting, and when he fought South Lancashire at the 1865 General Election, having just been unseated as MP for Oxford University, he had not been required to address his constituents for eighteen years (the hustings played no part in university elections, although Gladstone had campaigned unsuccessfully for his brother at Flintshire in 1857). But by late 1864 he had already gained a reputation for 'promiscuous public speaking' and was said to be redefining the role of the front-rank politician in British public life. After his return to the election platform in 1865, Gladstone's public reputation as an orator continued to grow. Particularly significant were two major speeches at Liverpool the following year in which Gladstone sought to rally public support for his beleaguered Reform Bill, then being savaged on the floor of the Commons by sceptical Liberal opponents of democratic change such as Robert Lowe. For a serving minister (Gladstone was Chancellor of the Exchequer) to seek to influence the legislative process by appealing to the higher authority of 'public opinion' was considered outrageous by many. But it cemented the perception of Gladstone, not only as the true champion of reform, but as a politician with the 'common touch'—a 'people's tribune'. Hence John Vincent's comment that 'others sowed for Gladstone to reap'. It was a remarkable transformation given his austere Peelite reputation in the 1850s.[30]

As one might imagine, 'respectable' politicians proved even slower to embrace *outdoor* speaking, given its close association with the radical demagogues of the post-Napoleonic era. Indeed, if anything the direction of travel was the other way. Radical leaders, keen to stress the orderliness and 'respectability' of their cause, increasingly brought their politics indoors—preferring to address ticketed meetings in large venues such as the Manchester Free Trade Hall—a building which came to symbolize the success of a more disciplined and rational mass platform after the repeal of the Corn Laws in 1846. Even a firebrand radical such as Joseph Cowen junior largely shunned the outdoor platform during the 1850s in order to dissociate his politics from the disorderly tumult of the streets. But as memories of 'dangerous' physical force radicalism began to fade, so self-consciously popular leaders such as Cowen and John Bright gradually became more willing to speak to large, outdoor audiences. Contemporaries had no doubt that what was at stake here was the class politics of public space—taking politics out of doors meant taking them to the poor and excluded. Hence when the radical trade union leader George Potter travelled to Dewsbury in 1868 to speak for Handel Cossham, the beleaguered official Liberal candidate, he was roundly condemned by local Radicals who declared that 'he should have given his address in the open air, not in the rich man's chamber [the town's Theatre Royal]'. Perhaps significantly, it was only after the franchise reforms of 1867 and 1884 that outdoor speaking came to be a staple of mainstream electioneering in Britain.[31]

But it was not just fear of 'disreputable' radicalism that held back the growth of the mass platform in the nineteenth century. By tradition, politicians were expected only to address meetings of their own constituents during an election—to intervene in another man's constituency was seen as an unacceptable intrusion on the close personal relationship between candidate and constituent. The gradual erosion of this convention during the later nineteenth century marked an important development in the history of electioneering. By the 1870s, party leaders regularly spoke at meetings across the country during a campaign, but it was still widely frowned upon for others to imitate their itinerant politicking. As late as 1884, Millicent Fawcett was writing to a Liberal candidate to explain that her blind, cabinet-minister husband would not be able to speak for him because,

> he has a very strong opinion that a candidate's chances of success are positively injured by speeches made by outsiders; he thinks constituencies regard such speeches as interference and dictation and resent them accordingly.[32]

But Fawcett was part of a dying breed. By the 1880s the rival party headquarters were already coordinating the supply of speakers to the constituencies, with front-bench ministers always proving a particular attraction to local parties keen to have a star name to maximize the impact of a set-piece meeting. That said, the party leaders were still used sparingly—when Gladstone chose to speak at the 1890 Bassetlaw by-election, rather than simply send a letter of support, his intervention was considered 'unprecedented'. Moreover, with more than 600 constituencies to be fought, party stars were inevitably spread pretty thin at a General Election, even before the 1918 reform act decreed that all constituencies would poll on a single day (until then polling had been spread over two or three weeks, partly to accommodate plural voters with the right to vote in two or more constituencies, but mainly as a hangover from early nineteenth-century fears that the forces of law and order might be over-stretched by simultaneous polling). Hence, one agent's warning, in 1905, that during a General Election 'each Constituency will have to depend very largely, if not entirely, upon its own resources'. We should not therefore exaggerate the impact of railways and the national press on the political platform before 1914—during a General Election campaign the political meeting remained largely the preserve of the candidate, assisted by a supporting cast of local volunteers of uncertain talent as public speakers.[33]

But for all that, the late Victorian cross-fertilization between the traditions of the ministerial platform, the radical mass platform, and the conventional election meeting still mattered, and once again it was Gladstone who played the decisive role. During the 1868 election, fought on the new urban householder franchise introduced by Disraeli's minority Government the previous year, Gladstone threw himself into the platform campaign in an unprecedented manner—addressing major election meetings in fourteen British towns. By all accounts he was a magnetic platform speaker, with a powerful, musical voice that retained the distinct Lancastrian 'burr' of his Liverpool upbringing. Interestingly, Gladstone made little use of the platform as Prime Minister between 1868 and 1874, but when he came out of retirement in 1876 to denounce the Bulgarian atrocities and Disraeli's continued support for their Turkish architects, the platform was as important as the pen in his political armoury. In particular, Gladstone used the mass platform to take his stinging attack on government immorality into the homes of millions via extensive reports in the national and local press. The demotic flair of his oratory confirmed him, over the heads of Lords Hartington and Granville, not just as 'the people's William', but as the only possible candidate for Prime Minister when the Liberals triumphed at the subsequent General Election in 1880. In the process Gladstone transformed the place of the platform and public oratory in British politics, making popular politics matter in ways that would still have been unimaginable at Palmerston's death in 1865. According to Lord Salisbury, the world-weary leader of Conservatism from 1881, political speech-making was 'an aggravation...which we owe entirely to Mr Gladstone'. It was also an aggravation that even Salisbury could not abjure, even if he was saved from the indignities of a popular election by the privilege of noble birth.[34]

2

The Fall of the Hustings
and the Rise of the Platform

1867 and all that

In 1867 Britain famously made a giant leap towards urban male democracy
with the passing of Disraeli's Second Reform Act, which introduced
a male householder (i.e. ratepayer) franchise to urban Britain. Drafted by
a minority Conservative Government, and much amended on the floor
of the House, the Act increased the English borough electorate from
under 500,000 to almost 1.2 million, rising to nearly 1.7 million by the
early 1870s as a combination of legislative changes and legal test cases
expanded the definition of the 'householder' franchise. Its impact in the
counties was much more modest—here the electorate in England and
Wales rose from 540,000 to 790,000, largely thanks to the reduction of
the occupier qualification from fifty to twelve pounds. Many felt that
Britain had made a great 'leap in the dark', enfranchising vast numbers of
poor urban voters who had been deliberately excluded from Gladstone's
ill-fated reform bill of 1866. Gladstone had intended a cautious extension of
the principles of 1832—enfranchising respectable artisans by reducing the
urban householder qualification from ten to seven pounds, but leaving the
urban poor (the so-called 'residuum') outside the 'pale of the constitution'.
Disraeli hoped to achieve a similar effect by imposing tough requirements
on householders if they were to qualify for the vote. But when Liberal
backbenchers succeeded in overthrowing these restrictive clauses the lurch
towards male democracy in the boroughs became more dramatic.[1]

One consequence of this great leap into the unknown was an increased
sensitivity towards the persistence of disorder in public politics. Observers
were convinced that the altered franchise had introduced a volatile new

element into elections, with inevitable consequences for public order. At Bristol, it was alleged that the elections of 1868 had been the most disorderly in the city since the bitter clashes associated with the reform crisis in the early 1830s. A by-election in April 1868 witnessed the reappearance of bands of armed 'roughs' outside polling booths, and the destruction of property on a grand scale by partisan mobs. It was widely alleged that the 'roughs' were in the pay of John Miles, the victorious Conservative candidate who was subsequently unseated for bribery on petition. But at the November General Election it was Liberal mobs that attacked the houses of prominent Conservatives throughout the city and destroyed the party's committee rooms in St Michael's parish. As in April, the election was marked by violent clashes between rival bands of supporters, many of them armed with makeshift weapons, leading to claims that some voters had been too frightened to come to the polls.[2]

According to one Bristolian observer, there was considerable anxiety that the Reform Act of 1867 had resurrected violent customs banished from the city with the passing of the first Reform Act in 1832. But it seems highly doubtful whether elections as a whole became more disorderly after 1867—events in Bristol seem to have followed their own, distinctly local, logic fuelled mainly by Miles's cavalier electioneering style (besides hiring 1,200 roughs he was alleged to have underwritten the supply of free beer to voters at 200 local pubs). If Bristol had enjoyed relatively peaceful elections during the mid-Victorian period, many constituencies had not. For instance in 1865, at the last Middlesex hustings to be held in Covent Garden, all three candidates, John Stuart Mill (Liberal), Robert Grosvenor (Whig), and W. H. Smith (Conservative), were pelted indiscriminately by the London 'mob' out for its election fun. At the same election a mob of 30,000 was said to have rampaged through Nottingham, smashing windows and sacking the Liberal party offices, while at Chippenham Liberal rioters greeted defeat at the polls by attacking the houses of fifty prominent local Conservatives.[3]

What changed after 1867 was not so much the level of disorder, as the political and social context in which disorder was understood. In many boroughs non-voters were for the first time in a minority, at least among adult males, and traditional rituals that had symbolized their inclusion in the political system, such as public nomination at the hustings and the ritual aspects of open public voting, came to be seen as dangerous anachronisms which threatened to impede the smooth absorption of the new voters into orderly and rational electoral politics. The incoming Liberal Government set up a Select Committee, chaired by Lord Hartington, to inquire into the conduct of both Parliamentary and Municipal elections. The committee heard evidence from nearly eighty witnesses, many of whom testified to endemic problems of bribery, intimidation, and violence in British electoral politics. It reluctantly concluded that only the adoption of secret voting ('the ballot') was likely to bring an end to the evils that had marred so many contests in 1868. The ballot, the committee argued, would not only promote 'tranquillity', but also 'protect voters from undue influence and intimidation', thereby introducing a 'greater degree of freedom and purity' into British elections. Many leading Liberals such as Gladstone and Forster followed the same logic—long staunch defenders of open voting, they came to accept the pragmatic case for the ballot as the best means to prevent intimidation and reduce disorder given the new enlarged urban electorate. In 1871 legislation to introduce the secret ballot failed in the Lords, but in 1872 it became law. Henceforth the British would cast their votes in secret—answerable only to their individual consciences. This was not what most Liberals wanted in 1872, they continued to believe in the moral superiority of open, public voting where electors would be answerable for their actions to their peers, but after 1867 they became convinced that too few voters were capable of living up to this ideal. The change undoubtedly marked an important landmark on the road to a more individualistic and privatized understanding of politics.[4]

The 1872 Act also abolished the ancient system of public nomination at the hustings—replacing it with a purely administrative system requiring the submission of signed nomination papers—even though the Hartington Committee had recommended retaining public nominations on the grounds that their abolition would 'fetter the free choice of the electors' and deny candidates a public platform from which they might refute misstatements about their character or opinions. However, the committee's earlier draft reports had signalled a radically different conclusion, thanks mainly to the influence of John Bright, the leading Radical reformer within the cabinet, and a strong advocate of both the secret ballot and the abolition of the hustings. It was Bright who originally persuaded the committee to denounce the 'serious inconveniences and evils' caused by public nominations, though in doing so he was merely reflecting the strongly expressed views of most witnesses, only two of whom spoke up in defence of the traditional public hustings. Like Bright, most witnesses felt that the hustings 'discredit our

electoral system' by causing 'tumult and disorder' without any obvious
positive benefit. Useful when few could read, and newspapers were dear,
opponents argued that public hustings were now irrelevant given that the
public could easily discover the candidates' opinions either directly, by
attending their election meetings, or indirectly through reports of their
speeches in the local press. Most also tended to agree with Bright that
household suffrage undermined the value of the traditional show of hands
at the hustings, although a few insisted that this made the hustings *more*
useful, since they could now give candidates a clear sense of the state
of 'public opinion' among the voters. In fact, in the aftermath of the
1868 election a number of local Liberal associations had experimented
with pre-election trial ballots in an effort to prevent rival candidates from
splitting the party's vote. Much like US primaries, these ballots represented
sophisticated means of testing a candidate's popularity compared with the
old hustings, although the experiment ultimately lost favour partly because
the Bristol petition of 1870 established that a candidate could be unseated
for corrupt or illegal practices in a pre-election ballot, but also because,
after the introduction of the secret ballot in 1872, it became impossible to
determine who was a bona fide party supporter—selection came to rest
instead with party members, or, more often, with the ruling committees
of local party organizations (although in recent years the Conservatives
have experimented with open 'primaries' in winnable seats, allowing all
registered voters to have their say over candidate selection, presumably in
an attempt, not only to court political legitimacy, but also to improve the
prospects of moderate candidates).[5]

But if the Select Committee ultimately proved too divided to call for
the abolition of the hustings, Hartington's colleagues in the Liberal Cabinet
were not so cautious. In Parliament few paid much attention to the
proposed abolition of public nomination—instead debate was dominated
by denunciations of the 'un-English' innovation of secret voting. One
exception was John Fielden, son of the famous tory factory reformer, who
spoke passionately in favour of the old ways. Fielden insisted that it was
spurious to claim that candidates' election meetings represented an adequate
substitute for the hustings. These, he insisted, were 'really private meetings
under a public name', whereas the hustings represented 'the greatest of
our public meetings'. Here he picked up on an issue that had bothered
Bright throughout the deliberations of the Select Committee; namely that
unlike the hustings, party election meetings were not necessarily open to

all-comers, and were almost never 'mixed meetings', that is meetings where candidates stood side-by-side on the same platform. In law they were indeed private occasions, and the public had no right to be there, let alone to question the speakers, except in so far as the organizers extended that right to them. Fielden was right to insist that only the hustings unequivocally provided 'the right of public meeting and the right of public discussion' (although in law any open-air meeting was public by virtue of being held on public space). Moreover, in a few constituencies, notably the more feudal parts of rural Scotland, candidates with powerful local connections still spoke only at the hustings, preferring to rely on 'influence' and the canvass, rather than words, to bring victory. Fielden was sure that Britain was about to abolish a vital bastion of political accountability, but few took much notice of his warnings in 1872.[6]

One reason for this indifference was that, in the aftermath of 1867, both the Hartington Committee and Parliament cared more about imposing order on public politics than about upholding ancient public 'rights'. It would be a mistake to imagine that their principal concern was to protect poor voters from bribery or intimidation by the rich and powerful. They were at least as determined to protect 'respectable' voters from intimidation by 'roughs' picketing the polling booths, or 'mobs' parading the streets, breaking windows and assaulting passers-by whenever they came upon the despised emblems of their political opponents. It was no accident that, alongside the Ballot Act, the government also introduced a bill to prohibit the use of public houses for election meetings or as committee rooms—the lavish supply of free beer was generally recognized to play a major part in electoral disorder. Nor was it an accident that the Act itself also introduced new powers to prevent disorderly behaviour in or around polling stations. Given the widespread fear of mob violence and intimidation at this point, it was perhaps hardly surprising that few politicians were prepared to speak up for the debased rituals of the hustings—for 'the once popular farce of "The Nomination"' as one jaundiced Bristolian observer put it in 1870. Confident that this would probably be the last such hustings to disturb the peace of his city, the writer mocked those, who, befuddled by drink, still found humour in the 'brutal horseplay' of the hustings; in 'blue and red powder, rotten eggs, and cabbage stalks'. What was needed, all agreed, was 'tranquillity' not 'tumult'—only this would allow Britain safely to absorb the new voters into the political system by taming the excesses of an official political culture that had hitherto pandered to the vulgar tastes of the politically excluded.[7]

According to Charles Seymour, 'the factor of violence disappeared almost entirely from electoral contests' after the legislation of 1872, although he acknowledges that where bribery was endemic the secret ballot made little difference beyond lowering the market rate for a vote (and making it easier to take money from both sides). Certainly, most contemporary observers were convinced that the combined effect of the ballot and the abolition of the hustings was indeed to increase the 'tranquillity' of elections. Sir Joseph Heron, town clerk of Manchester, welcomed the fact that election day excitement was now 'confined to a short period instead of having it during the whole of the day', although interestingly he believed that whilst there had been less excitement in 1874 than at previous elections, there had been greater 'interest' in the contest (though he would not be drawn when Charles Pelham Villiers suggested that this might be because, for many, the vote now belonged 'to them and not to somebody else'). However, not everywhere was so calm in 1874, and overall Seymour's picture is rather too rosy. True, henceforth no MP was to be unseated for intimidation, but it had always been notoriously difficult to prove intimidation in the election courts. Disorder and violence certainly did not disappear. Even in 1874, when disenchantment in Liberal circles did much to dampen partisan enthusiasm, there was still considerable election violence. At Wolverhampton large gangs of workmen picketed polling stations and attacked Conservative committee rooms in industrial townships such as Wednesfield and Willenhall, apparently in response to earlier incidents involving hired tory 'roughs'. There was also serious disorder at Sunderland, Norwich, Nottingham, Lincoln, North Durham, the Forest of Dean, Thurles, the Hartlepools, and across the Staffordshire Potteries. O'Leary identifies ten cases of serious rioting in 1874, but accepts the contemporary view of *The Times* that this still represented a significant diminution in electoral violence, and that 'Mobs, processions, favours, free-fights, and punch-drinking have become for the most part things of the past, and where rioting did occur ... it was probably not aggravated by any political duplicity.'[8]

The Times was registering an important shift in the tone of British elections, which henceforth would be much less dominated by the spontaneous enthusiasms of the crowd, but it was nonetheless overly sanguine in its predictions for the rapid decline of electoral disorder. If anything the 1880 election witnessed an increase in disorder and intimidation, thanks in large measure to the fact that radical enthusiasm had returned to fill the Liberals' sails. One contemporary account records eleven English election riots, including allegations that at Bath and Leamington large gangs of 'roughs' paraded through the streets smashing windows and brandishing clubs spiked with nails and screws. Some of this disorder was almost certainly purely mischievous in origin—the result of what Richter has termed 'spontaneous outbursts of sheer ebullience', targeting both sides (and the forces of order) without favour. For instance, at Manchester, both political parties were said to fear a Monday poll because the 'idle, drunken ... lower types' would amuse themselves by hanging around the polling booths, discouraging 'respectable workers' from coming to vote (many workers still extended the Sabbath by observing the decidedly unholy festival of 'Saint Monday'). According to this witness, it was 'irregular workmen' who 'make the rows, and that go about doing the shouting'. However, there were far too many incidents involving the deliberate targeting of known opponents and their property for this to stand as a general explanation of late Victorian electoral disorder.[9]

But even if electoral politics was not transformed overnight by the legislation of the 1870s, historians are right to see these changes as a deliberate attempt to tame the excesses of popular political culture. Between 1832 and 1872 almost all the traditional, ritualistic aspects of elections had been abolished. First the poll had been truncated to a single day, and dispersed by the need to institute multiple polling booths. Then, in the 1850s, Parliament began to chip away at the theatre surrounding electioneering by decreeing that both 'marks of distinction' (such as party cockades and ribbons), and all forms of music represented corrupt payments if financed by the candidate. Finally, the reforms of 1872 eliminated most of the surviving rituals of Britain's official election culture, including not only the open ballot and the nomination, but also, by default, the ceremonial procession to and from the hustings. As the official public rituals of electioneering became truncated, so inevitably the political parties moved to fill the void. Many have understood this in terms of the 'taming' or 'disciplining' of popular politics, but as we shall see, it is easy to exaggerate the control parties exerted over the electoral process down to the First World War. On the ground, much less changed after 1872 than one might imagine.[10]

In theory, only the official declaration of the poll survived as an inclusive public ceremony, but this did not mean that elections were suddenly stripped of their excitement or potential for tumult. Many customs survived despite their technical illegality, while others mutated to find robust expression in new forms. In Parliament politicians might be unambiguous about the need to reform popular politics and secure 'tranquillity' at elections, but they often sang to a different tune when face-to-face with the public in their constituencies. There appears to have been considerable popular resistance to abandoning the old ways of electioneering. At Sheffield in 1874, most voters made a mockery of the secret ballot by coming to the poll 'making their opinions and their favourite candidate known', while at Bristol not only were party favours generally worn, but brass bands played in the streets for days before the poll, and the rival candidates still made their ceremonial procession through the city in grand open carriages. Candidates knew that the public still wanted them to make a 'show' of elections, and they did their best to oblige—even if it meant bending the letter of the law. Down to 1914, it was recognized that the legal prohibition of 'marks of distinction' and hired music was all but a dead letter. The genius for improvisation did much to nullify the law's effect—with voters (and non-voters) dressing in their party's colours, making their own flags and favours, chalking the pavements and walls and sometimes painting their faces and bodies in party colours. But, as everyone knew, candidates also connived to subvert the law by secretly distributing party flags and cockades, and by hiring musical bands to liven up meetings and demonstrations. In 1906, W. J. Fisher, a defeated Liberal candidate, complained that it was still rare, especially in provincial towns and cities, for an election not to involve 'the employment of bands of music, torches, flags, banners and a general use of Party colours' despite the proscriptions of the Corrupt Practices Act. But then as one tongue-in-cheek guide to electioneering pointed out, candidates needed to ensure the widespread display of party colours in order to bring 'a little life' to something that the law threatened to make 'a very humdrum affair'. However, the law could and did sometimes put a stop to the show. At Walsall in 1892, the victorious Conservative candidate Frank James was unseated on petition because his agent had purchased 6,000 hat cards bearing the slogan 'Play up Swifts' alongside a picture of James (he was trying to capitalize on links to the town's popular football team which was elected to the football league later that year). Such cards were commonly used as a way of circumventing the law prohibiting 'marks of distinction' because it could be argued that it had not been intended that voters should wear them as partisan badges. However, James's bid to bring colour and amusement to the campaign backfired because his election accounts clearly identified the offending items as *hat*-cards.[11] The law did not make it easy for candidates to inject humour and excitement into politics by the late nineteenth century, but plenty still did their best to circumvent its restrictions.

True, candidates increasingly relied on others, such as full-time party agents and paid speakers, to act as intermediaries between themselves and the enlarged electorate, but these were most important in the period between elections. When it came to the campaign such intermediaries necessarily faded into the background. The candidate remained unrivalled as the central character in the electoral show. The election agent remained very much an invisible manager, keen to establish his credentials as a professional exponent of 'scientific' electioneering, but decidedly reluctant to steal the limelight from the candidate. Paid speakers, on the other hand, were highly visible figures, taking politics to those poor voters least likely to read political speeches and party propaganda, or to attend indoor ticketed meetings. However, they were no substitute for the candidate during a campaign, and in any case could not then legally be paid for their services. As the number of electors rose, so candidates' ability to conduct a full personal canvass or to monopolize the platform naturally declined. But if intermediaries necessarily came to take more of the strain, this did little to alter the highly personalized nature of late Victorian and Edwardian electioneering, which continued to be perceived as much a test of the candidates' character and fitness for office, as a test of national party programmes (indeed the whole notion of party 'programmes' in the modern sense remained ill-formed until the great battles of the Edwardian period between 'Tariff Reform' and 'Free Trade').[12]

Rise of the election meeting

Perhaps the most important arena for the expression of untamed popular participation in politics was the election meeting. As we have seen, even in the early nineteenth century the hustings was rarely the only show in town. During a campaign candidates often addressed constituents at impromptu outdoor meetings and in private clubs. Such meetings were usually intended to focus more narrowly on electors than the public hustings, which all agreed tended to be dominated by non-voters keen to 'have their say'. Candidates frequently spoke at special meetings organized by local clubs and societies, but open-air public meetings might also be held. At Chesterfield in 1832, Sir George Sitwell, a prominent tory supporter of the Ten Hours Movement, addressed a large open-air meeting for 'freemen, electors, and others' from the balcony of the Commercial Inn. All were free to ask questions, but as the lengthy account of the meeting makes clear, there was a strong bias towards freemen and other prominent local citizens among the questioners. In 1841, Rouse's *Manual for Election Agents* advised that candidates should make 'personal addresses' to the electors early in the campaign to explain their views, ideally on market days when they might reach the greatest number. But between the First and Second Reform Acts, it was the personal canvass rather than the public meeting which represented the candidate's first duty in the campaign. According to Rouse, if possible the candidate should personally canvass each voter, not least because most elections turned on the votes of 'doubtful men' with no strong allegiance to either side.[13]

The canvass was no less important in the large boroughs, but here there was a more sharply developed tradition of regular election meetings by the mid-1860s. Often these were indoor affairs, where the parties could exert greater control over proceedings—preventing the entry of known opponents, potential trouble-makers, and sometimes anyone who was not a voter. At Liverpool the parties were said to hold election meetings in music halls, school rooms, dissenting chapels, and even circuses. At Bradford both sides held campaign rallies in a large central hall capable of seating 4,000, but they also held dozens of meetings in each of the borough's eight wards—so that in all there must have been over two hundred meetings during the 1868 campaign. But such indoor meetings could still be disrupted by political opponents, or by those simply out to amuse themselves at the candidates' expense. In 1868, deep divisions among Manchester Liberals led supporters of Ernest Jones, the former Chartist leader, to seize control of the platform at the ward meetings of Mitchell Henry, who was standing as an independent, anti-Jonesite Liberal. At the same election, Staleybridge Liberals found their open meetings disrupted by supporters of William Murphy, the notorious anti-Catholic rabble-rouser who had recently stirred up sectarian tensions in the town. They responded by making most of their meetings closed, ticket-only affairs, but this both reduced their value as means of reaching 'doubtful men', and inevitably drew allegations that the Liberals were running scared of public opinion. At the same time, candidates continued to address market-day crowds from the relative safety of hotel balconies, and in towns such as Leeds they sometimes agreed to take part in unofficial joint hustings. Both were 'traditional' forms of outdoor oratory largely immune from the stigma of association with the Radical mass platform, which many still decried for its vulgarity and dangerous populism (at Manchester in 1868, Jones was attacked as an agitator unfit for the Commons precisely because his speeches were said to reflect the crude tastes of the mass platform).[14]

But it was only with the abolition of public nominations in 1872, that the election meeting came into its own as the focal point for face-to-face interaction between politicians and public. In essence, the election meeting took over many of the functions of the old hustings. Such meetings flourished because as well as enabling candidates to explain their views to the public, they allowed the public to interrogate the candidates, and to test their mettle by fair means or foul. Moreover, from the 1870s politicians became noticeably more willing to address the sort of outdoor mass meetings once seen as the preserve of 'unrespectable' radical demagogues. Even as Prime Minister Gladstone held outdoor meetings for thousands of constituents on Blackheath Common in the early 1870s, and later became famous for his impromptu open-air speeches during whistle-stop speaking tours. At Wolverhampton in 1874, the rival Liberal and Conservative candidates braved the February cold to address over 1,500 working men on waste ground near the town's largest engineering factory. They were effectively reproducing the format of the old hustings in order to reach working-class voters thought likely to shun stuffy indoor meetings, even in the depth of winter. Candidates always sought to ration their outdoor speaking, if only because poor acoustics made it very taxing, but it nonetheless became an increasingly important aspect of campaigning in the years after the abolition of public nominations.[15]

As we have seen, all major politicians came to embrace public speaking once Gladstone made it a central aspect of his political appeal during the 1860s. In the early 1870s, Disraeli used 'the platform' to proclaim his 'new' Conservative politics at major set-piece rallies such as those held at the Crystal Palace and the Manchester Free Trade Hall in spring 1872. However, the public platform embraced by the party leaders bore little resemblance to the rough and tumble politics characteristic of both indoor and outdoor election meetings. The parties' 'big guns' generally spoke at highly controlled, ticketed meetings where their audience was confined to the party faithful. Such meetings had a twofold purpose: to reinforce the bonds between the leadership and the party rank-and-file, and to take the leader's message to the wider public through near-verbatim press coverage of his speech. Except in the most elaborately choreographed sense, this ministerial platform was not about interaction with the public, and as such it stands in stark contrast to the election platform where interaction with the public was all important. Interestingly, Gladstone, the pre-eminent platform speaker of the age, was also one of the most carefully protected. When he spoke at an outdoor rally for more than 10,000 on Blackheath Common in 1871, party organizers used stewards and ticketing to control the event, even though the meeting was held on public land, and was intended to allow the Prime Minister to address his constituents. Similarly, in 1885 Randolph Churchill launched a fierce attack on Gladstone for speaking at 'packed' election meetings where questions from the public were strictly vetted.[16]

Gladstone's pre-eminence as a platform speaker was confirmed, above all, by his Herculean efforts of public oratory against British complicity in the Bulgarian atrocities of 1876. In his famous 'Midlothian campaign' of 1879, Gladstone transformed this attack into a general assault on the immorality of 'Beaconsfieldism' (Disraeli had become the Earl of Beaconsfield in 1876). Under the pretext of introducing himself to his new prospective constituency, Gladstone undertook a two-week speaking tour during which he addressed thirty meetings (including eight whistle-stop speeches on his train journeys north and south), and spoke for a total of fifteen and a half hours to a combined audience of just under 90,000 (many of the Midlothian meetings were small affairs in local kirks, although he also spoke to almost 20,000 at Edinburgh's Waverley Market). The tour was a national sensation, with massive coverage across the London and provincial press. But at the subsequent General Election Gladstone was far from alone on the platform, indeed many politicians, including Lord Hartington, his principal rival for the party leadership, addressed significantly more meetings. By 1885, so many front-rank politicians were travelling the country to address large election meetings that the party leaders could afford to take a back seat—Gladstone addressed only five meetings during the election, and Lord Salisbury just three (the Conservative leader was always a reluctant public speaker, but his activities were also restricted by the convention that peers should not interfere in elections to the House of Commons).[17]

Politics was entering an age when the set-piece meeting would come to dominate the lives of any aspiring politician. This usually meant elaborate preparation, especially as it was generally expected that politicians would speak from notes, rather than from a full transcript, but that they would nonetheless speak good prose for the next day's press. Only a few brilliant souls such as David Lloyd George dared trust to the moment and the spirit of improvisation—and even his efforts were often said to lack the necessary 'breadth and literary form' to read well the next morning. Most politicians rehearsed and redrafted their speeches painstakingly before a major meeting. Austen Chamberlain recalled an Edwardian weekend party at Taplow Court when guests found Lord Percy, Lord Hugh Cecil, and Winston Churchill all reciting their Monday speeches in different parts of the grounds. Although some, like Disraeli and Lord Salisbury, were able to memorize speeches so completely that they could speak without even notes, most followed the practice of the House of Commons, condensing their speeches into a series of prompts to ensure that they would not be blown off course should the meeting prove eventful. According to his son, Joseph Chamberlain would spend between three and five days of constant toil drafting and redrafting a major set-piece speech, before finally condensing it into note form.[18]

Actually delivering such speeches was also a major undertaking. In an age before amplification, only the strongest speakers could successfully address the vast audiences prepared to pay to come and hear the nation's political celebrities. Sometimes there might be a mechanical speaking aid, Lord Salisbury was known to make use of a sounding board that had to be specially erected in advance, but even so the physical strain of addressing audiences of up to 30,000—the number apparently squeezed into Birmingham's Bingley Hall to hear Gladstone in 1883—was very considerable (Gladstone records sipping egg-flip to save his voice, while, perhaps characteristically, Disraeli preferred large quantities of clear, white brandy—it looked like water even to the most keen-eyed temperance fanatic). The ability of party leaders to reach out to their followers in this way transformed politics, creating the basis for a more personal, charismatic, style of leadership, but it should be remembered that only a small proportion of the public, drawn overwhelmingly from the activist minority, could hope to see and hear their leaders in the flesh. Most Victorians consumed their politics at the breakfast table, in the lengthy press accounts of the party leaders' speeches (if they consumed them at all that is). This was why the short-hand reporters from the press and the news

Fig. 4. Gladstone addressing his constituents and reporters at an open-air meeting, 1874, *ILN*, 7 Feb. 1874, reproduced with the kind permission of the Syndics of Cambridge University Library

agencies always occupied a privileged position close to the platform, and it was why politicians sometimes succumbed to the temptation of allowing reporters access to advance copies of their speeches, in the hope of securing prominent coverage in the next day's papers. It was a practice that could occasionally backfire, as when *The Times* carried a full report of one of Gladstone's famous whistle-stop speeches even though a late-running train meant that the speech was never made (Fig. 4 shows Gladstone and the press corps at a meeting on Blackheath Common in 1874).[19]

Ordinary election meetings also thrived on press publicity. By the 1880s most constituencies had at least one daily newspaper prepared to cover candidates' meetings, and this provided a strong incentive for candidates to deliver a major speech every evening. Candidates were also advised to follow their opponents' speeches in the press so that they could quickly 'refute their arguments', and, judging by surviving collections of personal papers such as those of the Shropshire Conservative William Bridgeman, they took this advice seriously, amassing extensive scrapbooks of annotated cuttings from their opponents' speeches. Often rival local newspapers were directly owned by the opposing candidates or their close supporters, adding to the piquancy of their election coverage. But even where the press was more independent, it still played a vital role in shaping a genuinely interactive politics at constituency level—with controversies sometimes unfolding over many days of intense platform and press argument. But candidates could not rely solely on the press for their political intelligence. Reporters knew better than to repeat a slanderous attack in print, and candidates were therefore advised to make sure that they sent spies to opponents' meetings, preferably ones capable of taking short-hand notes, in case legal action should be required. Significantly, in 1895 Parliament amended the illegal practices laws specifically to combat the evil of election slander—henceforth an MP would be unseated if it could be proven that he had slandered a rival candidate. But since there was strong popular prejudice against a man who relied on the law to defeat his opponent, candidates were told that their best defence was to issue a personal letter to constituents refuting any false allegations, and attacking the foul methods of their opponent.[20]

The culture of election meetings

The first purpose of an election meeting was always to bring the candidate directly to the people; press coverage, however valuable, remained a secondary concern. Once the vote had been extended to the agricultural labourer in 1884, candidates in large rural constituencies would be expected to address at least one meeting in every village, even if this involved holding multiple meetings every night, and travelling vast distances on poor country roads in the process. In towns the candidate was expected to address meetings in every corner of every ward, often at outdoor pitches as well as in draughty local school halls. Sometimes logistics would defeat the election organizers in large rural constituencies and they would have to make do with a flying visit, rather than a full-blown meeting, in one remote hamlet or another, but everyone knew that such neglect risked fostering local resentment, and perhaps encouraging abstentions at the poll. If anything, the arrival of the private motor-car in the early twentieth century simply raised expectations, so that it became common for candidates to speak at five or more meetings in an evening—often relying on multi-car relays to fulfil their commitments. Where once a single appearance on the hustings would have sufficed, candidates now undertook dozens, often hundreds, of mini-hustings in every corner of their constituency. At each they would offer a short address on some burning topic of interest (at least to them), before fulfilling the primary function of such meetings—taking questions from the floor.[21]

Unlike set-piece ministerial meetings, it was absolutely essential that the election meeting should be genuinely open to all, just as the old public hustings had been. At major election rallies some tickets might be sold to help raise campaign funds, but the ordinary ward and village meetings that dominated a candidate's schedule had to be both open and free. Time and again, candidates were warned to avoid ticketing their meetings if at all possible—all agreed that a closed meeting was next to useless as a propaganda tool. Instead, they were advised to secure adequate stewarding to control troublemakers. They were also told to encourage women to attend in large numbers, as this usually improved behaviour (an interesting insight into the perceived chivalry of even the election 'rough'), and to ensure that likely troublemakers were sat near the front, where they could be watched, rather than in the shadows at the back. In a guide published by Conservative Central Office in 1890, it was suggested that one solution to persistent disorder might be to issue special invitation cards to local electors, thereby excluding the non-electors deemed by many to be the most likely source of trouble. But as the Shoreditch Conservatives discovered in 1880, such measures could offer little protection against determined opponents prepared to use forgery to gain entry to the other side's meetings. They also clashed with the customary expectation that election meetings, like the old hustings, were principally held to give non-electors the chance to 'have their say' before the poll. Down to 1914, approximately 40 per cent of adult men, and all women, remained excluded from the Parliamentary franchise, and the election meeting was recognized as almost their only chance to participate in the electoral process, and, perhaps more importantly, to interrogate their would-be representatives (see Fig. 5, which offers a gentle skit on the absurdity of many such exchanges).[22]

According to W. H. Rowe, of Conservative Central Office, it was precisely because audiences were 'always largely composed of non-electors' that meetings alone could never carry a campaign. Writing in 1890, Rowe acknowledged that meetings were indispensable, but counselled that their enthusiasm could be 'deceptive' and their effect 'over-rated'. According to Rowe, many voters, especially those who were 'doubtful' or 'indifferent', would never attend a public meeting, and therefore could only be reached by careful canvassing in their homes. A Primrose League election guide from 1914 took much the same line, insisting that 'personal persuasion' would always be more important than public meetings, not least because 'personal conversation affords opportunities for the discussion of points of especial interest to the individuals'. This worked best, League members were told, where the canvass could be 'personalised', with electors visited by acquaintances or people in the same trade as themselves. Although deference is often seen as the linchpin of Primrose League success before the Great War, this was not the face that it chose to turn to the wider public when votes were at stake. For one thing, the 'lady bountiful' canvasser was often deeply resented, as Stephen Reynolds and the Woolley brothers showed in a brilliant Edwardian sketch parodying the insensitive and condescending Mrs Balkwill as she tried to cajole Dave Perring, a poor but cussedly independent Devon fisherman, into voting for her candidate. But, the League also had to recognize that many wealthy supporters had no taste to go 'slumming' in pursuit of votes. Indeed, as early as 1869, Liverpool's pioneering 'tory democrat' Arthur Forwood frankly acknowledged that 'gentlemen' supporters would only canvass 'the best wards', leaving the bulk of the city to be worked by volunteers drawn from among the clerks and working men.[23]

One might well ask why candidates devoted so much time to meetings if they rarely brought victory, and if they were often the source, not just of physical exhaustion, but of inconvenience, abuse, and even physical pain. It might be tempting to blame vanity—some candidates undoubtedly relished the excitement of a tempestuous meeting, even more probably relished the sound of their own voices. But for many the constant round of election meetings in dreary halls was torture from beginning to end—yet still they persevered because everyone agreed that they had to—but why?

Fig. 5. Large and influential meetings at the 1885 General Election, *ILN*, 21 Nov. 1885, reproduced with the kind permission of the Syndics of Cambridge University Library

Above all, it was because, having filled the void left by the abolition of the hustings, the election meeting became a source of political legitimacy that no candidate could be seen to shun. Where once he had been expected to put up with the catcalls and abuse of the nomination crowd, now he was expected to endure a similar ordeal repeated daily in miniature across the constituency in the name of 'openness' and 'accountability'. Where once the hustings had been a great social leveller, now it was the election meeting. Certainly, many of the indignities of the hustings came to be routine features of the late Victorian and Edwardian election meeting. Both audiences and squib writers would seize on the chance to mock candidates who spoke poorly, or whose deportment on the platform fell noticeably short of the manly ideal. In 1880, a Liberal squib attacked Henry Allsopp, the Conservative candidate for East Worcestershire and a prominent brewer, as a poor speaker whose only hope of victory lay in 'the beer tap'. But it also mocked his weak, 'unmanly' persona at meetings: 'When the platform you sought and adventured to stand, | How gouty your step! and your visage how bland!' Candidates also continued to face the physical dangers once associated with the hustings. Bags of soot, or worse cayenne pepper, would sometimes be thrown to make 'speaking almost impossible', or improvised musical instruments would be smuggled in to drown the speaker in a cacophony of 'rough music'. Missiles were also regularly thrown, with firecrackers, eggs, fish, and rotten tomatoes favoured by those out for a little fun, while more malevolent audiences might turn to stones, ball bearings, or even the chairs they were supposed to sit on. Even in 1895, a generally rather low-key election thanks to the disarray in Liberal ranks, missiles were far from unknown, perhaps in part because the summer poll made vegetal ammunition unusually plentiful. At Oswestry, tory farmers were said to have caused trouble at Liberal meetings by throwing cabbages and tomatoes at the platform, while at Loughborough a rotten egg missed the Liberal candidate, but not his chairman or several lady supporters by his side.[24]

Like the hustings, the election meeting generated elaborate codes that shaped the actions of both speakers and audience. A good example would be the apparently bizarre tendency for candidates to plough on with a speech despite such vociferous disruption that they would be inaudible even to the strategically placed press reporters. In part this was simply a question of displaying that indomitable spirit the Victorians liked to call 'pluck', but it also reflected awareness of the customary belief that a meeting had not been 'broken up' if it lasted more than an hour. Moreover, although everyone knew that such disruption was rarely spontaneous, this did little to diminish the idea that an open public meeting represented a test of political legitimacy—and that any truly popular candidate would be able to rely on his friends and supporters to ensure a successful public meeting. True, organized disruption was generally deplored, but few candidates saw much to be gained by advertising the misdeeds of their opponents. When forced to explain the disruption of their meetings, they usually sought to portray the culprits as unsavoury hirelings from outside the constituency—before 1914 it was not sufficient simply to allege that an opponent's supporters were disorderly hooligans whose conduct proved that their cause was bankrupt. There was always particular sensitivity about attempts to 'capture' the platform, lest opponents should use it to pass hostile resolutions against the candidate and his cause. At Middleton, just north of Manchester, a Conservative meeting descended into farce in a dispute over whether the candidate would take questions from the floor. Amidst considerable pandemonium, the chairman declared the meeting officially closed, but neither side would leave the hall for fear that their rivals might seize the chance to pass partisan resolutions. In turn this dispute touched on two key facets of the election meeting that grew directly out of the old hustings: the audience's right both to ask questions and to express their opinions in a formal show of hands. Many insisted that the right to question the candidate should be unfettered, and the widespread custom of irreverent heckling in part fed off the belief that the candidate could be challenged at any point. The heckler was generally tolerated as a legitimate feature of election meetings, and many politicians insisted, not only that they thrived on such interventions, but that they used them to give structure and vigour to their platform performances. When things became particularly difficult, candidates might dispense with speeches altogether, simply throwing the meeting open to questions from the floor, although at the other extreme there were candidates who sought to preserve a modicum of order and control by insisting that they would only answer *written* questions (Gladstone and Churchill both favoured this method). Election guides also advised that if things got awkward organizers should ignore the custom of holding a show of hands for the candidate and his party, and instead simply move a vote of thanks for the chairman. But just as it was difficult to stop an audience from shouting out questions (and demanding answers), it was hard to stop them conducting their own show of hands.[25]

To understand why election meetings often involved bitter displays of party conflict, one needs to recognize the particular significance attributed to open public meetings in nineteenth-century Britain. In essence, such meetings sought to mimic the ancient custom whereby local leaders could convene parish, town, or county meetings to allow the public to air its feelings on a matter of burning concern. By drawing together the active, concerned citizenry such meetings purported to speak for their locality—and as such possessed a legitimacy that was widely recognized and respected. By holding open, public meetings political parties hoped to claim a similar legitimacy for their cause, and in doing so they gave licence to their opponents to mount counter-demonstrations. Interestingly, many of the most bitter confrontations between the parties focused not on election meetings, where the rules of the game were well known, but on protest meetings of more uncertain status, where one side or the other appeared to be trying to pass off a closed, party gathering as an open, representative meeting that purported to speak for the public as a whole. For instance in 1884, at the height of the crisis over the Third Reform Act, Birmingham Radicals broke up a Conservative mass meeting at Aston, incensed at a 'Tory ticket picnic being considered an expression of the voice of the Midlands'. Similarly, Conservative activists broke up anti-war meetings in 1878 and 1900, arguing that their proponents were falsely claiming to speak for the public at a time of national crisis. Disruption at election meetings sprang from the same logic—each side boasted of its ability to hold open meetings to demonstrate public acclaim for their man, and each side knew that success depended on mobilizing sufficient force, in the form of volunteer stewards, or sometimes covertly hired 'heavies', to ensure that their opponents would not be able to capture the meeting or break it up (see Fig. 6).[26]

As the Edwardian Liberal organizer Seymour Lloyd observed, perhaps the most remarkable feature of this widespread political disruption was not so much its near ubiquity, as the fact that 'in many constituencies the practice was looked upon rather as a harmless amusement by some of the minor politicians'. The American political scientist A. L. Lowell, made much the same observation in 1908, noting that the British generally saw a political meeting 'as a demonstration, rather than a place for serious discussion', and so tolerated counter-demonstrations despite the considerable disruption

Fig. 6. Disruption at an election meeting, 1885, *The Graphic*, 24 Oct. 1885 (part), reproduced with the kind permission of the Syndics of Cambridge University Library

they frequently caused. In part this reflected the view that disruption represented non-voters having their 'say' according to the time-honoured traditions of the old hustings, but tolerance of disorder was also sustained by a widespread belief, derived in part from classical traditions of civic republicanism, that a healthy polity depended on an active, vigilant (and male) citizenry. Better the occasional excesses of an over-excited public, than the dull apathy of a supine people incapable of defending their freedom and liberty. On the other hand, neither the state nor politicians should be openly implicated in disorderly politics—hence the determined efforts both to 're-form' official electoral culture and to penalize candidates found guilty of orchestrating electoral malpractice. Moreover, whilst in the constituencies Conservatives were fully integrated into the 'politics of disruption', and in radical mythology were the chief employers of prize-fighters and 'roughs' as hired muscle, nationally their leaders remained instinctively suspicious of the politics of mass mobilization. During the political crisis of 1884, Lord Salisbury famously dismissed Radical demonstrations in favour of reform by insisting that 'A party can speak by processions and demonstrations, but the nation can only speak at the polling booth'. Salisbury attacked the Liberal Government's willingness to 'descend into the streets' to bolster its case, and mocked the idea that '30,000 radicals going to amuse themselves in London on a given day expresses the public opinion of the country'. It was a view which did little to overturn the Victorian preference for active rather than passive manifestations of public opinion, but, in his stubborn resistance to the relentless march of mass democracy, Salisbury was nonetheless articulating a more circumscribed and orderly vision of citizenship which would ultimately come to dominate political life in the succeeding century.[27]

The restructuring of electoral politics, 1883–1885

As historians have long recognized, the context and character of British electoral politics were transformed by three major measures passed by Gladstone's second ministry between 1883 and 1885: the Corrupt and Illegal Practices Prevention Act (1883), the Third Reform Act (1884), and the Redistribution Act (1885). For the most part this legislative revolution simply accelerated existing trends (notably politicians' growing reliance both on the voluntary effort of local party activists and on the services of professional organizers and propagandists), but change was nonetheless so rapid that this moment deserves special historical attention. Writing early in the last century, Charles Seymour saw the legislation of 1883–5 as finally undermining the electoral dominance of the aristocracy, and establishing in its place a system firmly under the control of local party associations. By dramatically restricting how candidates could spend money during a campaign, and, perhaps more importantly, by greatly improving the mechanisms for supervising campaign expenditure, the Corrupt Practices Act gave a great boost to the role of the volunteer in electoral politics. John Gorst, the genius behind Disraeli's reorganization of the Conservative party after the defeat of 1868, saw this immediately, and recognized that the Act would transform the relationship between candidates and their local supporters. By outlawing the payment of canvassers and public speakers, and by strictly limiting the number of campaign staff who could be employed (all of whom were to be disfranchised by their employment), the Act ensured that even the most reluctant candidate would have to cultivate a strong 'voluntary party'. Conservative organizers in the Midlands drew the same conclusion, though more reluctantly. They worried over the danger of stimulating an 'abundance of zeal' among their supporters, but nonetheless concluded that the party had no choice but to create active mass organizations across the region if it was to compete under the new electoral system.[28]

Of course, the voluntary party was not a creation of the 1880s reforms. Throughout the 1870s, debate had raged about the pros and cons of the so-called Liberal 'Caucus' pioneered by the Birmingham Liberals in order to maximize their voting strength in School Board and Parliamentary elections (in the former electors cast multiple votes for slates of candidates, in the latter they cast only two votes for three seats—the so-called minority clause). The Birmingham model quickly gained ground among Liberals, not least as an antidote to the problem of multiple Liberal candidacies which plagued the party in many constituencies after 1867. Nor were the Conservatives complete strangers to the mass party before 1883. At Liverpool mass membership and a strong ward organization preceded the Second Reform Act. Indeed by 1869, the local party already boasted that volunteer workers were far more reliable than paid, and claimed that they were responsible for 95 per cent of the party's canvassing in the city. However, the Liverpool tory machine was not typical. By contrast, Birmingham Conservatives still relied almost entirely on paid canvassers in

1883, though less from choice, than because volunteer workers were so scarce in the capital of Chamberlainite Radicalism.[29]

The 1883 Act stimulated a plethora of election guides purporting to explain the new legislation to candidates and their agents, including notable contributions by the former Conservative principal agent John Gorst, and by the young lawyer and future Liberal Prime Minister, Herbert Asquith. It was testimony to the fact that, whilst *Blackwood's* might be right to argue that when it came to reforming electoral morals 'The voice in Parliament is not the voice out of doors', by the mid-1880s politicians appeared more willing to challenge popular feeling than in earlier decades. Writing in 1890, the secretary of the Conservative Central Office felt sure that the 1883 Act had 'raised the tone of election warfare, and stimulated and encouraged voluntary effort in a high degree'. Historians have generally endorsed this optimistic assessment of the Act. According to Cornelius O'Leary, the Corrupt Practices Act was responsible for a marked reduction in the level of disorder at British elections in the late nineteenth century. And while O'Leary probably overstates the diminution of violence by making too little of the increased legal barriers to mounting a petition for 'intimidation' after 1883, and by ignoring evidence that disorder and even riot often remained endemic at constituency level, it seems doubtful whether any subsequent election ever witnessed disorder, or indeed corruption, on the scale of 1880 (though the election of January 1910 ran it pretty close).[30]

Contemporaries were always deeply divided on the extent to which the 1883 Act cured British voting of corruption. Many insisted that the direct bribery of voters became much rarer in the late nineteenth century, partly because the Act transformed election agents from poachers into gamekeepers, but also because popular attitudes towards corruption were beginning to change. Historians have generally endorsed this view, although Hanham placed greater emphasis on the disfranchisement of notorious corrupt boroughs through the effects of redistribution, and Kathryn Rix has recently argued that the key factor was the gradual emergence of a new class of professional agent dedicated to bending rather than breaking electoral law. On the other hand, money continued to exert great influence over electoral politics, most notably through the practice of 'nursing'—that is, the large-scale donations that prospective parliamentary candidates regularly made in support of local churches, clubs, and charities. But even this was beginning to fall from favour in political circles by the early twentieth century, as we shall see in Chapter 3.[31]

The radical redistribution of seats that accompanied electoral reform in 1885 also did much to transform the structure of British elections. It was only from this point that the majority of electors found themselves represented by a single Member of Parliament—until then most constituencies had returned two members, and Birmingham, Leeds, Liverpool, and Manchester had each returned three. Under the redistribution of 1868 just over ninety English constituencies had returned a single MP to Westminster. But after 1885 the single-member constituency became the norm, with just two dozen double-member seats surviving in boroughs with populations between 50,000 and 165,000 (towns such as Bolton, Leicester, and Sunderland—ten of which survived as double-member boroughs down to 1948). One consequence was that it became much harder for local powerbrokers to strike private deals to avoid a contest. Rival parties would still sometimes agree to give each other a clear run in particular divisions, but deals became all but impossible *within* parties—the days of Whigs and Radicals sharing the Liberal ticket were over, and the scope for accommodating the growing demands for labour representation within the Liberal fold was much reduced. At the same time, many small boroughs were either amalgamated into the surrounding county, or else significantly enlarged. In consequence, many local parties suddenly found themselves facing greatly increased electorates—Swaddle estimates that the median borough electorate rose from 3,790 in 1880 to 8,269 in 1885, greatly reducing the scope for individualized campaigning in many constituencies. However, whilst the most extreme discrepancies were removed, there was no effort to equalize constituency electorates. York, with a population of 60,000, retained two MPs, while nearby Middlesbrough with 72,000 inhabitants returned only one. Even within a single borough such as Liverpool, which was carved into nine single-member divisions by the Act, there was considerable variation between the largest and smallest electorate (Everton had 9,439 voters compared with barely 7,000 in the Irish-dominated Scotland Division—while Manchester North-West boasted 12,685 voters compared with only 8,579 in the adjacent North-East division). Even most radicals objected to strict equalization on the grounds that it would destroy the individuality and historical integrity of British constituencies. But something had still been lost in the larger towns and cities, which now became a patchwork of apparently arbitrary subdivisions. Lubbock and Courtney resigned from the Liberal Government over the issue, convinced that subdivision would destroy the 'individuality' of boroughs and reduce MPs to mere 'delegates of ward interests'. In his memoirs, the former Liberal minister Augustine Birrell echoed their complaints, arguing that the Act had 'ruined the romance' of an election in his native Liverpool. Here at least it seemed as though the representation of mere agglomerations of individuals had triumphed over older ideas about the representation of coherent communities and their interests. In theory the new constituency boundaries were drawn to reflect the 'pursuits of the people', but this was always a highly subjective concept, and, despite claims to the contrary, it did not simply involve the recognition of pre-existing geographically and sociologically distinct 'communities'. Rather, as a series of recent studies have demonstrated, even the newly created suburban divisions were so-cially and politically diverse—if many became bastions of so-called 'villa toryism' this owed more to sustained hard work by local parties, than to brute sociological logic.[32]

Finally, we need to look at the impact of reform itself. The 1884 Third Reform Act extended the borough householder franchise of 1867 to the counties, and was proclaimed by all sides as inaugurating the political emancipation of the agricultural labourer. Older county franchises, including the notorious 40-shilling freeholder franchise responsible for the generation of so many manufactured 'faggot' votes, survived alongside the new mass franchise, but henceforth something approaching adult male democracy would operate in the counties as well as the towns. In total the county electorate more than doubled between 1883 and 1886—increasing from approximately 960,000 to over 2.5 million. It marked the beginning of a radical transformation of rural politics. Within a decade elected county and parish councils existed alongside the new, more democratic Parliamentary divisions and the parties found themselves dragged inexorably into a competition for the farm labourer's vote. Reform heralded an explosion of political meetings across the countryside. As late as 1884 one still finds local Conservative parties such as the Oswestry Association holding no political meetings at all outside elections for fear that they might stir their quiescent radical foes into action. But once 'John Hodge' had the vote such an approach was unthinkable, not least because agricultural labourers were thought to be all but immune to traditional means of political persuasion. Canvassing posed a particularly tough challenge because labourers were commonly supposed to say 'yes' to both sides, not just to ensure a quiet life, but because the habit of *appearing* deferential to 'the likes o' they' was so deeply engrained in the labourer's psyche. Similarly, it was assumed that his limited formal education meant that John Hodge was more likely to be swayed by platform oratory than fine prose. Time and again politicians were reminded to keep things simple for 'indifferent and ignorant voters' and never to assume knowledge in party literature. But this was by no means a story confined to the 'backward' shires. Politics as a whole was becoming more, rather than less, populist at the close of the nineteenth century, as the parties grappled with the challenges of the new mass politics. At Westminster politicians might seek to tame popular political customs through legislative reform, but in the constituencies they tended to bow to the logic of electoral necessity. This meant cultivating the 'common touch' (or a reasonable semblance of it) and avoiding any action likely to offend popular sensibilities. By the Edwardian period electoral politics were probably more volatile, and more shamelessly populist, than at any time in living memory. Many politicians felt profoundly uneasy about the tenor of the new democratic mass politics, but as we will see in the next chapter, they also felt powerless to change things in the years before the Great War.[33]

3

Money, Men, and Mayhem: Electoral Politics before the First World War

The triumph of populism

Historians have often stressed the growing civility and rationalism of public politics in Britain in the decades before the First World War. According to Cornelius O'Leary, after 1880 elections lost 'much of their colour and festive character. The exercise of the franchise was at last regarded as a solemn duty, a right of citizenship, but also a responsibility.' In a similar vein, Colin Matthew has written of the emergence of 'an integrated political community' in late Victorian Britain where 'public oratorical accountability was the link between Westminster and a politically fascinated national constituency'. By contrast, after the war, Matthew argues, politics came to be dominated by what Wallas termed the 'deliberate exploitation of sub-conscious, non-rational inference', and in this debased and polarized climate Liberalism naturally lost out to the more elemental, materialist politics espoused by Labour and the Conservatives. But, in truth Edwardian elections were more fiercely fought, more disorderly, and more shamelessly populist than those of either the late Victorian or the inter-war era. Perhaps more importantly, Liberal heavyweights such as Lloyd George, Churchill, and even Asquith showed themselves to be supreme masters of this new uncompromising mass politics.[1]

Perhaps the epitome of the Edwardian Liberals' embrace of vulgar populism was their exploitation of the so-called 'Chinese slavery' issue in the run-up to the 1906 election (indentured Chinese labourers were being transported to work the Transvaal gold mines in the wake of the

1899–1902 Boer War). In theory this was a classic liberal issue embodying internationalism, humanitarianism, and an abhorrence of the evils of slavery and imperial exploitation—and this is undoubtedly how many leading Liberals discussed the issue from the platform. However, this was not how it played in the populist Liberal press, nor, crucially, how it came to be represented in official party propaganda or in heated constituency contests. Recalling the election in the 1930s, the former Liberal minister Augustine Birrell decried 'the spectacle of hired men dressed up as Chinese labourers, dragged out from one Liberal platform to another'—he made no excuse for these 'disgusting' re-enactments, merely observing that, 'Electioneering is a vulgarizing pursuit'. Pro-Liberal newspapers such as *Reynolds's Newspaper* and the *Morning Leader* took things even further—representing Joseph Chamberlain, the former Unionist Colonial Secretary, as 'the Rt. Hon. Chowseph Chamerstein'—one-part Chinese labourer, one-part Jewish financier. Official Liberal propaganda never quite plumbed these depths, but it did deliberately fuel resentment that jobs on the Rand were to go, not to white Britons, whose army had won the war, but to foreigners willing to work in appalling conditions. One leaflet spoke of Chinese 'slaves' come to 'take the bread out of the mouth of the British workman', while a colour poster from the 1906 election depicted a ghost-like British soldier trying to rouse the sleeping John Bull to the sight of a stereotypically Jewish financier overseeing three Chinese labourers with their hands tied(?) behind them. The poster was entitled 'The War's Result: Chinese Labour', and included the caption: 'Voice of Tommy Atkins (from the shades): "Is THIS what we fought for?' Technically there was no mention of 'slavery' here, but in the context of the 1906 campaign there hardly needed to be for the message to strike home.[2]

By most measures the two elections of 1910 were even more intensely fought and 'vulgar'. The first election, in January, was especially note-worthy. Rarely had a General Election been so close, and never had such a large proportion of the electorate been mobilized to vote. Turnout across the United Kingdom reached an all-time high of 86.8 per cent, and the two main parties ended up in a near dead-heat—274 Liberal MPs to 272 Conservative/Unionist—though 82 Irish Nationalist and 40 Labour MPs ensured that Asquith remained secure at Number 10. Only eight English constituencies saw unopposed returns, compared with 116 in 1895 and 151 in 1900. Moreover, the contests themselves were also decidedly more intense and volatile in 1910. A detailed study of campaigning in eleven

English constituencies between 1895 and 1935 recorded more than twice as many election meetings in January 1910 as in 1895—in part because the campaign was dragged out over a remarkable eight weeks. At the same time, election meetings were almost twice as likely to involve outside speakers, and also almost twice as likely to involve active opposition from the floor (30 per cent of meetings involved opposition, compared with 18 per cent in 1895, and approximately 10 per cent in 1922 and 1935, the two post-war elections studied). Perhaps for this reason January 1910 was also the election when meetings were most likely to involve both a visible police presence, and organized entertainment such as communal singing.[3]

But if the elections of 1910 marked the high point of partisan mobilization in modern British politics, this should be seen, not as a contingent artefact of the close and bitter party conflict of that year, but as the culmination of longer-term trends—trends that had been set in motion by the legislative transformation of electioneering in the 1880s. The mainstream parties responded to this transformation by adopting ever more populist methods in the hope of gaining the upper hand over their rivals. By historical standards, electoral turnout was high across the late Victorian and Edwardian period. In England, turnout at General Elections ranged from 74.1 per cent (1886) to 87.7 per cent (January 1910), and in the three elections fought on relatively young electoral registers (1885, 1906, and January 1910) it averaged 84.4 per cent—a figure matched only once in the remainder of the twentieth century (in the knife-edge contest of February 1950). During these years the political parties went to great lengths to enliven public politics in the hope that they might capture the interest of the new mass electorate. In essence, the parties were filling the void left by the legislative curtailment of the official election earlier in the century—although they were naturally also responding to the great increase in the size of constituency electorates under the Second and especially the Third Reform Acts. The populism of Edwardian public politics had its roots in these efforts to enliven party politics and thereby reach out to the new voters.

Contemporaries were particularly struck by the great increase in outdoor election meetings after 1885. Election manuals increasingly advised that the candidate must not let fears for the 'dignity of his position' prevent him from reaching out to the type of voter who would never come to an indoor meeting. As we have seen, in the larger boroughs this trend was already noticeable by the 1870s, but by the 1900s it had become all but universal.

However, some politicians never warmed to the hardships of 'outdoor work', with its exceptional demands on the voice, and limited scope for controlling hostile opposition from the crowd. Lord Salisbury, Conservative leader through the 1880s and 1890s, remained a reluctant performer even on the conventional indoor platform, and made few personal concessions to the need to chase votes—indeed his electoral strategy was premised on the need to contain rather than exploit mass democracy—so that 'popular Conservatism', which undoubtedly flourished in this era, was for the most part built from the bottom up. Interestingly, even Winston Churchill, who frequently appealed to the traditions of 'tory democracy' associated with his father, continued to have deep reservations about outdoor meetings until electric amplification became widely available in the mid-1920s. Churchill's aversion to outdoor speaking may have been shaped in part by his experiences at the 1908 Dundee by-election, when his outdoor meetings were wrecked by a female suffrage campaigner wielding a large railway porter's bell. With both the crowd and the law on her side, the Liberal stewards were powerless to act and Churchill's outdoor meetings collapsed into farce. In 1918 Churchill was still insisting on his 'rule against open air meetings', perhaps because he found that, with the opposition weak, the town's 'extremists' flocked to his meetings to 'let off steam'. But he was quick to break his rule when the local shipyard workers asked him to address a lunchtime meeting at the docks. Not even a heavyweight like Churchill could afford to pass up such an opportunity, however weak the opposition might be—to do so would have played into the hands of the 'Bolshies and Conshies' (as he put it) who were causing trouble at his meetings.[4]

But perhaps what was most remarkable about the late Victorian explosion of outdoor speaking was how rarely crowds overstepped the mark. True, unruly crowds might sometimes push and harass, but despite candidates' obvious vulnerability election crowds generally refrained from causing them serious harm. Of course, this was not entirely a matter of goodwill—only the most foolhardy politician would appear without a 'bodyguard' of partisans to ring the platform, and some, including Churchill, occasionally hired undercover detectives to supplement the forces of the local constabulary. But given the continued volatility of electoral politics, self-restraint must also have played its part. It is as though an unspoken compact existed between crowd and politician—with the former recognizing the symbolic significance of the candidate's willingness to abandon the relative safety of an indoor meeting (and, one might add, of a privileged life), to take up the rigours of open-air politics. Deference was part of the story here—it mattered that the candidate taking politics to the people in this way was seen as a 'toff'. When it was just a so-called 'freak' candidate, such as the maverick independent Arthur Hunnable, who intervened in a series of by-elections during 1907 and 1908, different rules applied—although even Hunnable was more often mocked than harmed (Fig. 7). By contrast, when Churchill and Chamberlain found their carriage trapped 'in an immense hostile crowd' at Oldham in 1900, both were confident that for all the excitement, and the 'groaning and booing', they were in no physical danger. Similarly, at nearby Manchester North-West in 1906, a press photographer captured William Joynson-Hicks, the future Conservative Home Secretary, standing precariously on a flimsy wooden chair with little more than his suit, stiff collar, and tie to protect him from a large, and judging from the man in the foreground, decidedly hostile audience (Fig. 8—note, too, the two elegantly dressed ladies apparently seated behind 'Jix' and presumably also confident that they would come to no harm). Surveying more than three decades of electioneering experience in 1931, Churchill praised the 'good sportsmanship' of British voters, and insisted that even the most hostile crowds 'very rarely try to hurt you', however much they might shout you down or attack 'your personal character'.[5]

On the other hand, social prestige was not always sufficient to protect a candidate from the crowd. Augustine Birrell's experience of the 1900 election in Manchester was much less happy than Churchill's, culminating on polling day with him and his wife being followed through the streets by a hostile mob that spat on them and spattered them with mud from the dirty streets (although even this rough treatment was aimed more at humiliation than actual bodily harm). Candidates were also warned not to overdo the symbols of social prestige—audiences expected a candidate to dress 'respectably', not least as a marker of respect for them as an audience, but this meant the sober attire of the middle-class professional, not the more flamboyant and overtly class-inflected dress of upper-class leisure. Seymour Lloyd was convinced that even in small town and village meetings, 'the arrival of a platform group in white ties and shirtfronts has a tendency to emphasize class distinctions in a way which is hardly consistent with good taste, and, from an electioneering standpoint, is hopelessly bad tactics'. The point of the election meeting was to exploit class distinction by appearing to deny its significance as a barrier between candidate and public. As such,

Fig. 7. Tormenting Arthur Hunnable at Jarrow, 1907

Fig. 8. William Joynson-Hix ('Jix') campaigning at North-West Manchester, 1906

anything that appeared to betray a sense of social superiority undermined the democratic symbolism of the meeting. This meant speech and manner, as much as dress. As Seymour Lloyd put it, 'A platformer on a pedestal is a ghastly failure—and deservedly so … People do not go to political meetings to be lectured by a fine gentleman who feels himself miles above their heads.' On the contrary, they went to political meetings to hear fine gentlemen talking to them as equals—even if the more successful platform performers knew that this meant modifying their language to hide the class gulf embedded in a Latinate as opposed to Anglo-Saxon vocabulary. Some also went to shout abuse at their social superiors, but that was usually the limit of their class revolt. Writing to her husband in the midst of the bitter 1922 election at Dundee, Clementine Churchill was adamant that 'even in the rowdiest, foulest place of all[,] the people were really good-natured'. The convalescing Churchill was less confident—when he finally arrived in Dundee one meeting was so disorderly that he asked his private detective to sleep across his hotel doorway. That said, a decade later he too would be celebrating the restraint that generally characterized even the rowdiest British meeting.[6]

From the 1880s, the need to reach out to the new voters also fuelled a revolution in the printing operations undertaken at party headquarters. Three main factors drove this propaganda revolution: first, technical innovations such as offset-lithography and rotogravure which allowed printers to break free from the constraints of traditional letter-press printing; second, the so-called 'yellow press' revolution on Fleet Street associated with titles such as the *Daily Mail* and *Daily Express*, which highlighted the mass appeal of sharp layout and punchy journalism; and third, the growth of commercial advertising which heightened awareness of the need for visual impact in mass communications. Of course, much party propaganda remained dense and uninspiring, but there was nonetheless a discernible shift in both the quantity and quality of printed party 'literature'—as all sides insisted on describing their printed propaganda—from the mid-1890s. The Liberal Publication Department, established in 1887 to provide local Liberal parties with a reliable source of centrally produced leaflets, pamphlets, and posters, produced over 10 million leaflets at the 1892 General Election. This figure had risen to 25 million by 1895, and over 40 million at its pre-war peak in January 1910. Conservative Central Office more than matched this prodigious effort, distributing no less than 46 million leaflets in January 1910, when the total British electorate stood at under eight million—that is, more than six leaflets for each voter. Since local parties continued to produce their own 'literature' on a massive scale, and there was also a proliferation of non-party election material generated by assorted pressure groups, it can be seen that the Edwardian elector was probably at greater risk of drowning in a sea of paper than in a sea of free beer. Whether it was all read is another matter. H. C. Richards certainly doubted it, arguing that whilst party literature was usually read in the counties, it was 'often wasted by being scattered broadcast in the towns'. Similarly, despite the party's great propaganda effort of January 1910 the *Liberal Agent* nonetheless felt that 'The leaflet can never be so effective as the human voice' since the hard-working elector would always prefer to hear a lively speaker in the flesh. There is evidence that the Conservatives in particular were seeking to refine their propaganda techniques on the eve of the First World War, producing special leaflets targeted at specific groups such as shopkeepers, railwaymen, and building workers. This was to become a staple of inter-war electioneering, although given the relative paucity of the information most parties had about individual electors it always tended to work better in theory than in practice.[7]

The political poster also came into its own in this period. In 1880 election posters still relied almost entirely on bold verbal messages using traditional letterpress printing, but simple line-drawings gained ground over the next decade, usually in the form of political cartoons, and in the 1890s the first full-colour election posters appeared, mimicking the revolutionary impact of Pears Soap's 'Bubbles' campaign of the late 1880s. From 1900, the central parties began to sell large-format, full-colour posters direct to local parties, and a revolution in pictorial campaigning began. The Liberal Publication Department sold 175,000 posters in 1900, over 500,000 in 1906, and approximately one million for the two elections of 1910. Conservative figures are not directly comparable, but suggest an even more precipitate increase, with the party issuing almost four million posters in 1910. Moreover, by 1910 a vast array of pressure groups, many such as the Budget League and the Tariff Reform League only nominally independent of party, were issuing their own election posters on a grand scale. In the run-up to January 1910 the Budget League distributed half a million posters, and the Tariff Reform League managed a combined total of over 53 million leaflets, pamphlets, and posters. But even so, most election posters remained locally produced and simple in format—not least because they were destined, not for the expensive commercial billboards capable of displaying high-quality 16 and 32 sheet posters, but for clandestine night-time fly-posting by party activists. It was common for both sides to indulge in fly-posting on a grand scale, and the repeated over-postering of opponents' propaganda was said greatly to add to the cost, not to mention the annoyance, of a campaign. There were many who doubted the wisdom of all this effort. Some felt that national posters were often unsuited to local conditions, while others had more pointed complaints, such as the Labour candidate who complained that his local association had been charged for thousands of unusable posters on which his name had been misspelled. In the towns, it was claimed that pictorial advertising was so ubiquitous that it had ceased to have much impact, while in the countryside it was said to be hard to find effective poster sites at all. Professional bill-posting was also very expensive—a fact which probably explains why, after the costly 1910 elections, there was a proliferation of local pacts barring full-size posters in future contests. Finally, there was the considerable problem of how to find a universal language of political communication in a highly stratified society. Politicians were warned of the danger of giving offence with vulgar posters, but they were also told that simple slogans and humour represented the most effective way of getting their message across to 'indifferent and ignorant voters'.[8]

On the whole vulgarity won out in Edwardian politics. Locally produced leaflets and posters were often crude in both form and content. At Salford South in January 1910, even Hilaire Belloc, the writer and Liberal MP, relied on bold slogans such as 'Vote for Belloc and Hands off the People's Bread'. As with 'Chinese Slavery' in 1906, unofficial Liberal propagandists sounded the most shamelessly populist notes—perhaps because they had less reason to fear alienating 'respectable' opinion than the party propagandists. In January 1910 the Liberal *Daily Chronicle* published cartoons and leaflets proclaiming 'Tariff Reform means Dog Meat' alongside an image of a German butcher selling 'first-class horse and dog meat'. Such images were disseminated, not by the mainstream parties, but rather by the various partisan pressure groups which sprang up in Edwardian Britain such as the Free Trade Union, the Budget League, and the Tariff Reform League. Unlike Victorian political pressure groups such as the Liberation Society (Church disestablishment) or the United Kingdom Alliance (temperance), the rationale of these organizations was to promote causes that had already become central to the political programmes of the main parties—they were essentially auxiliary organizations in the mould of the Conservatives'

Primrose League, rather than pressure groups seeking to move an issue up the political agenda. With good reason, historians have generally discussed their role in terms of how the parties gradually learned to exploit loopholes in the 1883 Corrupt Practices Act. Auxiliary organizations could spend vast sums on political propaganda without it needing to be returned in the candidate's official expenses. Hence the millions of posters distributed by these groups at the elections of 1910, and hence too their high-profile role in Edwardian by-elections, where resources could be targeted on a single constituency. When Leo Amery fought, and nearly captured, the staunch Liberal seat of East Wolverhampton in 1908, the rival pressure groups were quick to move into the constituency. Amery recalled 'shop windows displaying dumped foreign goods or revolting illustrations of Germans feeding on horseflesh and black bread'. At the same time, the constituency was apparently swamped in a deluge of posters, leaflets, and street-corner orators—all funded by the rival pressure groups. But as well as making a mockery of attempts to control election expenditure, the Edwardian pressure groups also allowed the parties to plumb the depths of political vulgarity by proxy.[9]

After 1906, Conservatives went out of their way to try and neutralize Liberal propaganda by attacking the shameless 'lies' that their opponents had supposedly peddled to secure their landslide victory. Fighting the East Wolverhampton by-election in 1908, Leo Amery issued a detailed attack on the Liberal Government for its exploitation of the so-called 'Chinese slavery' issue, alleging, in the process, that the Liberals had not only continued the policy in South Africa, but had also introduced a more coercive version of the scheme to the New Hebrides. By 1910, Unionists found themselves on the back foot on the issue of old-age pensions, with Liberal candidates across the country alleging that because Unionists opposed the 'People's Budget' it followed that they also opposed the recently introduced state pension that it was intended to underwrite. In Shropshire, William Bridgeman faced a 'stiff contest' mainly because his opposition to pauper disqualification was 'misrepresented' as outright opposition to state pensions, though he hit back hard issuing leaflets that blamed Liberals for the hated 'character test' imposed on pensioners. Chamberlain's Imperial Tariff Committee issued an election handbook offering Unionist canvassers advice on how to refute 'the Dear Loaf Lie' and 'the Old Age Pensions lie'. The Tariff Reform League produced posters highlighting the increased cost of 'free trade' bread since 1906, and Conservative Central Office published its own leaflet denouncing the 'old-age pensions lie', which Leo Amery, for one, evidently considered important enough to include with his election address in a special mailing to every elector. Here the voters were told to, 'Remember the Chinese Slavery and the Big Loaf Frauds. Do not be fooled again BUT VOTE FOR THE UNIONISTS, FAIR-PLAY AND OLD-AGE PENSIONS.' Of course, the Unionists were not above pushing their own populist slogans—alongside dump shops and parades of unemployed workmen, candidates such as Amery embraced pithy slogans such as 'British Work for British Men' and 'Work not Charity' to argue that trade protection was the real issue facing the nation in 1910. But all this meant was that whilst Unionists might freely attack their opponents' message, it became much harder to attack their methods, as these were now their own.[10]

Political parties also sought to reach out to the new and supposedly fickle electors through less brazenly populist means. In the 1890s there was a craze to enliven political meetings with magic lantern shows, which involved the projection of full-colour images much like a modern slide projector. These devices were especially popular at village meetings, where it was argued that they did much to educate 'the rural mind' on the issues of the day (Conservatives were especially fond of showing stirring scenes of imperial adventure). However, most agreed that lantern shows were unsuited to electioneering; not only was the equipment involved both expensive and delicate, but it was considered positively foolhardy to switch the lights out on an election crowd. By the 1900s some political parties were experimenting with the technology in an effort to make it more suitable for elections, for instance by projecting poster-size images onto the walls of public buildings—most often party offices or clubs. There was also pressure to make indoor meetings as pleasurable as possible. Between elections, when it was legal, parties were encouraged to lay on professional musical entertainment to liven up their meetings and encourage enthusiasm. Even the socialist ILP played this game, which appears to have been as much about ensuring the commercial success of ticketed meetings, as about sweetening the pill of political speeches. When the Bristol ILP organized a large fund-raising rally featuring Keir Hardie and George Lansbury in 1909, they still agreed to pay a guinea to two professional singers who would be advertised as performing at the beginning and end of the meeting. In a similar vein, local parties were advised to decorate meeting halls with flags, posters, and even plants to help make the whole experience more 'attractive' to the public.[11]

Women and electioneering

But perhaps the most striking and important development in late nineteenth-century public politics was the growing prominence of women as active, and often independent, political campaigners. Women had never been wholly absent from electoral politics, but, as we have seen, their role was sharply circumscribed for most of the nineteenth century. A candidate's female relatives might sometimes speak on his behalf, particularly if he was unable to address a gathering in person, but most steered clear of full-blown politicking even then. Gladstone's wife Catherine was widely credited with establishing the fashion for wives to act as their husbands' visible, public champions—travelling with them throughout a campaign and sitting beside them on the public platform. But, as Lady Frances Balfour confessed (having played the part for her brother-in-law Gerald at Leeds in 1885), being the candidate's helpmate reduced women to little more than passive ornaments. However, there were exceptions to the rule, including most famously Jennie Churchill, Winston's Brooklyn-born mother, who in 1885 not only stepped in to organize her sickly husband's ministerial by-election at Woodstock, but also played a leading role as both canvasser and platform orator. As when the Duchess of Devonshire campaigned for Fox in the 1780s, much was made of Lady Churchill's skilful manipulation of her feminine charms to woo the male electorate. But in contrast to the late eighteenth century, tory election songs now celebrated a female campaigner who 'marshalled all her forces' and 'took the hearts and votes of all Liberals in the town'. Even opponents celebrated her panache. Writing to congratulate her after the poll, Sir Henry James teased that if all he had heard about her campaigning was true he must surely introduce a second Corrupt Practices Act.[12]

But, before the turn of the century, few politicians' wives chose to emulate Jennie Churchill. On the contrary, the impetus for increased female involvement in late Victorian politics came mainly from the grassroots. After the legislative changes of the mid-1880s, political parties began to place increased emphasis on the need to mobilize women as volunteer election workers. At first the emphasis was mainly on women as routine party workers, helping to maintain the electoral register, compiling the canvass, addressing envelopes, contacting out-voters and the like. But through organizations such as the Women's Liberal Federation (1886), the Women's Liberal Unionist Association (1888), and the Conservatives' mixed-sex Primrose League (1883), women gradually began to assume a more prominent role in all aspects of public politics. In part this was driven from below, as women sought to find fulfilment in new public roles, but it also reflected a growing recognition within the parties that women could bring more excitement and novelty to politics than any number of lantern shows or full-colour posters. Although Conservatives often decried the 'unfeminine' antics of Liberal and socialist women speakers, they too made eager use of 'Ladies vans' and women's cycling corps to proselytize the party's message. This was largely a matter of pragmatism. In the early 1890s female propagandists such as Enid Stacy, Carrie Martin, and Katherine Conway proved fiery evangelists for the socialist cause—able to draw large audiences of adult males to impromptu meetings in a way that more conventional (male) speakers found impossible except at election time. But Conservatives managed to convince themselves that their own 'lady orators' were somehow of a different stamp—that what made the female platform 'unseemly' and degrading was not women speaking in public, but rather women articulating radical, 'unfeminine' causes such as women's rights and sexual equality. It marked an important milestone in the transformation of British public politics—women were emerging from the shadows of the political culture to become active participants in the dialogue between politicians and public. Active, but *not* equal; as the Edwardian suffragette campaign underlined, public political space was still highly gendered—it was male space in which women participated as a sexed 'other'. When women broke the rules of their conditional participation—most obviously by aping the male tactic of political disruption—participation itself could swiftly be withdrawn. When Asquith addressed a mass meeting at Birmingham's Bingley Hall at the height of the 'suffragette' campaign in September 1909 the audience of 13,000 was confined entirely to men—as was the audience at the Albert Hall three months later when Asquith launched the Liberals' General Election campaign.[13]

However, this was not the whole story. For one thing the 'necessity' of excluding women from meetings was widely deplored by all parties—it was in no sense seen as 'natural' for political meetings to revert to being all-male occasions (indeed even at Asquith's Bingley Hall meeting women sat alongside the Liberal leader on the platform, as if to refute claims that Liberals were anti-female). Nor was the reassertion of male exclusivity by any means universal. For one thing, most meetings remained immune to suffragette disruption—the 'militants' targeted only two types of meeting: Liberal ministers' ticketed, set-piece meetings and by-election meetings for Liberal candidates. Moreover, in both cases their interventions were deplored less because they were women 'who dared to intrude...into a man's meeting' (as Emmeline Pankhurst put it) than because the militants were offending less gendered customs surrounding the political platform. By disrupting the ministerial platform they were importing the rough-house tactics of elections into a very different political world where leading statesmen were expected to be able to discourse rationally on the issues of the day, not just to audiences of the party faithful, but to the nation through the verbatim reports of their speeches in the daily press. Disrupting such meetings was seen as a constitutional outrage, more than an outrage to gendered notions of propriety. On the surface, disrupting Liberal by-election meetings would appear to be less controversial, but again suffragettes often caused outrage for the wrong reasons—resented not as women invading male terrain, but as 'outsiders' seeking publicity by interfering in a local contest. For generations, candidates had blamed disruption at their meetings on hired troublemakers from outside (so as to discount the idea that the local populace was hostile)—and the suffragettes fitted that bill all too well. The suffragette campaign certainly generated a great deal of brutal, misogynist violence against female mili-tants, but we should not therefore assume that the polity as a whole became more unequivocally male in consequence. If anything the reverse was true.[14]

Pat Jalland argues that women's role in election campaigns grew im-measurably after 1900, both as behind-the-scenes organizers and as public speakers. In particular, far more wives and daughters began to emulate Jennie Churchill's example two decades earlier by throwing themselves headlong into the daily grind of campaigning. Some did so willingly, even eagerly, but others appear to have been reluctant converts to the campaign trail, pushed into the fray by the growing expectations of local organizers and party workers. In 1906 the *Illustrated London News* claimed that 'in no former Election have women played so prominent and effective part...Even the platform is theirs now.' A detailed study of electioneering in eleven English constituencies found that the number of candidates able to call on regular support from their wives more than doubled between 1895 and January 1910—from 14 per cent to 36 per cent. The number of meetings at which women spoke also doubled, although this still represented barely 8 per cent of all meetings—the 'lady orator' was less ubiquitous in Edwardian politics than contemporary accounts sometimes suggest. Many factors lay behind the trend, including the desire of elite women not to be outdone by their sisters in the burgeoning female auxiliary organizations. But one must also wonder whether another factor was the desire of male politicians to surround themselves with their womenfolk in an attempt to refute suggestions that they were anti-woman, and perhaps even to provide protection from the attacks of suffrage militants. However, one thing is certain—reaction to the suffragette campaign did not drive women from British political life.[15]

Certainly by the 1900s only a few local parties still represented bastions of male exclusivity. One such was the Oswestry Conservative Association in Shropshire. At a by-election in 1904 William Bridgeman, the future cabinet minister, failed to hold this rock-solid seat for the Conservatives. Shocked by defeat, he set about overhauling the local party machinery with the help of Joseph Chamberlain and the Birmingham tariff reformers. Chamberlain immediately identified the absence of women's organizations as a major source of weakness, and this was confirmed in a subsequent report on the constituency compiled by William Jenkins, who told Bridgeman 'you practically had no lady helpers in your recent contest'. Bridgeman responded quickly to the findings, and by the close of the year there was a strong Women's Unionist Tariff Reform Association taking the fight to the recently victorious radicals. Despite the Liberal landslide in 1906 Bridgeman regained the seat with a majority of five hundred. The organization of a strong Women's Tariff Reform movement was also said to have played a key part in Captain Morrison-Bell's success in consolidating his hold on Mid-Devon after a close and bitter by-election victory in 1908. On the eve of the First World War the Association was said to boast almost 5,000 women members, compared with a total (male) electorate of approximately 12,000. In an age when women could still not become individual members of the mainstream parties, the auxiliary organizations which proliferated in Edwardian England appear to have played a vital role in mobilizing female partisanship in a more decidedly political manner than the Primrose League or even local Women's Liberal Associations had done at their outset in the 1880s.[16]

This mass female activism, which was by no means confined to Conservative circles, reflected in part the decisive shift of political controversy towards bread and butter issues of domestic consumption after 1900. The bitter party battles over the relative merits of Free Trade and Protection placed the housewife at the centre of political debate, and encouraged both political parties to lay renewed emphasis on the need to reach out, not only to the male householder, but also to his wife. Mass women's organizations, such as the local Women's Unionist Tariff Reform Associations, were at the forefront of this effort to reinvigorate house-to-house visiting in response to the increasingly domestic focus of political debate. Women activists targeted wives as much as husbands, and they carried out the bulk of their visiting in 'peacetime' (i.e. between elections) when it was claimed that only women's quiet, unassertive doorstep proselytizing could take the party's message into the 'enemy' camp. In 1904 Chamberlain was adamant that only 'personal efforts' could bring back the labourers, and especially the labourers' wives who had been swayed by their opponents 'lies about the big and little loaf'. As the Primrose League told its volunteers in 1914, the object of such 'personal efforts' was to 'endeavour to get into friendly conversation with the voter or his wife', and never to start by asking about their politics. Inevitably many have seen 'undue influence' at work in such visiting, especially when it was conducted by Church or charity workers. Marc Brodie has recently stressed the skilfully directed role of malicious gossip in such informal political communication, but, historically, perhaps its greatest significance lay in the fact that by 1914 women already represented the backbone of party organization across much of Britain even though they remained excluded not only from full citizenship, but even from full membership of the parties their efforts sustained. It would be foolish to suggest that the Edwardian suffrage campaigners were pushing at an open door, but the logic of electoral competition played its part in ensuring that the door was not firmly bolted against them.[17]

The politics of the crowd

Even in the Edwardian era—when partisanship appeared to structure almost every aspect of daily life, cool heads recognized that large swathes of the electorate were not convinced supporters of either side. Canvass returns demonstrated that there was 'always a large doubtful or unknown quantity' among the electorate—those 'who have no definite opinions, but who may be influenced by the arguments addressed to them; others who are wholly indifferent to public questions, and who require to have their interest aroused...'. These were the people that politicians sought to reach through magic lantern shows, house-to-house visiting, clever cartoons, and well-drafted 'literature'. But for all the innovations in political communication that characterized the era, it remained the platform and the soapbox that dominated electioneering before 1914. Commenting on his experience of Edwardian elections at Bristol North, Augustine Birrell recalled that he never canvassed a single elector because 'in those days elections were merely speaking matches'. At first glance this is not easy to explain. It was generally acknowledged that most electors would never attend an election meeting, that audiences were often dominated by non-voters, including women and children, and that the environment of an election meeting was rarely conducive to persuasion even if open-minded voters should be present. But none of this really mattered. As we have seen, meetings consumed the bulk of the candidate's schedule partly because they secured him extensive coverage in the local press, but mainly because they were the principal means by which he could demonstrate the 'manly' virtues of openness, good humour, and courage that had once been tested at the public nomination hustings. But if politicians put up with the indignities of the election meeting in order to demonstrate their equanimity and pluck, this did not mean that they welcomed the persistence of disorder in Edwardian electoral politics. Rather, it reflected the fact that they felt powerless to do much about it without alienating the voting public.[18]

Politicians seem to have viewed disorder at their meetings as an inescapable fact of life—much like the weather. For instance, in 1900 William Bridgeman reported holding a 'dull' meeting at Woodbridge in Suffolk even though sections of the audience had thrown missiles at him. True, parliament rushed through the Public Meeting Bill at the height of the suffragettes' campaign of political disruption in 1908, but this did nothing to prevent the 1910 elections being the most disorderly contests in living memory. The legislation was aimed at preventing disorder at all public meetings, but it contained special provisions making organized disruption during an election an 'illegal practice'. It was a classic example of politicians at Westminster trying to use the law to reform their own actions in the constituencies—or rather to reform the electoral customs that they felt obliged to uphold when face-to-face with their own electors. However,

the legislation was little used before 1914. It may have increased politicians'
wariness about being openly identified with disruption (although conniv-
ance in such things had long been frowned upon), but the old adage
that 'political prosecutors are not popular with voters' was not forgotten.
The same was true of election petitions as a whole. As one successful
election lawyer later recalled, the belief that any successful petitioner was
'certain to be a loser at the following election' because 'it was thought not
good form ... to turn out your opponent on petition', acted as a powerful
deterrent—especially when it cost more than a pound a minute to bring a
petition (equivalent to a labourer's weekly wage in 1910).[19]

However, whilst there remained powerful barriers restraining politicians
from reforming political custom and practice before 1914, there was
undoubtedly a growing concern about the health of Britain's emerging mass
democracy. In his 1908 study *Human Nature in Politics*, Graham Wallas laid
great emphasis on the irrational factors underpinning the electoral process.
Rejecting the tendency of the nineteenth-century Liberal intelligentsia to
celebrate an idealized democracy of rational individualism, Wallas insisted
that politicians had to engage with the people as they were, rather than as
they should be. This meant accepting that 'most of the political opinions
of most men are the result, not of reasoning tested by experience, but
of unconscious or half-conscious inference fixed by habit'. Wallas's work
was immensely influential, and is often taken as signalling a decisive
shift towards a more consciously manipulative style of electioneering.
However, it is important to recognize that Wallas saw himself, not as a new
Machiavelli, but as a clear-sighted critic of present tendencies. He wrote the
book against the backdrop of 'Chinese slavery', dump shops, and the big
loaf, and in the light of his own grim experiences as a Progressive candidate
for the LCC in 1907—he knew all too well that political organizers had no
need of an advice manual in the techniques of mass manipulation. Nor was
Wallas alone in his forebodings about the tendency towards irrationalism
in democratic politics. In his 1909 study *The Condition of England*, the
Liberal junior minister C. F. G. Masterman, suggested that the by-elections
of 1908, which had gone so badly for the Government, had witnessed the
birth of a new politics of 'the crowd'—a debased politics which appealed
to the sensations, not the intellect. Apparently forgetting the parades of
Chinese 'slaves' and the big and little loaves of 1906, Masterman lambasted
'the new electioneering' for trying to hypnotize the crowd with vulgar
stunts such as processions of supposedly unemployed workers (the victims

of Free Trade), and trolleys bearing big and little coal sacks (to highlight the impact of Government policies on fuel prices).[20]

But whilst Masterman was undoubtedly right to argue that 'clever men' were seeking to harness the techniques of mass persuasion to political ends, he was wrong to equate this with the politics of 'the crowd'. Leaning heavily on contemporary fascination with so-called 'crowd psychology' and the mass mind, and borrowing freely from Hobson's 1901 critique of Jingoism, Masterman painted a bleak picture in which 'Humanity has become the Mob'—brought into the streets to do the bidding of 'the strong man', but with a latent potential for brutal, indiscriminate violence. But as we have seen, Edwardian politicians went to considerable lengths to distance themselves from the vulgar populism of 'the new electioneering', not least by drawing a clear line between the ministerial platform and the activities of proxy organizations such as the Tariff Reform League and the Free Trade Union. Those, such as Lloyd George, whose platform style echoed the sensationalism and populist excesses of the pressure groups, faced severe censure from 'respectable' opinion. If anything, it was becoming *less* acceptable for politicians to identify themselves with the mob in this era—perhaps in part because Wallas, Masterman, and others were doing so much to publicize the evils of demagogic politics. Significantly, in the study of constituency campaigning discussed earlier, there was only one measure on which the January 1910 election appeared less intense than that of 1895—the propensity of candidates to take part in crowd events such as organized processions. Defeated candidates, in particular, proved decidedly less inclined to hold processions after the declaration than in 1895. Intense partisanship may have played a part here—it is not clear that it would always have been safe for a defeated candidate and his supporters to parade the streets in 1910—but it seems likely that many politicians also felt less comfortable marching at the head of a boisterous election crowd. In victory it might be hard to resist being swept along by the moment, but in defeat it was all too easy. Of course, such rituals did not simply disappear overnight—they remained a feature of campaigning in many constituencies down to the Second World War, but torchlight processions, and similar events that brought crowd and candidate into close proximity, were already in decline by the 1900s.[21]

It is striking how often Edwardian accounts of election disorder focus on heroic individuals seeking to tame the disorderly masses. Echoing Grego's account of Thackeray at Oxford in the 1850s, some still celebrated the manly hero who tamed the crowd by force of arms. In 1908 a biography of Colonel Fred Burnaby, adventurer, soldier, and sometime Conservative candidate, presented its Victorian hero leaping into audiences to teach unruly 'roughs' a lesson and 'revelling in the melee' of a free fight. As with Thackeray, much was made of Burnaby's physical and moral superiority to the crowd. At one moment he is portrayed hoisting two puny hecklers from the audience on outstretched arms, at another he is said to have quelled a seething mob simply by showing he had no fear of it. But whilst Burnaby and Thackeray are depicted as Olympian figures—as untainted masters of the crowd—there is no sense that their mission is to transform the crowd in their own image. But this is precisely the note that many Edwardian accounts of electoral politics began to strike. In his 1907 account of life as an itinerant Liberal propagandist, Joseph Howes makes much of his attempts to bring the light of Liberal reason to the staunchly Conservative villages of north Fylde during the 1880s and 1890s. Time and again, he emphasizes that the Liberals refused to descend to their opponents' level by engaging in free fights—despite considerable provocation. According to Howes, after prolonged Liberal campaigning only two villages remained bastions of the 'brutality and rowdyism' that local tory leaders had thoughtlessly encouraged—and even here the tables were turned as the farm lads had learnt to boo and hoot at all politicians—tory and Liberal alike.[22]

Nor was this narrative of political enlightenment a purely Liberal affair. In Mid-Devon, Conservatives wove similar myths around Captain Ernest Morrison-Bell, their heroic victor over Charles Buxton at the notoriously disorderly by-election of 1908. Morrison-Bell later recalled facing 'a yelling mob' at Newton Abbot's Butter Market, where opponents tried literally to sweep him from the platform using a long pole. When he captured the seat by 559 votes on a 90 per cent turnout, Liberal anger was so intense that he was warned he should forgo the victor's traditional tour around the constituency. This was probably sage advice given the fate of his twin brother Arthur, who, mistaken for the candidate, was trapped in the Conservatives' Newton Abbot headquarters for hours while a Liberal mob smashed every window in the building. The Liberal crowd also turned its anger on Emmeline Pankhurst and her supporters, who had come to Mid-Devon to oppose Buxton as part of their campaign against the Government's refusal to grant votes for women. Pankhurst was roughly handled and rolled in the mud by her assailants, who then besieged her inside a shop where she had sought refuge.[23]

On the surface, Morrison-Bell was undoubtedly a manly hero in the
Burnaby mould—six foot two, mentioned in dispatches in South Africa,
and just 36 when first elected in 1908. By his own account, he relished
turning the tables on his attackers during the 1908 by-election—he even
boasted of throwing a man through the glass door of a local hotel. But
by 1913, one observer insisted that 'though many a "tough" down here
can testify [to] his respectable biceps', it was not through force of arms
that Morrison-Bell had triumphed over 'the methods of barbarism and
personal brutality' which had previously tarnished Mid-Devon politics.
According to this writer, who recalled the 1908 by-election for a 'savage
kick in the groin from a hobnailed boot [which] made me go a-limping
for the best part of a year afterwards', Morrison-Bell had inculcated a new,
calmer temper in constituency politics. Locals credited him with having
transformed Newton Abbot 'from a den of roaring lions ... [into] a cage of
sucking doves'. By the 1920s, the *Totnes Unionist* recalled Morrison-Bell,
who had stood down in 1918, as having 'transformed it from a division
notorious for rowdyism into one of the most orderly in the country,
even in the heat of an election'. Similarly, suffrage campaigners seized on
violence such as that at Mid-Devon to denounce the underlying brutality
of the existing male polity. To this end they were undoubtedly aided
by the reluctance of newspaper proprietors and politicians to publicize
the considerable personal violence which characterized the militants' own
campaign—physical attacks on ministers, in particular, were played down,
probably in part from fear of reviving Fenian violence. This helped mask
ambiguities at the heart of the suffragette campaign, which might otherwise
have diluted its critique of the existing, macho male polity. There was, in
short, a broad range of voices proclaiming the need to 'reform' Britain's
electoral culture on the eve of the First World War. And whilst the
turmoil of the 1910 elections should remind us that there were still plenty
of forces pulling in the opposite direction, this growing sense of disquiet
would prove influential in the very different context of post-war electoral
politics.[24]

Money and class

One might imagine that one area where the old ways survived largely
unchallenged before the war was in the influence that money continued to

exert over electoral politics—particularly through the practice of 'nursing'
constituencies between elections. In 1906 W. J. Fisher, who had failed
to capture Canterbury despite the Liberal landslide of that year, wrote a
stinging attack on the 'electoral abuses' that still blighted British political
life. According to Fisher it was all too easy to 'drive a coach and four
through' the 1883 Corrupt Practices Act—free or heavily subsidized beer
was still widely available in many constituencies, publicans still boasted
of controlling large blocs of voters, and election petitions had failed even
when, as at Haggerston and Lancaster, it had been proven that free beer
had been dispensed on a large scale. Fisher also insisted that election agents
continued to spend far in excess of the legal limits set by the 1883 Act.
He claimed that 90 per cent of printing costs were never put through
the books, with the balance of printers' invoices paid in cash 'on the
nail'. Such claims, which remained widespread in the Edwardian period,
are by their nature impossible to verify, but the same cannot be said of
the complaint that the law also gave politicians great leeway to indulge
in the systematic 'nursing' of a constituency. Would-be candidates, often
now bearing the title of *prospective* Parliamentary candidate, were free to
spend lavishly to endow their chosen constituency with public amenities,
and to support its various charitable causes. They were usually warned
to avoid either giving directly to individuals, or using party machinery
to administer their largesse, but in practice some candidates who did
both still managed to survive election petitions. There remained, in short,
a strong sense that wealth could exert legitimate as well as illegitimate
forms of influence. Both bribery and 'treating' were widely perceived as
'illegitimate' by the late nineteenth century, even if many voters disagreed,
but lavish 'nursing' of a constituency was seen as no more than a natural
expression of social responsibility by the rich and powerful. Of course
the reality was very different, as internal Unionist party guidelines issued
by George Lloyd at Staffordshire West in 1911 make clear. Before any
donation was made, officials were told to ask 'What return, from a Party
point of view, is likely to be got out of the giving'. And in case the
message was unclear, the guidelines concluded by stressing 'It should
be borne in mind that these subscriptions are given with the object of
making our Member more POPULAR and to bring forward the PARTY and
to further its interests, and in the case of every application it is essential
that these points should be kept in view.' Moreover, in 1913, when Lloyd
announced that he would not fight the seat again, he immediately ended

his support for forty-six local clubs and societies and instructed that all new applications should be forwarded to his proposed successor as Unionist candidate. The crude calculus behind 'nursing' could hardly have been more explicit.[25]

It would be wrong to imagine that men like Lloyd relished the chance to spend their wealth in this manner. On the contrary, in private most appear to have shared Fisher's distaste for the 'bleeding' of candidates by 'greedy young men unwilling to pay for their own pleasures'. Lloyd clearly resented having to provide subsidies to the activities of local groups such as Catholics and United Methodists who 'never vote for us', and he was livid when he had to find over £50 to cover the bad debts of a Unionist sub-agent at Cannock to stop the matter becoming a public scandal. But it was well known that MPs who refused to play the game, like Gladstone's son Willy at Whitby, often found their tenure at Westminster abruptly truncated. On the other hand, apart from being very expensive, nursing was beginning to gain a bad name thanks to the perceived emergence of a new class of super-rich plutocrats prepared to use their vast fortunes to buy seats with which they had not the slightest personal connection. Hilaire Belloc exposed the system mercilessly in his 1908 novel *Mr Clutterbuck's Election*, where the hapless plutocrat is fleeced by wily party organizers, and made the unwitting accomplice to corruption when the so-called 'Bogey Man' pays off his election workers from a bag of gold sovereigns. But perhaps most decisively, as with other electioneering rituals, the growth of Labour politics from the 1890s, also began to undermine the old ways. By definition too poor to 'nurse' a constituency, Labour men challenged the whole concept of nursing as debased—their goal was 'social rights' not private perks. Thus, whilst custom, and the law, remained remarkably tolerant of money's supposedly 'legitimate' influence over electoral politics, its sway was already in decline before 1914. Even wealthy politicians were increasingly anxious to find ways to reduce the cost of politics—only fear of offending public sentiment constrained their legislative instincts.[26]

Labour candidates, and to a lesser extent the growing number of so-called 'carpet-baggers' (men of modest means sponsored by the central parties as 'rising stars'), challenged more than just the custom of 'nursing' constituencies. These candidates from humble backgrounds destabilized the simple social hierarchies of Victorian electoral politics. In particular, they challenged election rituals which presupposed that the candidate was a man of status, wealth, and usually local influence. For have no doubt, from the outset Labour politics was about challenging the emblems of traditional class dominance in British politics. When John Burns stood as a socialist at Nottingham in 1885, one of his hand-bills proclaimed the dawn of 'the innings of fustian and corduroy', and declared that the 'Frock coats and high hats had had their time'. This was undoubtedly wishful thinking in 1885, even in Britain's large industrial cities, but it did signal the excoriating challenge that Labour would mount to the old, paternalist mode of politics. No longer would it be taken for granted that the rich should rule over the poor—nor that the best one could hope for from politics was therefore to profit from the rich man's largesse whenever 'the voting' came round. In an important sense Labour politics represented not the beginning but the end of class politics in Britain—henceforth it could no longer be assumed that a vast social and economic gulf separated the candidate from most ordinary voters. In consequence, rituals which fed off class distinction, and the symbolic disavowal of social difference through face-to-face public contact in meeting halls, on the doorstep, or in the street, began to lose some of their cultural power. As many Labour pioneers would discover to their dismay, there was still often a great cultural and ideological gulf between themselves and the voting public—indeed the very fact of being a candidate, or even a platform orator, tended to set one apart from 'ordinary people'. But even so, the rigid hierarchies of social class no longer structured this awkward cultural interaction in the same way once the Labour pioneer and the professional carpet-bagger took to the electoral stage.[27]

4

War, Women, and the 'Silent Majority'

Politics and the mass media

Historians have generally assumed that the growth of radio and cinema as new means of mass communication transformed public politics in inter-war Britain. According to A. J. P. Taylor, 'Men and women heard the voices of leading statesmen in their own homes. They ceased to attend meetings, except those held by the advocates of minority views which were denied expression over the airways.' Taylor was equally convinced that the new media transformed the character of politics by demanding a 'gentler, more intimate style' which 'the oldtimers, trained on audiences, could not manage'. There is a grain of truth to both claims—politicians did come to doubt the ability of conventional public meetings to reach more than a fraction of the new mass electorate. Perhaps more crucially, they increasingly became convinced that meetings were unable to reach the uncommitted voters most likely to sway an election—the so-called 'silent majority'. At the same time public politics did show signs of becoming less disorderly and demonstrative between the wars. The dominant tone of inter-war politics was low-key and homely; it was the domesticated politics of Baldwin and Attlee that typified the age, not the more flamboyant, platform-honed style of Lloyd George, Churchill, or Mosley. But we should be wary of ascribing these changes to the inevitable impact of new technology. For one thing, the vulgar populism characteristic of Edwardian elections was already losing favour before cinema or radio came on the scene. Three main factors were crucial here: the political and cultural lessons drawn from 'total war' and its chaotic aftermath, the impact of female enfranchisement in 1918, and reactions to Labour's sudden post-war breakthrough—themes taken up at the end of this chapter in the discussion of inter-war Britain's claims to be considered a 'peaceable nation'. Moreover, many of the technological developments of the inter-war period had the potential to enhance rather than diminish the scope for demagogic politics. This was especially true of advances in the electronic amplification and relaying of speech, but radio and cinema could also be mobilized to support a very different, more demagogic style of politics, as events in Nazi Germany would make all too evident. If we are to understand the transformation of public politics in Britain between the wars we must look beyond technological determinism for our answers.[1]

But this is not to deny that the new mass media were beginning to transform the way that ordinary people interacted with politics and politicians. True, it was not until the 1935 election that radio reached a majority of British homes (in 1924, the year of the first election broadcasts, less than one in five homes possessed a set), but contemporary accounts suggest that those who heard politicians' election broadcasts were often deeply moved by the experience. A working man from Dagenham wrote to Baldwin in 1935 explaining that he had heard every broadcast the Conservative leader had made since 1926—'so although I have never met you I feel I know you quite well ... I feel I can trust you ... you typify in yourself that innate steadiness and probity that is Britain.' Baldwin's files contain many such letters from self-styled 'humble' voters, most of whom clearly felt that Baldwin had been speaking directly to them in their own homes. One voter tells him 'In your own words of last Monday, we *do* know you Sir, and we *do* trust you.' From the outset, one peculiar feature of broadcast politics in Britain was that, unlike in America or mainland Europe, the intimate 'fireside' chat possessed a near monopoly of the airwaves. The public rarely heard live transmissions from the party leaders' public meetings. This is often attributed to the widespread perception that Baldwin had triumphed in 1924 by heeding the advice of the BBC chairman John Reith that an election broadcast would come across best if it was delivered in the style of a studio talk (see Fig. 9). MacDonald and Asquith, by contrast, chose to let the BBC broadcast live extracts from their scheduled evening meetings. In both cases the result was woeful—not only were such performances considered too declamatory for home consumption, but neither politician had yet mastered the art of speaking into a microphone (another technology that was still in its infancy in 1924). But just as important as the supposed 'lessons of 1924' was the fact that the BBC operated a complete moratorium

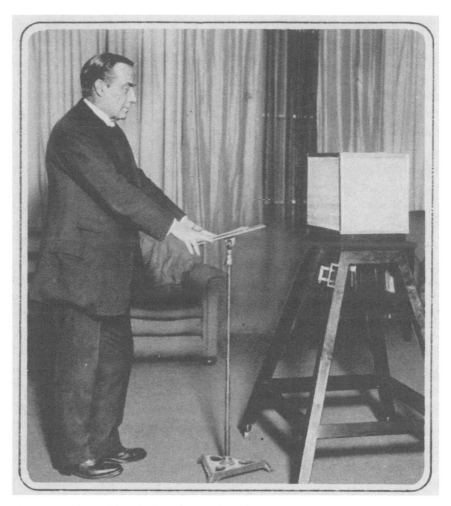

Fig. 9. Stanley Baldwin's first election broadcast, 1924, *ILN*, 17 Oct. 1931, reproduced with the kind permission of the Syndics of Cambridge University Library

on election news until well after the Second World War. Apart from the party's allotted election broadcasts, British radio was essentially a politics-free zone during a General Election. Moreover, even outside elections, live news coverage remained decidedly under-developed between the wars thanks to the BBC's fear of angering the powerful interests on Fleet Street.[2]

A similar story can be told for cinema. Many commercial newsreel makers and film distributors maintained close relations with Conservative

politicians between the wars, but they were nonetheless reluctant to court
controversy by using their screens for overtly party political purposes.
The cinema had become an important tool for Government propaganda
during the First World War, but few wished to see this sort of overt
political propaganda continue in the post-war world—indeed historians
too often forget just how negatively all sides viewed overt 'propaganda' in
the aftermath of war. Only the Conservatives sought to make propaganda
films on any scale between the wars, and they soon found that their only
hope of getting an audience for such material was to take it direct to the
people by purchasing their own mobile cinema vans, and in 1928 their
own sound film system (Phonofilm). Baldwin recorded a short 'talkie' for
the 1929 election (incongruously filmed with Baldwin standing informally
by a desk in the garden of Number 10 Downing Street, see Fig. 10), and
Winston Churchill apparently used the technology to cover his enforced
absence from Epping at the start of the campaign. But commercial adoption
of the new technology was relatively slow, and it was not until 1932 that
all British newsreels carried soundtracks. In consequence, although leading
politicians such as MacDonald and Baldwin made soundtracked appeals to
the nation in 1931, it was only at the 1935 General Election that cinema
came into its own as a medium through which the party leaders could speak
directly to millions of British voters. By the mid-1930s cinema newsreels
were reaching a remarkable 20 million Britons every week. As with radio,
it was Baldwin who emerged as the acknowledged master of the new
medium. John Ramsden reminds us that thanks to cinema, Baldwin was
probably the first premier 'with whom the electors actually became familiar,
the first premier whose voice, appearance and characteristic gestures would
have been seen and heard by a majority of his countrymen'. In many
respects Baldwin's 1935 newsreel appeal to the nation anticipated the
post-war televised election broadcasts that would become such a staple of
British electioneering. Baldwin famously had no qualms about employing
scriptwriters to hone striking phrases, and in 1935 he stole a march on his
rivals by using a roller mechanism similar to the modern autocue to help
him appear natural and unscripted in front of the camera. According to one
correspondent, his address was the only one to be applauded in her local
Wood Green cinema, where a working man was overheard saying 'What
I likes about Baldwin, 'e don't sling no mud.' Historians have perhaps
exaggerated the extent to which Baldwin was the architect of the inter-war
reaction against 'personalities' and strident partisanship, but he instinctively

Fig. 10. Stanley Baldwin's first 'talkie' election appeal, 1929, *ILN*, 4 May 1929, reproduced with the kind permission of the Syndics of Cambridge University Library

understood the new public mood, and in becoming its greatest champion he also became its master.[3]

Both the national and the provincial press were also changing rapidly between the wars. Politicians were generally convinced that change was for the worse, but it is important to remember that newspapers remained the principal source of political information for most Britons throughout the inter-war period. In a report on public attitudes to the press, Mass Observation commented that 'Almost everybody reads newspapers, whether regularly or irregularly.' However, the report also identified widespread scepticism about the reliability of press coverage, concluding that 'people regard newspapers as a source of the day's topics of conversation, and not as a source of truth about events'. Similarly, a 1939 inquiry into 'broadcasting in everyday life' found that over 95 per cent of respondents 'gave more credence to the broadcast News' than to what they read in the press (interestingly only 54 per cent of its mainly working-class sample bought a newspaper every day).[4]

For the provincial press, the broad trend was towards consolidation and nominal independence. Whereas in the Edwardian period most constituencies had boasted rival Liberal and Conservative newspapers, usually published as dailies in the larger boroughs, by the 1930s many were dominated by a single title, often with a wide regional distribution. Commercial logic dictated that such papers generally adopted a non-party, 'independent' stance (although their ethos was nonetheless often distinctly anti-socialist). On the whole this meant that they tended to cover party politics, including election meetings, fairly neutrally (in stark contrast to the more overtly partisan Edwardian press), with only editorials displaying political bias. In theory, this increased the utility of the local press as a means of reaching the uncommitted voter, especially given that in some towns, readership levels reached 70 or even 80 per cent of households. However, there were also strong pressures running in a counter direction. Regional super-titles such as the *Liverpool Daily Post* or the *Birmingham Mail* served too many constituencies to give local contests extensive coverage, while the rise of the so-called 'new journalism', with its emphasis on human interest stories and strong pictures, also worked against blanket coverage of local campaigns. Increasingly, local papers preferred to run illustrated 'features' about candidates' activities, or 'exclusive' personal interviews, rather than just report their speeches at meetings. Most papers confined themselves to reporting only one meeting per issue for each candidate, but candidates continued to hold multiple meetings in different parts of their constituency every evening. Popular demand, rather than media coverage, remained the principal rationale for holding meetings between the wars.[5]

The London daily press was also changing. The thirst for news during the Great War had encouraged many households to take a national newspaper for the first time, and this trend continued apace between the wars as the main Fleet Street titles fought intense circulation wars—enticing readers not just with lively journalism, but also with incentives such as free insurance. Although individual titles, such as the 'diehard' *Morning Post* or the Liberal *Daily Chronicle* and *Westminster Gazette*, might struggle, overall both the 'quality' and popular press saw its net circulation rise between the wars. In 1920 5.5 million households took a London daily newspaper, but by the 1930s that figure had risen to over 10 million. After a period of steady decline in the 1920s, the *Daily Telegraph* enjoyed unprecedented growth through the 1930s, reaching a circulation of almost 800,000 on the eve of war. Similarly, the revamped *News Chronicle* was selling over 1.2 million copies daily throughout the 1930s. But most politicians focused on the more dramatic advance of popular titles such as the *Daily Mail* and *Daily Express*. During the 1920s, Rothermere's *Mail* was the pre-eminent London daily, with a circulation touching two million by the end of the decade. In the 1930s it was overtaken first by the re-launched *Daily Herald*, and then, more spectacularly, by Beaverbrook's *Daily Express*, which was selling 2.5 million copies daily by the late 1930s. During the First World War, Fleet Street's 'press barons' (Northcliffe, Rothermere, and Beaverbrook) had rightly gained a reputation for making and breaking governments, and they remained as interested in making as reporting political news in the post-war era. Throughout the 1920s first Lloyd George and then Baldwin found himself at loggerheads with Rothermere and Beaverbrook and their respective titles. This confrontation came to a head between 1929 and 1931 as both newspapers mounted sustained campaigns to ditch Baldwin and his cautious brand of 'safety first' Conservatism. Duff Cooper's victory at the Westminster St George's by-election in March 1931 is often held up as the decisive turning point in this struggle. It was here that Stanley Baldwin famously declared that the press barons sought 'power without responsibility—the prerogative of the harlot throughout the ages'. Cooper's triumph helped set the scene for the formation of a cross-party National Government just months later, and marked a decisive turning point in the political pretensions of the popular press. In 1935 it was possible for a supporter to write to Baldwin to congratulate him on 'taming' the *Mail* and *Express* without compromising his ability to capture the 'large silent vote, belonging to no party, which often swings elections'. Indeed by the late 1930s many were lamenting that the press had been transformed into supine accomplices of Government attempts to sell appeasement to a doubtful public. But throughout the inter-war period one thing was certain—the popular London press could no longer be relied upon, either as a barometer of public opinion, or as a reliable means of influencing that opinion. One should be careful not to exaggerate here. During an election much of Fleet Street was all too willing to act as an extension of Conservative Central Office's publicity department, as the furore over Labour 'rowdyism' and the Zinoviev letter demonstrated during the 1924 campaign. However, even during an election the popular press displayed no inclination to carry lengthy reports of politicians' speeches, while at other times they proved even less pliable. Indeed, one reason why Baldwin displayed such sustained interest in radio and cinema was his deep frustration with the capriciousness of Fleet Street.[6]

Here lay the true significance of radio and cinema—not as an alternative to the political meeting, which survived in pretty rude health between the wars, but as an alternative to an unreliable and, in part, discredited press. The notion that the public suddenly stopped attending meetings is simply unsustainable. It is true that outside elections, politicians complained that it was difficult to attract decent audiences across much of Britain, but this was not a new phenomenon. Before the First World War Seymour Lloyd had lamented the difficulty of holding public meetings in London and other great cities outside elections, and had described how one supposed 'monster demonstration' managed to attract just seventeen people to a 'huge hall' in London. Similarly, writing in the early 1930s, Cecil Emden observed that 'the number of political gatherings, unconnected with parliamentary candidatures, has much diminished in the course of the last half century'. Unfortunately, historians have missed this distinction between the long-term decline of ordinary public meetings, and the continued vitality of the election meeting. One reason is their tendency to dismiss election meetings as debased imitations of the 'true' public meeting because at election time rational argument supposedly had to be sacrificed to flattery and vulgar populism. They are right, of course, but as we have seen, election meetings also provided almost the only occasion when politicians came face-to-face with the general public, rather than just their admiring supporters. It was this which helped preserve the election meeting's importance well beyond the emergence of radio and cinema as rival claimants on mass leisure time.[7]

Golden age of the meeting?

If anything, the inter-war period witnessed the heyday of the election meeting thanks to technological innovations such as amplification, instantaneous relay, and more reliable modes of transport (Edwardian politicians had made extensive use of motor cars, but private diaries suggest that they were all too often left stranded by the roadside). These developments allowed candidates to address multiple meetings more easily, and it became common for politicians to address six or more meetings in an evening.

Writing in 1930, Ramsay Muir, the former Liberal MP for Rochdale, argued that the number of meetings and speeches had 'enormously increased' and that 'the flood of political oratory has become so immense that it cannot be reported'. He also felt that 'the gap between the authoritative leader and the ordinary speaker has narrowed' with the decline of verbatim reporting in the press—thereby increasing the significance of candidates' local election meetings. By the 1930s, some commentators were beginning to worry that leaders' election broadcasts were producing a 'diminution of the interest in ordinary election meetings', but they remained convinced that meetings offered electors something distinct and exciting that they could not find elsewhere. As the Conservative organizer Philip Cambray put it in 1932: 'the spoken word has to-day all the force in political warfare which it possessed in the past'.[8]

Mobile loudspeakers—built into cars, vans, and small lorries—began to be used to facilitate outdoor speaking almost as soon as the technology became widely available. As with cinema vans, the Conservatives led the way, partly because they had more money to spend on electioneering than their rivals, but also because they hoped that new technologies would help counter Labour's perceived advantage in conventional soapbox oratory. By 1929 Conservative Central Office already ran at least ten cinema vans, a small fleet of loudspeaker vans, and had approximately one hundred portable PA systems available for hire. They were also devoting considerable resources to training local activists as public speakers, conscious that even cinema vans proved most effective when supported by a strong platform speaker, and that in any case they had to do what they could to match Labour's dominance of old-style street-corner oratory. In 1931 a Labour election guide boasted that the party had 'held its own against these innovations [mobile cinema and loudspeaker vans] by the superior quality of its outdoor platform speaking.' The Conservatives appear to have agreed: in October 1928 their Principal Agent was advising the party leadership to call an early spring election specifically to avoid being dragged into a long summer of open-air campaigning which would 'place us at a disadvantage'. The advice was heeded, though the election was still lost.[9]

During the 1920s outdoor speaking became even more central to electioneering, consolidating a trend that could be traced back to the franchise reforms of the late nineteenth century. Candidates took some of the strain here, but the parties were generally wary of allowing them to over-tax their voices at tough open-air pitches. Frank Gray, briefly a maverick Liberal MP, claimed to have held sixteen large open-air meetings across Oxford on the eve of poll in 1922. In five strenuous hours he reckoned to have addressed 12,000 voters, two-thirds of whom were probably non-partisans, whereas his Conservative opponent would have managed to reach only 2,500 at his indoor rally, almost all of whom would have been loyal supporters. The lesson was obvious it seemed; in the age of mass democracy, politicians had to take to the streets if they were to be effective. Labour also advised its candidates to make regular appearances at outdoor pitches, although they were told to limit themselves to a few words of encouragement or thanks, leaving speech-making itself to iron-lunged supporters. One factor here was that Labour was slow to accept amplification for outdoor speaking—in 1931 the party's official electioneering guide was still arguing that it destroyed the intimacy between speaker and audience. Outdoor speaking was all about taking politics to the people, and for Labour candidates this had to be done on the basis of strict equality. Amplification threatened to destroy that equality by accentuating the exotic, 'outsider' status of the speaker, and it was not until the later 1930s that Labour began to make routine use of the new technology. At first many Conservatives remained reluctant to follow Labour onto the streets at all; indeed in the early 1920s a party electioneering guide still warned of the dangers of 'cheapening' the candidate with outdoor speaking. But as amplification became widely available, so these qualms evaporated. By 1932 Cambray was adamant that, far from being 'undignified', open-air speaking represented 'a return of the old practice of hustings' and to the traditions of Victorian statesmen like Gladstone. Conservatives had less to fear from accentuating social difference (for most it remained an integral part of their public identity), and, perhaps in consequence, they displayed few qualms about embracing outdoor amplification. Indeed some, like Harold Macmillan at Stockton in 1929, proved happy to rig the new systems to their own private cars—thereby displaying not only their considerable wealth, but also their confidence that this need not prove an insurmountable barrier to engagement with the voters (Fig. 11).[10]

But amplification really came into its own for the party leaders' great set-piece meetings. Lloyd George, the greatest platform orator of his generation, was the pioneer here. In 1922, campaigning as the outgoing premier, he made extensive use of relay systems so that his speeches could be heard by vast overspill audiences. At Bristol, where Lloyd George addressed an audience of 2,000 at the Hippodrome, a crowd of 20,000

ELECTIONEERING UP-TO-DATE.

Capt. Harold Macmillan, the Conservative candidate for Stockton, addressing a street corner audience in Ewbank-street, through a microphone and loud speaker.

Fig. 11. Harold Macmillan with mobile loudspeaker at Stockton, 1929 *North-Eastern Daily Gazette*, 25 May 1929, p. 3 (© The British Library Board. All Rights Reserved)

gathered outside to hear the ex-Prime Minister's speech relayed by a Magnavox system (though by all accounts the system was not up to the job, and most heard little or nothing). During the 1923 election Lloyd George addressed a series of vast open-air meetings across the north of England using powerful new amplification systems to address unparalleled crowds—30,000 were said to have heard him at Bolton and 40,000 at Rochdale, numbers that even Gladstone could never have hoped to reach through outdoor oratory. An incident at Rochdale underlined the power of the new technology. Lloyd George was developing an argument about Lancashire's historic connections to Free Trade when he asked an aide 'What about Cobden, was he Lancashire?'—suddenly the whole square burst into laughter, as well they might given Cobden's famous connection to 'Manchester School' Liberalism. A chastened Lloyd George was left to bemoan the 'mischievous instrument' that had exposed his ignorance of Liberal party mythology. Inevitably others were quick to follow in the Welsh wizard's footsteps. Baldwin's first experience of the technology was in July 1924 when he addressed a meeting of 20,000 at Manchester's Belle Vue stadium. Baldwin complained of having to 'ascend a scaffold' above the vast throng who were packed 'like sardines in a tin, no interruptions and no movement'. The equipment itself was off-putting—he described having to 'stand stock still and speak into a thing like a beehive'—worse was the anonymity of the whole process: 'you establish no personal contact with your audience nor do you know if they are gripped'. But there was no turning back. Three years later Baldwin was happily addressing a vast crowd of over 70,000 at a Conservative rally in the grounds of Welbeck Abbey in Nottinghamshire, and during the 1929 election he was said to have addressed 200,000 on Blackpool beach via an elaborate relay system. Such events became a staple of the leaders' itinerary in the late 1920s, with care spent to ensure that the events were also visually striking, in order to maximize coverage both by the newsreel companies and on the picture pages of the popular press. In 1929, improvements in relay technology enabled both Lloyd George and Baldwin's major campaign speeches to be relayed at great expense to multiple venues across the country (although the BBC's news moratorium meant that no part of them would be relayed to people's homes). The leader's meeting thus remained integral to political communication; it was simply adapted to make the most of new technologies.[11]

However, despite the proliferation of both ordinary election meetings and elaborate mass rallies between the wars, it must be acknowledged that politicians increasingly began to doubt their efficacy as a means of reaching the all-important uncommitted voter. The growth of open-air meetings was directly linked to the recognition that most electors would never be persuaded to venture inside a conventional meeting hall. It was the same logic that saw all three parties organizing seaside propaganda campaigns every summer—here, surely, they would find the elusive 'silent voter' (though whether holidaymakers really wanted to be found is another matter). With the average constituency boasting almost 50,000 voters by 1929 it was obvious that even intensive public speaking, both indoor and out, would probably reach only a minority of the electorate—but the symbolism of face-to-face politics remained vital. Politicians knew that voters expected to see, hear, and, most importantly, be able to interrogate the rival candidates during an election campaign. Faced by considerable disruption at Birmingham Ladywood in 1924, Neville Chamberlain wished that he could abandon traditional indoor meetings altogether and confine himself to touring the courts and factories of his poor, inner Birmingham constituency. But he knew that if he did so 'it would be said that I was afraid of meetings and of questions and I should eventually be driven into holding them after all'. Similarly, Harold Macmillan, recalling his campaign at Stockton in 1923, acknowledged that meetings had often been gruelling experiences, but he had no doubt that they remained 'vastly important, even decisive'. When things got especially difficult Macmillan would abandon any pretence at delivering a speech and simply field questions from the floor, since this, he quickly realized, was what people really came for anyway. Labour organizers took a similar view, arguing that the ordinary election meeting remained indispensable because it appealed to the 'human or personal' side in a way that radio, cinema, and even the amplified mass rally never could. Most importantly, it provided the 'added excitement of heckling and questions' which still appealed to so many between the wars.[12]

The campaign transformed

But if the meeting remained as a focal point of elections, there was nonetheless much that changed on the campaign trail after 1918. For one thing, the campaign itself was dramatically shorter than before the war. Campaigning was now concentrated in the last two weeks before polling. Houston and Valdar, writing in 1922, talked of 'these days of short and intensive campaigns'. Candidates had traditionally indulged in long campaigns of public speaking in the run-up to an election, but after 1918 there was neither the money nor, apparently, the public appetite to sustain such an effort. Before the war the Manchester Liberal Federation, confident that an election was in the air, had held thirty major public meetings by Christmas 1909, even though Parliament was not actually dissolved until 10 January 1910. By contrast, in 1931 Stafford Cripps held no public meetings at Bristol East until ten days *after* the dissolution of Parliament, although he then addressed two or three each night over the last week and a half, culminating in seven public meetings across the constituency on the eve of poll. This pattern is confirmed by the findings of a survey of meetings in eleven English constituencies between 1895 and 1935. While the total number of meetings changed little across the period, by the 1930s they were generally simpler, shorter affairs squeezed into the last fortnight of the campaign.[13]

Set-piece election rallies remained an important feature of local campaigns between the wars, but they became rarer partly because election expenses had been severely squeezed by the 1918 'Fourth' Reform Act, and partly because candidates now had a legal right to the free use of local elementary schoolrooms during the sixteen days between writ and poll. Indeed, it seems likely that it was the combined effect of these legal changes, coupled with the introduction of a common election timetable and polling day for the whole country, that did most to determine the shift to a distinctly shorter (if still intense) campaign after 1918. But school halls were not conducive to the survival of pomp and ritual in electoral politics. As Harold Macmillan recalled of his first meetings in Stockton, adults squeezed into tiny schoolroom furniture were likely either to listen passively, as though to a lecture, or else to prove hostile and irritable. Either way they could be 'very difficult'. Increasingly, candidates appear to have favoured simple, pared-down meetings as the best way to manage such audiences. Mosley famously sought to emphasize his 'modern' credentials by dropping anything that could detract from his direct relationship with the audience—platform dignitaries, chairmen, and formal votes of thanks or confidence were all dispensed with. Few mainstream politicians were prepared to go quite so far, but evening-long meetings, with teams of speakers became rare, and increasingly formal rituals with roots in the old hustings, like votes of confidence, were also dropped.[14]

Meetings were not the only aspects of electioneering affected by the financial restrictions of the 'Fourth' Reform Act. According to Michael Dawson, the 1918 Act more than halved the amount a candidate could spend per voter even before allowing for the effects of rapid inflation—general prices more than doubled between 1914 and 1919, and the price of some key electioneering staples such as stationery and printing rose more than fourfold. Deflation eased the situation a little in the 1920s, but the lavish spending of the Edwardian era never returned; hence Cambray's comment in 1932 that election costs had been cut so fine that it was now hard to run 'an effective campaign' within the law. Moreover, there were also signs that the super-rich candidate, prepared to spend on a lavish scale to woo a constituency, had become an endangered species—perhaps in part because of the inroads of higher taxes on wealth and income, but perhaps also because Labour's post-war breakthrough had transformed the political and social context both of electioneering and of being an MP. Politics was ceasing to be a 'game for gentlemen'. Again legislative changes accelerated this process of social levelling by drastically reducing the cost of politics. In 1911 Labour had won an important victory over traditional conceptions of the 'gentleman leader' by securing MPs an annual salary of £400. In turn, the 1918 Act transferred the payment of official election expenses from candidates to the Treasury and allowed all candidates one free 2-ounce mailing to each elector (equivalent in value to 40 per cent of total legal expenses in a borough in 1918). The law on agency was also tightened in an attempt to stop the Edwardian practice of lavish spending by outside pressure groups. Writing in the 1930s, Cambray was convinced that these restrictions had 'removed much of the gaiety of elections. They are now dull affairs by comparison with those of the generation preceding the war.' But others pointed out that the 1918 restrictions were anything but watertight—as long as candidates were not mentioned by name there was still little to stop outside bodies from intervening in a constituency campaign. That only maverick newspaper owners now sought to intervene in this way was therefore testimony to a shift in political temperament as much as political law.[15]

But for all that, money continued to matter. Even within the new tighter limits, Conservatives could still generally outspend their rivals at both the national and local level between the wars. Conservatives recognized that money was probably their greatest asset in the battle to control the radicalizing tendencies of mass democracy. The Conservatives' financial edge was seen not just in their greater use of new technologies such as mobile loudspeakers, relay systems, and cinema vans, but also in more established fields of propaganda such as advertising, leaflets, and also local campaigning, where the Conservatives spent vastly more than their opponents on paid assistance (some said, probably unfairly, because unlike Labour, they had to). This disparity was at its most extreme after 1927, when the Conservatives' Trades Dispute Act, passed in the aftermath of the General Strike, starved Labour of vital trade union funds at national and local level by insisting that members must contract into, rather than out of, the political levy (it was reversed by Labour in 1946). In 1929 Conservative candidates outspent their Labour counterparts on average by two to one (£905 against £452), and in 1935 the gap was wider still despite a reduction in overall expenditure (Conservatives now spent on average £777 compared with £365 for Labour). At the same time the party was also spending vast sums on nationally co-ordinated propaganda. In 1927 they distributed almost twenty million leaflets, including nine million intended to neutralize the TUC's campaign against the Trades Dispute Act, and in 1929 they sent copies of the party manifesto to 8.3 million homes and hired the advertising agency Benson's to devise a sophisticated campaign that included almost half a million billboard posters (by contrast at the 1955 election the three main parties managed just 6,000 between them). They also bent the law by allowing posters put up before the election, often on donated billboards, to remain on display throughout the campaign without being declared in candidates' election expenses. Conservative strategist Philip Cambray argued that public opinion should be moulded by continuous party advertising campaigns, and that the law on campaign advertising should be tested in the courts, but neither was tried between the wars. It would not be until 1957 that Conservatives experimented with a sustained pre-election advertising campaign, and not until 1974 that the Liberals demonstrated the legality of a national advertising campaign *during* an election.[16]

Increasingly the parties' propaganda efforts became focused on what came to be known as the silent majority—the vast numbers of less partisan, largely inactive citizens whose votes were said to decide elections under the new franchise (one Labour guide termed them the 'hesitant electors'). The key means of reaching these voters was believed to be not the human

voice, but the printed word—itself testimony to the parties' limited faith
in new technologies between the wars. Daunted by the sheer scale of the
new post-war electorate, as well as by its supposed lack of settled political
convictions, evangelism rather than organization became the watchword
of political strategists. According to Frank Gray, after 1918 approximately
half the electorate was of no fixed politics—compared with at most a third
before the war, which meant that almost any constituency was up for grabs
to a candidate who could organize an effective, well-judged local campaign.
This was certainly how the Conservative organizers Houston and Valdar
saw things in their massive tome on *Modern Electioneering Practice* written
shortly after the passing of the 'Fourth' Reform Act. Pointing out that
'only a relatively small section of the public is possessed of settled political
convictions', they insisted that the modern party agent had to be first and
foremost 'a publicity expert' since 'Elections to-day are mainly won by the
printed word.' Long before the Conservatives turned to Benson's, Houston
and Valdar were arguing that 'Winning elections is really a question of
salesmanship little different from marketing any branded article'—the key,
they argued, was to understand the cumulative power of propaganda on
'the large majority whose political opinions are more vague and less deeply
rooted'.[17]

Increasingly the written word, rather than the platform, dominated
the parties' propaganda efforts between elections. Leaflets, pamphlets, and
especially party newsletters came to be seen as the principal weapons in
a publicity war aimed at swaying the volatile public mind. Nor was this
just a question of long-term, incremental influence—well-judged printed
propaganda was believed to have proved decisive in swinging key inter-war
elections. For instance, many Conservatives were convinced that in 1923
last-minute Liberal leaflets on food prices and war pensions had swung the
campaign against them. In 1924 the party sought to secure a similar effect
by exploiting the Zinoviev letter's supposed revelations about Labour's
links to Soviet Communism, although in this case Fleet Street proved a
decisive adjunct to the party publicity machine. But for all that, it was only
in 1929 that party propaganda matched the extraordinary levels seen in
1910. In 1924, despite the Conservatives' concerted attempt to discredit the
outgoing Labour Government, they still issued ten million fewer leaflets
than in January 1910, despite there being three times more voters. But in
1929 the party distributed a remarkable 93 million leaflets (twice the level
of 1910) though all to no avail; unless, that is, one believes party chairman

J. C. C. Davidson, who insisted that without this colossal propaganda effort the party might easily have lost more heavily. Davidson was convinced that in 1929 the decisive factors saving the party from a heavier defeat had been, first, that the party had concentrated its efforts on the seats considered to be most 'in danger', and, second, that, unlike their Labour opponents, they had avoided 'highbrow' appeals in favour of the 'simpler and more easily understood propaganda leaflet'. Indeed, though it is the avuncular poster of Baldwin calling for 'Safety First' that is now usually cited, the party published an array of striking posters in 1929, many in the bold style that would be associated with the work of Saatchi and Saatchi half a century later. In one MacDonald is depicted as a gun-totting, masked gangster demanding higher taxes from the hapless voter (Fig. 12).[18]

Of course there was nothing new about vulgar electioneering tactics, indeed the inter-war period threw up nothing as striking (or crass) as the Edwardian parades of Chinese labourers and unemployed workers, or the rival displays of 'Free Trade' and 'Tariff Reform' loaves. Houston and Valdar might advocate bold visual 'stunts' to influence voters' 'mass psychology', but this was not the dominant tone of inter-war electioneering. As early as 1920 observers were commenting on the more 'sober' tone of post-war elections, and in 1922 a national organizer for the Labour Party was insisting that 'It is our business not to depend on "stunt" methods…but to take advantage of the fact that people do read in these days to a far greater extent than ever before.' When elections went badly, Labour strategists might be found wondering whether voters would only respond to irrational stunts, but ordinarily the party stuck to its faith in the power of reason. In 1931 the party's official guide to electioneering was adamant that 'Political education is spreading and rising, and the platform appeal has correspondingly to be revised and adapted.' Indeed even a broadly cynical Conservative like Philip Cambray was happy to acknowledge that by the 1930s far more people were informed about political issues and the workings of Parliament than had been the case fifty or even twenty-five years before—a fact he attributed largely to the growth of the popular press. Moreover, there was a widespread recognition that the rapid growth of non-party, mass organizations such as the Women's Institutes, the Towns Women's Guilds, the British Legion, and the League of Nations Union signalled the blossoming of a dynamic civic culture outside the political parties, which offered a bedrock of democratic stability. Writing in 1945, the Labour organizer Harold Croft argued that it was the combination of broad-based party coalitions and the

Fig. 12. Conservative election poster, 1929, *ILN*, 25 May 1929, reproduced with the kind permission of the Syndics of Cambridge University Library

dense network of voluntary associations and single-issue pressure groups that
sustained British democracy. As Helen McCarthy has recently suggested, in
many respects inter-war voluntary associations defined themselves against
the bitter divisiveness of conventional party politics. Perhaps significantly,
when he found himself at odds with the League of Nations Union in 1934
over the question of the 'Peace Ballot', Baldwin sought to undermine the
organization's initiative by suggesting that it would allow 'unscrupulous
propagandists' to use 'the cause of peace for party politics of the lowest
kind'. But in the midst of the 1935 General Election, with war crises
in the air, he sought to ally his government with the emotions that the
ballot had stirred by making a high-profile 'non-party' speech to the Peace
Society that was seen by millions thanks to its coverage by British-Gaumont
newsreels.[19]

But whilst inter-war politicians had good reason to be wary of becoming
closely associated with vulgar stunts, this did not stop them throwing
themselves whole-heartedly into the election scares that loomed so large
in campaigns between the wars. Party strategists concluded that shorter
campaigns coupled with a mass franchise made it easier, as Cambray
put it, 'to stampede the electorate' with a 'last-minute lie'—especially
if, as with the Zinoviev letter, the press could be persuaded to spread
the lie to every corner of the country. In 1929 some Labour candidates
were said to have raised the cry that Conservatives were 'baby-killers'
because the Government had cut the grant providing free milk to nursing
mothers, while in 1931 Philip Snowden famously rounded on his former
Labour colleagues by suggesting that, had they stayed in office, savings
would have been raided and the unemployment fund exhausted. Historians
have sometimes been sceptical about the influence of such tactics—and
only a fool would suggest that Labour would have triumphed in 1931
but for Snowden's intervention—but Neville Chamberlain, for one, was
convinced that Snowden had a strong claim on office 'as he has done so
much to win us the election'. However, precisely because the last-minute
lie was believed to be so potent, the parties also worked hard to inoculate
their supporters against its influence. In 1935 the Conservatives sought to
run scares about Labour's threat to building societies and personal savings,
while in turn Labour held up the bogey of massive rearmament and military
conscription, but by all accounts neither issue stirred much interest among
an electorate that was learning to discount 'party politics of the lowest
kind'. Much more effective was Baldwin's 'above party' intervention at the

Peace Society. Neville Chamberlain considered it 'one of the finest things he has ever done', and acknowledged that Baldwin's contribution was vital to 'retaining the floating vote'.[20]

Managing mass democracy

As this emphasis on 'mass psychology' and 'scares' suggests, politicians initially felt profoundly daunted by the post-war mass electorate, not least because they believed that old election techniques, such as registration work and intensive canvassing, could no longer prove effective. In the immediate post-war years many constituency parties all but abandoned canvassing in despair at the sheer size of the task before them, and it was generally accepted throughout the inter-war period both that a complete canvass was now all but impossible, and that in any case the electorate was so unsettled in its politics that the canvass could offer little guide to final voting intentions. Worse, the register itself was also worryingly unstable; as one seasoned organizer observed, not only did an agent now have to organize perhaps five times as many voters, but 'from one fifth to a quarter may change with every new Register'. This shifting, mass electorate was thought to be beyond either direct personal influence or the indirect influence of party organization. The sheer weight of numbers was mesmerizing—how could meetings count for much when there were 50,000 voters, and the biggest local hall might hold two or three thousand at most? Restless, spirited souls like Frank Gray might feel that the answer lay in the street-corner stump and a manic programme of house-to-house visiting (he boasted of having visited nearly every house in Oxford in the run-up to his successful campaign), but few politicians possessed either his stamina or his boundless optimism. For them the evangelism of the printed word seemed more practicable and decidedly less onerous. Much better, they reasoned, to embrace the doctrine that the leaflet war was now 'the really vital feature of the campaign'—that victory lay in the grasp of the candidate who understood the need for 'bright, snappy reading, lightened with catchy headlines in attractive type'.[21]

But in practice party propaganda often fell far short of this ideal. Whilst willing to acknowledge that some efforts, such as Snowden's attacks on his former colleagues in 1931, could represent decisive interventions in the campaign, Cambray argued that 'in post-War years, political Parties seem to have favoured mass production of "literature" to the detriment of effectiveness, but to the benefit of waste-paper dealers'. Centrally drafted 'literature' was often seen as inappropriate to local needs, but constituencies also struggled to find anyone remotely capable of producing the bright, snappy copy demanded by modern tastes. The local newsletters widely produced by constituency Labour parties during the 1920s were praised both for their 'modern' styling, and for their skilful blending of national and local copy. Here, Labour appears to have had the edge for much of the inter-war period, although, as Laura Beers has argued, during the 1920s this dynamism was in many respects a necessary corollary of the party's antagonistic relationship with the 'capitalist' press, and its reluctance to allow the TUC-owned *Daily Herald* to be run on purely commercial principles. Moreover, Davidson was not alone in believing that Labour's literature had been too 'highbrow' in 1929—Arthur Henderson for one apparently agreed. Similar criticisms were voiced internally in the wake of the 1931 and 1935 election defeats, and even in the early 1940s one Labour figure was still bemoaning the ineffectiveness of party literature with 'its unattractive printing, its pedestrian language' and its lack of striking images. But of course, Conservatives also frequently got the pitch and tone of their propaganda wrong. Bob Boothby recalled the output from Conservative Central Office as a 'torrent of nonsense' during the 1945 campaign, while well into the late 1940s Conservative party branches expressed a strong preference for locally designed posters, rather than the ineffective copy produced by Central Office.[22]

In short, there was widespread frustration that large swathes of the mass electorate were simply beyond reach—that neither street-corner oratory nor snappy leaflets promised to reconnect politicians with the mass electorate. Heading for defeat in 1929, Steel-Maitland wrote of his frustration that in the 'immense new districts' of his Birmingham constituency he and his wife found it impossible to get enough workers 'to get to know us' to break down the view that he was 'a monster of inhumanity' because of his time as Minister of Labour. Worse, though deeply distrusted by all sides, it was Fleet Street that appeared to exert the greatest sway over the new mass politics. During the Zinoviev 'scare' of 1924 this influence had been exerted to the benefit of Conservatism, but neither Baldwin nor Conservative Central Office trusted the maverick, independent Conservatism espoused by Rothermere's *Mail* and Beaverbrook's *Express*—and with good reason. Both papers were lukewarm about Baldwin's brand of Conservatism, and in 1929 offered the Conservatives only half-hearted support. One defeated Cornish Conservative, shocked by the loss of five seats in the county, railed against the press for promoting Lloyd George's radical programme among that 'big and solid lump of Liberals who never come to meetings and won't listen to argument'. Recoiling from a worse defeat in 1931, Labour also railed against the 'capitalist newspapers' which had 'stampeded' the electorate to vote National. One Labour agent blamed the 'great national newspapers and the wireless' for creating a 'mass psychology' which meant that 'propaganda tends to become de-localised'. It was a bleak assessment, and one that Labour leaders generally rejected in happier times, but it nicely captured a growing fear that what we would now call 'mediated politics' was beginning to come between candidates and constituents.[23]

The inter-war period saw a number of ingenious attempts to break down the anonymity of mass politics that anticipated the direction party politics would take after 1945. Perhaps the most striking of these was the tendency of Labour MPs, along with some maverick Liberals, to pioneer what we would now call MPs' surgeries. Frank Gray claimed to have run a weekly advice service throughout his brief spell as MP for Oxford in the early 1920s, but the trend really took off from 1924, when MPs became entitled to free rail travel between their constituencies and Westminster. Most MPs continued to make infrequent journeys back to their constituencies, relying on the local association, the post, and the telephone to keep abreast of constituency problems, but increasingly some MPs (mostly Labour) began to adopt a more hands-on approach, spending most weekends in their constituencies dealing with problems and making appearances. Harold Macmillan claimed to have been one of the few Conservative MPs to adopt the practice in the late 1920s, mindful that his depressed industrial seat of Stockton was both highly marginal and over-brimming with hardship cases for him to try and solve. These diligent MPs were trying to shore up the local bases of politics in an age when impersonal, national forces appeared to hold greater and greater sway—but it is important to remember that in doing so they could still tap into important sources of resistance to the nationalization of politics: local pride was one, but perhaps more tangible was the ability of a vibrant local press to provide vital publicity that could counter the corrosive influence of Fleet Street. Cambray felt that Labour MPs had 'made themselves slaves of their constituents' between 1929 and 1931, spending 'almost every weekend among the electors, always accessible'—and for what? In 1931 almost all had been swept away in the great national tide of opinion against their party. But surgeries did not disappear in consequence. Indeed, by 1938 the young Conservative Quintin Hogg was reintroducing the MP's surgery to Oxford in the wake of his famous victory in the post-Munich by-election. Surgeries would not become general for decades, but the uncertainties thrown up by the new mass franchise, and particularly by the apparently weak partisanship of so many voters, had played an important part in their genesis.[24]

Another important strategy sought to overcome the anonymity of mass politics, not by developing new forms of face-to-face contact, but rather by breaking the electorate down into distinct sub-groups and interests. Variously known as targeted or stratified electioneering, the idea was that parties should tailor their political language to specific audiences, rather than struggle to find an elusive 'mass appeal'. David Jarvis has shown how this approach helped Conservatives to overcome the psychological shock of facing the new mass working-class electorate after 1918. He shows how Conservatives learnt, or rather re-learnt, to think in terms of the 'working classes' rather than 'the working class'—recognizing that workers had diverse interests, many of which could be represented as sharply at odds with the redistributive and egalitarian instincts of socialism (the scares about Post Office savings and building societies are two obvious examples of this approach, but there were many subtler variants). But targeted electioneering was about more than identifying issues that could appeal to distinct interest groups—it was also about targeting propaganda selectively to different audiences. Parties had always done this in the sense that candidates from the same party would routinely tailor their appeal to the character of their constituency. But targeted electioneering was about differentiation at the level of the voter rather than the constituency, and was primarily about explaining the implications of the party's national programme to specific groups of voters, rather than about allowing candidates to deviate sharply from that programme in the name of constituency interests. Conservative Central Office had begun advocating targeted campaigning before 1914, but it was in the 1920s that it came into its own. At the local level it meant parties compiling lists of voters in particular trades or occupations, or particular age groups, as a basis for targeted mailings of literature and personal correspondence from the candidate. At the national level it meant tailoring political messages to the specific demographic characteristics of a newspaper or magazine's audience. From the start Labour was as interested in such techniques as its opponents, with Sidney Webb in particular a strong evangelist for the scientific logic of what he termed 'stratified electioneering'. Labour candidates routinely sent out special letters to groups such as teachers, clergymen, shopkeepers, co-operators, and trade unionists, but this was about as far as the technique ever went since local parties generally struggled to collect comprehensive individual-level information. Perhaps significantly, though Webb had first proclaimed the need for 'stratified electioneering' in 1922, more than two decades later Labour's official electioneering guide was still arguing that 'something of this more scientific approach to the electorate may have to guide our agents in the future'. Clearly we should not overstate the revolution in campaigning between the wars—most candidates still relied on scatter-gun rather than targeted propaganda—reinforced, as ever, by a fortnight of talking themselves hoarse on the platform. That was what they knew, and in the absence of serious research to the contrary, there was no reason to think that anything else would work better.[25]

Peaceable nation?

Concerns about the character and temper of the new mass democracy also played a decisive role in transforming the culture of public politics after 1918. Although overall the 1918 election was probably most notable for its lack of excitement (turnout was just 57 per cent), there were nonetheless local hot spots of serious disorder. Contesting Dundee as a Coalition Liberal, Churchill complained of facing 'the most turbulent meetings I have ever addressed', which he attributed largely to 'this enormous electorate composed of so many of the poorest people in the country'. Similarly, in 1922 Austen Chamberlain felt that 'everywhere there was a bitter extremist element out for revolution, men and women alike'. According to Churchill, who lost his Dundee seat fighting as a 'National Liberal', 'they were "spewed out of the slums—the kind of women who would spit in your wife's face" ' (they apparently did just that when the be-pearled Clementine Churchill sought to deputize for her convalescing husband at a series of rough meetings across the city). To Chamberlain, who was still smarting from the collapse of his hopes for a permanent anti-Labour Coalition, the signs were clear: here was 'A dangerous element, & new, I think—bitter, fanatical, ready for violence if they saw a chance.' Nor were such comments wholly fanciful. The pre-war householder franchise had been biased against the urban poor, whereas after 1918 the impact of universal male suffrage was amplified by the abolition of pauper disqualification and the relaxation of restrictive residence requirements. But 1918 had merely increased the 'slum vote', not created it. As John Davis has demonstrated, plenty of very poor voters had made it onto the register from the 1880s onwards. Politicians' post-war fears spoke to a larger truth: the breakdown of confidence in social hierarchy. Where disorder had once been seen merely as evidence of high japes or rough manners, it now tended to be interpreted as 'class war' (Labour's advance was crucial here—not because it preached class war, it didn't, but because it fundamentally disrupted the class dynamics of public politics: elections were no longer about choosing which gentleman should rule over you, though by the late twentieth century most would be again). According to C. E. Montague, writing in 1922, the war had mercilessly exposed the failings of Britain's ruling class, so that 'it lives, since the war, in a kind of contempt'. Nor did this sense of social dislocation quickly pass. When Labour won six seats at Birmingham in 1929, Austen Chamberlain again explained things in stark class terms: 'the working classes have been nourishing a silent resentment more like class hatred than anything I have experienced in my life time. The old people still supported us but the young were sullen & resentful & voted socialist almost solidly.' These were dangerous times—for most Conservatives full democracy could not have come at a worse moment—old certainties were in flux and class enmities had apparently never been deeper. No wonder Baldwin talked of the need 'to educate them before the crash comes'. (Fig. 13 reminds us how stark the class dynamics of electioneering could still be between the wars; Viscount Weymouth is stooping to canvass an unemployed miner at Frome in 1931. His efforts were not in vain—he recaptured the seat for the Conservatives with a majority of 7,110.)[26]

It was not just Conservatives who feared the temper of the new democracy. Most Labour leaders had long thought in terms of educating the people to make them fit for socialism, and experience of the wartime patriotic crowd had merely strengthened their distrust of 'the mob' and disorderly street politics. Writing in 1919, MacDonald argued that the old party politics had been content to teach the people how to 'enjoy an election', but Labour's mission must be to help them think intelligently about politics. It was a viewpoint only strengthened by his first-hand experience of electoral disorder at the notorious Woolwich by-election

Fig. 13. Stooping to conquer: Viscount Weymouth canvassing the unemployed at Frome, 1931, *ILN*, 24 Oct. 1931, reproduced with the kind permission of the Syndics of Cambridge University Library

of March 1921, which ended in MacDonald's defeat at the hands of a Conservative war hero from humble origins who had been strongly backed by Horatio Bottomley's scurrilous popular weekly *John Bull*. In its analysis of 'The Woolwich Fight' the *Labour Organiser* concluded that, henceforth, the party 'must adopt quieter methods' if it was to succeed with the new electorate. Enthusiastic meetings and colourful trade union demonstrations were said to bring little benefit—if anything they threatened to alienate the new voters. According to the journal,

> The quiet, ordinary citizen who keeps his politics to himself, hearing the shouting and singing of the demonstrators, or attending the meetings to find himself in the midst of a cheering gathering, is not impressed with the power of Labour to govern; for governing is not done by shouting...

During the 1920s this concern for the sensibility of the 'quiet, ordinary citizen' often placed Labour politicians in conflict with their own more exuberant supporters, many of whom still saw an election as a chance to have some fun at the tories' expense. But the fact that their opponents seized on every opportunity to highlight, and often to exaggerate, examples of 'Labour rowdyism' suggests that the leaderships' instincts were sound. Where once candidates had sought to ignore disruption, or if that was impossible, to blame it on hired outsiders, they now saw it as something to publicize as proof that their opponents were unfit for office. Indeed, on the eve of the 1923 election the *Conservative Agents' Journal* openly argued that ' "Prevention of free speech" is a fine "gag" ' that could be made to 'stick to your opponents like tar' during an election. Conservative Central Office ran stories about Labour 'rowdyism' for all they were worth during the 1924 election, shifting their focus only when the even better 'gag' of the Zinoviev letter hit the news. Significantly, Labour did not respond, as once they might, by claiming that such disorder merely reflected voters' spontaneous anger at tory lies—instead they sought to blame disorder on others—on Communists, Irish republicans, and hooligans—or else tried to highlight counter-examples of 'tory rowdyism'.[27]

But was behaviour at elections changing as rapidly as attitudes? This is not an easy question to answer. We have seen that many contemporaries were struck by the more 'sober' tone of post-war politics, by the diminution of colour and excitement, but should we take such statements at face value? Didn't politicians always look back to a golden age when the public really cared about politics? Well, yes, up to a point, but one needs to remember that few commentators hankered after a return to the days when candidates were regularly spattered by mud or bombarded with dead animals—indeed most were clear that change was for the better. But that still leaves the question of how great change really was. The gag of 'rowdyism' only worked because disorder persisted at elections. But for all that, the trend was towards quieter, more orderly contests where the clash of rival bands of partisans became the exception rather than the rule (unlike before the war). Michael Dawson has shown that elections became markedly more orderly in the rural south-west after 1918, and contemporary newspapers can be found making similar claims for many parts of Britain, including Labour strongholds such as central Scotland and south Wales. My study of elections in eleven English constituencies between 1895 and 1935 drew similar conclusions. Judging from local press reports, at least one-third of meetings involved some degree of active opposition from the floor in January 1910; three times the level recorded for both the 1922 and 1935 contests. Perhaps the controversial elections of 1924 and 1931 would have produced somewhat higher levels of disorder, but even these contests failed to generate the sustained popular enthusiasm characteristic of Edwardian elections. Neville Chamberlain, for one, reported in 1931 that he had 'never before had such crowds to address nor so little interruption ... even the Socialists remain quiet and subdued', while apart from Mosley himself, most New Party candidates appear to have been met by curiosity and gentle mocking, rather than violent hostility. Hence, too, the slow build-up to Stafford Cripps's 1931 campaign at Bristol East, despite the fact that, outside greater London, his was the only southern borough seat to resist the anti-Labour flood tide. True, many 'National Labour' renegades could tell a different tale of 1931, but their experience was not typical.[28]

Significantly, elections appear to have become quieter, less disorderly affairs before either radio or cinema had emerged as significant players in electoral politics. Writing in 1921, Morris observed how 'the old street corner rowdyism, armies of hired canvassers, great numbers of imported speakers, highly colored motor cars, and carefully staged torchlight processions were things of the past'. Similarly, in 1922 Montague commented on the 'limp apathy that we see at elections'. Many accounts told the same story of the 1929 election. At Bishop Auckland, Cuthbert Headlam found his meetings unusually 'quiet and orderly', even in the mining districts, but concluded that it was a sign, not of conversion, but of 'boredom' (rightly so as he lost his seat). William Bridgeman, who had spoken for Headlam, took the same view, noting that in seats where once he could 'hardly get a hearing', audiences now 'listen without a sound, and with tremendous interest'. But he too doubted that they had been converted—rather the workers were simply 'puzzled and repressed ... having lost faith in their leaders' remedies'. Perhaps significantly, Macmillan recalled the 'apathy and listlessness of the electors' at Stockton when he lost in 1929, whereas two years later he regained the seat comfortably despite considerable disorder. As in 1924, the Conservatives appear to have prospered amidst the inflamed feelings surrounding the fall of the minority Labour Government. Higher turnout was one factor—this tended to help Conservatives throughout the inter-war period, even in municipal contests. But another factor may well have been that stories of Labour disorder did just what Conservative strategists had predicted: they alienated the 'silent majority' and confirmed fears that Labour was 'dangerous' and unfit for office. But if so, it was a trick that was running out of steam by 1935. Although the popular Conservative press again ran frequent stories about Labour rowdyism, giving maximum coverage to the desperate plight of the few beleaguered National Labour candidates, one observer concluded that 'even by exaggerating every little incident they could make little capital out of it'. But then it was said to have been 'the quietest and most orderly [election] ever held'—in this context even the *Daily Mail* could not whip up a credible moral panic about Labour rowdies.[29]

But most politicians turned their backs on disorder, not just because they feared conjuring up the demons of class war and the 'submerged tenth'; they also feared alienating the new female voters. In 1922 Houston and Valdar declared that 'women have sounded the death-knell of mud-slinging and unfair tactics in elections'. When politicians talked of the 'silent' or 'hesitant' voter who had no time for riotous politics and shouting matches, the new female voter was rarely far from their mind. In the early 1920s, all parties went to extraordinary lengths to try and reach out to women voters: holding regular women-only public meetings, ensuring that women played a prominent role in all their public activities, and paying respectful attention to the lobbying efforts of local women's groups. Writing in the *Sunday Graphic* during the 1929 election, Baldwin celebrated the fact that the contest was 'being conducted with a sanity and an absence of emotion that would do credit to a board of directors', and argued that it was 'the influence of the women electors' that had created this 'absence of excitement'. Of course Baldwin was no neutral observer here—having ushered in the equal franchise a year earlier, he was keen to ensure that Conservatism reaped the maximum benefit from Britain's first majority female electorate. But the fact that in doing so he naturally equated a feminized polity with a peaceable polity is nonetheless significant. Not everyone was so positive. A deep strain of misogyny ran through Conservative politics between the wars, and when things went badly plenty of men were on hand to blame the women. One irate Conservative blamed his party's defeat at Huddersfield in 1929 on 'hundreds of girls [who] voted for Mabane because he had "curly hair"', adding, 'Many of them thought he was single because he had no women on the platform with him.' On the other hand, Austen Chamberlain took the opposite, if hardly less condescending view, that those Conservatives who had bucked the trend in industrial districts had 'literally danced themselves into safety with the Flappers'.[30]

But it was not just a question of the female vote. The parties also continued to rely heavily on women as party workers. After 1918 even the Conservatives accepted that women must be recognized as full members, and the party moved swiftly to co-opt the network of Women's Unionist Tariff Reform Association branches to form the basis of a new nationwide women's organization. But even in the late 1920s, party chairman J. C. C. Davidson found himself at loggerheads with men at party headquarters 'who still believed that politics was a masculine profession'. Things were often no better in the constituencies, although the pre-war trend for wives to become near full-time party organizers continued. Neville Chamberlain's letters from the 1920s are full of references to his wife Annie's sterling work visiting the Birmingham poor and co-ordinating the efforts of the constituency women's section in the slums of Ladywood. Both she and Clementine Churchill were also among the many politicians' wives persuaded to speak at the special women-only meetings so common in the early 1920s. At the same time, it also became common for ministers' wives to hold the fort at constituency meetings, leaving their menfolk free to speak in more marginal constituencies. Leo Amery, another inner-city Birmingham MP, seems to have done this routinely throughout the 1920s. But there were still old-guard local parties that resisted change. After the Conservatives lost Westminster St George's to an Independent Anti-Waste candidate in June 1921, the party discovered that there were just 275 members, almost all wealthy men living in the constituency's most exclusive wards. Little more than a year later, after a concerted effort to draw in women and the less affluent, there were nearly 1,300 members including 477 women. For Labour too the story of women's mobilization in constituency politics was decidedly uneven. There were heartland constituencies where, for years, Labour politics remained synonymous with the union lodge, so that no one, man or woman, could exert any influence as an individual member, but there were also seats where powerful women's sections came to set the agenda of Labour politics, especially at the municipal level where they often pioneered a dynamic approach to public service provision. But as Duncan Tanner has shown, even male-dominated local parties often pursued an advanced line on issues such as birth control and maternal health—reminding us that the party as a whole placed a strong emphasis on the politics of (household) consumption, rather than (male) production in this period. The image of an aggressive, male-centred Labour party faced by a moderate, feminized Conservatism is thus profoundly misleading—it is, in truth, an artefact of Conservative propaganda, which sought to paint

Labour with the brush of narrow trade union sectionalism and macho 'rowdyism'.[31]

For all that, 'rowdyism' was not simply a myth spun by Conservative propagandists. Even in 1935 there was serious disorder, although it was mostly confined to contests involving the hated champions of 'National Labour' including MacDonald himself, who had a gruelling time in the process of losing his Durham mining seat of Seaham to Manny Shinwell. But across Britain's large conurbations—particularly in London, Glasgow, Birmingham, and Liverpool—electoral disorder had put down deep roots, and persisted throughout the inter-war period. Here attempts to construct a new vision of Britain as a 'peaceable kingdom', with an electorate that was quiet, rational, and above all orderly, made little impression on deeply entrenched customs that upheld the public's right not only to interrogate, but also to torment, their would-be political masters. At the same time, politicians in the big conurbations remained more willing to connive in the organization of disorder than was the case elsewhere. At Birmingham in 1922, Austen Chamberlain was plotting to stop trouble at his meetings by bringing in hired roughs from local public houses. When told that there would be a 'free fight' he claimed to have replied 'I don't mind that ... if the right heads are broken too—& thoroughly!' Two years later Austen's half-brother Neville was locked in a bitter struggle for Ladywood with Oswald Mosley. Mosley, who would go on to raise political force to an art form in the 1930s as leader first of the New Party (with its notorious Biff Boys) and then the British Union of Fascists, appears to have been the chief instigator of disorder (in the 1930s his failure to register changing attitudes towards rabble-rousing would do much to put him 'beyond the pale' even before his movement turned explicitly towards Nazism and anti-Semitism). But at Ladywood in 1924, Neville Chamberlain was still quite happy to respond in kind—encouraging his supporters to 'retaliate' by shouting Mosley down wherever he spoke. Similarly, there is evidence from Glasgow of links between Protestant street gangs and local Conservatives, while Maxton and the Glasgow ILP were also well-known champions of the city's robust street politics. We also know that both in London and Birmingham, local Conservatives, faced by persistent disruption, turned to proto-fascist organizations to beef up their stewarding arrangements during the mid-1920s. While at Islington in 1931, a group of navy ratings stamped out bottle-throwing at Patrick Donner's meetings by half-drowning one culprit in a lavatory bowl. Indeed, taken together, these exceptions suggest an intriguing possibility: that the decisive factor shaping the transformation of electoral politics may have been public opinion, or at least politicians' perception of public opinion, rather than any deeper shift of sensibility among politicians. Where public opinion continued to tolerate disorder so did politicians, at least through the 1920s. However, there were signs of change even in the big cities—it became possible for candidates to hold closed, ticket-only meetings as a way of highlighting the disorderly conduct of their opponents, or even to abandon formal meetings altogether in favour of impromptu street-corner gatherings, as the Conservative candidate did at the Peckham by-election in 1936 (though he still lost).[32]

But we must be wary of romanticizing the stubborn persistence of electoral disorder in urban Britain. Often what it involved was simply rowdy, drunken young men excluding others, especially women, from the political arena by their boorish and violent behaviour. That such behaviour had been tolerated for so long is perhaps a bigger mystery, than that it rapidly lost favour after 1918. The secret of its longevity must surely be found, first, in the fact that election meetings were widely acknowledged to be the direct successors of the old hustings—and were thus seen as arenas for the ritual display of rival partisanships; second, in the related fact that non-voters were believed to possess a legitimate right to 'have their say' at such meetings (as they once had had at the hustings) precisely because they could not express their views at the poll; and finally, in the relative indifference to behaviour likely to marginalize women while Britain remained a sex-exclusive, male polity. After 1918, all this changed—only youths remained non-voters (at least among men), and electoral politics ceased to be a male preserve—all that survived to sustain the old ways was a distant link to the unruly traditions of partisanship once associated with the public hustings. That this was enough to sustain the politics of disruption in much of urban Britain for another generation was a testimony to how deeply the traditions of the hustings had impressed themselves on popular political culture.

We should also be wary of arguing that rejecting an aggressive, disorderly public necessarily meant rejecting an *activist* public. Most inter-war politicians wanted to substitute a deliberative for a demonstrative model of citizenship, but this did not necessitate breaking with political traditions that stressed the importance of a vigilant, publicly minded citizenry. Politicians hoped to encourage 'peaceable-ness' not passivity in the democratic electorate. Hence their keen cultivation of the non-party associations that flourished between the wars, since it was believed that these bodies promoted a model of rational, engaged citizenship which promised firmly to anchor Britain's fledgling democracy in a vibrant, healthy civil society. True, one can argue that inter-war politicians placed considerable emphasis on home-centred conceptions of citizenship, and made special efforts to reach out to the 'silent' or 'hesitant' voter who would not come to meetings, but they also worried profoundly over social trends that seemed to suggest that community and voluntarism were in decline, especially in the supposedly atomized, materialist suburbs. Though such fears were certainly overdrawn—neither private suburbia nor the new council estates were really wastelands of anomie—they remind us that, between the wars, few people welcomed the idea of a passive, armchair democracy. But on the other hand, if associational life remained rich, it was increasingly divorced from formal party politics. Even Conservative politicians were nervous about their ability to reach out to the new, more secular and non-party culture that flourished in the suburbs; its contours were unfamiliar and unstable, and not obviously open to either the old techniques of an evangelizing, face-to-face politics, or the new techniques of one-size-fits-all national propaganda. In *English Journey*, J. B. Priestley commented that, 'Unlike nineteenth-century England' the new England emerging in the suburbs was 'not politically-minded'. According to Priestley, 'One of its most familiar jokes is the ironical demand to know what Mr. Gladstone said in 1884.' Priestley feared that such an apolitical culture might all too easily fall prey to 'an iron autocracy'. But perhaps Neville Chamberlain was nearer the mark when he concluded, in the midst of the 1935 election, that, if henceforth 'non-party men and women [would] decide the nature of governments', it was reassuring to know 'that they are not swept off their feet by Lloyd Georges'—but preferred, instead, the quiet, consensual politics of a Baldwin.[33]

5

Towards the New Jerusalem

Labour's breakthrough

Labour's historic landslide victory of July 1945 was heralded not with a bang but with a whimper. Although many politicians would subsequently remember the election as marking the high point of post-war popular enthusiasm, at the time most were more struck by the unusual calm that descended over the first General Election for a decade. Hugh Dalton, soon to be appointed Chancellor of the Exchequer in the first majority Labour Government, recorded that it had been a quiet election, notable not for displays of popular enthusiasm, but for the spirit of seriousness and intelligent interest that had gripped the voters. Recalling the election in the late 1950s, after his retirement from Westminster, Dalton continued to insist that a new mood had gripped voters in 1945 and that it had been a defining feature of Labour's breakthrough election. Other big beasts of the Labour movement took a similar view. Herbert Morrison, Labour's wartime Home Secretary, recalled the remarkable silence at packed election meetings, and declared, not entirely disinterestedly, that 'A new sort of John Bull was preparing to go to the polls, and however he was to vote I liked him and was proud of him.'[1] After winning a by-election at Smethwick in October 1945, Patrick Gordon Walker drew similarly optimistic conclusions about the transformation of the British voter. Though twenty years later, after his defeat in the infamous Smethwick 'race' election of 1964 he may well have taken a rather different view, at this moment of heady expectation he declared,

> the people of Britain has politically grown up. It is a different people from ten years ago. It knows what it wants, it is not going to be diverted by stunts and personalities...Because the people have grown up it pays to be frank.[2]

Not all Labour politicians were quite so sanguine about the public's low-key mood in 1945. Some might claim to detect a new, more rational voter preparing to give informed consent to the building of the socialist 'New Jerusalem', but others were not so sure that the battle for minds had been decisively won. Within a few years, as economic problems mounted, Morrison himself was stressing the pragmatic basis of support for Labour in 1945, while Woodrow Wyatt, Labour MP for Aston, was arguing that the party must face up to the fact that 'the great mass of the people [are] ... almost entirely non-political'.[3]

Fighting Leeds South in 1945, Hugh Gaitskell, then one of Labour's young rising stars, was clearly surprised by the muted response to the party's dramatic local gains (Labour won five of the city's six seats, and came within a whisker of completing a clean sweep). Trying to re-enact the pomp of old-style elections, the five victorious Labour candidates paraded round the city in a motorized cavalcade, Gaitskell waving to bystanders as he precariously forced his upper body through a car sunroof. At the time, Gaitskell put the lack of public enthusiasm down to the undemonstrative Yorkshire temperament, commenting that the celebrations 'would have been more amusing in the south' (he had been chaired at an eve of poll rally at Chatham in 1935). With hindsight, though, it seems more likely that the future Labour leader was enjoying his first intimate acquaintance with the docile post-war electorate.[4]

For the most part Conservatives shared their opponents' assessment of the 1945 election. Having represented Stockton-on-Tees for nineteen of the previous twenty-one years, Harold Macmillan, the future Conservative Prime Minister, found that his three weeks of wartime campaigning 'passed quietly, much too quietly'. Meetings, though well attended, proved 'dull and uneventful', while the declaration, delayed three weeks here, as everywhere else, by the logistical complexities of incorporating the votes of overseas servicemen, had been 'a dull formality' without crowds or visible evidence of enthusiasm. Successfully defending the more promising north-east seat of Newcastle North, Conservative backbencher Sir Cuthbert Headlam noted a 'general apathy and lack of interest in the election', which he blamed on the pernicious influence of radio.[5] Conservative party organizers trying to make sense of their party's humiliating defeat pointed to 'the continuing and ominous calm with which the electors in so many constituencies went about their business'. True, some candidates had experienced rowdy opposition (at Kingston upon Thames John Boyd-Carpenter,

a future Cabinet Minister, complained of a sustained heckling campaign
led by disgruntled servicemen), but party organizers were clear that taking
the country as a whole 'no election was ever more quietly conducted'. At
Leicester West, where he stood as a 'National' candidate, Harold Nicolson
found that even the Communists 'listened quite politely' at his meetings.
The Nuffield College election study, the first instalment of that venerable
series introducing Britons to the delights of 'psephology', drew the same
picture. Although the Beaverbrook press had tried to revive the old cry
of 'Labour rowdyism' during the campaign, the authors of the Nuffield
study concluded that such incidents were wholly untypical and were, in
fact, often the result of deliberate provocation by Beaverbrook and his
associates. The real story of the election, they concluded, was 'the quietness
of the campaign' and the worrying signs of voter apathy. Even in Glasgow,
where, as we have seen, popular politics had remained far from tamed
throughout the inter-war period, meetings were often thinly attended and
the old soapbox orator was said to be absent from the street corners.[6]

There is something paradoxical about accounts of electioneering in 1945.
Contemporary sources tend to stress not only the calmness of the campaign,
but also the public's indifference to every effort to instil enthusiasm.
Retrospective accounts generally tell a different story. With the benefit
of hindsight, many felt the first post-war election to have represented a
golden age of mass politics and popular enthusiasm. Roy Jenkins recalled
how, fighting his first campaign in the unpromising Conservative bastion
of Solihull, he had nonetheless been able to draw crowds of two or
three hundred, night after night, to local schoolroom meetings. For the
Conservatives, Julian Amery recalled his first election contest (at Preston)
as the liveliest campaign he ever fought, with standing room only at most
meetings and volleys of heckling throughout his speeches. On the other
hand, at the time Amery's impulsive Conservative running mate Randolph
Churchill (the Prime Minister's son), felt there was 'too much apathy' in
the town. His yardstick here was almost certainly the two lively elections
he had fought in Liverpool during 1935, particularly the West Toxteth
contest where even his mother, Clemmie, had faced fireworks and wild
disorder at public meetings. Churchill apparently wanted to liven up the
proceedings at Preston by hiring two elephants from Manchester Zoo so
that the Conservative candidates could make a real stir as they rode through
the constituency. When the 'narrow-minded, middle-class provincials' of
the Preston party vetoed his plans, Churchill and Amery had to make

do with a more orthodox cavalcade of open-top cars (flamboyant to the last, Churchill borrowed his from the exiled King of Yugoslavia). As these examples demonstrate, in 1945, politicians had not yet abandoned hope of reaching ordinary, uncommitted voters through public meetings—and a few, like Churchill, still believed that an old-fashioned political stunt might do the trick.[7]

Despite claims that the soapbox was absent from the streets of Glasgow in 1945, it would be quite wrong to imagine that outdoor speaking had disappeared from British politics. In fact, in areas like suburban London, where war damage and requisitioning meant that there was often an acute shortage of indoor venues, the reverse was often true. Here, some politicians recognized that the only way they could hope to reach electors would be to defy suburban sensibilities which decreed outdoor meetings 'undignified'. Indeed, the long summer days and the ubiquity of the loudspeaker encouraged many politicians to make extensive use of outdoor speaking throughout the 1945 campaign. Factory gate meetings remained a staple of British electioneering, sometimes drawing boisterous crowds thousands-strong during workers' lunch breaks. Rather more novel was the colonization of the bomb-sites of war-torn urban Britain as a perfect setting for impromptu outdoor politics (see Fig. 14, which also nicely conveys the gulf between Bill (Lord) Buckhurst and his East End audience). For a few years, until urban redevelopment gathered pace, the bomb-site meeting became a new staple of British electioneering—and not just for the obscure local crank with his soapbox. During his whistle-stop tour of northern England and Scotland in June 1945, Winston Churchill was said to have addressed a crowd of over 50,000 on a blitzed site near Piccadilly in central Manchester, and in 1947, Anthony Eden addressed 3,000 on a Liverpool bomb-site during the Edge Hill by-election.[8]

As can be judged from Churchill's reception in Manchester, the 1945 General Election also demonstrated that voters would still flock to see party leaders 'in the flesh', despite unparalleled access to their speeches on the radio. Although it was estimated that the twenty- to thirty-minute nightly election broadcasts reached an *average* audience of 45 per cent, with one of Churchill's four efforts reaching a remarkable 59.2 per cent of the population, there were still massive crowds whenever either party leader appeared in public.[9] Churchill's triumphal election tours proved a particular draw. Often people waited hours for a chance to see, and hear, the man who had helped guide the nation's destiny through the dark years of war.

Fig. 14. 'Bill' Buckhurst campaigning on an East End bomb-site, 1945, Kurt Hutton, 'A Lost Cause', Hutton Archive (3062682 RM), (Getty Images)

Like Gladstone in his heyday, Churchill frequently stopped to give short impromptu addresses to small knots of people waiting by the roadside to catch a glimpse of his motorcade. The result was that he invariably arrived late for scheduled rallies. At Leeds, a crowd of approximately 25,000 was said to have waited patiently for three hours outside the Civic Hall. At Preston, the Market Square was packed for two and a half hours, with the crowd 'entertained' by a string of speeches from local politicians, until finally Churchill arrived to make a brief address from the steps of the Free Library. His reception appears to have been no less euphoric on the final leg of his four-day national tour, which took him through central Scotland. But the Churchill magic did not always work—at least not in London. Here, a number of Churchill's open-air speeches were marked by vociferous heckling, most famously a rally at Walthamstow stadium, and there were even minor incidents of stone-throwing. Given that the Conservatives did no worse in London than in the rest of Britain in 1945 it seems likely that Churchill's very different reception in the capital merely reflected the fact that here his appearances lacked the novelty and sense of public occasion that they enjoyed in the provinces, although there is also some evidence that the capital represented the last bastion of old-style political disruption in post-war Britain.[10]

Attlee's national tour was no less successful, though by comparison it was a low-key affair. Whereas Churchill toured with a massive entourage, using specially hired trains and a variety of different limousines, Attlee was driven around Britain in the family saloon—his wife Vi, a famously bad driver, behind the wheel. Attlee was not troubled by roadside crowds desperate to catch a glimpse as he sped by, but like Churchill he did speak to packed meetings wherever he went. At Swansea tickets to hear Attlee were over-subscribed fourfold, and the local party called on Ian Mikardo (a 'toughie with a loud voice') to entertain the crowds waiting in the open-air for a chance to see and hear the Labour leader. There were similar scenes wherever Attlee spoke—with halls forced to close their doors early, and vast crowds left outside hoping for an impromptu word. This was the story at Cardiff, Northampton, and across the Midlands and north-west, where Attlee and the other Labour leaders were said to have drawn crowds 'on a scale not hitherto known'.[11]

But despite the enormous popularity of the leaders' election rallies, big set-piece meetings continued to decline as a feature of British electioneering. In some areas this must simply have reflected the limited availability of halls, but there also appears to have been a growing sense that big campaign rallies merely attracted die-hard supporters who might be better occupied canvassing on the doorsteps. Most local parties appear to have held only two or three big meetings during the 1945 campaign: an adoption meeting to kick things off in style, an eve-of-poll meeting to whip up enthusiasm for the big push on polling day, and, if party headquarters looked kindly on the constituency, a high-profile public meeting addressed by a big-name national speaker. Privately, it was recognized that the rationale for such meetings was to enthuse party workers and to gain good press, rather than to win converts among the general populace. Adoption meetings were often explicitly party occasions, although one also finds evidence of candidates holding nominally open meetings at which party activists would be encouraged to masquerade as ordinary voters gripped by sudden enthusiasm for the cause (a trick now reproduced at walkabouts instead).[12]

The big question, of course, is what lessons can we draw from the watershed election of 1945 about our key area of interest: changing relations between politicians and public? In the mid-1940s both radio and cinema were close to the peak of their influence with the British public. Cinema attendance had risen sharply during the Second World War, reaching an all-time high in 1946, when per capita attendance was higher even than in the United States. Radio was also at the peak of its influence. Before the war, the maximum audience for a party election broadcast had probably been about 25 to 30 per cent of the adult population (for Baldwin in 1935). In 1945 the *average* audience was 45 per cent. This figure fell at subsequent elections, slowly in the early 1950s, and then precipitately in 1955 (38 per cent in 1950; 36 per cent in 1951; and just 15 per cent in 1955).[13] But despite these powerful diversions, Britain still possessed a distinctly activist public in 1945. Large numbers remained keen to meet candidates in the flesh as well as to catch party leaders on the radio or cinema newsreels. Direct personal contact remained central to electioneering, although it must be doubted whether, even in 1945, candidates ever reached more than a fraction of their constituents by such means. Conservative organizers warned that doorstep canvassing must not be neglected since candidates would never reach more than *half* the electorate directly through meetings and outdoor speaking—though perhaps more realistically, Labour organizers felt reaching one-eighth this way represented a good showing.[14] By the mid-1950s, by contrast, few politicians expected to reach even that many electors through direct campaigning, and there was also growing despair at the prospect of reaching *any* of the electors who really mattered: the so-called 'floating voters' whose enigmatic character would come to dominate political discourse even more than between the wars.

Even in 1945 most observers agreed, first, that public participation was down on pre-war days, and second, that the public had largely turned its back on the rowdy displays still characteristic of elections in much of urban Britain between the wars. To many, it seemed that the electorate had internalized the idea that public politics should be about rational argument and instruction, rather than entertainment. Indeed, according to the first Nuffield study, hostility to charismatic leadership had become so strong among electors that politicians felt obliged to abandon old-style platform oratory in favour of a sober, almost conversational style of delivery. Britons had spent six years telling themselves that they would never have fallen for the wild rhetorical excesses of the fascist dictators, and far longer decrying the glib oratory and hollow promises that had won Lloyd George the 1918 'Coupon' election. Perhaps it was no wonder, therefore, that in 1945 many were prepared to celebrate the fact that 'political debate had fallen from the heroic to the conversational level'. Gallup found that 42 per cent of electors disapproved of the way the 1945 campaign had been conducted, and that of these a majority specifically objected to mud-slinging, political stunts, heckling, and rowdyism. Similarly, the people-watchers of Mass Observation found voters to be hostile to candidates who resorted to 'personalities', even though their own judgements about politics were strongly influenced by ideas about politicians' character and personality. The big question, of course, was whether public politics, stripped of the visceral thrill of live entertainment, would have a long-term future once the sober, optimistic mood of 1945 had been tempered by the harsh realities of post-war reconstruction. Writing in 1951, Harold Macmillan remained amazed at the willingness of audiences 'to listen to reasoned and often heavy argument' with only 'a little wit and a few mild jokes ... to coat the pill'. But whether such dry fodder had a long-term political future was quite another matter.[15]

Party politics triumphant, 1950–1951

In many respects the two General Elections of 1950 and 1951, held twenty months apart, represent the apogee of party politics in the modern era. Both elections were extremely close. In February 1950 Labour saw its majority fall from 146 in 1945 to just five. Labour secured slightly over 46 per cent of the popular vote, its principal Conservative opponents and their allies 43.4 per cent. In 1951 Labour again won a larger share of the popular vote: 48.8 per cent against 48 per cent for the Conservatives, but it fared less well in key marginal seats, partly thanks to the collapse in the number of Liberal candidates (down from 475 in 1950 to just 109). At 77 Winston Churchill found himself once again Prime Minister, this time with a slim but workable overall majority of seventeen.

If turnout is any measure of public engagement with politics, then these elections established a new high-water mark for British democracy. Both elections were fought on old registers, and yet turnout was well over 80 per cent on each occasion—a threshold not passed at any other election since the introduction of full democracy in the wake of the First World War. Allowing for deaths and technical inaccuracies in registration it seems likely that the effective turnout was close to 90 per cent at both elections.[16] At the same time, this was also the golden age both of two-party politics and of mass party membership. In 1951 the two main parties accounted for almost 97 per cent of the total vote across the UK—again a record for the post-First World War period. They could also claim millions of voters as paid-up party members. The Conservatives had responded to defeat in 1945 by overhauling party organization and initiating a series of membership drives which swelled the ranks of the 'voluntary party'. By 1951 they could claim approximately two and a half million members, peaking at 2.8 million a year later. Labour also sought to boost individual party membership in this era, conscious that the nominal membership of many trade unionists was difficult to translate into political activism. In 1951, alongside the 4.9 million workers affiliated to the party through the trade union political levy, Labour could also boast 876,000 individual party members, almost 400,000 more than at the end of the war. Labour membership also peaked the following year—at 1,014,000. All membership figures need to be treated with caution because constituency parties often had strong incentives to distort recruitment figures, but they nonetheless offer a fairly credible index of basic trends. After the early 1950s the trend was slowly but surely downwards for both parties.[17]

But if these figures all point to a golden age of political engagement and partisanship in the 1950s, it did not feel like it at the time. Observers, including both Attlee and Churchill, generally agreed that the intensely fought and nail-bitingly close elections of 1950 and 1951 were also the quietest and dullest on record. In Newcastle North, Headlam was unusual in reporting larger audiences than in 1945, but even he was struck by the quiet nature of the campaign, and the complete indifference of the public to gimmicks such as cinema vans. At Preston, Julian Amery had no doubt that things were 'much quieter than in 1945', while Labour's agent at Bristol South-East reported meetings that were 'all packed with thoughtful but quietly enthusiastic supporters'. A full-scale study of Glasgow's fifteen constituencies concluded of the 1950 election that 'as elsewhere, it was a quiet campaign' with little evidence of voter interest until the last few days. In 1951, a similar study in Bristol North-East celebrated 'the advances in political knowledge, maturity and sobriety' over the previous fifty years which meant that 'General Elections today are no longer the noisy affairs that they were'. Recalling the 1950 campaign after he had retired, Harold Macmillan drew similar conclusions despite his own flirtations with boisterous public politics in pre-war days. Alluding to Churchill's description of the campaign as 'demure', Macmillan welcomed both the eclipse of 'the old knockabout politics' and the electors' new-found 'serious approach to their responsibilities'.[18]

But how should we explain this apparent paradox of widespread public indifference and high voter turnout? One answer would be that party organization provides the key: that the new, mass-membership parties were simply able to corral a largely apathetic electorate to the polls. However, as we shall see, mass parties could do little to breathe life into the 1955 election (turnout fell to 76.8 per cent despite a relatively young register). Nor should we exaggerate the ability of parties to translate mass membership into mass activism. Constituency studies from the 1950s suggest that local parties could generally mobilize only a tiny fraction of their nominal membership to undertake vital electioneering tasks such as canvassing, leafleting, or knocking up. In 1955, H. J. Hanham found that in Bury Labour had less than 100 active party workers out of a total membership of 3,000, while at Bristol North-East they could muster fewer than 40 canvassers out of a party membership of 1,200. Both parties were dominated by sleeping members, and it therefore seems likely that high levels of party membership were a consequence of voter partisanship, rather than its cause. This may be one reason why party membership peaked for both parties in 1952—buoyed by the unparalleled electoral mobilization of 1950 and 1951.[19]

But the question therefore remains, how could elections have become so 'demure' when partisanship was so strong? A number of factors can help explain the apparent paradox. Not for the first time, legal changes played an important part in the story. The Representation of the People Acts of 1948 and 1949, through which Labour finally ushered in strict one-person-one-vote democracy by abolishing business votes, university seats, and the few remaining two-member boroughs, also further reduced allowable election expenses, despite rising post-war prices. In 1945 a candidate fighting a borough seat with 60,000 electors could spend up to £1,300; in 1950 that figure was just £850. There were also new restrictions on the use of private cars for electioneering purposes. All cars had to be officially registered and their number was restricted to ensure greater equality between the parties. In some constituencies it was also wrongly assumed that they had to be stripped of party adornments such as posters and ribbons (presumably this confusion arose from the long-established prohibition on parties distributing 'marks of distinction'). The new limits on expenses hit harder than expected in the early 1950s because acute paper shortages led printing and publicity costs to rise much faster than general prices. Parties were forced to economize on election literature. Production values were compromised, while the volume of literature also fell. Many candidates abandoned the custom of sending a copy of their election address individually to each elector, relying instead on one posting per household. But perhaps the most striking consequence of the financial squeeze was the massive reduction in the use of visual forms of communication. The cost of full-size, 16-sheet commercial posters increased by 50 per cent between the 1950 and 1951 elections, leading to a significant reduction in their use by both parties. According to Nuffield, the number of hoarding-sized posters declined at each election between 1945 and 1955. In 1951, approximately 10,000 such posters were displayed nationwide (7,000 by the Conservatives). In 1955 there were just 6,000 posters, of which the Conservatives were responsible for all but 1,000.[20]

In Glasgow in 1950, posters were said to be much scarcer across the city than in previous elections. One factor was the growing scarcity of hoardings with the rise of long-term block bookings by commercial advertisers, but another was cost in an era when it was still assumed that any poster had to be charged to the local candidate. To compound the problem, fly-posting, so long a prominent feature of electioneering in Britain, had been outlawed by the 1947 Town and Country Planning Act, thereby denying local parties access to cheap alternative forms of publicity. Observers were struck by the contrast with pre-war elections with 'their wealth of posters, stickers, and bills, in which every available space seemed to have been utilised', and concluded that the change 'tended rather to emasculate the election campaign'. Even in 1945 it had been common for large swathes of a constituency to be plastered in night-time poster raids (with rival party headquarters always a special target). This ceased after 1947—election organizers proved keen to police opponents' misdemeanours—where fly-posting survived it was generally conducted on a small-scale, freelance basis. When the young Robin Cook was caught fly-posting at Edinburgh North in the 1960s, the Labour agent disowned him and apparently threatened to tell the police that the materials he was using had been stolen from the party's office.[21]

Elections were becoming less colourful and less visual in other ways. For some time observers had been commenting on the declining role of pageantry and show in British electioneering. This seems to have gathered pace during the 1950s. By 1950 it was already possible to argue that the public procession had become the preserve of fringe groups like the Communists and Fascists, having 'ceased to be respectable' as a mainstream electioneering device. The motorized cavalcade was also less evident in the early 1950s, though this probably reflected the direct impact of petrol rationing, as much as any deeper cultural shift. Observers in Glasgow recorded that 'there was little colour or originality—hardly any processions, no groups of urchins, as of old, chanting "Vote! Vote! Vote!"; only one band was out on the eve-of-the-poll'.[22] Once again the parties played their part in this transformation. As late as 1945 Labour organizers were reminding local parties that one way to 'rouse the masses' was to get the children on your side. Coyly, they refused to 'spoil' their pages by saying how this was done—though the lavish distribution of free sweets was usually the preferred method (certainly this was my father's introduction, aged 5, to the electoral politics of East Bristol in 1931). But when almost the same article was re-published on the eve of the 1950 election all mention of mobilizing children was dropped. Labour activists were again implored to 'rouse enthusiasm', but the means suggested were rather modest. They were told to ensure a good display of window cards early in the campaign, to pack their meetings with party activists, to use loudspeaker tours to drive home the candidate's name, and finally to ensure a 'splash of colour' by decorating party cars and making sure key workers wore rosettes in public. This, they were assured, would have far greater impact than 'buying expensive poster sites'.[23]

However, this 'dulling down' of British electioneering was not just a question of limited resources and sober audiences. It was at least in part a question of imposing dullness on the people. Contemporary accounts of election meetings and party rallies suggest that these were often unbelievably badly organized. The local schoolroom meeting, the staple of electioneering since before the First World War, was often particularly depressing. Electors frequently found themselves squeezed uncomfortably on tiny chairs, or wedged into school desks complete with inkwells. Little was done to decorate school halls—even the ubiquitous newspaper posters of the inter-war era were said to be fading from the scene in some constituencies. In the east end of Glasgow, observers reported that the only decoration in many halls was a large municipal notice decreeing 'No Spitting'; and at a Labour meeting in London during the 1951 election Robert McKenzie found that the only decoration was a *Daily Herald* poster pinned to the speaker's table by two unwashed milk bottles. Big political meetings were usually somewhat better organized, but these too remained low-key affairs. There was no adornment at all at Clement Attlee's first public meeting of the 1950 campaign—just a stage with a row of collapsible chairs behind a trestle table and two posters imploring 'Vote for Attlee'. Even Sir Winston Churchill was said to add only a dispatch box to the normal furniture of a British political meeting: the table, chair, and jug of water. In 1950 he was also said to have toned down his platform performances to be more in tune with the sober age. At Edinburgh's Usher Hall he apparently spoke for an hour to an audience of 3,000 'lifting his head and hands only to make a point'. When Anthony Eden spoke at Glasgow's St Andrew's Hall there was at least some concession to showmanship. The platform was decorated with bouquets of flowers, the audience entertained by organ and piano recitals, and the whole event elaborately stage-managed, but it was still very far from being a Nuremberg (or even an Olympia) style rally—and it was intended to be. Observers claimed that in 1950 none of the big Glasgow meetings came close to evoking 'that mass emotion that was a feature of large public meetings fifteen or twenty years ago'. Labour's efforts were said to be particularly disappointing. Clement Attlee and Sir Stafford Cripps both addressed packed halls, but their meetings were said to lack orchestration or any sense of dramatic climax—apparently frustrating 'the evident desire of the audiences to become enthusiastic'. Some politicians were still prepared to whip up an audience, but their style was widely considered to be both anachronistic and vulgar. Despite Gaitskell's frequent complaints about unresponsive northern audiences, he was disgusted when he had to follow one of Manny Shinwell's 'knock-about music hall turns' at Leeds Town Hall in 1951. Gaitskell records that his wife Dora 'almost vomited' having to sit through Shinwell's speech, but the audience clearly loved it, and became 'so drunk by the emotional nonsense that Shinwell had talked that it was impossible to make them think at all'. Here Gaitskell was eliding the widespread suspicion of demagogic platform oratory, which had its roots in the inter-war rejection of flamboyant politicians such as Lloyd George and Mosley, with a more thoroughgoing rejection of vulgarity, sentiment, and emotion in public politics. His embrace of austerity in politics, as in life, was more absolute than that of most voters. Indeed, one might also argue that during the 1950s Gaitskell and his supporters distrusted their left-wing opponents, such as Aneurin Bevan, Jennie Lee, and Michael Foot, as much for their ability to stir powerful emotions from the platform as for their policy disagreements with the Labour leadership.[24]

But if the majority of political meetings were so resolutely dull, one must surely ask why anyone bothered to go. For go they most certainly did. In 1951, Gallup found that 30 per cent of British voters claimed to have attended at least one indoor or outdoor political meeting during the General Election. By contrast, local constituency surveys conducted during the General Elections of 1950 and 1951 all recorded significantly lower figures (7 per cent in Greenwich, 11 per cent in Bristol, and 14 per cent in a group of six London marginals).[25] One factor was simply that constituency surveys tended to be more careful than the early pollsters about including the elderly and housebound in their sample, but another was that these constituency surveys all focused on divisions of big city boroughs where candidates' meetings reached a smaller proportion of the electorate than in rural areas and provincial towns. This was a point explicitly acknowledged by researchers at Bristol North-East who pointed out that not only were there far more meetings in the adjacent county constituency of South Gloucestershire, but that when Clement Attlee visited the seat to support Tony Crosland he managed to address more than 10 per cent of electors at a single outdoor rally. At East Dunbartonshire, on the Clyde, Willie Whitelaw, a future Home Secretary under Margaret

Thatcher, found that public meetings remained all-important and that they were still invariably packed. This was also the impression of a group of American political scientists who studied the 1950 election. They found that 'meetings were generally jammed', with the doors having to be closed well before the advertised start of most meetings. Writing in the midst of the 1950 campaign, Lord Woolton, the Conservative Party chairman, was convinced that 'public meetings have played a most important part in these critical weeks'.[26]

One reason people went to meetings in such large numbers was that meetings were indeed 'all-important'—apart from the politicians' disembodied radio broadcasts, they were still the only show in town (in 1951 the first televised election broadcasts had been shown, but only 12 per cent of electors saw even one of these transmissions). Accounts of political meetings still made up a large proportion of election news coverage, which, thanks to the continuation of the BBC's news moratorium, could only be followed through the pages of the local and national press. In the circumstances, it is perhaps not surprising that politically interested voters chose in large numbers to hear things for themselves, rather than rely solely on newspapers that were widely viewed as politically biased. But this largely informative, even instructional style of meeting was not to everyone's liking; the young in particular showed little interest in these sober post-war gatherings. Between the wars, political parties had sometimes resorted to banning youths from their meetings in an attempt to control 'rowdyism' and 'hooliganism'. By 1950 this was largely a non-issue, not so much because rowdyism had disappeared—the occasional meeting still descended into uproar and anarchy—but because across much of the country young people had simply ceased to attend political meetings, apart, that is, from small bands of earnest Labour Youth and Young Conservatives acting as stewards or distributing party literature. Fighting Bristol South-East in 1951, Tony Benn lamented the conspicuous absence of young voters from his meetings, while at Greenwich, meetings were said to be dominated by middle-aged voters, although observers noted that when there was heckling it was mainly by youths. The 1950 survey of Glasgow also found a strong bias towards older voters at many meetings, with questions about pensions prominent in consequence. Glasgow politics had remained unusually volatile into the 1930s, but in 1950 its 'didactic' meetings were said to be dominated by 'restrained, intent citizens'. It seems that the type of voters (and non-voters) who had once gone to meetings for a bit of light entertainment, often found at the speaker's expense, could now afford to seek their fun elsewhere. Esmond Wright, one of the co-ordinators of the Glasgow study and later a Conservative MP for the city's Pollok constituency, felt sure that full employment, good wages, and the competing attractions of bar and cinema had drawn away 'those unconvinced spectators who, in the past, have acted as a chorus to the hecklers, and given excitement to election gatherings'.[27]

In the early 1950s most politicians were quite pleased to see the back of the 'unconvinced spectator' who was interested more in frivolity and entertainment than political argument. For decades political leaders had been trying to mould a more rational, deliberative public politics; sadly they had also moulded a drab, lifeless politics that was perfectly suited to the post-war age of austerity. On the verge of television's political revolution, British elections had never been so lacking in colour, visual stimulation, or platform drama. Most politically active voters appeared perfectly content with this state of affairs. After a week electioneering in Lancashire and the Midlands in 1951, Macmillan telephoned Churchill to tell him that 'The people seem in a serious mood and prefer to listen to serious arguments'.[28] The big question was whether this appetite for rational public politics would long survive the emergence of television as a rival medium embracing the same mission to educate and inform, but in a brighter and decidedly more convenient form.

6

The Decline of the Platform

Core voters and floating voters

David Butler has described electioneering in the early 1950s as a bizarre political battle in which the parties appeared almost oblivious of one another's existence, each 'manoeuvring on a different battlefield against straw armies of its own devising'.[1] The image is a brilliant one and nicely captures the essential artificiality of post-war electioneering. However, things had not always been thus. On the contrary, the rise of the daily provincial press in the later nineteenth century had shaped a platform style that had been genuinely interactive—with candidates using the near-verbatim reports of their speeches in the local press to maintain a constant dialogue both with the electorate, and with their political opponents. In the 1950s, on the other hand, front-rank political figures such as Harold Macmillan and Hugh Gaitskell were happy to give the same speech time and again during a campaign, paying no attention to the claims of rival candidates, and only minimal regard to the needs of the press for fresh copy. One might imagine that this reflected the debasement of local journalism in the post-war era, but this would be mistaken. Local newspapers continued to give extensive coverage to local campaigns throughout the 1950s, including detailed reports of candidates' speeches.[2] This was less true of the big city dailies that increasingly assumed a regional role akin to the London evening press, but in most constituencies there were still plenty of column inches to be filled locally. The key change seems to have been that politicians began to take seriously the nostrum that political opponents should be ignored at all times in order to starve them of 'free publicity'. The argument itself was hardly new, what gave it a new edge was a broader shift in campaign thinking. Increasingly alert to the findings of political scientists and opinion pollsters, election organizers began to argue that the campaign should be focused on mobilizing core supporters rather than converting the uncommitted or hostile. Post-war surveys suggested that up to four-fifths of voters were sufficiently partisan never to switch allegiance—although many identified only weakly with 'their' party, so that they still needed to be mobilized—or in the parlance of the day 'organized'. Moreover, of those who did acknowledge changing allegiance, hardly any switched directly between the two main parties, and only a tiny minority (perhaps one in twenty of all voters), claimed to make up their mind *during* the election campaign. Add to this the finding that these crucial 'waverers' or 'floating voters' were the people least likely to read party literature or attend political meetings, and one can begin to see why many organizers lost faith in the politics of persuasion in the 1950s. Much better, many felt, to concentrate on strategies for maximizing the core vote. This meant conducting an extensive door-to-door canvass to identify party supporters, preferably in advance of the poll. It also meant using leaflets, posters, window-bills, and loudspeaker-work to try and ensure that these supporters knew the candidate's name, because until 1969 ballot papers included no mention of party affiliation. Finally, it meant having efficient systems on polling day to identify those who had not voted to ensure that they went (or were taken) to the poll.[3]

Of course none of this was new—the point was rather that these technical aspects of electioneering came to loom larger as proselytizing and general propaganda began to seem old-fashioned and largely pointless. Increasingly, social class and social geography were embraced as the vital determinants of largely fixed party allegiances, creating a geography of partisanship etched on the mental map of every activist—'these are our streets', 'that's enemy territory'. Social surveys repeatedly suggested that between 55 and 65 per cent of manual workers voted Labour while between 60 and 80 per cent of non-manual workers voted Conservative.[4] Moreover, beneath these stark politics of class lay an even starker politics of place, since non-manual workers living in predominantly manual neighbourhoods were found to be decidedly more Labour, while the reverse was true in the non-manual heartlands of suburbia—here manual workers were more strongly Conservative.[5] Neither political scientists, nor political leaders, were blind to the fact that support from across the social divide might still be crucial to electoral success (Conservative leaders in particular never forgot that half their support came from manual workers). But this did not prevent activists on the ground from thinking in terms of 'Labour streets' and 'tory streets'. Even in 1950, researchers in Greenwich found that both party agents discouraged canvassing in 'enemy strongholds' because it wasted scarce resources. In consequence, only a socially mixed, central section of the constituency was canvassed equally by both parties. This became party gospel in the 1950s. When *Labour Organiser* reviewed the first Bristol constituency study in 1955 it drew a simple conclusion: 'Instead of trying to win over opponents, a properly planned election campaign will be directed at supporters.' Conservative organizers took the same line during the 1950s. At Bolton East the local agent insisted that the key to victory in 1955 had been the 'concentration of effort in the areas we knew would vote well'. At the by-election in Liverpool Garston three years later Conservatives went further by ensuring that known Labour strongholds were 'blacklisted' so as 'to avoid arousing the Socialists' vote during the campaign'.[6]

In many respects this whole approach to electioneering was constructed on the shakiest of foundations. For one thing, even in the best organized constituencies canvassing tended to be far from an exact science. Observers generally agreed that the parties' canvassing efforts peaked at the 1951 election, but even then polls suggested that they visited only 53 per cent of British households, and probably directly canvassed only about 20 per cent of individual voters. In the low-key 1955 General Election just 44 per cent of households were canvassed, although in the livelier 1959 election the figure rose again to reach exactly 50 per cent. Constituency studies of canvassing revealed wide discrepancies between party claims and voter experience. At Bristol North-East in 1951 Labour claimed to have conducted a complete fresh canvass and to have marked off 80 per cent of households. However, researchers found that among their sample barely 20 per cent of voters recalled having been visited by Labour canvassers during the campaign, suggesting that party workers must have relied heavily on second-hand information and folk memory to construct their street returns. Constituency studies also suggested that canvassing could be wildly inaccurate. At Greenwich in 1950, Labour's canvass suggested that one district would vote 60 per cent Labour, 25 per cent Conservative, whereas the survey suggested that it actually voted 31 per cent Labour, 45 per cent Conservative. In another district Conservative canvassers gave Labour a 3 per cent lead, whereas the survey suggested Labour's lead was actually 15 per cent. It was hardly a ringing endorsement for a strategy that was premised entirely on first identifying one's core vote.[7]

There were, of course, some politicians who never accepted the logic of what came to be known as 'selective campaigning'. For instance, when Edward Heath became the prospective Conservative candidate for Bexley in 1949, he refused to accept the agent's advice not to canvass 'Little Moscow' (an estate built to house munitions workers in the First World War). Sure enough, he found the local residents amazed to see a tory on their patch, but he also soon realized that few were actively hostile, not least, he deduced, because they probably never saw Labour politicians either. Kenneth Baker, the future Conservative Home Secretary, experienced similar bemusement when he and his friends insisted on canvassing the docklands areas of Poplar in 1964. But these were still very much lone examples. Closer to the spirit of the age was Ian Mikardo, Baker's opponent at Poplar in 1964, and the Bevanite MP for Reading from 1945 until his defeat in 1959. Mikardo was a passionate champion of selective campaigning whose 'Reading system' had revolutionized the process of 'knocking up' Labour promises on polling day (for decades Labour activists would call their carbonized pads of partly crossed-off promises 'Mikardoes'). On the eve of the 1959 election, Mikardo wrote a piece called 'Know and deliver your vote' for the *Labour Organiser*. In it he advocated not just selective canvassing, but also selective propaganda. According to Mikardo, Labour should avoid sending its loudspeaker vans into any area where the marked register contained less than 50 per cent Labour promises. He also recommended only leafleting households known to be 'for' or 'doubtful'—partly to save money, but mainly to avoid stimulating the Conservative vote.[8] Here was selective campaigning taken to its logical conclusion, but it was not an approach well-suited to the emerging television age. For one thing, it was clearly ridiculous to worry about stimulating the opposition vote once, as happened in 1959, the broadcast media began to offer blanket news coverage of the national campaign. Indeed, in the longer term, television would play a decisive role in eroding the clan-based party loyalties that underpinned the whole ethos of selective campaigning. Even in 1951, surveys had suggested that only half of Labour and Conservative supporters identified strongly with their party; by 1979 that figure had declined to approximately one quarter. Similarly, the two-party share of the popular vote declined from 97 per cent in 1951 to just 75 per cent in February 1974—by 2005 it stood at barely two-thirds.[9]

1955: The first television election?

The television age was hardly in full swing in 1955, even though many contemporaries labelled this 'the first television election'. That said, whilst a majority of British homes still lacked television, it was nonetheless apparent that this was the first election in which television made a significant impact on political campaigning. Unlike in 1951, when, on average, party broadcasts on radio had commanded an audience more than three times greater than television, by 1955 the two media reached almost equal numbers of electors (radio claimed an average audience of 15 per cent, down from 36 per cent in 1951, while television managed 14 per cent). Radio's influence was clearly declining more sharply than television's was rising, perhaps because this was an election that strikingly failed to capture the popular imagination. But despite the innovation of a full programme of televised election broadcasts, this was, in truth, the last election fought wholly in the old mould—the last election when the parties' national campaigns consisted of little more than a manifesto launch followed by three weeks of more or less uncoordinated speech making around the country by the front-rank leaders. In addition, the 1955 election was almost without doubt the dullest election to date—suggesting that with or without the dawn of the television age, old-style public politics was more or less played out in Britain by the mid-1950s.[10]

According to the Nuffield study, the 1955 election was 'the most apathetic yet seen in twentieth-century Britain'. Harold Macmillan agreed, noting in his diary that 'There has never been a "quieter" election'. Hugh Dalton, fighting the last of his ten elections, was more scathing, describing it as 'the most tedious, apathetic, uninteresting, and I think, worst organised' contest he had ever known. Given the Conservatives' clear victory in 1955—their Parliamentary majority increased from seventeen to sixty, and they out-polled Labour by 49.7 to 46.4 per cent—one might imagine that widespread apathy was borne of a general sense that the election would be no contest. This certainly played a big part in subsequent lacklustre campaigns such as those of 1966 and 2001. However, early opinion polls did not suggest that a Conservative victory was inevitable. On the contrary, Gallup's first poll suggested that the 1955 election would be at least as close as those of 1950 and 1951. It showed the Conservatives on 47.5 per cent compared with Labour on 47 per cent, and it gave Labour a narrow lead when 'don't knows' were pressed to make a choice. Few people seem to have been convinced. A month earlier, Gallup had found that only 22 per cent of voters expected Labour to win the next election, and this sense of looming defeat appears to have hung over the party's campaign throughout the election. Perhaps significantly, a few days after Eden announced the election, Richard Crossman noted in his diary that the *Daily Mirror* had decided to hold back from supporting Labour till the last week because 'at present the people are too apathetic'.[11]

At the time some blamed television for the public's indifference to the election. But in the marginal seat of Bristol North-East, researchers found that television ownership had no influence on whether or not people attended meetings. Moreover, it is important to recognize that, in 1955, television was in no sense a direct rival to either the public meeting or the press as a means of informing oneself about the issues at stake in the election. As at every election since the inception of broadcasting, the BBC again imposed a moratorium not only on news coverage of the campaign, but also on the broadcasting of any material that could be considered in any sense controversial or likely to influence voters. During this so-called 'closed period', current affairs programmes such as *Press Conference* and *In the News*, which had recently begun to pioneer political discussion and direct interviews with politicians, were taken off the air, and news bulletins dealt only with the formal technicalities of nomination and polling—otherwise, the viewers were left with nothing but the seven official party election broadcasts.[12]

Nor did these official party broadcasts demonstrate any marked flare for exploiting the potential of television as a medium. Commentators generally agreed that the parties' efforts were unadventurous and, frankly, rather dull. In his memoirs, Harold Macmillan recalls his performance as the anchor man of the first Conservative broadcast as 'weak and jejune', and he calls the party's second effort, which tried to imitate *Press Conference* by assembling a panel of ten journalists to interrogate five leading Conservative politicians, 'amateurish'. In her memoirs, Grace Wyndham Goldie, a long-time BBC executive in current affairs programming, insists that throughout the 1950s leading politicians such as Eden and Macmillan remained half-hearted about television. Unlike leaders of the previous generation such as Churchill and Attlee, they recognized that television had to be accepted and utilized, but she insists that they still never took it seriously as a means of revolutionizing political communication. Goldie's principal criticism is that politicians became so mesmerized by the idea that television could give them access to millions of viewers in their own homes, that they tended to think in terms of addressing 'the masses', rather than of addressing individuals. She doubtless has a point, but at the time commentators were more struck by the speed with which politicians seemed to be adapting to the new technology. Regular televised party broadcasts had only begun in March 1953, and yet it was generally agreed that Sir Anthony Eden's effort at the close of the 1955 campaign was an unqualified triumph. In a post-mortem on the campaign which asked 'Was this a TV election?', Anthony Wedgwood Benn had no doubt that Eden's simple broadcast, speaking direct to camera for fifteen minutes, had been a revelation: 'he did what no other political figure to-day is trained to do—a fireside chat on the screen'. Conservative Central Office had established its own television studio in 1951 to train party leaders for the new medium. Benn was clear that Labour had to move fast to catch up, but he also acknowledged that in 1955 no party had come close to using television to its full potential; they had seen it as just 'an adjunct to other forms of propaganda' when it should have been used 'to set the pace of the campaign'.[13]

As Benn and others observed, television had done little to shape the 1955 campaign, and could hardly be blamed for the public's poor response to more traditional methods of electioneering. Indeed, some politicians had tried to revitalize traditional campaigning by introducing the glamour of television. Some sought to relay television broadcasts at public meetings, others obtained films of the broadcasts for subsequent screening alongside more traditional party propaganda. Those of a more defeatist temperament simply chose to end their meetings early so that the audience could rush home to catch the broadcast. However, almost everyone agreed that the public meeting had reached a new low point in 1955. Heckling was said almost to have disappeared from British political life, while meetings as a whole were described as poorly attended and wholly unexciting. According to a post-election Gallup survey, only 12 per cent of electors claimed to have attended at least one political meeting (compared with 30 per cent in 1951). In Bristol North-East, researchers recorded a drop from 10 per cent in 1951 to 6 per cent in 1955, and concluded that the political meeting could no longer be considered 'an open forum for debate', having become instead 'a rallying point for the faithful' dominated by a 'stage army' of party activists and hangers-on. At Baron's Court in London, Labour held just three conventional indoor meetings, although it did also organize two rallies for big name guest speakers. At Bury in Lancashire, Labour did even less—holding just three meetings throughout the campaign—the minimum necessary to secure coverage in the local weekly newspaper. These meetings drew a total audience of approximately five hundred—less than one per cent of the electorate. The Conservatives, by contrast, held twenty-four meetings attracting over 2,000 electors (though this still represented only a tiny fraction of electors).[14]

But this was not a universal experience. Elsewhere, particularly in rural areas, the political meeting remained a vibrant force throughout the 1950s and beyond. Here even loyal party supporters considered their vote conditional on the local community being honoured by a visit from the candidate. Tiny hamlets might sometimes be expected to make do with a flying visit by car, or a meeting held without the candidate, but it was generally recognized that such pragmatic compromises could easily cost votes on polling day. This urban/rural difference was confirmed in the 1959 constituency study of Newcastle-under-Lyme, which recorded significantly higher levels of attendance at meetings in the scattered, rural parts of the borough. Many market towns also continued to have lively political meetings throughout the 1950s. When Robin Day stood for the Liberals at Hereford in 1959 he found himself in the middle of a 'first-class, full-blooded knockabout argy-bargy'. Writing in the News Chronicle he declared, 'Has TV killed the hustings? No, not a bit of it. Anyone who says straightforward, man-to-man, street-corner electioneering is dead is talking through his hat.' Day was particularly struck by the seething, open-air crowds that gathered in the centre of Hereford on Saturday evenings to hear the party candidates put their case. However, as locals acknowledged, the survival of Hereford's raucous High Town hustings already set the city apart from its sleepier neighbours such as Leominster. Even so, the wild scenes in 1959 were nonetheless exceptional, and seem to have had their roots in a bitter dispute between the Conservatives and Labour over the order in which candidates should speak. By the time it was Day's turn the pubs had turned out and the hustings had descended into near anarchy, with partisans determined to ensure that no one got a hearing. Day's platform was overrun and his microphone broken. Whether these dramatic events proved, as Day supposed, that old-style electioneering was alive and well in the heartlands of the nation is another matter.[15]

Hereford's full-blooded street politics were unusual, but there were still plenty of politicians capable of packing a public meeting in the 1950s.

Flamboyant personalities such as Sir Gerald Nabarro, the Conservative MP for Kidderminster, might use television and the press to develop a high-profile public 'image' (the buzzword of the hour), but this did not mean that they neglected traditional constituency politics. Nabarro was a regular on BBC radio's *Any Questions*, and, with his distinctive handle-bar moustache, was also a familiar sight on television and in the papers, but he nonetheless prided himself on exemplary attention to constituency correspondence and local surgery work. He also continued to hold public meetings on a grand scale—insisting that television actually increased the popularity of his meetings in the late 1950s and 1960s. Party leaders could also still count on drawing a large crowd. In 1955 both Eden and Attlee again undertook significant nationwide speaking tours during the campaign. Eden apparently insisted that his meetings should not be all-ticket affairs, and he addressed a number of open-air mass rallies, including the Birmingham Rag Market where he spoke to a crowd of approximately 10,000. Once again Attlee was driven around the country by his wife Vi. They covered 1,200 miles in nine days, with Attlee speaking at forty major meetings. In 1959 Hugh Gaitskell and Harold Macmillan undertook even more arduous speaking tours, and drew even greater crowds. Six hundred supporters were turned away when Gaitskell spoke at the Colston Hall in Bristol, while at Trafford Park, near Manchester, Labour claimed that he addressed a mass rally of 20,000. Gaitskell might not offer his audience a Shinwell-style music-hall turn, but as party leader with a high profile on television he remained someone to be seen and heard in the flesh if the opportunity arose.[16]

Supplanting the platform

But if the message from Hereford, Kidderminster, and Trafford Park was that the political meeting was not yet dead, there can be little doubt that at constituency level it was often decidedly poorly. Politicians of both parties had been complaining of falling attendance for decades, but there is nonetheless evidence that they were right to suspect a precipitate fall during the 1950s. On the eve of the 1955 election, the two main parties estimated that attendance at meetings had fallen by 50 per cent since 1951. As we have seen, figures from the General Election suggest that if anything this was probably an under-estimate. In Bristol South-East, Tony Benn found his meetings so poorly attended that he began to think hard about new ways of connecting with the public. Benn lamented that 'the old days of petitions, indoor meetings, 100 per cent canvasses and the rest, are probably dead and gone for ever', and he identified four ways he could reconnect with his Bristol constituents. Two involved playing a more active role in the local Labour party, underlining that it was not just voters from whom he felt detached. But Benn also decided to begin a programme of regular MP's surgeries and a rolling personal canvass of the constituency. There is little doubt that Benn loved the thrill of the platform, and genuinely regretted the need to downgrade the meeting, but not everyone shared this sentiment. Like many MPs, Sir Henry 'Chips' Channon, the Conservative MP for Southend West, hated 'the electoral plunge' feeling that it left him 'squeezed dry ... [of] every ounce of vigour and vitality'. Even Macmillan was beginning to feel like this by the 1950s, though he had once revelled in the livelier side of English electioneering. In 1951, he declared: 'What a horrible 3 weeks and more lies before us! I hate elections more and more,' while in 1955, freely acknowledging that he did much less campaigning than in pre-war days, he still complained that he found it 'all very tiring'. Similarly, Gaitskell always found the constant round of speaking obligations during a campaign 'intolerably boring'.[17]

Of course there was nothing new in such sentiment; politicians had been complaining about the hardships and indignities of campaigning since elections began. The big difference in the 1950s was that they increasingly began to doubt whether there was any point continuing to treat election campaigns as marathons in public speaking. Party agents had long been sceptical about the value of public meetings, and after 1955 they not only had hard evidence from social surveys to support their claims, but also politicians' own memories of half-empty halls and unenthusiastic audiences. In the circumstances, most politicians were only too keen to follow Benn's example and consider alternatives to the public meeting.[18]

Over the following years politicians experimented with both direct and indirect means of reconnecting with voters. Perhaps most widely used throughout the 1950s and 1960s was the mobile loudspeaker system. This technology had been available since the 1920s, but it only became the mainstay of electioneering after 1945. Cost was one factor in the proliferation of the mobile speaker system, but another was undoubtedly the continuing decline of the public meeting. If the voters refused to come to political meetings, it seemed logical to take the meeting to them. However, from the outset it was recognized that this was easier said than done. Firstly, it was clearly hopeless to make a conventional political speech from a loudspeaker car, especially if it was on the move. Unless a crowd could be persuaded to gather around the stationary vehicle, the most that could be attempted was crude party sloganeering alongside the constant reiteration of the candidate's name and party affiliation. Even at the time, it was difficult not to see something faintly desperate about these attempts to force politics on an indifferent and disengaged public. But with research suggesting that in some constituencies less than one in three voters read even a single election pamphlet, parties hoped that a few well-chosen, and well-amplified, slogans might reach the electorate holed up in their domestic bunkers. Intriguingly, the advent of portable reel-to-reel tape decks increased the possibilities of the mobile loudspeaker. In Greenwich, Labour used the technology to take its message into the courtyards of municipal housing blocks—only children bothered to listen to the speeches, but squads of canvassers found the 'show' helped them to persuade tenants to take window bills. In Bristol South-East, Benn used his loudspeaker car to play ten-minute recorded speeches while he conducted personal house-to-house canvassing. Remarkably, in some county seats there were even stories of politicians recording entire speeches to be played in absentia at public meetings held in remote villages. But a tape recorder was no real substitute for the candidate—it could not be questioned, and if heckled it would not lose its temper. Perhaps predictably, such hi-tech experiments were not popular.[19]

From the outset there was considerable anxiety about how the public would respond to the intrusive use of loudspeakers. It was one thing to use loudspeakers as an aid to public speaking on traditional pitches such as public parks, town squares, or bomb-sites, but it was quite a different matter to take the same equipment into shopping centres, or worse residential areas. In some constituencies local by-laws against public nuisance were deemed to outlaw loudspeakers, or at least to bar their use on moving vehicles. Elsewhere, parties voluntarily agreed to limit or even ban loudspeakers. At Bury there was said to be 'a local convention between the parties which prohibits the use of loudspeakers on cars', while elsewhere local parties tried to capitalize on the unpopularity of amplified politics by making unilateral declarations of abstention. In one unspecified Midland seat the Conservative candidate refused to have anything to do with loudspeakers or political slogans. At Liverpool Wavertree in 1950 the Labour candidate proclaimed his abstention on the grounds that many of his constituents were shift workers who would be trying to sleep during the day. Others sought merely to limit their use. In Dorset a Conservative candidate placed advertisements in the local press announcing that he would not use loudspeakers after 6.30 p.m. so as not to interfere with children's bedtimes. At the Leeds South-East by-election in February 1952, Dennis Healey and his Conservative opponent stopped using loudspeaker cars as a mark of respect after the death of King George VI. At the Gainsborough by-election in 1956, Conservatives insisted that loudspeakers must only be used to advertise meetings, or to draw a crowd on the candidate's 'whistle-stop' tours. All were signalling the basic fact that there was something rather vulgar, and perhaps counter-productive, about loudspeaker politics. This was certainly how it had seemed to the researchers studying the 1950 General Election in Glasgow. Here it was the Conservatives who made greatest use of loudspeaker cars, particularly in two marginal riverside seats of Govan and Scotstoun, which they went on to capture from Labour. But despite these victories, the research team concluded that the apparent value of the loudspeaker car was 'deceptive ... it is doubtful if it wins many votes, and it certainly loses some'.[20]

The problem was simple: far from closing the gulf between politicians and ordinary voters, amplification, even in the guise of the simple megaphone, underlined the 'otherness' of politicians—their remoteness from people's everyday lives. Normal people didn't shout at each other through speaker systems. The technology might well allow a candidate to grab the attention of the uncommitted voter in his or her home, or at the shops, but it was far from clear that it would do anything but alienate that voter. Even at political meetings amplification was often considered a barrier between politician and audience. Labour still harboured considerable reservations on this score, and in 1950 its activists were advised that amplification should not be used for outdoor speaking because it destroyed the intimacy of the human voice, thereby preventing the speaker from developing a rapport with his or her audience. Indeed, for this reason amplification was sometimes shunned even at large indoor rallies. In 1955 Attlee and Bevan and a clutch of London Labour politicians addressed almost a thousand supporters at the King's Theatre in Hammersmith without the aid of a speaker system. Unfortunately for them, a determined group of perhaps thirty hecklers was also present and managed to prevent the speakers from being heard. All, that is, except the irrepressible Bevan, who apparently 'managed to dominate his opponents in the audience', despite provoking more interruptions than anyone else. Eventually technology would advance to the point where amplification barely altered the tone and timbre of the human voice, but by then, sadly, both Bevan and the traditional election meeting would be long gone.[21]

The 1950s witnessed other strategies for reaching voters who were no longer prepared to come to conventional political meetings. One was to reinvent the public meeting. This took a number of forms. Politicians became increasingly keen to accept invitations from local interest groups, such as churches, trade bodies, and voluntary organizations—even if this meant sitting on a panel with rival candidates (something that was otherwise almost never countenanced). Election campaigns also witnessed the proliferation of visits to local institutions such as universities, hospitals, schools, and old people's homes, again sometimes alongside rival candidates. This was partly about taking politics to the voters if the voters wouldn't (or couldn't) come to you, but it was also about politicians' growing awareness of the need to cultivate the media through what came to be known as 'photo-opportunities' (of which more later). After the 1955 election, the young Edward Heath and his agent pioneered a different approach to the problem. Instead of calling public meetings that attracted only the hard-core party faithful, Heath decided to organize a series of invitation-only meetings for particular occupational groups such as doctors, dentists, teachers, and clergymen. These meetings, which were hailed a great success, were held between, rather than during, elections, but they nonetheless highlighted the perception that the traditional political meeting was played out by the mid-1950s.[22]

The other great innovation of direct campaigning in the 1950s was the 'walkabout', though the term itself was not used at this time. In 1970 Harold Wilson, and to a lesser extent Edward Heath, began to make informal public appearances in an attempt to gain good, positive television coverage of them interacting with 'ordinary voters', but, by the mid-1950s, the basic tactic was already commonplace among lesser political figures anxious that they were losing touch with electors. Once again the idea was simple—candidates cut back on conventional meetings, particularly on daytime open-air speaking tours, in favour of informal outdoor appearances in places where voters were likely to congregate in large numbers. Shopping centres were always a favourite choice, though as Roy Jenkins found at Birmingham Stechford, in suburban constituencies it could prove very difficult to know where one's voters actually shopped. At the Ipswich by-election in 1957, John Cobbold, the Conservative candidate, held many fewer meetings than at the recent General Election, preferring instead to conduct elaborately planned daily tours of the constituency which he claimed allowed him to meet thousands more electors. On a much humbler scale, in 1961, Tony Benn experimented with canvassing morning commuters while they waited at bus stops (and in 1963 began boarding the buses for the same purpose). Given that both by-elections were part of Benn's campaign to renounce his peerage, there was clearly potential here for good media coverage, but his diary entries nonetheless demonstrate that it was the chance to meet and talk with 'ordinary' voters that excited the reluctant 'Lord Stansgate'. Benn described Bristol buses as 'public meetings criss-crossing my constituency all day just waiting to be addressed' and wryly observed that 'people can't easily walk out on you when the bus is moving' (see Fig. 15). Similarly, Roy Jenkins came to see elections as a challenge 'to shake as many hands' as possible, though he was perhaps unique in devising a clicking machine to count how many voters he had managed to 'tick up' during the campaign (he apparently reached 'almost exactly 2000' in February 1974).[23]

This urge to reconnect with ordinary voters affected politicians' behaviour between, as well as during, elections. Like Benn in Bristol, many began to conduct a continuous rolling canvass of their constituency. This activity would be billed as disinterested 'visiting', but the aim was always to improve the marked register in readiness for the next election. Hence when Stan Newens first fought Epping in 1964 he claimed to go into the contest with a fresh 75 per cent canvass already in place. But perhaps the greatest change of the post-war era was the massive increase in constituency case work—both for serving MPs and for aspiring candidates. Political scientists have tended to see this as a peculiar feature of late twentieth-century 'post-industrial' politics, driven by factors such as improved levels of education, voter 'dealignment', and the decline of the 'amateur' politician, but, in truth, its roots should be traced back to Labour's pioneering of grass-roots politics between the wars.[24] All but the most feckless of 'amateur' politicians had always taken constituency correspondence seriously, even if this simply meant paying someone else to deal with it. What was new in the post-war era was, firstly, the massive increase in the volume of such correspondence and, secondly, the willingness of more and more politicians from all parties to make themselves personally available to hear their constituents' problems first-hand at MPs'

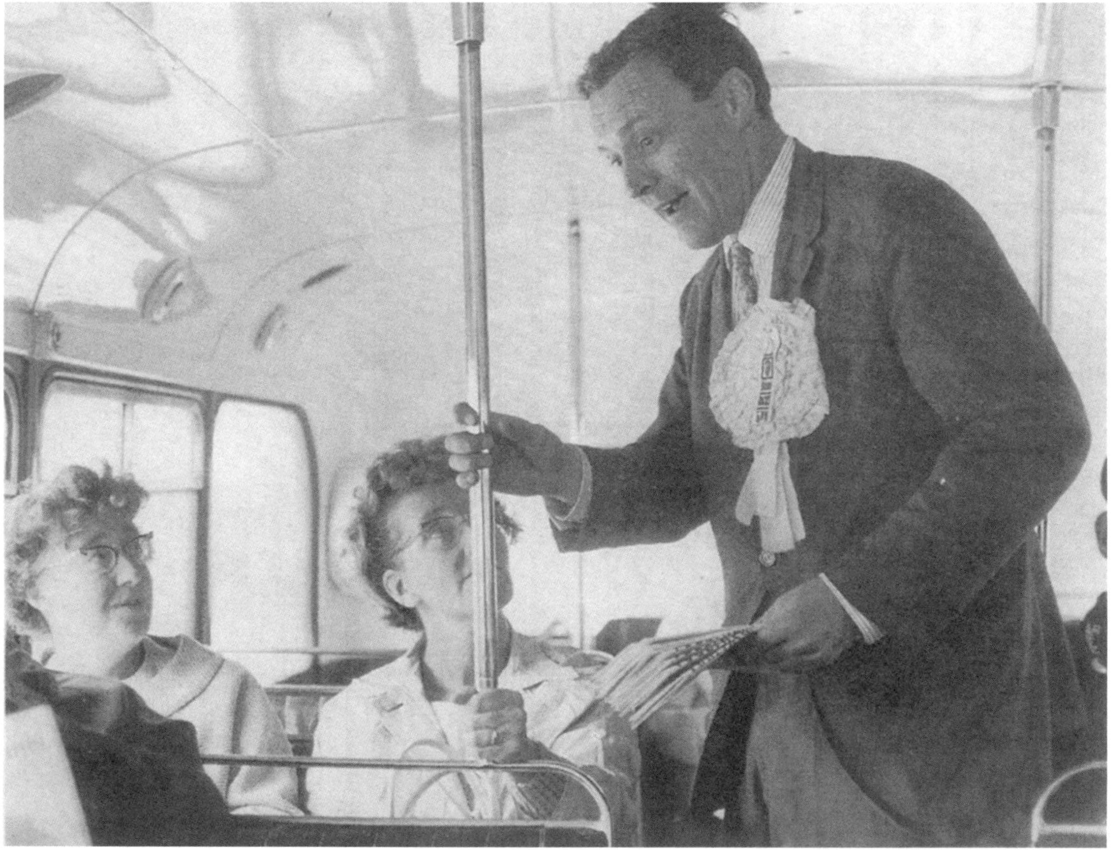

Fig. 15. Tony Benn campaigning on the buses, Bristol, 1963, reproduced with the kind permission of the Rt. Hon. Tony Benn

'surgeries'. In the immediate post-war era the constituency surgery was still a minority taste. In 1945 Joseph Binns, the new Labour MP for Gillingham, considered his introduction of a monthly 'personal consultation service' newsworthy, although he nonetheless acknowledged that *some* MPs already held such sessions on a weekly basis. Significantly, Binns also claimed that constituency correspondence had increased sixfold on pre-war days. There were also assiduous constituency MPs among Conservatives. At Bury in Lancashire, Sir Walter Fletcher's regular surgeries were said to have helped him hold this largely industrial seat even in the Labour landslide of 1945. At Greenwich the prospective Conservative candidate began holding regular 'Advice Bureaus' in 1949, forcing the sitting Labour MP to raise his own profile in the constituency. But the pressure to be a good constituency MP was by no means overwhelming at this point. As late as 1958, the recently ennobled Earl Attlee felt able to write a scathing attack on the growing trend for MPs to spend every weekend 'dealing with constituency cases'. Similarly, Roy Jenkins described himself as sitting as 'an old-style member' for Birmingham Stechford. There was apparently no suggestion that he might live in the city, nor even take a pied-à-terre, and it was agreed that he need only visit the constituency once a month. But by the late 1950s it was becoming more difficult for an MP not to hold frequent surgeries. In Bristol South-East, Benn still felt he could run surgeries on a three-week cycle, but others complained that every weekend was now devoted to hearing hardship cases in the constituency. Attlee, for one, deplored the fact that 'the M.P. is expected to be guide, philosopher and friend, not to mention Poor man's lawyer, to his constituents', and boasted that he had never held 'surgeries' in his Limehouse constituency, only dealing with hardship cases that were passed on by local councillors or other responsible agencies. Writing in the mid-1960s, Reginald Bevins, the former Conservative Postmaster-General, was quite clear that 'the near eclipse of the public meeting' had encouraged the majority of MPs to adopt weekend surgeries as a means of maintaining 'personal contacts' in the constituency. Having lost his Liverpool Toxteth seat in 1964 he was also pretty scathing about the long-term benefits of being a good constituency MP: 'I had given most of my weekends to those in trouble. In the result that counted for nothing.' The importance of constituency 'service-work' has continued to grow since the 1960s, not least because MPs have emerged as the key point of mediation between highly centralized state services and individual voters, but it is nonetheless important to recognize that its origins lay in part in the decline of alternative, more public, forms of political interaction in the immediate post-war era.[25]

The mass media and politics in the 1950s

However, post-war politicians were not only interested in new ways of connecting with voters 'in the flesh'. Surgeries, walkabouts, and personal canvassing were not the only shows in town. Politicians knew that it could be just as important to reach voters indirectly, through party propaganda, and increasingly also through the independent, non-party media: press, radio, and television. As we have seen, politicians had long seen the press as a vital means of influencing voters, and had been keen both to ensure that journalists had good facilities to report political speeches, and that they were fed with lively copy for news and 'features' items. Politicians had also long complained that political meetings received inadequate coverage in the national and local press, but by the 1950s there appears to have been growing substance to the charge. Douglas Jay, a cabinet minister in Wilson's first Government, recalled that it was in the 1950s that 'Fleet Street discovered that there was no value in reporting most political speeches'; from then on a politician's finest efforts would go unnoticed 'beyond the fifteen persons actually present' in some chilly provincial school-room.[26] However, editors continued to view elections as 'good copy', and one finds extensive press accounts of candidates' election meetings throughout the 1950s. That said, human interest 'news' was becoming increasingly important for both local and national newspapers in the post-war years. Meetings qua meetings were no longer considered hard news—at least not unless something controversial was said, or something dramatic happened. Newspapers wanted a story, and politicians began to come up with increasingly ingenious ways of providing them with one. There was nothing new about the election 'stunt' of course—Churchill's elephants were testimony to that—but during the 1950s there was a new emphasis on the need for local politicians to be more assiduous in cultivating the media: feeding them stories, if possible even getting a weekly column in the local newspaper. The photo-opportunity also came of age in the 1950s. A decade before Margaret Thatcher famously clutched a new-born calf for nearly fifteen minutes to please the media pack during the 1979 campaign, Gerald Nabarro was already commenting that he wished fewer politicians would allow themselves to be 'photographed holding piglets upside down by their back legs'. During the 1950s party organizers frequently advised politicians on how best to 'get into the news and stay there'. The 'action picture' (our 'photo-opportunity') was seen as the surest way to ensure newspaper interest. In 1951 Conservatives were told, 'Make your candidate do something, even if it is only jumping over a five-barred gate or wrapping a rug around his agent's feet.' As one would imagine, such events were often highly stage-managed, but they could still end in failure. Tony Benn recalls how, during the 1959 General Election, a local child was meant to be photographed handing him a black cat (for luck), but because the child would not stop screaming its mother had to step in to save the day.[27]

But this keen interest in the techniques of media manipulation did not mean that politicians had given up trying to address the electorate directly through party propaganda. The great virtue of propaganda was, of course, that politicians retained absolute control of the message, even if this did increase voters' suspicion of what was being said. As we have seen, between the wars, the Conservatives had experimented with cinema, and official party broadcasts had also grown in importance, but the backbone of political propaganda remained the poster and the leaflet. In the 1920s many politicians felt that written propaganda, particularly in the form of the party news-sheet, was taking over from the spoken word as the principal means of reaching voters. This faith in the printed word declined markedly after 1945. Again research on voter behaviour played its part in this story. In Bristol, researchers found that almost half the electorate had failed to read any party literature during the 1951 campaign. In the low-key 1955 election this figure rose to three in every five voters. Things were even less impressive at Greenwich. There only 28 per cent of voters claimed to have read even one election pamphlet during the 1950 campaign (although 40 per cent claimed to have read a candidate's address). Worse, these studies all found that undecided voters—the people who would ultimately determine the outcome of most contests—were the ones least likely to bother reading anything that came through the letter-box. Writing in 1957, a Conservative election agent echoed the view of the cabinet minister Dr Charles Hill that, 'leaflets are of little value in present day life'. The electorate, it was believed, could no longer be stampeded to the polls. What mattered, it seemed, was not 'election platform issues or last minute scares ... [but] the general climate of public opinion built up over the preceding two years', and this would be shaped, not by party literature, but by the broadcast media and advertising, with a little help from the press.[28]

Again, there was nothing particularly new in the call for continuous propaganda—this was already a truism between the wars. The difference was that now the claim was backed up by survey evidence demonstrating that whilst the majority of voters were party loyalists, amongst those less fixed in their partisanship, far more changed allegiance between elections than during the frantic few weeks of campaigning. The other big difference was that by the late 1950s one party, the Conservatives, was prepared to act decisively at the national level to co-ordinate a massive pre-election propaganda campaign aimed at the key 'waverers'. The Conservatives had long been prepared to innovate in the field of propaganda, but their advertising campaign of 1957–9, shaped by the commercial agency of Colman, Prentis, and Varley, nonetheless raised the game to a new level. The length and cost of the campaign were both unprecedented, with billboards and advertisements in the national press running almost continuously for two years until Macmillan called a General Election in September 1959. At the national level, the Conservatives spent twenty times more than Labour on advertising in 1959, and at one point they were actually the largest press advertiser in Britain. The campaign culminated with two posters conveying scenes of prosperous family life, and the telling slogan: 'Life's better with the Conservatives. Don't let Labour ruin it'. Moreover, in the run-up to the 1959 election, the Conservatives' message was reinforced by a massive PR campaign against nationalization organized by private business interests.[29]

Interestingly, Gallup sought to track the impact of party publicity campaigns throughout 1959. Their polls always indicated that more people had seen Conservative than Labour posters. Awareness of party advertising was highest between May and July, but at no stage did a majority of respondents claim to have seen one of the parties' advertisements. Intriguingly, Gallup also asked if people had 'taken action' as a result of seeing party advertising; in May 1959 9 per cent claimed that they had done so, though sadly they were not asked what they had done! One thing we do know, however, is that if opinion polls are any measure, support for the Conservatives strengthened during this PR blitz, though so too did the British economy. During 1957 the Conservatives had, on average, trailed Labour by nine percentage points on the Gallup Poll. In March 1959, Gallup still had Labour one and a half points ahead, but by September they put the Conservatives in a seven-point lead. In the October General Election, Macmillan's Government was returned with an overall majority of exactly one hundred, having polled 49.4 per cent compared with 43.8 per cent for Labour. Many factors had contributed to Labour's heavy defeat, which was its third loss in succession, but one thing was clear, relying on local organization and 'getting the vote out' was no longer sufficient. *Labour Organiser* noted that whilst it was now a cliché to argue that 'elections are won between elections', Labour had done precious little to act on this adage between 1955 and 1959.[30]

But of course the greatest revolution in political communications was the emergence of television as a mass medium. In 1955 approximately 40 per cent of British homes had television. By 1959 that figure had risen to over 70 per cent, but perhaps more importantly television had also begun to throw off the shackles which until then had severely curtailed its political influence. The key here was undoubtedly the emergence of commercial television (ITV) as a direct rival to the BBC. Unlike in the USA, the new independent television companies were not allowed to carry paid political advertising, but they did help to shake up political broadcasting. ITV pioneered new, harder-edged forms of news and current affairs coverage, including much less deferential interviews with leading politicians, such as the first full-scale Prime Ministerial interview when a young Robin Day quizzed Macmillan in February 1958. This was also the month when Granada TV led the overthrow of the moratorium on election news coverage by running two half-hour programmes on the Rochdale by-election. Political parties were uneasy with the innovation, but did not stop it. Both the Liberal and Labour parties were principally anxious to ensure there would be no television coverage of public meetings, perhaps from fear that this might encourage organized heckling (as indeed it did in 1964). Conservative Central Office was doubtful about the whole legality of coverage, fearing, with some reason, that programmes could be construed as a chargeable expense to each candidate given that broadcasters, unlike the press, had not been exempted from the strict rules on third-party expenses in the 1949 Representation of the People Act. Although these uncertainties remained unresolved, the absence of any decisive legal challenge opened the floodgates to political television in Britain. The broadcasters and the political parties spent the next eighteen months feverishly planning how best to handle extensive television news coverage of the looming General Election. Few politicians appear to have welcomed the revolution that was unfolding, but that did not stop them planning how best to capitalize on the chance to reach voters through this powerful new medium, including, as Macmillan quickly demonstrated, taking seriously the need for what would now be called image 'make-overs'.[31]

The introduction of broadcast election news transformed electioneering at the national level. The morning news conference was born to feed the appetite for fresh election news stories, though it was not yet televised. Serious day-to-day news management had arrived, although it should be acknowledged, firstly, that it was initially aimed more at the press than at broadcasters, and, secondly, that the parties had been organizing broadly comparable events at by-elections for some time. Richard Crossman, chairman of Labour's Campaign Committee at Transport House, was clear from the outset that he was at the centre of a political revolution. For the first time Labour had a genuine election *strategy*, devised and co-ordinated from the centre; previously 'Everybody has been saying and doing what they felt like in the constituencies, with a few tours of famous speakers.' In turn, the Conservatives had developed a highly centralized publicity effort to run their pre-election advertising campaign, and were well placed to adapt this to election purposes. The age of the national campaign had arrived.[32]

Interestingly, in 1959 many felt that television coverage of the election had not only boosted popular interest in politics, but had also encouraged voters to venture out to see these new celebrities of the small-screen 'in the flesh'. Attendance at public meetings rose sharply from the disappointing levels of 1955, though there was no return to the levels of the early 1950s. Gallup found that 18 per cent of voters claimed to have attended an indoor election meeting, and 9 per cent an outdoor meeting (compared with 12 per cent and 5 per cent respectively in 1955). Again constituency studies produced markedly lower figures. In 1959 a survey in the neighbouring seats of Pudsey and Leeds West found that 11 per cent of electors claimed to have attended an election meeting, while in Newcastle-under-Lyme the figure was 9 per cent. Politicians from both parties, including Richard Crossman and Gerald Nabarro, reported that meetings were more enthusiastic than for many years, and there were even reports of considerable heckling in some constituencies. However, at North Kensington, where Oswald Mosley sought to revive British fascism by exploiting the fallout from the recent Notting Hill riots, all sides agreed that indoor meetings were useless.

The Labour and Conservative parties concentrated almost exclusively on canvassing, while Mosley and the Liberal candidate threw themselves into sustained campaigns of outdoor speaking. But both men lost their deposit, suggesting that, at least in inner London, with its shifting population and threadbare local press, the political meeting was already dead by 1959.[33]

Nationally the picture was rather different. As has been noted, the two main party leaders, Hugh Gaitskell and Harold Macmillan, each embarked on major speaking tours. Macmillan travelled over 2,500 miles and gave more than seventy speeches—twice the number Eden had managed in 1955. In turn Gaitskell gave over fifty speeches, again many more than his predecessor in 1955, including a number of massive outdoor rallies. More importantly, such meetings continued to shape the course of the election. When Macmillan made his decisive attack on Gaitskell's credibility over taxation he did so at an election meeting in Glasgow, not at a morning news conference. That said, the party leaders were careful to ensure that their words would be recorded, not just by the national and provincial press, but also by the television cameras that now began to follow them about the country. This was why so many front-rank politicians began to speak at the beginning, rather than the end, of evening meetings—it meant that the television companies could process their film in time for the late evening news bulletins (still the only BBC programmes to carry significant election news). Perhaps judging that they were unlikely to secure much airtime anyway, Liberal campaigners decided that neither their leader, Jo Grimond, nor any of the five other Liberal MPs, would take part in a speaking tour during the 1959 campaign. In the end, Grimond's hi-tech helicopter tour of Liberal target seats did grab some headlines (and some great pictures), but otherwise the Liberals relied heavily on their two election broadcasts to reach a mass audience. Although the two main parties were allotted nearly four times more airtime, Gallup still found that half the electorate claimed to have watched a Liberal broadcast. The Liberals' 1959 strategy anticipated the looming age when television would dominate campaigning—and indeed all forms of political communication.[34]

Audiences for individual television election broadcasts still fell well short of the levels that radio had secured in 1945, but the proportion of the population seeing at least one broadcast was nonetheless high. Nationally, Gallup found that 61 per cent of voters claimed to have watched at least one party broadcast, and local surveys tended to return broadly similar findings. As in earlier elections, the party broadcasts were extensively reported in the press, thereby becoming election news in their own right. But in 1959, for the first time, other television programmes also became news. To the surprise of many there were no great set-piece interviews during the campaign—these were still considered too high-risk by party leaders. Perhaps more surprisingly, a number of companies, notably Associated-Rediffusion in the south-east and the BBC, cancelled scheduled programmes that might touch on controversial political topics. Broadcasters also agreed that there should be a 'television truce' on the eve of poll—a sort of mini-'closed period'. On the other hand, 1959 also saw the birth of the 'election special'. The BBC came up with *Hustings*, a series of programmes with a regional focus in which politicians from each party answered questions from a partisan audience. Associated-Rediffusion used the panel format to foreground women candidates quizzed by women voters and young candidates quizzed by young voters. Another ITV company, Granada, proved particularly innovative. During the campaign it ran *Marathon*, an ambitious programme which gave every candidate in the Granada region the chance to make a direct appeal to constituents on air (although for legal reasons only if their opponents also agreed to appear). By all accounts it did not make for great television, but it was at least a valiant attempt to remind viewers that they would be voting for individual politicians, not just well-packaged party tickets. On the day before the truce, Granada also produced *The Last Debate*, a programme that proved anything but dull. During the campaign, a number of the BBC *Hustings* programmes had been described as 'gladiatorial' confrontations where politicians faced 'politically hostile' audiences, but *The Last Debate* took audience participation to new levels. Filmed in a large, galleried studio to mimic a real public meeting, the audience apparently 'interrupted and heckled on such a scale that at times the speakers were shouting to try to make themselves heard...'. It was as though broadcasters were trying to reproduce the most dramatic aspects of platform politics in the over-heated television studio. Perhaps significantly, the producer of *The Last Debate* described it as not only 'unquestionably the best and most exciting programme of the campaign', but also as 'a fine election meeting'. But the politicians, including two front-bench heavyweights in Selwyn Lloyd and Barbara Castle, did not come across well, reduced to shouting their points at each other and at members of the hostile audience.[35]

Given the limited use of 'vox pop' interviews in 1959, programmes like *The Last Debate* represented one of the few ways in which electors managed to find a voice 'on the box'. But the fact that the voice heard was so discordant and partisan raised problems for broadcasters and politicians alike. For broadcasters the main problem was that the theatre of unscripted political controversy could easily descend into chaos—full-scale shouting matches came across poorly on the small screen. For politicians the problem was greater. They found it difficult to combat heckling with quick ripostes since it was impossible to judge the mood of the audience that really mattered: the viewers. Indeed, it was difficult to know whether viewers would even have heard the offending intervention from the audience. Compared even with the set-piece interview, this was television at its most unpredictable and messy. The parties' response was decisive. During the elections of 1964, 1966, and 1970 they maintained a united front against participating in programmes that involved live studio audiences—the spectacle of senior politicians losing their cool on *The Last Debate* lived long in the memory. Of course, politicians continued to resent the pretensions of the professional television interviewer—their implicit claim to speak on behalf of the absent viewer/voter, and their mimicking (some said usurping) of Parliamentary procedures of accountability—but they recognized that these interactions were nonetheless easier to manage (and manipulate) than confrontations with real voters. Interviewers were, after all, ultimately unelected hirelings, and their claim to 'speak for the people' could be successfully contested by the skilful politician. But this is to anticipate how campaigning evolved after the first 'television election' of 1959. The innovations in 1959 had been important but limited. It was not until the next election, in 1964, that British politicians, led by Labour's dynamic new leader Harold Wilson, began to focus more on the opportunities posed by television than the threats.

7

The Local Campaign in the Television Age

The eclipse of the local campaign

The years after 1960 witnessed a decisive shift away from both direct, face-to-face electioneering and the local, constituency-based campaign. As late as 1955, H. J. Hanham could describe the General Election in Lancashire as being characterized by 'a series of isolated electoral units'. But by the mid-1960s observers were agreed that 'at the local level every general election is basically the same'—a question of organization, not politics, in which contact with voters was perfunctory at best, and opponents were almost completely ignored. This largely organizational approach to electioneering had become dominant during the 1950s. Both main parties came to believe that their primary task during a campaign was to mobilize their party's latent vote, since there were thought to be few 'floating' votes to be won, and little prospect of getting voters to switch through local propaganda. When television finally emerged as a significant medium for political communication between 1959 and 1964 politicians were quick to seize on its potential for bringing the campaign directly into the homes of the mass electorate. In a sense the official party political broadcasts had being doing this since 1951, but only in a partial, rather articifical, manner. It was only when broadcasters lifted the moratorium on election news in 1959 that the campaign proper began to be seen on television. In 1959 exposure was still limited and viewers essentially saw a televised version of a traditional campaign, though one heavily slanted towards the activities of Macmillan and Gaitskell as party leaders. In 1964, for the first time, they saw a campaign fought *through* television, and the campaign they saw was resolutely a national campaign dominated by snippets from the party press conferences in London and from leaders' speeches on the stump.[1]

Once controls had been lifted it was inevitable that the power of television would further diminish the significance of face-to-face campaigning; what was not inevitable was that the local contests in Britain's six hundred plus constituencies would come to be wholly overshadowed by the national campaign 'as seen on TV'. To understand why this happened—why by the late 1960s activists could feel that their local efforts merely distracted voters from the 'real' campaign on television—we need to look beyond purely technological explanations, after all parochialism has continued to thrive in US electioneering, despite that country's supremely televisual political system. We must focus instead on the political, legal, and media context within which television's coverage of politics has evolved in Britain since the 1960s. We also need to look more closely at constituency campaigning itself. This has been more dynamic than is often imagined, particularly since the 1970s, when politicians rediscovered that there were votes to be won, as well as organized, during a campaign.[2] Four main factors determined that after 1959 Britain's television revolution would coincide with, and in many respects cause, the near-total eclipse of local campaigning. First, the relative weakness of local and regional media in comparison with their national counterparts (particularly in the field of broadcasting); second, the fact that television emerged when the 'tribalist' model of campaigning, with its emphasis on organization over persuasion, was at the height of its influence; third, the nature of the electoral system itself, which effectively ensured that victory or defeat nationally would be determined by a minority of 'undecided' voters in one hundred or so marginal constituencies; and fourth, and perhaps most importantly, the severe legal and financial constraints imposed upon candidates at the local level, but not upon the parties nationally.

Turning first to the structure of the mass media, perhaps the most striking feature is the weakness of provincial broadcasting in Britain, especially before the growth of local radio in the 1970s, and the severe legal constraints on its coverage of elections. From the outset both the regional ITV companies, and to a lesser extent the BBC, mounted discussion programmes with a regional flavour, but during elections these were obliged, for legal reasons, to avoid discussing locally controversial issues. As we have seen, the legal status of political broadcasting had been left unclear by the 1949 Representation of the People Act. In 1964 a test case brought against the Conservative leader Sir Alec Douglas-Home established that candidates were not legally liable for the cost of television programmes so long as the primary purpose of their appearance was not to make an appeal to their own constituents. The absurd result of this ruling was that during the 1960s broadcasters felt able to show politicians campaigning anywhere but in their own constituencies. After 1969 the coverage of local campaigns was placed on a clear legal footing by a new Representation of the People Act, but there remained powerful legal constraints on broadcasters which prevented them from covering local campaigns in the same depth, and with the same sophistication, as the national campaign. Local campaigns could now be covered either if all candidates participated, or if one or more candidates indicated that they were happy for a programme to go ahead without them (although no programmes could be made before nominations closed, leaving broadcasters with only a ten-day window). Over subsequent decades these restrictions were further relaxed, particularly by the ruling that broadcasters did not need to seek candidates' formal permission to film them campaigning. But even so, the coverage of local electioneering remained such a legal minefield that broadcasters often preferred to provide 'local colour' by filming the party leaders on whistle-stop visits to the provinces, rather than have to worry about how to provide balanced coverage to all candidates in a particular local constituency.[3]

By contrast the press, both local and national, remained wholly unfettered in its reports on constituency campaigning. Indeed the constituency profile became an increasingly prominent feature of election news coverage in the up-market national press from the 1960s. But whilst this was undoubtedly an interesting trend in political journalism, what mattered most to candidates was the coverage they could garner in the local press serving their own constituency. But by the 1960s, local newspapers varied greatly in the extent to which they provided parliamentary candidates (and sitting MPs) with publicity for their campaigning activities both between and during elections. Whilst consolidation meant that many daily titles no longer devoted much space to constituency-level politics, some local newspapers remained vital links between party politics and local voters. At Smethwick, in the West Midlands, the weekly *Smethwick Telephone* boasted a circulation of 20,000 in a town where there were barely 22,000 households. In the early 1960s the paper provided extensive coverage of the local Conservative party's campaign against the effects of immigration on the town. During the infamous 1964 election, when Labour's shadow Foreign Secretary Patrick Gordon Walker lost his seat to the Conservatives on a massive (and wholly untypical) swing of 7.2 per cent, over 70 per cent of the *Telephone*'s election news stories were mainly or partly about immigration. The potential intimacy of the link between the local press and party politics was also underlined by the case of highly marginal Reading. Here, the launch of a new daily paper in the mid-1960s led all three parties to hold more meetings because it was widely believed that the fledgling paper was hungry for copy. But where there was only a weekly paper it was now normal for parties to hold just one public meeting per week, not least because, as at Swansea in 1964, editors made it clear that that was all they would cover. Candidates were also told bluntly that they must be brief at all times because 'very few people are going to read dollops of speeches'. At Coventry in 1970, the local paper told candidates that it was dropping all coverage of election meetings in favour of in-depth interviews, illustrated feature stories, and guest columns by candidates. Immediately Richard Crossman's local party agreed to abandon its long tradition of opening and closing the campaign with a major rally. Whereas once meetings had been held because the public demanded them, now across much of Britain they existed only to secure free publicity; when that was withdrawn their rationale disappeared.[4]

To make matters worse, television had erupted onto the political stage at a time when many commentators discounted the need to make political appeals to the electorate at all. As we have seen, the 1950s and 1960s represented the golden era of the narrowly organizational approach to electioneering—what mattered was not persuading the 'doubtfuls', but corralling one's known supporters to ensure that a maximum number went to the poll. Although both parties embraced this depressingly mundane approach to politics with enthusiasm, it was Labour that raised it to near-gospel status. Harold Wilson's inquiry into party organization, held in the wake of the 1955 election defeat, concluded that 'even a limited improvement in organization would have won us the election' despite having trailed the Conservatives by sixty-eight seats. Wilson's report started from the assumption that Labour had a natural majority among the voters, and that therefore the key to electoral victory lay in the perfection of party machinery to get these voters to the poll. After the massive Conservative public relations campaign of 1957–9, and Macmillan's subsequent landslide election triumph, attitudes slowly began to change, but a greater openness to 'PR' did little to breathe political life into local campaigning. Instead, the assumption was that political success would come from a combination of national propaganda and local organization. The principal exception was by-elections in the run-up to the 1964 General Election—when party professionals such as Percy Clark, the national Publicity Officer, would descend on a constituency to help create an 'image' for their candidate, much as they sought to mould Wilson's image for the national media. Jeremy Bray, the young ICI scientist chosen to fly the flag of Labour's technological revolution at the Middlesbrough West by-election in 1962, confessed to George Brown that 'It's a terrifying business having one's image created, but no one could be better at the job than Percy.' But in Labour's debates in the early 1960s about how best to reach 'floating' voters there was very little talk about the role that local campaigning might play in the process. When Len Williams, Labour's General Secretary, outlined the contribution that local parties could make to the 'Let's Go with Labour!' campaign of 1963–4—Labour's first great experiment with public relations—he focused solely on organizational issues, particularly the need to amass sufficient Labour 'promises' to be confident of victory before the election was even called. It would take another decade, and the growth of Liberal 'pavement politics', for this narrow thinking seriously to be questioned within the two main parties.[5]

Local campaigning was also hard hit by the remorseless logic of Britain's first-past-the-post electoral system. By 1964 researchers were already finding that the advent of television had encouraged parties in safe seats to campaign less vigorously, holding fewer meetings and conducting a less thorough canvass, apparently on the assumption that television coverage and national propaganda campaigns would be sufficient to 'get the vote out'. In safe seats, the need for an active campaign was further reduced when the 1969 Representation of the People Act decreed that henceforth ballot papers would include a candidate's party allegiance alongside the bare information of name, address, and occupation. Overnight the massive effort spent trying to drum home the message 'Vote for Bloggs, the Blah party candidate' became redundant, and in many rock-solid seats there seemed little else to justify more than the most minimal electioneering effort. At Greenwich in 1950 only one in four voters had known their Labour MP's name before the campaign began, but intensive campaigning meant that with ten days to go 90 per cent of Labour voters knew his name, whilst 80 per cent of

Conservatives knew the name of his challenger. By contrast, in February 1974, Gallup found that 23 per cent of voters claimed not to know the *parties* standing in their constituency, let alone their candidates' names, while at the end of the 1987 campaign approximately 40 per cent of voters did not know who was standing in their constituency. At the same time, national party strategy tended to emphasize the irrelevance of the local campaign in all but a small number of so-called 'critical' (or 'marginal') seats. And within these hundred or so marginal seats the voters who really mattered, the people who would always determine who formed Britain's next Government, were a minority within a minority—the 25 to 30 per cent of voters who were broadly unaligned, and might therefore be swayed by propaganda. Historically, party organization was often strongest in safe seats where supporters were plentiful and victory more or less certain, and much shakier in the key marginals. There were exceptions, of course, such as Faversham in Kent, where Labour had built a mass party over many decades which helped it hold a difficult marginal seat continuously from 1945 to 1970. But party leaders knew that it was hopeless to wait till every local party embraced the Faversham model. Instead, they placed their hope in 'mutual aid'—whereby activists from safe (and also hopeless) constituencies would be encouraged to divert much of their energy to campaign in nearby 'critical' seats where the result might prove decisive in national terms. Mutual aid always worked much better on paper than in practice, but the strategy undoubtedly placed an official stamp on the idea that campaigning hardly mattered in most 'ordinary' constituencies.[6]

Certainly, the decline of local party organization since the 1960s has been striking, whatever measure one takes. In the early 1950s the Conservatives had a full-time party agent in almost every constituency, and the Labour party could claim approximately 50 per cent coverage. By the mid-1980s the Conservatives had fallen back to 50 per cent coverage, and Labour organization had collapsed to the point where barely one in ten constituency parties could support a full-time agent. Figures for individual party membership, though somewhat less reliable, also register steep decline. After 1957 Labour artificially boosted its figures by insisting that local parties affiliate on the basis of a minimum membership (initially 800, raised to 1,000 in 1963). Even so, declared membership declined from over one million in 1953 to 790,000 in 1960, 680,000 in 1970, and just 266,000 by 1988. Conservative party membership probably followed a similar trajectory, although official figures are sketchy and membership itself was often a very loose concept at constituency level. In 1952 party leaders boasted that their great post-war membership drives had raised membership of the 'voluntary party' to a staggering 2.8 million. By the late 1960s it was estimated that membership stood at something over 1.5 million; and by the early 1980s internal studies suggested a membership of approximately 1.2 million, although more sceptical commentators estimated that the true membership was probably much lower, perhaps under half a million. A clearer barometer of the decline of local activism has been the collapse of canvassing since 1960. As late as 1959, half the British electorate claimed to have been visited by at least one party canvasser during the course of the General Election. This fell sharply, to 38 per cent, at the next election in 1964. By the 1970s pollsters were finding that less than 20 per cent of households appeared to have been canvassed, although in the marginals the figure was often much higher—with 70 per cent or more claiming to have been canvassed. Interestingly, the level of canvassing appears to have risen again during the 1980s—with approximately 30 per cent of households claiming to have been canvassed in both 1983 and 1992, and a remarkable 49 per cent in 1987. This probably reflects the re-emergence of three-party politics since the 1970s, as this has led both to the proliferation of marginal seats and to a growing interest in the community-based 'pavement politics' associated with the Liberal revival. The significance of this recent 'rediscovery' of local campaigning is discussed more fully below.[7]

Finally, in trying to understand the decline of local campaigning after 1960 we need to explore the special legal and financial constraints which curtailed electioneering at constituency level. Rooted in the realities of nineteenth-century campaigns, British election law long recognized only the separate contests between individual candidates in the country's six hundred plus constituencies. By contrast, the national campaign evolved outside of, and largely unconstrained by, electoral law until the Political Parties, Elections and Referendums Act, 2000 finally set national limits on party campaign expenditure, albeit at a very generous level (just over £19 million in the twelve months prior to the 2005 General Election for a party contesting every seat). We have already seen how electoral law encouraged broadcasters to pay greater attention to the antics of national rather than local politicians, but it also meant that cash-strapped local parties found that there was little they could do to construct a distinctive, localized campaign.

There were frequent complaints at the failure to uprate permissible election expenses in line with inflation, particularly from Conservative agents who tended to be more confident about their ability to raise funds where necessary. In real terms the legal expenses declared by candidates had fallen almost continuously during the twentieth century, having reached a high point in the intensely fought General Elections of 1910 (a high point, that is, for elections fought after the introduction of the 1883 Corrupt Practices Act). After allowing for inflation, Conservative candidates spent on average just 43 per cent of the 1910 levels in 1929, 24 per cent in 1945, 12 per cent in 1964, and a miserable 8 per cent in 1979—with other parties registering a similar decline in the level of expenditure across the century. That said, by the 1970s it was only in the marginals that most candidates tended to spend anywhere near the permitted maximum. In February 1974, candidates spent on average only about 60 per cent of the amount permitted by law. As parties economized on campaigning, local posters, still immensely popular in the 1940s and early 1950s, appear to have lost out to leaflets and newspaper advertisements as the principal means of reaching the voters. In February 1974, Labour found that more than 90 per cent of local parties had made use of press advertising. The elections of 1974 also witnessed a massive increase in the use of election leaflets tailored specifically to local campaign issues, thanks largely to the rapid spread of inexpensive litho-printers among local parties. It was this technology, later reinforced by the growth of PCs and desk-top publishing, that underpinned the new 'pavement politics' of the 1970s, and which can therefore be said to have helped resuscitate local campaigning, at least in the marginals.[8]

It was also in 1974 that the national campaign finally came of age. Until then, national campaigning had consisted of two elements—the statutory party election broadcasts and the media coverage party leaders gained through press conferences, studio appearances, and campaigning activities in the country. But in February 1974 the Liberals unleashed an electioneering revolution with their 'Take Power!' campaign of press and poster advertising which ran throughout the General Election. Previously, national propaganda campaigns had been halted before the formal declaration of a General Election, with local parties instructed to assume legal responsibility for any posters still displayed in their constituency. Given that the legality of national advertising campaigns during an election had been upheld as early as 1952 (in *R. v. Tronoh-Malayan Mines*), one can only assume that the parties proved slow to test this legal loophole because they doubted the value of short-term propaganda offensives. Certainly, this was the dogma which dominated the thinking of the PR advisers who shaped both the Conservative campaign of 1957–9, and the equally innovative 'Let's Go with Labour!' campaign of 1963–4. In the late 1960s Conservative strategists were using sophisticated polling techniques to identify potential waverers among Labour's core vote (notably skilled workers and women under 35), but they still believed that these voters had to be swayed by long-term propaganda, rather than by the election campaign itself. But when 'late swing' appeared to have brought Heath victory in 1970, attitudes began to change. Previously it had been assumed that any fluctuations in voting intention during the campaign would simply cancel each other out, but in 1970 many observers, rightly or wrongly, believed that Heath's battling campaign had turned the election. The supposed Liberal surge of February 1974, which saw the party gain up to eight percentage points during the campaign in some polls, appeared to remove any doubt about the new-found volatility of British voters. Given the prominence of the Liberals' controversial 'Take Power!' campaign, it also suggested that advertising could pay big dividends during an election. Once the Liberals' campaign had gone unchallenged at law it was all but inevitable that the other parties would also embrace large-scale campaign advertising. When Wilson called a second General Election in October 1974 all sides were ready with plans to use press and poster advertising to woo the floating vote. They have never looked back.[9]

But if elections since 1974 have been characterized by massive central advertising expenditure during the few short weeks of the campaign, we should not forget that this is largely a function of the legal constraints on other, potentially more fruitful, ways of influencing voters. There can be little doubt that if parties were free to do so they would spend their millions locally, in the key marginals that decide a General Election. Indeed, if the law allowed they would doubtless spend the vast majority on local television commercials, as happens in the United States. From the 1970s to the 1990s the parties spent vast sums on national press and poster advertising, in the hope that this would have some impact on the voters who really matter. In 1979, the first election to witness a truly mass advertising campaign, the parties were advised that so long as they kept their propaganda resolutely national—avoiding candidates' names, specific local issues, and the targeting of key seats—they could do more or less as they liked. In 1979 money was spent fairly evenly on press and poster advertising, with the Conservatives also spending heavily on cinema advertisements targeted at the youth vote. In the 1980s the level of central party expenditure rose sharply, reaching almost £9 million in 1987, with the great bulk of this money spent on massive press advertising campaigns. In 1987 the Conservatives alone spent more than £2 million in the final five days following 'wobbly Thursday' (when a slight blip in polling returns seemed to suggest that victory might not be assured). In the 1990s spending fell back slightly in real terms, and the parties began to place greater emphasis on high-impact poster campaigns, with more money again being spent in the run-up to the campaign after academic research suggested that the six months prior to the 1987 campaign had seen decisive shifts in voter allegiance (this came to be known as the 'near term' campaign after John Major made decisive use of co-ordinated pre-election campaigning to pull off his surprise 1992 victory). By 1997 80 per cent of all central party publicity expenditure was devoted to poster sites—with the parties doing all they could to bend the law against targeting their effort on the marginals.[10]

What no one could say, however, was whether any of this massive expenditure made the slightest difference, but then rational, profit-maximizing behaviour had never been at a premium in the inner circles of party strategists. What mattered was less winning votes, than being seen to try and win votes. Denied access to paid television advertising (the medium most likely to sway voters on a large scale), election propaganda in Britain tended to be as much about maintaining party morale and lifting the spirit of one's supporters, as about seeking to convert wavering voters to the cause. What is not in doubt, however, is that in the late twentieth century this massive PR effort underscored the dominance of the national, media-dominated campaign over the efforts of candidates and activists on the doorsteps in Britain's six hundred plus constituencies. The introduction of statuary limits on national party expenditure in 2000 did little to change this because the limits set were so generous, although the legislation did bring the national campaign, and the party machines that run it, firmly within the sights of the law for the first time. At the same time, there has been a notable renaissance of the local campaign since 2001, with the two main parties turning to new technologies to co-ordinate their national and local campaigns to an unparalleled degree, a theme explored more fully below.[11]

Innovations in local campaigning

The traditional constituency campaign may have been eclipsed by the rise of television, but local campaigning resolutely refused to die, at least in the marginals. For one thing, those maverick candidates whose spirits revolted at a narrowly organizational interpretation of campaigning never wholly disappeared. Fighting the giant south Essex constituency of Epping in 1970, Norman Tebbit boasted of having fought a strongly personal campaign against the sitting left-wing Labour MP Stan Newens. Tebbit's back-room organization appears to have been fairly chaotic (his agent went on a prolonged drinking binge during both 1974 elections), but his flair for controversy was already well developed, and he secured maximum publicity both for his belligerent attacks on Newens and for his high-profile walkabouts in 'enemy' strongholds such as Harlow new town. Traditionally, party strategists had decried personal attacks, partly for fear of the legal consequences, but mainly because it was held to be bad policy to offer 'free advertising' to the other side. Though never wholly vanquished, such thinking lost much of its power in the 1970s. Changes to the ballot paper reduced the importance of name recognition, and the use of 'knocking copy' emerged as a key feature of the resurgent Liberals' strong local campaigning style—the so-called 'pavement' or 'community' politics. Faced by a strident Liberal challenger in Des Wilson at the 1973 Hove by-election, Tim Sainsbury hit back in kind. Breaking with Conservative tradition, Sainsbury won out against Wilson's community-based politics by fiercely attacking his opponent's credibility and insisting that the real issues facing voters were national rather than local. In the process, both sides made extensive use of cheap in-house litho printing to conduct a leaflet war that in many respects was reminiscent of the old interactive 'platform wars' of the pre-Second World War era. Local politics was back with a vengeance. After narrowly losing Ipswich in February 1974, Ken Weetch paid tribute to his Conservative opponent's excellent publicity machine, but lambasted the 'pernicious effect' of his willingness to pander to the voters' 'unbelievably parochial' instincts (dark arts that Weetch himself went on to master so well that he managed to hold the seat even in the Labour meltdown of 1983, though not in 1987).[12]

There were other attempts to bring interest and excitement back to local electioneering, though not all can be judged a striking success. At Nelson and Colne, in east Lancashire, Labour activists resurrected the tradition of holding an eve-of-poll torchlight procession through the constituency in 1970, perhaps influenced by Harold Wilson's famous triumphal marches through Liverpool in the 1960s. Recognizing that they were trying to take politics 'back to the old days', the organizers stressed that the spectacle was a great tonic for party activists, regardless of whether it gained any votes. By contrast, across the Pennines, Labour activists in one Yorkshire constituency sought to liven up the 1970 General Election by organizing a pop concert in the local park—with their candidate making short speeches between sets to a crowd claimed to number 1,200. Similarly, in 1979 Labour activists in Yorkshire organized a multicultural festival combining colliery brass bands with steel bands in an effort to overcome the 'drab and uninspiring' nature of modern electioneering. But whilst some sought to find alternatives to television, others embraced innovations that were directly parasitic on the medium. Perhaps least convincing were those that sought simply to mimic television—such as when Fulham Labour party showed a film including vox-pop interviews with party loyalists at a party rally in 1964. More successful were attempts to enliven electioneering by mobilizing the showbiz glitz of television celebrities. Labour proved particularly adept at this game in the 1960s. At Baron's Court in 1964, the young Vanessa Redgrave helped organize a widely publicized 'celebrity canvass' for Ivor Richard, while in the Hull North by-election, which prepared the way for Wilson's triumphant 1966 election campaign, Clive Dunn and Alfie Bass spearheaded Labour's celebrity challenge. In 1966 itself, the previously impregnable Conservative bastion of Hampstead was overcome with a little help from a group called 'T.V. Stars for Whitaker' (Labour's barrister candidate)—quite fitting given that from 1992 the seat would be represented for Labour by Glenda Jackson, probably best known for her appearances on the *Morecambe and Wise Show* and in BBC costume dramas such as *Elizabeth R*. In 1974 Tony Benn had Sylvia Sims canvassing for him at Bristol South-East, while at Blackburn Barbara Castle had Frankie Vaughan singing 'Moonlight' in the market place. A decade later, on his way to defeat at Bristol, Benn was determined to shun such 'razzmatazz' in favour of a 'low-key local campaign [with] no frantic handshaking, no loudspeakers ... [and] the absolute minimum of television', but his new-found puritanism could not hope to stem the tide of superficial, media-driven politics. At the Chesterfield by-election which returned him to Parliament the following year, Benn refused to hold press conferences or make any other concessions to the 'media circus'. Press and broadcasters were told 'to follow us around the constituency as we canvassed and addressed public meetings', but the result was not coverage of the real campaign, as Benn hoped, but rather a permanent media scrum that made it impossible for Benn even to meet ordinary voters.[13]

In flirting with 'celebrity politics' candidates hoped to hijack the 'media circus' to their own ends—gaining good publicity by capitalizing on the ability of fame to generate media interest. But for the most part innovation in local campaigning was considerably more prosaic: it was about refining traditional techniques rather than taking a giant leap into the modern media age. In the 1960s 'impact canvassing', and its near cousin the 'walkabout', caught on as attractive, upbeat alternatives to the loudspeaker raids that had been such a staple of electioneering since 1945. Where the loudspeaker car emphasized the gulf between politician and public—and the one-way nature of their political interaction—it was hoped that these new, more informal techniques would help politicians re-establish a personal rapport with voters. Many felt that Charlie Morrison, a flamboyant member of the Wiltshire gentry, had caught the mood of the 'swinging' sixties at the 1964 Devizes by-election by surrounding himself with teams of attractive female canvassers. By 1970 Richard Crossman and his fellow Labour candidates found themselves swept up in the vogue for the 'walkabout canvass'. Crossman records being involved in 'another round of meeting the people, with eight or nine helpers going along both sides of the street while I rushed from side to side shaking people's hands'. Crossman added that 'even poor old Maurice Edelman [a Coventry MP since 1945], who up till now had merely been loudspeakering, finally got out of his car for the first time in three weeks and actually walked the streets'.[14]

By the mid-1960s, with fewer voters strongly fixed in their allegiance, and more apparently switching sides during the campaign, activists began to rethink the utility of traditional canvassing. Most agreed that it remained important, but there was more emphasis on canvassing as an end in itself. Information about voting intention was still sought, but simply 'meeting the people' came to be seen as the overriding purpose. Orpington Conservatives, seeking to rebuild their base after the shock Liberal victory of 1962, highlighted doorstep canvassing as the best means of reconnecting the party with ordinary voters. A decade later, Cheshire Conservatives proclaimed that the key to regaining Hazel Grove from the Liberals had been the decision to throw their energy, not into canvassing, but rather into out-producing and out-delivering the Liberals in the local leaflet war. In the process, their election agent observed that 'the value of canvassing has changed from seeking support to providing us with a point of political contact between us and the electorate'. Labour strategists drew similar conclusions in the wake of their shock 1970 defeat—arguing that canvassing needed to be about more than mere data collection—it had to be a vehicle for emphasizing 'the personal and proselytising aspect of campaigning'.[15]

The 1960s and 1970s also saw a new openness to American campaigning techniques, with much talk (not for the first time) of reorganizing election-eering along 'scientific lines'. At the national level this meant greater use of advertising, PR, and private polling, and hence greater reliance on the pro fessionals trained in these fields (as satirized by Peter Cook in the 1970 film *The Rise and Rise of Michael Rimmer*). But at the local level it generally meant taking a fresh look at familiar campaign activities. There was a vogue for training volunteers in the art of so-called 'survey canvassing'—essentially techniques borrowed from market research to increase the accuracy of the doorstep canvass in an age of three-party politics. The Conservatives proved particularly assiduous followers of developments Stateside, and in the later 1960s they tried to incorporate a version of the American 'cell system' into their strategy for capturing the 'critical seats' necessary to unseat Wilson. The idea was to identify and influence small groups of 'opinion formers' who would then boost the party's fortunes with the wider elect-orate. Pushed hard in the run-up to the 1970 election, the Conservatives dropped the idea in subsequent years mainly because it proved impossible to obtain reliable political intelligence about 'opinion formers' from local parties. Instead they fell back on more conventional propaganda techniques such as selective mailing—identifying groups of voters that might prove susceptible to a targeted appeal based on their putative common interests. Target groups might include council house tenants, young voters, married women, or, if the local intelligence was particularly strong, even groups such as NHS workers, the elderly, or private tenants.[16]

The idea of selective mailing had been around since before the First World War, but it entered a new era after 1974, as local authorities gradually went over to the use of computerized electoral registers. Henceforth local parties would be able to buy pre-printed address labels for every voter, saving hundreds of hours of laborious work hand-writing address labels for the candidate's Freepost delivery. It was the beginning of a revolution in local campaigning. By the mid-1980s local parties could buy the register in machine-readable form for use on relatively inexpensive personal computers. Suddenly, selective mailing entered a new era as local parties were able to combine database and mass mailing software to send out increasingly sophisticated personal mailshots to 'target' voters. Perhaps predictably the possibilities opened up by such new technologies tended to be explored only in a minority of key marginal constituencies, but here at least there was no longer much doubt that the local campaign mattered. All three parties also began to make extensive use of tele-canvassing, often organized from national party call centres. Much of this work was conducted before the election began—preparing the ground for targeted mailshots and doorstep visits—but by 1992 there was widespread suspicion that tele-canvassing was continuing throughout the campaign, without being declared on candidates' election expenses. There has also been a growing tendency for parties to use database technologies to organize national mailshots of floating voters in key marginal constituencies, thereby circumventing tight controls on local campaign expenditure. In 2005 the Conservative party raised this tactic to a new level when it bought the 'Voter Vault' software that had helped steer George W. Bush to victory in the US presidential race the previous year. In theory, this software would make it possible to manipulate voter-level social, economic, and cultural data to send targeted mailshots to various sub-groups of supposedly Conservative-leaning voters. However, Britain's tough data protection law denies parties access to the sort of information about individuals that is commercially available in the United States. In consequence, Voter Vault had to work mainly with postcode level data bought from marketing companies (notably Experian's 'Mosaic' database)—useful, but still a rather blunt instrument when one considers that on average each postcode includes fifteen separate households. It seems likely that 'Voter Vault', along with some skilfully targeted direct funding from wealthy supporters such as Michael Ashcroft, did help the Conservatives in key marginals in 2005, but even with another low turnout it could not work the psephological miracle that its champions had hoped for. Yes, in theory, just 150,000 voters switching allegiance would have been enough to wipe out Tony Blair's massive 2001 majority, but even this new hi-tech constituency campaigning could not come close to targeting voters with that sort of precision, especially when the other side was playing a very similar game in exactly the same seats. Labour apparently sent out ten million direct mailshots from its national campaign centre at Gosforth, while its tele-canvassers made two million calls. The party also sent locally themed DVDs to a quarter of a million voters in sixty key marginals—sharing the cost between the candidate and the national party—this was local campaigning only in name.[17]

Moreover, in this hi-tech guise local campaigning remains focused largely on enumerating and targeting voters more scientifically, rather than on reinvigorating the local campaign as a vital point of contact between politicians and public. New technology allows the parties to deliver the sort of highly focused, 'selective' campaign effort that apostles of the organizational approach to electioneering could only have dreamt of in the 1950s and 1960s. The personalized letter and the telesales call have taken over from the scruffy leaflet and the window sticker—politics appears simultaneously more individualized and more privatized, even though it is increasingly co-ordinated on a mass scale from remote national campaign centres. The basic passivity of the average voter is taken for granted. Were it not for the proliferation of mobile phones, ex-directory listings, and call screening, which are all eroding the reach of the party phone banks, face-to-face interaction might easily vanish from the local campaign. As it is, the doorstep call remains the only way to be sure of reaching many critical swing voters. It is all a far cry from the days of tumultuous election meetings and boisterous polling day crowds, but as the next section explains, those days were already long gone by the time Michael Howard brought Voter Vault to Britain.[18]

The death of the election meeting

We have traced the mutation and gradual decline of the election meeting across the twentieth century in previous chapters, but it was only in the 1960s and 1970s that the meeting ceased to play a significant part in British campaigning. The proportion of electors claiming to have attended an election meeting halved between 1959 and 1964. By then it was already widely dismissed as a marginal and largely ritualistic aspect of electioneering, which diverted party activists from the 'real' work of identifying and mobilizing the party's maximum potential vote. But whilst there may have been a sharp drop in attendance in 1964, there was also evidence that the

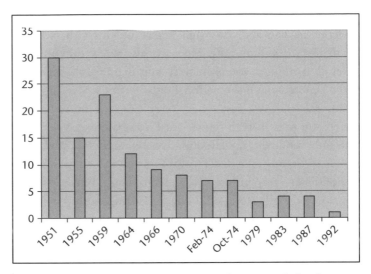

Fig. 16. The proportion of electors claiming to have attended at least one public election meeting during the General Election, 1951–92
Source: Gallup (ed.), *Gallup International*, vols. 1 and 2; *News Chronicle, Behind the Gallup Poll*; David Butler *et al.*, Nuffield British Election Studies series, 1951–92.
Note: Since Gallup often recorded figures separately for attendance at indoor and outdoor meetings it has sometimes been necessary to estimate the number attending one or other. Other surveys such as the BES record the same basic trend, though figures for specific elections vary.

intrusion of TV cameras into high-profile meetings stimulated a revival of earlier customs associated with the meeting, such as aggressive heckling and even organized disruption. Thereafter, attendance at meetings appears to have declined slowly but consistently through the remainder of the 1960s and 1970s before recording a second precipitate fall in 1979, when just 3 per cent of electors claimed to have attended a meeting; barely one-tenth the percentage recorded in 1951 (see Fig. 16).

Such figures need to be viewed with considerable caution, but there is no reason to doubt that they register the broad trend of attendance at meetings since the 1950s; that trend was almost continuously downwards after 1959. The big question of course is why? Was this simply an inevitable consequence of the rise of television—both as a diversion for audiences and as a superior means of communication for politicians—or were other factors at work? To answer such questions we need to look in greater detail at what was happening in the constituencies from the 1960s to the 1980s, at efforts to revive or repackage the election meeting, and at the factors which finally led to its almost total eclipse after 1979. The early 1960s represented a transitional phase in our story during which there was enormous variation across Britain. At Finchley, in suburban north London, the Conservatives placed great emphasis on public meetings as a means of advertising their dynamic and attractive young candidate Mrs Margaret Thatcher (MP since 1959). Mrs Thatcher held ten public meetings drawing a total audience of approximately 1,300, just 2 per cent of the total electorate, but still respectable by London standards, where the indoor meeting had been in steep decline since before the war. By contrast her Labour opponent subscribed to the 'modern' view that public meetings were a waste of everybody's time. He held only one meeting throughout the campaign—a traditional eve-of-poll rally to boost supporters' morale before the big push on polling day.[19]

In the 1960s it was quite common, as at Finchley, for rival candidates to adopt completely different strategies. In general, Conservatives seem to have persisted with meetings for longer than their opponents, both in urban and rural constituencies, but there was no iron law. At Brighton Kempston in 1966 it was the Labour candidate who held a full round of public meetings, while his Conservative opponent concentrated almost exclusively on canvass work, while at the 1962 Middlesbrough West by-election Labour candidate Jeremy Bray put considerable personal effort into organizing three large meetings with national speakers to address weighty topics of the day: the Common Market, development, and disarmament. When Labour captured wealthy Hampstead in 1966 the party organized an extensive programme of meetings—boasting that audiences averaged 250 per meeting, including large numbers of undecided voters. By contrast, at Brixton and Islington, both parties held only one meeting to 'show the candidate' in 1964, although at Brixton the candidates did also appear at two open platforms organized by local non-party bodies. At Rhondda West in 1966 only the Communists bothered to hold any formal public meetings—Iorwerth Thomas, defending a massive 69 per cent Labour majority, contented himself with impromptu visits to local social clubs. Perhaps surprisingly, outdoor speaking still remained an important part of electioneering in the 1960s, particularly in large conurbations where it was hard to draw an indoor audience, but also in scattered rural areas where there was often nowhere to put one. For instance, in parts of London where candidates had long held only one token public meeting, local parties still devoted enormous energy to securing good outdoor pitches, particularly for the traditional Saturday harangue.[20]

By 1964 it was widely recognized that only a few big-name politicians could attract large audiences, even during a general election. The two main party leaders were always the biggest draw, even when, like Gaitskell or Home, they were not exactly scintillating platform performers. By the early 1960s leaders' meetings had become an integral part of the television election. With the party leaders followed around the country by rival camera crews, these were as much media as political events. Significantly, these were also the main meetings that still regularly attracted trouble in the 1960s, with both Wilson and Home (especially the latter) subjected to considerable 'rough heckling' in 1964. But this is really part of a different story concerning the complex and shifting relationship between political leaders, the media, and the public in the television age—a story that will be explored at length in the next chapter. For have no doubt, the cameras were *agents provocateurs* at leaders' meetings in the 1960s—without their ability to transform a politician's temporary inconvenience into a dramatic national news event one suspects that the leaders' meetings would have been almost as dull and uneventful as everybody else's.[21]

By 1970 it was claimed that only seven politicians could still reliably draw crowds of over five hundred: besides Wilson and Heath (the party leaders), these were Jim Callaghan and George Brown for Labour, and Enoch Powell, Quintin Hogg, and Sir Alec Douglas-Home for the Conservatives. By then the average attendance at an election meeting was said to be between forty and fifty, with even prominent cabinet ministers sometimes attracting audiences in single fingers. At the Leicester South-West by-election in 1967 Richard Crossman found himself speaking to an audience of four (plus considerably more reporters) for 55 minutes until finally the candidate and his canvassers arrived swelling the audience to a 'respectable' thirty. Whether there was much point in Crossman addressing a meeting dominated by hard-core Labour activists is another matter. Increasingly political strategists in all parties felt that the answer was an unequivocal 'no'—political meetings had outlasted their usefulness. Stan Newens recalled abandoning meetings in 1970 after realizing that 'they took 50 activists to organize and drew audiences of only 15 committed supporters'. Similarly, in the aftermath of the party's 1964 defeat the *Conservative Agents' Journal* had argued that candidates needed to put much more effort into cultivating the print and broadcast media, and much less into speaking to the converted at formal public meetings. But the Conservatives' problem was that in far-flung constituencies there were often many strong local branches who believed that it was their right to hear the candidate at least once during the campaign. Well into the 1970s Conservative strategists were still lamenting that whilst the meeting might be 'finished' for practical political purposes, it was very difficult to wean local activists off the idea that the daily meeting was an essential part of a good campaign. In large rural seats it was still routine for candidates to boast of addressing over one hundred meetings during a campaign, sometimes many more. In holding North Cornwall for the Liberals in 1970 John Pardoe claimed to have spoken at more than 280 meetings, though almost all of these were outdoor affairs. At a time when it was becoming unusual for an urban candidate to hold more than three or four meetings in total, it remained normal for rural candidates—even Labour ones—to hold three or four meetings a night. However by 1979 the Conservatives were said to be alone in persisting with this level of activity, even in rural England.[22]

Even at the time, many saw George Brown's last great marathon speaking tour during the 1970 General Election as the swansong for old-style campaigning, not least because of the pathos of Brown losing his own marginal seat of Belper in Derbyshire after selflessly speaking for others throughout the campaign. In 1966 Crossman already felt that Brown's rumbustious electioneering was 'more Pickwickian and old-fashioned this year than ever before'. Four years later, against the backdrop of shock defeat, critics were even harsher. Many noted that for all his tireless speech-making, Brown had garnered precious few column inches in the national press, and almost no extended television coverage. The media happily mined Brown's raucous, and often chaotic, meetings for good election images, but his arguments were almost never heard beyond the confines of the meeting—and by all accounts sometimes not there either. Even the supportive *Labour Organiser* acknowledged that Brown's forceful banter with hecklers would have swayed few floating voters, and that his meetings sometimes provided opponents with a chance to engineer dramatic 'stunts' for the press and TV cameras. Although this journal, at least, still celebrated Brown's defiant bid 'to make politics human' again.[23]

Even after 1970, not all candidates were happy to see the meeting disappear from urban politics, but there was often little they could do to revive the tradition. At Bristol South-East, Tony Benn always held a full programme of public appearances, ending his campaign with a series of eve-of-poll meetings in the different parts of his constituency followed by a late-night rally in St George's Park illuminated by the headlights of supporters' cars. In this he was maintaining a local Labour tradition that could be traced back to the party's first victories in the constituency between the wars. But by the mid-1970s not even Benn could guarantee a decent audience. When he arrived at Redfield School for the first meeting of the February 1974 campaign, he found TV crews from various British and European broadcasters, reporters from a string of major national newspapers—and no audience. According to his own account, he leapt into the loudspeaker car and toured the nearby terraced streets telling people to come along to put their questions direct to the nation via the BBC—though even then only a few good citizens chose to take up the opportunity. At the same election Barbara Castle found that whilst her new-found status as a TV celebrity meant that she was 'mobbed for autographs' wherever she went, she still could not attract decent audiences for indoor political meetings. After two poor meetings at the start of her campaign she cancelled the rest and focused instead on informal public appearances around the constituency. Voters might be thrilled by the chance to meet a TV personality 'in the flesh', but this did not mean that they were prepared to trudge out on a dark winter's evening to hear the same person talk politics in a local municipal hall or schoolroom. As Michael Pinto-Duschinsky observed, commenting on the 1974 elections, 'people are not generally interested in the views of the constituency candidates'—even when, as in Barbara Castle's case, those candidates were front-rank political figures of cabinet status. To most voters elections were fought primarily through the mass media, pre-eminently through television, and since this presented the election in resolutely national terms—mainly as a presidential-style contest between the rival party leaders—the local campaign ceased to register as something in which one might become actively involved. Austin Mitchell complained that 'the local candidate is an intruder on the national campaign, knocking on doors and interrupting' as voters tried to follow the 'real' campaign on television or in their newspapers.[24]

By 1979 it was said that only Thatcher and Callaghan, the party leaders, could attract full halls anywhere in the country. Even such charismatic figures as Denis Healey, Chancellor in the outgoing Labour Government, often drew only a few dozen to an evening meeting. To make matters worse, at the start of the 1979 campaign, the terrorist assassination of Airey

Neave, Conservative MP for Abingdon and a close Thatcher ally, placed formidable new constraints on the traditional open public meeting. It is conceivable that the sharp drop in attendance registered in 1979 reflects this fraught security context—though if so, it was not a trend to be reversed in subsequent years. Indeed, by the late 1970s there was evidence that where the public meeting survived at all, it did so mainly because some politicians, and some local activists, still cherished the opportunity to talk politics face-to-face, rather than accept that electioneering had now become merely an endless series of walkabouts and 'media friendly' visits to local hospitals and schools. Both Labour and Conservative MPs could be found declaring that it remained essential for voters to have the chance to 'cross examine the local candidate' in an open public forum. They doubtless meant what they said, but one should also give credence to Roy Jenkins's frank recollection that by the 1970s he had come to view the main purpose of meetings as 'bolstering the ego of the candidate'; 'without them', he observed, 'electioneering is flat, low-pressure work'.[25]

Jenkins was one of the old generation—having fought his first election in 1945. As such the meeting was in his blood, and it was one of his proudest boasts that, though it was widely dismissed as a 'media party', in its early days the breakaway Social Democratic Party (SDP) had been a party of public meetings. Jenkins recalled that 'For a time we restored the public meeting to a position in British political life which it had been steadily losing for the previous thirty years.' He claimed that as leader of the new party, pledged to 'break the mould' of British politics, he found he could draw audiences four times larger than when he had been Labour Chancellor in the late 1960s. In 1981, when the party was launched, Jenkins found himself addressing old-style overspill meetings in unlikely places such as Wantage, while in leafy Guildford 1,700 braved a severe downpour to hear the SDP message first-hand. But even the SDP magic could not work everywhere. At Glasgow Hillhead, which Jenkins won for the SDP in March 1982, he reckoned to have reached a quarter of the electorate during a full programme of meetings, but in his earlier by-election campaign at Warrington, on the Cheshire/Lancashire border, audiences had been poor. Jenkins concluded that Warrington was simply 'not that sort of a town', and that the only way to reach the voters here was for the SDP's 'gang of four' to 'cavalcade around the constituency' waving at shoppers from an open truck. Despite Jenkins's claims to the contrary, it seems likely that the 'media circus' surrounding the launch of the SDP played a large part in the revivalist spirit that infused so many of the party's early meetings. If so, this might also help to explain the contrast Tony Benn noted between his 1984 by-election contest at Chesterfield, when the 'media circus' was out in force, and the subsequent 1987 General Election. During the 1984 campaign, Benn found himself addressing an over-spill meeting of a thousand in the town's historic square, whereas in 1987 a speech in the market place drew a modest audience which applauded like a crowd at a 'village cricket match when somebody scores a run'. Warrington showed that even the 'media circus' could not breathe life into the meeting everywhere, but by the 1980s it was pretty clear that meetings thrived only as an adjunct to media exposure. There was undoubtedly something positive about this—people went to hear Jenkins or Benn because they wanted to know more about their views than they could glean from television. On the other hand, without the TV coverage that made them political celebrities it is doubtful that many voters would have felt such curiosity at all. The recent commercial success of speaking tours by political figures, which began with Benn's nationwide tours in 2002–3, and has since seen the promotion of 'An Audience With…' Alastair Campbell, William Hague, and latterly George Galloway, should probably be understood in this light—not as a revival of the old public meeting, but as an intriguing political variant of 'celebrity' culture (most are masterminded by Clive Conway Celebrity Productions). That said, this can still spill over into elections—as at Cambridge in 2005, when Charles Kennedy drew so many to the city's Guildhall that he was obliged to address an overspill meeting of six hundred.[26]

However, there remains little doubt that by the mid-1980s public meetings had largely disappeared from urban Britain. According to the Nuffield election study there were now many towns, including marginals, where candidates held no public meetings at all, except perhaps those organized independently by churches and other local groups. The Conservatives held just two public meetings at Epsom in 1987 compared with twenty in 1964, though at nearby Surrey South-West Virginia Bottomley was still holding well-attended nightly election meetings, apparently because the local Conservative Association's 8,000-strong membership demanded them. Front-bench politicians were now rarely wasted on political meetings, even in highly marginal constituencies—instead they were asked to take part in media 'events', walkabouts, and mass canvassing drives in the marginals in the hope of gaining good coverage for themselves and local candidates on regional news bulletins. In 1979 the BBC ran a late-night television programme called *Hustings* offering extended excerpts from that day's main evening speeches. Four years later, not only had the programme been relegated to the relative obscurity of late-night talk radio, but perhaps more significantly, the producers found that it was becoming increasingly difficult to find enough substantial speeches to justify extended excerpts. Of course a few politicians continued to insist on holding public meetings into the 1990s, but the results were often profoundly disappointing. In 1992 one Labour candidate claimed to have held eleven meetings which attracted a total audience of just eighty-four—including two meetings where no one at all turned up. It is perhaps hardly surprising, therefore, that when Geoffrey Howe, writing at the turning of the century, recalled two eve-of-poll rallies at Reigate in 1983, he commented wryly: 'how old-fashioned that now seems'. The traditional open political meeting might have been in decline for decades, but its final eclipse was nonetheless a rather rapid affair.[27]

Most commentators have assumed that the decline of the meeting was simply a function of the growing sophistication of the mass media. There is much to commend this view, particularly in relation to the rise of political television as a rival, and decidedly more convenient, source of political information. However, this is not the whole story. We need to remember that the meeting had been stripped of much of its excitement and popular appeal even before the emergence of political television. We also need to remember that the platform's main function, besides providing voters with an opportunity to 'have their say', had been to provide a forum for political interaction between candidates. Candidates rarely, if ever, met in public—but they did read each other's speeches in the local press, and, when necessary, responded vociferously to an opponent's challenge or perceived offence. This worked best where there was a daily paper with a circulation confined to only a few parliamentary constituencies. Such papers existed on a large scale between the 1880s and 1930s, but became much rarer in the second half of the twentieth century with the rise of regional super-titles to dominate the daily provincial market. With little prospect of getting copy into the local press on a regular basis, and even less chance of receiving more than token exposure via the broadcast media, candidates increasingly turned to the in-house leaflet as the best means both of setting the campaign agenda and of countering the claims of their political opponents. Interactive campaigning was not dead—but it had shifted from the platform to the cheap local leaflet. At the same time, the highly interactive national campaign, with its welter of charges and counter-charges, became increasingly dominant through the influence of the mass media—often completely overshadowing the squabbles between rival candidates at local level.

Working the constituency

There had long been a tradition of prospective parliamentary candidates working their constituencies in order to win voter allegiance before the election. In the nineteenth century it had been usual for wealthy candidates to 'nurse' a constituency by spending prodigious amounts of money funding local good works and making donations to myriad recreational and charitable associations. Giving on this scale died away during the twentieth century, but politicians did not cease to 'work' their constituencies—instead they turned from the ethic of charity to the ethic of 'service'. As politicians came to have less and less contact with voters in formal public settings such as the meeting, so they saw more of them in the private setting of the MP's consulting room or 'surgery'. Increasingly, MPs (and prospective parliamentary candidates) sought to bridge the perceived gulf between politicians and public not by holding meetings that few, if any, ordinary voters would ever attend, but by making themselves available as troubleshooters capable of solving the problems that beset voters' everyday lives.

As we have seen, the fashion for MPs to hold regular local 'surgeries' took off during the 1950s, though individual MPs had been providing such a service much earlier. In the 1950s there were still many MPs who confined their constituency service work to handling correspondence and acting as a lobbyist for constituency interests at Westminster. Those who held constituency surgeries, often did so fairly infrequently. Gerald Nabarro, the flamboyant Conservative MP, made much of his assiduous constituency work, but was nonetheless holding only a monthly surgery even in the late 1960s. Harold Wilson also held monthly surgeries, though it is perhaps significant that whilst he handed over other constituency business to his agent on becoming Prime Minister in 1964, he continued to hold his Huyton surgeries in person, acting as his own secretary so that he could continue to see constituents in private. In 1963 a survey of nearly seventy MPs suggested that one in five still held no surgeries, and only one in three held fortnightly or weekly surgeries. However, the new generation of MPs—those first elected in the 1960s when the idea of the surgery was already well established—tended to work to a more demanding schedule. Peter Walker, first elected for Worcester in 1964, boasted of spending every weekend in the constituency holding surgeries and canvassing. Walker claimed to have seen 30,000 constituents at his surgeries over a quarter-century, and was convinced that it was this, above all else, that allowed him to build 'a strong personal following' in the city. At Hornchurch, Alan Williams also introduced weekly surgeries after capturing the seat for Labour in 1966. Perhaps conscious that this might not be enough in a sprawling suburban seat with over 90,000 voters, he also bought a caravan and mobile loudspeaker system so that he could combine a weekly fixed surgery, with a mobile 'surgery on wheels'. It was a good example of the new mentality—of politicians going 'out to the people' because they no longer felt any confidence that the people would come to them. By 1967, when Barker and Rush conducted an extensive study of MPs' constituency work, only 2 per cent claimed to hold no surgeries for constituents, over 90 per cent said they held 'regular' surgeries, and nearly half said that they held surgeries at least every fortnight. By 1979 the figures had risen further, with 93 per cent claiming to hold regular surgeries, and 58 per cent holding surgeries at least every fortnight, but it appears that the sharpest increase in surgery work occurred in the mid-1960s, driven by the large intake of new (mainly Labour) MPs in 1964 and 1966.[28]

As Walker recognized, politicians' greatest task was always to make sure that the public knew how much they were doing in the constituency. With a London study in the early 1970s suggesting that an MP might see only 120 surgery cases in a year, and a more detailed Midlands study suggesting that a Labour MP saw ten constituents per month at his surgeries (with perhaps another 25 cases coming to him by other means), it was clear that only a tiny proportion of voters would ever be touched directly by the MP's service work—and not all of these would be satisfied by the help or advice received. At this rate, an MP might hope to 'serve' perhaps 3 per cent of the electorate during a full Parliament—with most studies suggesting that between one-quarter and one-third of these cases would end unsatisfactorily for the constituent. It was therefore crucial to make sure that the surgeries were well advertised in both party literature and the local press. Press advertisements served a dual purpose—generating both awareness and 'custom' (in the Midlands study the majority of people attending surgery were self-referrals who had found the details in the local press). As long as confidentiality was preserved, party literature could also be used to highlight success stories. Indeed, at Bristol in 1964 Tony Benn used his free election mailing to send out a special insert about his advice service. On the other hand, Dingle Foot wisely drew the line at allowing Anglia TV to televise his Ipswich surgery work in the late 1960s, partly because it would destroy confidentiality, but also because he feared that some people would relish the opportunity to air their perceived grievances in public. Another approach was to move away from the narrow emphasis on the MP as service provider. At Lewisham West in the early 1970s John Selwyn Gummer, who would later become famously embroiled in the BSE crisis, experimented with a constituency-wide advice system involving neighbourhood volunteers who would provide the first point of contact for any constituent in need of help or advice. Gummer explained that although he held a weekly advice session in the constituency, he realized that 'many people don't find the help and information that they need'. The scheme was therefore presented as an imaginative attempt to reach out to local people in difficulty, and much emphasis was placed on the 'non-party' status of the volunteers and experts who would be working with Gummer. It was also a well-publicized attempt to ensure that an MP in a highly marginal London seat would be *seen* to be doing something for local people. It encapsulated what Dinnage, writing about advice work in a similar London seat in the early 1970s, called 'the quasi-symbolic significance' of the surgery—its ability to symbolize 'the availability of "them" to "us" '. But since Gummer still lost in February 1974, one has to recognize that such symbolism could not work miracles.[29]

There were always a good many politicians ready to ask whether constituency service paid electoral dividends. A study of Sheffield MPs in the mid-1960s had suggested that assiduous constituency MPs did no better in elections than MPs with a more traditional, Westminster-centred approach to politics. On the other hand, even in the 1960s, when the idea of the remorseless and impersonal nature of 'national swing' was rarely questioned, there was evidence that incumbent MPs tended to do better than newcomers by between 1.5 and 3.5 points of 'swing' (and a suggestion that popular incumbents might do even better). In the 1980s a large volume of research began to confirm this picture, suggesting that constituency service could allow MPs to develop a significant personal vote to insulate them from national swing. But even before such research became widely disseminated, studies showed that the mere *possibility* of generating a personal vote was enough to persuade most MPs to throw themselves assiduously into constituency work. Prudential rationality was doubtless a factor here, but so too was the desire not to alienate a powerful local party keen to see their representative active in the constituency. Alan Clark's bitter outbursts in his diaries against 'mendicants' clogging up his surgeries, and his deep loathing of everything to do with constituency work, cannot be separated from the maverick MP's burning resentment at the constant demands on his time from Plymouth Conservatives. Clark despised the pressure for MPs always to be seen to be doing something in the constituency, convinced that this had more to do with massaging the egos of local councillors and party functionaries than actually serving the voters. By contrast, Oona King's diary of life as MP for Bethnal Green and Bromley shows a woman all but overwhelmed by the sheer scale of human misery clamouring for her help. Most of King's cases clearly sprang from dire poverty, especially among the elderly and migrants, but there is often also a 'care in the community' dimension to surgery work which can be no less demoralizing—though that hardly excuses the decision of one Conservative MP, defeated in 1997, to give his opponent's home telephone number to 'my three mad women—the three truly deranged constituents who came to every surgery'.[30]

By contrast, MPs' correspondence has always been a largely invisible form of service work with little scope for the local party to interfere unless, as with Wilson at Huyton, a local officer was asked to field the work on the MP's behalf. Hence, even gross neglect could easily go undetected by the local party, as when Alan Clark found a five-year-old bundle of unsigned letters to constituents while clearing out his Westminster locker. In one 1970s study it was found that 44 per cent of voters contacted their MP by post (compared with 26 per cent using the surgery). A detailed study of Tony Benn's constituency correspondence at Bristol South-East during 1972–3, found that, in an average week, he received 41 constituency letters and sent out 54—and that, despite regular surgeries, 85 per cent of his case work was based purely on correspondence (interestingly, in February 1964 Benn claimed to be receiving 100 constituency letters per week, and sending out 200, suggesting, if true, that constituency work could also be decidedly cyclical). Moreover, even Benn's 1964 postbag fell far short of record-breaking standards. In 1966 *Labour Organiser* reported that there were three large suburban seats in the south-east where MPs claimed to receive up to 100 letters in a single day: Hitchin (Shirley Williams), Epping (Stan Newens), and Billericay (Eric Moonman)—all with electorates of over 90,000. Such a vast workload could only be handled with considerable office support, and even then necessarily precluded any follow-up work beyond a letter of reply outlining the action taken on the constituent's behalf. By the late 1960s it was estimated that 87 per cent of MPs were receiving more than 25 letters per week, with a little under half claiming to receive more than 50. The growth in constituency correspondence has been prodigious since then. A study in the mid-1980s, before the email revolution had really begun, estimated that MPs received on average 33 letters per day, with roughly half of these coming from constituents.[31]

However, according to party organizers, the most important way to work the constituency was to keep oneself constantly in the news, which for most politicians meant cultivating the local press for all it was worth. As we have seen, this was much easier in constituencies still served by genuinely *local* 'local' newspapers, though even here it was increasingly unlikely that a politician could simply hope to find his or her public utterances reproduced verbatim in the press. This still happened in some remote areas, such as parts of rural Scotland, where small-scale newspapers with skeletal staffs only survived by publishing press releases almost un-edited, but across most of Britain local journalism was decidedly more 'modern' in its approach to political reporting by the 1960s. Politicians would only get good coverage if they did something—preferably some-thing unusual and visual—rather than if they just said something. Although Labour was often particularly suspicious of the capitalist press, there were striking exceptions. In marginal Baron's Court, Labour had a dedicated publicity officer in the 1960s whose sole purpose was to keep the pro-spective Labour candidate's name constantly in the local papers. As Alan Clark testifies, Conservative MPs were under similar pressure to 'work' the local press. He writes disparagingly of the constant demands from his Plymouth Sutton party for greater 'impact' in the press 'by which they mean, not what they call "the London papers", but the bloody *Herald*'. Clark was characteristically unimpressed by the hyperbole about publicity—observing bluntly, after a series of bad local election results in 1985, that 'Janet Fookes, whose vast arse is seldom undisplayed in the

Herald, did in fact suffer an almost identical swing in her part of the city [Plymouth Drake].'[32]

Perhaps predictably Clark never displayed much enthusiasm for the travails of electioneering proper, any more than he did for the tiresome business of working the constituency between elections. Clark saw the absurdity of frantic walkabouts and loudspeaker raids—suspecting that these impositions on ordinary people's lives were both unwelcome and unproductive. At his first election in February 1974 Clark found that on walkabouts he was mainly 'pinioned by a few grumblers', while during the October election he noted that most voters 'avoid my eye, or start up conversations with each other'. If this was taking politics to the people, then they rarely seemed grateful. Gyles Brandreth, another flamboyant Conservative MP and diarist, was equally sceptical about many strategies for reaching out to the voters. Fighting his first contest at marginal Chester in 1992, Brandreth hated 'bearding half-awake commuters' at the station and 'badgering the mums at the school gates'—though he professed rather to like less intrusive forms of interaction such as 'straightforward street-walking and door-knocking'. In 1997, he insisted on controlling his own itinerary and immediately axed both the railway station and school gates from his schedule. By contrast, Clark's loathing of political interaction was more total, although perhaps to his credit he singled out the hollow rituals of the loudspeaker tour, with its constant repetition of inane slogans, for special hatred. On one occasion, the whole thing became too much and he digressed into a rambling monologue in a mock Devon accent, stopped only by his wife slamming on the brakes and telling him he was making himself 'utterly ridiculous'. Clark always hated what he termed the 'democratic overhang' of 'mendicants' and other 'constituency detritus', but he also knew that these were the very things that gave legitimacy to a politician. In the 1980s he often envied Lord Young, then a rising Thatcherite star, for being unencumbered by the burdens of constituency correspondence, sleeper trains, and, of course, periodic elections. But he also knew that these were badges of honour essential to success within the British political system. When Lord Young was still on the up, Clark advised him that he must find a seat quickly if his career was to prosper. In 1990, when Lord Young was on the slide, Clark recognized that people took special pleasure in the peer's downfall because 'he had never served an apprenticeship in the Commons, with all the hateful and long drawn-out rituals of late votes and constituency pressures'.[33]

No one could hate 'constituency pressures' more than Clark, but even he knew that ultimately they were what gave him credibility as a political figure; indeed recognition of this brutal fact doubtless did much to fuel Clark's loathing of the whole business. But if serving 'the people' still bestowed political legitimacy, and the 'democratic overhang' had to be endured, this no longer meant that politicians had to engage meaningfully with their constituents at elections. To Clark's credit he knew this well, and clearly felt repulsed by the artifice of democratic rituals—pretending to make oneself accessible to the people by marching along the High Street with an entourage of supporters, concocting a photo-opportunity for the local press, or parading around the constituency in a loudspeaker car. It was something that another Conservative politician, Sir Peter Rawlinson, Heath's Attorney-General in the early 1970s, claimed to be the greatest tragedy of modern democratic politics in his aptly named autobiography *A Price too High*. According to Rawlinson, as soon as he retired from active politics in the late 1970s he began to see why so many people recoiled from it. He also 'began to realise that politicians never actually talk to anyone. They either lecture or they canvass.' It was a stinging indictment of the new world of electioneering that had succeeded the public meeting as the focal point of political interaction between candidate and voter. The meeting itself had been far from perfect as a forum for political exchange, but most of the innovations to post-war campaigning seemed to preclude any meaningful political interaction. Constituency service was clearly valuable, but it was rooted in a provider–client relationship where voters appeared as powerless individuals in need of help, rather than as citizens demanding representation. Other innovations, such as 'impact' canvassing, the 'walkabout', and 'loudspeakering' tended to emphasize purely superficial forms of political interaction—they were intended to create positive 'buzz' for a campaign, not to persuade voters by argument, let alone to give those voters a chance to argue back. Revealingly, Labour's confidential 'Walkabout Guidelines' for the 1992 campaign stated that party workers 'should fan out ahead of the two principles [*sic*] screening who should be introduced'. A favoured technique was for the volunteers to hand out party stickers—that way the candidate and accompanying 'star' would know who was 'at least friendly enough to wear a Party sticker'. Here 'meeting the people' was clearly about creating a good impression, especially for the cameras, not contacting the undecided and hostile to win them over. It was a clear example of how, in the age of media politics, semblance was more important than substance. In 2005 Labour was accused of taking this game to a new level by bussing photogenic party supporters around the country to ensure friendly, cheering crowds for visiting party leaders. But even so, as the next two chapters discuss, we should not assume that the rise of mediated politics has had a wholly negative impact on popular participation—the very fact that politicians still feel the need for a semblance of popular acclaim means that the Westminster bubble can never be hermetically sealed. At an election there is always strong pressure to let the people inside the gates.[34]

8

Broadcasting Politics

Understanding mediated politics

From the earliest days of political television, one can identify shared interests between politicians and broadcasters, but this is only one part of the story of their relationship. Arguments that stress a cosy conspiracy against the public are too simplistic. Relations between politicians and broadcasters have frequently been fraught, and have always been inherently unstable. In the 1960s, broadcasters, particularly at the BBC, judged that their 'public service' remit demanded that they should press politicians to discuss important issues, such as immigration and Europe, which they would rather avoid—a practice widely attacked as 'producerism' or 'agenda setting'. In turn, the parties sought to rein in the broadcasters by making tough pre-conditions for the involvement of politicians in television programming, including for many years an absolute veto on public participation. In the 1970s the parties relaxed these restrictions on public involvement, but in turn broadcasters largely abandoned agenda setting in favour of more reactive, news driven, or analytical approaches to the coverage of elections.

Since the 1960s the parties have constantly experimented with techniques intended to secure better media images than their rivals: more televisual rallies, better groomed politicians, better organized and timed public engagements. From 1964 to the mid-1970s the two parties were fairly evenly matched, but after Harold Wilson's retirement in 1976 the Conservatives had an unchallenged lead over their rivals for almost a decade. Wilson had been a consummate media performer, but his triumphs had been largely personal, masterminded from his private office. Crucially, Wilson never tried to win the battle for PR within the wider party, which reverted to type at the first opportunity (Michael Foot took the blame for this

in 1983, but it was really a deep-seated organizational failure). On the
Conservative side, both Heath in the late 1960s and Thatcher in the late
1970s wholeheartedly embraced the advice of PR and media experts. The
key difference was that, unlike Heath, Thatcher kept her team together
after victory, and was therefore well placed to take advantage of the post-
Falklands euphoria that sealed her electoral fortunes in the early 1980s.
Since Mandelson's 'red rose' revolution the two parties have again been
evenly matched in the fight for good PR. Each has proved aggressive in
its battle with broadcasters to secure 'fair' coverage, helped no doubt by
recurring uncertainties surrounding the legal and financial status of both
the BBC and the independent television companies. In some respects
relations between broadcasters and politicians have become increasingly
adversarial with the rise of the political 'marketeers'. In the 1960s high-
minded broadcasters might seek to set the news agenda, but their coverage
of election 'incidents' generally presented politicians in a favourable light
(except when live feeds precluded such generous editing). By the late 1980s
'incidents' were the life-blood of television news, and politicians could
be certain that any slip, any awkward fracas with voters, would receive
maximum news exposure—aided, of course, by technical developments
such as ENG (electronic news gathering) and the later spread of digital
recording equipment.

At one stage, after the rumbustious elections of the mid-1960s, it seemed
possible that the parties would effectively isolate their leaders from any
further contact with the 'dangerous' voting public. The public had been
banned from studio programming since the fracas on Granada's *The Last
Debate* in 1959, and now it seemed that the traditional public meeting
was to be similarly purged. In 1970 both parties placed great emphasis on
vetting audiences and controlling every aspect of televised political events.
Campaign organizers sought to minimize meaningful interaction between
party leaders and voters in order to control the images that television would
relay to the all-important *viewing* public. However, there were always
limits to this strategy. Sometimes, the public would break through the
protective shield, either by crashing a media event or at the direct behest
of broadcasters through phone-ins and audience participation programmes,
which flourished again from 1974. And sometimes, as in 1992 and 2005,
politicians anxious to re-establish their connection with voters would seek
out the public as a conscious strategy to gain political legitimacy. John
Major's famous soapbox exploits in the second half of the 1992 election

fed off television's power to convey symbolic images of a leader 'facing the music' at the centre of seething crowds. But, as we shall see, it also gave Major the chance to associate his opponents with public disorder. Nonetheless, it demonstrated that face-to-face interaction continued to be perceived as a source of political 'legitimacy'—and hence that politicians who preferred to seal themselves inside the Westminster/media bubble courted potential disaster at the polls.

Politicians continue both to fear and to crave televised interaction with the voting public in almost equal measure; indeed, one might argue that it is no accident that the rise of the phone-in, the walkabout, and the studio grilling coincided with the precipitate decline of the traditional election meeting. Of course politicians in full control of their destiny, such as Margaret Thatcher in 1987, can afford largely to avoid media-engineered interactions with the voting public (though not without incurring considerable criticism), but for politicians in difficulty, such as Major in 1992 or Blair in 2005, the political legitimacy to be derived from high-risk interactions with the public often proves impossible to resist. In this and the following chapter, we will therefore explore not only how television has undermined traditional forms of face-to-face interaction in politics, but also how it has opened up new opportunities for popular involvement. Far from creating a virtual election, remote from real voters—what post-modernists would call a mere 'simulacrum' of democracy—the broadcasting revolution since the 1960s has generated new methods for demanding public accountability of politicians, methods that in some respects are more powerful than those of the old hustings and election meeting because they reach a much broader audience, and are less easily monopolized by a boorish male minority.[1]

The rise and fall of the TV election

But before exploring the shifting relationship between politicians, broadcasters, and the public in greater detail, we must begin by identifying the key landmarks in the history of political broadcasting in Britain since the late 1950s. As we have seen, there are strong grounds for arguing that 1964, not 1959, was Britain's first true television election. In 1959 television cameras had effectively filmed a fairly traditional British election campaign dominated by party leaders touring the country to make set-piece speeches at evening meetings; the only major innovation, apart from Labour's slick political broadcasts, had been the introduction of more formal morning press conferences as a key means of feeding copy to both the press and the new broadcast news programmes. Five years later, the election was effectively fought on and through television—with Labour's new, young leader, Harold Wilson, emerging as master of the medium. Learning lessons from the image-makers around President Kennedy even more than from Macmillan's skilful make-over since 1957, Wilson was presented as a 'man of the people' from humble origins who retained his simple tastes: HP sauce, Huddersfield Town, and his trade-mark pipe (though it was said that the former Oxford don often preferred to smoke cigars in private). The contrast with the patrician style of Macmillan, and even more that of Home, could not have been greater, and television was now the vital means of conveying this message. By 1964 the medium allowed politicians to speak directly to almost the entire population—television ownership had risen from 70 to 90 per cent since 1959, and the proportion of the population claiming to have seen at least one party election broadcast was up from 57 to 74 per cent (with electors seeing on average 4.5 party broadcasts compared with 3.1 in 1959). There was also more politics actually on television in 1964. The main evening news bulletins gave much fuller coverage to the election than in 1959—so that, in turn, two-thirds of voters claimed to have watched election news at least three or four times per week in 1964, compared with only one in three voters in 1959. For the first time viewers watched live feeds from the leaders' evening election meetings, and saw the party leaders being interrogated in the studio (notably by Robin Day and others putting viewers' questions in *Election Forum*). They also received an early introduction to the game of manufacturing 'pseudo-events' specifically for the television cameras. Keen to match the positive images that Home would derive from his final cabinet meeting, Labour arranged for veteran party leader Clement Attlee, now 80, to visit Harold Wilson to wish him well for the campaign. As Benn noted at the time, the aim was simple: to make sure that 'we should be in the news too'.[2]

In 1964, after the improvised scheduling of the 1959 election, politicians laid down strict rules governing the basis on which they would cooperate with television broadcasters. The parties asserted their right to control who appeared on television, what they would talk about, and how programmes would be organized—including a complete ban on audience participation and the right to veto the involvement of neutral experts. Hence the stilted format of *Election Forum*, where viewers' questions had to be posed second-hand by professional journalists, and the programmes had to be made before Parliament had been dissolved (and hence before the campaign proper had really begun). Little had changed in 1966, but there were signs that broadcasters were beginning to resist these stifling constraints on their role. Steeped in their organization's strong public service ethos, producers at the BBC sought to push politicians to deal with major issues that they would rather ignore for fear of exposing internal party differences. In 1966 this meant trade union power and Europe—or rather attitudes to the European community. In 1970, when for the first time the BBC merged its news and current affairs departments for the duration of the campaign, it meant immigration and the challenge of 'Powellism'. As an Opposition backbencher Enoch Powell had no official status, but it was estimated that his skilfully managed interventions captured 20 per cent of television news coverage during the 1970 campaign. Broadcasters also sought to encourage party debate by increasing the number of head-to-head confrontations between leading politicians. In 1964 there had been only one such tele-vised exchange, in 1966 *Campaign Report* alone carried twenty-two studio confrontations. A new form of election theatre had been born, though again not without considerable resistance from the party machines. In 1970, when Richard Crossman suggested staging a head-to-head discussion of social security, the Prime Minister told him curtly that 'it has been arranged between the parties that confrontations are undesirable'. Crossman got his way, but he was disturbed by the party organizers' determination to avoid substantive discussion wherever possible. With some prescience he wrote, 'running the campaign on these lines is terribly dangerous. We attract frivolous, superficial support which a shock could blow away.' It did; Heath was swept to power, and Crossman never held office again.[3]

The 1970 election was also notable for the first colour television cover-age, though at this stage few homes possessed colour TV sets (barely 1 per cent), and many television studios continued to work in black and white—denying the Conservatives the full benefit of their new television-friendly, professionally designed blue sets. This was also the election at which politics took a back-seat to football on British television, at least until England was knocked out of the World Cup by West Germany on the Sunday before polling. Party election broadcasts were shortened to ten minutes, and ran later in the evening, with the result that average audiences declined (though more than nine out of ten electors still claimed to have seen at least one party broadcast). By contrast the February 1974 election saw what many considered to be saturation coverage. In the fevered atmosphere of Heath's 'crisis' election, broadcasters extended their lunchtime and evening news bulletins, and produced a mass of special programmes devoted to discussion and analysis. Jeremy Thorpe's Liberals fought a well-planned media campaign, including an expensive live TV link between London and North Devon (where Thorpe was defending a precarious and sprawling marginal seat that required old-fashioned hands-on campaigning). The two General Elections of 1974 also witnessed both the return of live studio audiences and a series of innovative phone-in programmes that brought politicians into direct contact with the public. However, polls suggested that despite these innovations, the public was less than happy with the new, more intensive television coverage. In 1970 only 17 per cent of viewers felt that 'far too much time' had been devoted to the election, but in February 1974 that rose to over 30 per cent, amidst widespread criticism that the broadcasters had succumbed to election 'overkill'. Television companies cut back their coverage for the October election, and kept it at a reduced level in 1979, but it again increased markedly during the 1980s, partly thanks to the 'ENG' (electronic news gathering) revolution which increased the scope for live feeds from the campaign trail. By the 1987 election over 70 per cent of electors were complaining that there was too much politics on television, and in 1992 this reached a remarkable 78 per cent.[4]

Ironically, one of the factors driving the growth of television election coverage in the 1980s also worked to weaken its impact—namely the proliferation of channels. Britain's third channel, BBC2, had been created as early as 1964, Channel 4, the second commercial station, was launched in 1982, and Channel Five in 1997. In 1983, for the first time, party election broadcasts ceased to be shown simultaneously on all channels, making it easier for voters to opt out of the parties' television wars. Thereafter the growth first of video (VCR) ownership, and then of specialist programming on satellite and cable channels, made opting out increasingly easy (digital 'catch-up TV' is just the latest nightmare from the party strategist's perspective). As early as 1974 opinion polls had found that 37 per cent of British voters claimed not to have been following the campaign at all one week before polling (in France the comparable figure was 9 per cent). The explosion of choice brought by technological advance simply made it easier to escape politics without having to switch off altogether. And so, ironically, as ENG, breakfast television, and finally the launch of 24-hour news channels in the late 1980s, brought media campaigning to saturation point, large swathes of the public voted with their remote controls by choosing to miss the whole damn thing. In 1987 the BBC's flagship *Nine O'Clock News*, which had been doubled in length for the election, recorded a 25 per cent fall in viewers. By 1997, when the *Nine O'Clock News* lost one-third of its viewers during the campaign, 20 per cent of households had the option of turning to multi-channel, satellite, or cable television. Since the audience for these channels doubled (to almost one-quarter of total audience share) on evenings when the main terrestrial channels offered blanket election coverage, one must assume that large numbers chose to exercise this option. As various commentators have noted, politics was entering a 'post-modern' age, where terrestrial television channels operating under a strong public service ethos were losing market share to less tightly regulated broadcasters for whom political news was a lower priority—not least because their audience was strongly biased towards those escaping the election. Add to this signs that the British press, though still distinctly partisan by international standards, was becoming less strictly aligned than at any stage since the Second World War, and one can see that the party gurus of modern, 'strategic communications' worked so hard at news management and public relations precisely because the context within which they were working was so difficult—and sure to become more so as multi-media entertainment proliferated. By 2005, terrestrial television channels were still responsible for approximately two-thirds of all viewing in British homes (16 hours per week), but the two main terrestrial channels, BBC1 and ITV1, which could still claim 85 per cent of all viewing when Channel 4 was launched in 1983 had seen their market share shrink to just 40 per cent. The golden age of top-down media politics had clearly passed.[5]

Politicians and broadcasters in the 'golden age'

The General Elections of 1964 and 1966 generated considerable controversy over the manner in which television chose to present the party leaders to the public. As we have seen, these elections led to widespread concern that television was acting as an *agent provocateur* in British public politics. In both elections the main party leaders continued to hold a large number of open public meetings, much as they had done for more than half a century. Thanks to the power of the British press such meetings had always been organized with a national as well as local audience in mind, but the introduction of television cameras provided a very different kind of national media coverage. Unless something extraordinary happened, national newspapers generally favoured short, simple reports that concentrated on the most newsworthy aspects of a politician's speech, not on the more 'theatrical' aspects of meetings such as badinage between heckler and speaker. Television was different—not only did it thrive on the visual and theatrical, but it also thrived on immediacy. In 1964 both television channels experimented with live feeds from the party leaders' meetings, and put considerable effort into ensuring that film from recorded meetings would be available for same-day broadcasts. With both Wilson and Home addressing open mass meetings it was perhaps inevitable that opponents would seize on the opportunity to cause maximum embarrassment and disruption for the cameras. Sir Alec Douglas-Home faced a particular dilemma. Anxious to defuse criticism that his twelve years in the House of Lords had rendered him unfit to lead a mass democracy, Home embarked on a widely publicized programme of so-called 'meet the people' meetings. He was, by all accounts, not a natural 'man of the people', and from the outset he struggled to come to terms with irreverent heckling. A week before polling day, television viewers watched Sir Alec all but overwhelmed by raucous opposition from sections of the crowd at an unticketed meeting for 7,000 at Birmingham Rag Market. Wilson also faced considerable organized opposition, particularly when speaking out against racist opposition to immigration, but most agreed that he handled such situations with much greater skill than his aristocratic opponent. Indeed in 1966 Wilson was accused of deliberately provoking hecklers, conscious that his sharp ripostes from the platform came across well on television. Wilson was a consummate platform performer who quickly learnt to adapt his art to the television age. In 1964 he exploited the innovation of live transmission by preparing short, pithy statements which he would slip into his speech as soon as he saw the cameras' 'on air' lights illuminated. He was also quick to realize that television's unidirectional microphones picked up little of the hustle and bustle of a traditional public meeting. This meant that viewers would be none the wiser if a politician simply chose to ignore opposition from the floor, but that witty ripostes from the platform would fall flat unless the original interjection was first repeated for the benefit of viewers at home. Wilson mastered this technique to brilliant effect in the 1960s, perhaps most famously at a 'rematch' Birmingham Rag Market meeting in 1966 when ITN ran a five-minute, uninterrupted live feed of Wilson dominating a hostile crowd of 10,000.[6]

Compared with Wilson, there is little doubt that Home floundered before the television cameras in 1964, especially in live transmissions where broadcasters could do little to massage the images relayed to the public (it was widely believed that producers deleted unflattering scenes from pre-recorded footage to ensure that politicians were shown 'at their best'). Less clear is, firstly, whether Labour played any part in orchestrating this disruption, and, secondly, whether the Conservatives sought to play up televised disruption as a means of discrediting the rejuvenated Labour opposition. Home and Quintin Hogg, the chief Conservative victims of political disruption, were adamant that the whole thing was a Labour plot. Lord Blakenham, the Conservative party chairman, was a little more circumspect, laying the blame not on Labour itself, but on left-wing youths connected to the Campaign for Nuclear Disarmament (CND) and Labour's 'Young Socialists'. Wilson, in turn, denounced the disorder as the work of 'a sub-stratum of hooligans with loyalty to neither side', while Frank Byers, the Liberals' campaign manager, tried to show that he was 'with it' by claiming 'this sort of chant gives the impression you are at a Beatle session rather than a political meeting'. Perhaps predictably Home and other Conservative party leaders seized on the wild scenes from Birmingham and elsewhere to conjure up parallels with the excesses of Nazi Germany, and to suggest that disruption revealed that Labour was still unfit to govern. It seems unlikely that they were doing more than making the best of a bad situation, but this was not the view of two American researchers studying the marginal west London constituency of Baron's Court. They were adamant that local Conservative organizers had calculated 'that a few rowdies displaying poor campaign manners might help to prevent a shift of some middle-class voters to Labour, especially if there was good television coverage of their behaviour'. Accordingly, when Home came to address a large outdoor rally at Hammersmith Broadway they cleverly transposed the platform at the last minute so that Home faced a crowd of sympathetic supporters, while hecklers, who had been waiting all day to have a go at the Conservative leader, were trapped at the back of the stage, powerless to put him off, but in full view of the television cameras. The same researchers also insisted that Labour activists were 'somewhat distressed' when they learnt that Quintin Hogg had faced serious disruption at Hammersmith Town Hall a few days earlier.[7]

Commentators were probably right to suspect that the presence of television cameras encouraged those of an exhibitionist temperament to show off in public. Indeed, there was evidence that an American television company actually planted its own hecklers at one of George Brown's meetings to make sure it captured some 'typically' lively British election scenes (in 2005 BBC3 producers were accused of repeating the trick at two meetings addressed by the Conservative leader Michael Howard—their rather unconvincing defence was that they were making a programme about the history of heckling). But it was not just television that raised the temperature of British politics in the 1960s. No less important was the re-emergence of youth as an important and volatile presence in public politics. Almost everyone agreed that the organized bands of protesters stamping their feet and chanting at political meetings in 1964 consisted almost entirely of youths, most of whom would have been non-voters (it was Labour that finally lowered the voting age from 21 to 18 in 1969). In the 1950s there had been frequent complaints that young people had abandoned political meetings as boring and irrelevant—now they were back with a vengeance. In 1964 it was Home's support for the Polaris missile programme that angered radicalized youth, but later in the decade, as the student protest movement gathered momentum, Labour became equally anxious about the re-emergence of 'direct action'.[8]

Although research suggested that Home's popularity suffered little, if at all, from television's intrusive eye, this was not the lesson that Conservative party strategists drew from 1964. On the contrary, the myth developed that the publicity given to disorderly meetings, particularly the Birmingham Rag Market meeting, had cost Conservatives the election. In 1966, party organizers were determined to ensure that Edward Heath, their new leader, would address only carefully vetted, all-ticket gatherings. Moreover, when they realized that Heath's performances were rather lacklustre in this sterile environment, they decided to liven things up, not by allowing the public free access, but by planting friendly 'hecklers' in the crowd to keep Heath on his toes (Labour had apparently done something similar in 1964 to make sure Wilson got to use his best put-downs). The same attitude prevailed in 1970. Douglas Hurd, then Heath's young private secretary, recalled how 'we novices were often regaled by the veterans with tales of the damage which this [the 1964 Birmingham meeting] had done'. Conservative organizers were determined that Heath must be kept 'at arms length from violence at all times', even if this again meant all-ticket meetings and a ban on questions from the floor. By contrast, in 1966 Wilson had still been happy to mix it with real hecklers—despite pleas from party strategists that he should stay out of the fray to capitalize on his Prime Ministerial status. Richard Crossman recalls finding Wilson 'enormously elated' the morning after his Birmingham Rag Market meeting despite having been confronted by '10,000 people booing and jostling', and despite the slight injury to his wife Mary caused by a missile from the crowd (Wilson apparently hoped to exploit the incident as a way of highlighting that he *had* a wife, unlike Heath).[9]

By this time Richard Crossman was already deeply anxious about the impact television was having on British politics, complaining that 'bitty TV treatment' was creating the sense of a 'frivolous election'. According to Crossman, television 'concentrates so on personalities and leadership and gimmicks that the viewer gets a picture of bickering politicians and no real understanding of the issues involved'. But others felt that the real problem was not that television ignored issues, but that it always wanted *new* issues—encouraging frenetic 'issue-a-day' politics which paid too little attention to the parties' campaign agendas. In the years following his dismissal from Heath's shadow cabinet, Enoch Powell proved particularly adept at exploiting the media's hunger for controversy and a newsworthy story. The party front benches sought to ignore both Powell and the race issue that had made him so controversial after his 1968 'rivers of blood' speech at Birmingham. When Tony Benn broke ranks by delivering an emotive speech linking Powell to 'the flag that fluttered over Belsen', Wilson was furious. Benn's sin was to have brought 'the racial question' centre stage, rather than stick to his ministerial brief. But when Benn followed his leader's advice the results were predictable. Billed to speak on 'Industrial Policy' at Uxbridge, Benn found that the television crews simply packed up and left once it became clear that he would be discussing the intricacies of new technology rather than the infamy of Enoch Powell. Reflecting on the reaction to his original attack on Powell, Benn concluded 'The trouble is that the mass media will not report anything you say other than the sensational or trivial, or personal things. To this extent the media do dictate the nature of the campaign.'[10]

From the politician's perspective the mass media were simultaneously trivializing politics and seeking to impose their own agenda. Perhaps inevitably, broadcasters saw things rather differently. Television producers, particularly those at the BBC, believed they were asserting their independence by encouraging controversy and by refusing to allow the front benches to bury awkward issues such as Europe and the unions (1966) or immigration and race (1970). In short, by making professional judgements about 'newsworthiness' they were seeking to play a more active, agenda-setting role in British elections. All three main parties naturally resented this perceived usurpation of their role, but it was Labour that felt most threatened and therefore reacted most strongly. After his comfortable victory in 1966, Wilson famously refused an interview with the BBC amidst acrimonious allegations of high-handedness and bias. Labour leaders had come to rely on the broadcast media as their best chance to bypass a largely hostile press, and they deeply resented broadcasters' efforts to supplement straight news reporting with analysis, discussion, and comment (notably in the late-night BBC programme *Campaign Report*). Labour wanted its message to reach the electorate unmediated, and the new trends in broadcast journalism clearly threatened that goal. For a while it seemed possible that Labour would turn to the law to impose tighter restrictions on the broadcasters, but this threat never materialized—instead the parties largely adapted their campaigning tactics to the new order.[11]

In 1970 the Conservatives made a concerted effort to manipulate the 'issue-a-day' mentality of the news broadcasters through better co-ordination of press conferences and evening speeches. However, they found broadcasters less than pliant —issues trailed by the party were simply ignored unless they matched the journalists' criteria for 'newsworthiness'. Apart from Powell's antics, the media paid little heed to anything but economic issues in 1970, and by default Heath was forced to fight his battle on this terrain. Other campaign innovations worked more smoothly in 1970. Labour organizers were now as keen as their opponents to protect political leaders from awkward public confrontations. The late 1960s had seen a series of violent demonstrations against Labour ministers at British universities, with Rhodesia and support for US policy in Vietnam particularly emotive issues. Largely in response, Wilson and his inner Cabinet decided to drop traditional, set-piece meetings that might prove easy targets for student protest, in favour of last-minute 'walkabouts' and visits to meet party workers in the field; events intended to create warm news images for the viewing public. This also suited Wilson's low-key, 'steady as she goes' approach to the election. On the other hand, Conservative hopes depended on rekindling the sense of crisis that had dogged Labour for much of its time in office, and so Heath embraced more resolutely political tactics. His media-centred campaign was built around two formal platforms that allowed him to attack the Wilson legacy: the morning press conference and the evening political meeting. The meeting, in particular, was given a thorough make-over for the television age in 1970. Geoffrey Tucker, Conservative director of publicity since 1968, had repeatedly driven home the message that 'the election will be won or lost on television', and he was therefore determined that Heath's meetings would be as telegenic as possible. The watchword was professionalism. With help from Roger Boaden, Tucker ensured that Heath's campaign tours were planned with the same meticulousness as the party's election broadcasts. Venues were checked out in advance to ensure that cameras would be cited to show Heath at his best. A special mobile set was designed so that Heath would always be seen against a high-quality blue backdrop. Tight restrictions on admission and questions were imposed to ensure that the party retained total control of the images that would appear on voters' televisions, although these were in fact relaxed when the anticipated trouble from left-wing students and miscellaneous far-Right groups failed to materialize.[12]

Ironically, in a closely fought election both sides gradually became convinced that their opponents' tactics were gaining the best exposure on television. Heath's aides were impressed by Wilson's informal, 'folksy' campaign style, feeling that it made their own leader seem remote as he jetted about the country in his hired DART plane to deliver 'solitary set speeches'. Their response was to build impromptu walkabouts and photo-ops into Heath's schedule, usually squeezed in before his evening meeting. Predictably these hastily arranged events often went badly wrong. At Norwich it was half-day closing when Heath tried to go 'walkabout' around the city centre, while at Edinburgh a microphone picked him up telling aides 'I think that's enough for them, don't you?' As Jim Prior, a Cabinet Minister under both Heath and Thatcher, later recalled, organizers were wrong 'constantly to think up these gimmicks for Ted: they always turned sour'. At the same time, Wilson's aides gradually became frustrated at the poor organization and lack of professionalism associated with their leader's impromptu provincial visits and walkabouts. Compared with Heath's slick campaign, theirs seemed ill-planned and chaotic. Worse, they came to feel they were generating 'messy' television, which, as Crossman had warned, conveyed little of political substance to the public. There was not much that Labour could do to improve matters in 1970—time was too short—but at the next election in February 1974 Labour ran a much more tightly organized campaign deploying many of the presentational techniques pioneered by Heath's team in 1970. That said, even in 1974, Labour organizers found many local parties deeply sceptical about prioritizing the needs of television over those of the live audience, with some reluctant to sacrifice good seats just so that cameras could be sited to get the best shot of Wilson in full flow.[13]

The 1970 election again raised questions about television's coverage of political disorder. Many complained that the broadcasters paid undue attention to trouble at Enoch Powell's volatile meetings, just as they paid too much attention to his speeches, but in other respects coverage was rather low-key. With broadcasters keen not to be accused of encouraging violent direct action, viewers saw little of the rough and tumble of the campaign which some Labour figures denounced as the dirtiest since 1931. Despite keeping his movements secret until the last minute, Wilson had fourteen eggs thrown at him during his 'meet the people' tours, and he and his wife were also bombarded with flour and ketchup. It was the first of these egg-throwing incidents that prompted Heath to make his only famous political joke. Pointing out that Wilson had been attacked during an unannounced, last-minute visit he suggested that this raised the disturbing prospect that men and women were walking the streets of Britain, armed with eggs, 'on the off-chance that they'll meet the leader of the Labour Party'.[14]

Overall, the 1970 election marked an important stage in the development of media politics in Britain. Both Wilson and Heath made considerable use of photo-opportunities throughout the campaign, though these were still often poorly conceived and executed. At the same time, Heath and his advisers transformed the leader's meeting into a carefully planned media event, where it was the television audience, not the live audience, that mattered most. Political meetings would never be the same. In 1973, speaking at the Lincoln by-election caused by Dick Taverne's decision to break with Labour, Tony Benn, to his horror, found everything geared around the needs of television. At one meeting, the speakers were even obliged to redo their entrance 'for the benefit of the cameras'—with the audience left in darkness except for the glare of the television lights. Benn complained that 'It was an illustration of just what happens when the media takes over. A by-election belongs to the people not the mass media, and I didn't like it a bit.' Like Powell, Benn was seen as a controversial, and hence 'newsworthy', figure, and so remained squarely in the media spotlight whilst other, more senior, Labour politicians were frequently ignored. Having once portrayed himself as the party's media guru, Benn was now firmly in the traditionalist camp. In 1974 he was horrified by Wilson's new, media-focused campaign style, which seemed to revolve entirely around morning press conferences and glitzy ticket-only meetings. Benn was unimpressed by Wilson's expensive mobile set, his use of make-up artists, and his grand theatrical entrances (made possible by the use of professional PA systems and cut-out microphones). Benn found 'the whole personality cult a bit offensive', and felt sure Wilson was wrong to prioritize polished television visuals over 'meeting the people'. He wrote, 'Wilson is really fooling about on the fringes, seen at press conferences and ticket-only meetings; whereas Heath is on the streets in walkabouts, giving a sort of de Gaulle impression.' Heath held only six major rallies, compared with eleven in 1970, and undertook nineteen walkabouts. His campaign organizers considered most of these to have been 'highly successful', but they did encounter problems managing the media scrum, and on at least one occasion fighting between rival cameramen and photographers caused such a severe crush that the walkabout had to be abandoned. In consequence, Heath played down the walkabout in the final week, convinced that it was generating chaotic television images which detracted from his central message that this was a crisis election called to resolve the question 'Who governs Britain: Parliament or the unions?' Throughout the campaign both sides tried hard to shape media coverage to reflect their campaign priorities. At their political rallies Heath and Wilson both trailed the key passages from their speeches in press releases, in the hope that they would be used by the broadcasters in their evening news bulletins. But Wilson initially found his efforts frustrated by the media's preference for focusing on his trademark jokes, rather than his carefully scripted 'soundbites'. Wilson's aim was to strike a resolutely high-minded, statesmanlike tone in the style of his predecessor Hugh Gaitskell, and to this end he finally resolved to strip everything light or amusing from his speeches so that only the serious message would be left for transmission.[15]

But, whilst broadcasters displayed some scepticism towards Heath's claim that trade union power was the single issue before the electorate in February 1974, this was not so much agenda-setting, as recognizing that Heath's opponents were determined to fight the election on a much broader range of issues. In fact agenda-setting as such was in clear retreat by 1974, perhaps in part because of the furore caused by the BBC's decision in 1971 to air a controversial exposé of the Labour leadership as part of its current affairs series *24 Hours*. Provocatively titled *Yesterday's Men*, the programme was widely viewed as a deliberate attempt to undermine the folksy, down-to-earth image of Wilson and his fellow Labour ex-ministers by presenting them as driven above all by money and personal ambition. Wilson apparently never forgave David Dimbleby for his part in the programme, and he in turn was convinced that the fall-out from *Yesterday's Men* led to a 'hideous softening' in the way television presented politicians for years to come.[16]

The October 1974 election, which Wilson hoped would secure him a working majority after the inconclusive result in February, saw party leaders again experimenting with new means of utilizing the power of television. The Liberals, buoyed by their strong showing in the February election, adopted a high-profile, glitzy campaign intended to portray their leader, Jeremy Thorpe, as an equal to Wilson and Heath on the national stage. Thorpe was seen hurtling around the country by helicopter, train, and even hovercraft, as he visited the dozens of constituencies suddenly labelled Liberal target seats. But many felt Thorpe had overreached himself. Hoping to use television to maintain the bandwagon momentum of the February campaign, Thorpe instead faced stinging criticism that his 'flying circus' made him look lightweight and marginal compared with the main parties' two 'big beasts'. Wilson stuck pretty faithfully to his February formula—though he now had two travelling sets (making it easier to ensure that each venue was configured for optimum television impact in advance). He also concentrated more narrowly on the marginal Conservative seats that Labour had to capture to form a majority government. Heath, by contrast, sought to introduce a series of bold campaign innovations. He further reduced the role of major set-piece rallies (addressing only four in three weeks), cut back drastically on walkabouts and 'whistle stops', and placed renewed emphasis on small-scale, informal meetings and daytime 'Question and Answer' sessions with special interest groups such as ratepayers, farmers, industrial workers, and young voters. Heath was keen to strike a less confrontational tone than in February in order to woo floating Liberal voters, and it was hoped that these meetings would convey an atmosphere of rational debate, rather than strident assertion. At most meetings he sat in a swivel chair and took off his jacket—much as John Major would do, with equally comic results, during the 1992 election. Like Major's 'Val Doonican' sessions, most commentators agreed that Heath's innovation lacked 'newsworthiness' and made for very dull television. The discussions often degenerated into technical question and answer sessions that left viewers cold, and frequently bemused. Worse, the sessions lacked credibility because they relied on invited audiences, under-lining the artificiality of the whole exercise, and fuelling suspicion that, far from addressing ordinary members of the public in open debate, Heath was fielding soft questions from party supporters. Roger Boaden, Heath's election tour organizer, acknowledged that mistakes had been made. At Aldridge-Brownhills, in the West Midlands, he felt that the audience 'was too obviously Party supporters' leading the press to become 'very cynical' early in the campaign. The next two meetings, with Reading ratepayers and Tottenham Young Conservatives, merely compounded the problem, so that few took any interest when Heath later conducted genuinely tough question and answer sessions at venues such as Old Trafford industrial estate.[17]

In the aftermath of defeat, Boaden acknowledged that most of the innovations in October had been 'ill-considered'. However, it is wrong to suggest that they were simply dropped once Margaret Thatcher replaced Heath as Conservative leader in February 1975. On the contrary, the hastily improvised experiments of October 1974 were rethought and refined over the following five years. 'Informality', 'the daily picture', 'the daily story', and 'special interest activities'—ideas that had been central to the October campaign—would become integral to the Conservatives' media revolution in the late 1970s. As in 1970 (but *not* 1974), the Conservatives spent years meticulously planning their campaign strategy after the election of Thatcher as party leader, drawing on the resources of a high-calibre team of media professionals in the process. Gordon Reece, Thatcher's publicity director and a former television producer, worked tirelessly to perfect the photo-opportunity (known internally as 'special interest activity') as a controlled means of generating warm images of the party leader among 'ordinary voters'. Compared with the anarchy of the typical walkabout, these carefully choreographed media events generated strong images that worked equally well on television and in the press. The photo-opportunity itself was not new of course—it had been a staple of news management for almost half a century (one thinks of Chamberlain waving his piece of paper at Heston Airport or Churchill defiantly touring bomb-sites in 1940), but it nonetheless entered a new era with the Conservative campaign of 1979. Each day's activity was elaborately planned. Organizers gave careful consideration both to timing and to 'visuals', and they produced detailed briefing notes to ensure that Thatcher, and everyone else, always knew exactly what was happening, and why. These almost regal visits to factories, shops, and hospitals became a hallmark of British electioneering over the next decade, but it was perhaps Thatcher's visit to a Suffolk farm early in the 1979 campaign that generated the most enduring images when photographers spent nearly fifteen minutes filming the Conservative leader awkwardly clutching a new-born calf. By all accounts campaign managers, and the pliant farmer, were much relieved when it became clear that the calf had suffered no ill-effects from its drawn-out media ordeal. Interestingly, whilst campaign files make it clear that the farm had been chosen to generate 'warm' images of Thatcher seen alongside farm animals (it was one of the few farms with livestock in the area), the iconic image of Thatcher and calf appears *not* to have been pre-planned. The genius had been to put Thatcher into a situation where the media could shape its own vision of the perfect image (Fig. 17).[18]

Conservative interest in exploiting the potential of the photo-opportunity appears in part to have been driven by strategists' assessment of how best to break down what one internal memo termed the ' "sexist" objections' to Thatcher as the first female party leader. Believing that criticisms of Thatcher's voice, accent, hair-do, dress, and manner were rooted in sex prejudice, they reasoned that rather than challenge such thinking, their best option would be to 'allow for it by emphasising Mrs Thatcher's femininity' (although they also spent a good deal of time trying to modify these same facets of her persona—most famously by encouraging her to lower the pitch of her voice). So was born the project to reinvent Thatcher, the career politician married to a millionaire businessman, as the housewife superstar determined to bring the principles of good housekeeping to bear on the nation's finances. A key facet of this strategy was the determination to maximize the media exposure Thatcher received on location, meeting people going about their daily lives, and displaying her 'natural warmth and strength, which comes across so powerfully'. Hence during the 1979 election, Thatcher was filmed wielding a new broom while visiting a Kleeneze factory in Bristol, sewing pockets while visiting a Leicester textile factory,

Fig. 17. Margaret Thatcher and Suffolk calf, 1979 (PA photos)

and shopping for groceries in Halifax. As one internal party memo put it, 'The television audience needs to see a relaxed woman in "soft" situations, recognisable surroundings—supermarkets, factories, streets—out in the country.' However, in late 1978 Reece became increasingly concerned that this strategy was being undermined by the prominence broadcasters were now giving to Thatcher's abrasive contributions at Prime Minister's Question Time. Reece was particularly concerned by the use of recorded excerpts in television news bulletins, arguing that these needed to be countered 'by encouraging Mrs Thatcher to be seen in the country as was done very successfully between 1975 and the first half of 1978'. For the most part Thatcher was happy to oblige both the party strategists and the media, as one Suffolk calf would discover, but she did put her foot down when it was suggested that to maximize the flow of 'soft' news images during the campaign she should spend more time away from London, and hence away from the morning press conference. She was not prepared to dilute her dominance of the 'hard' politics of the Westminster bubble, however much she might sympathize with the strategy of courting 'soft' news images. In

1983 and 1987, now very much her own woman, she insisted that her campaign itinerary should never take her away from London overnight.[19]

But the traditional walkabout was far from dead in 1979. Thatcher's team had spent almost eighteen months perfecting meticulous itineraries that would build strong photo-opportunities into their leader's town centre walkabouts. They also tried to ensure that pictures would be available in time for the early evening news bulletins, 'soft' news slots watched by a higher proportion of floating voters than the more prestigious main evening bulletins. One cardinal rule for the campaign (one personally endorsed by Thatcher) was that the 'first engagement [must] be geared especially to publicity'.[20] James Callaghan, Labour leader since 1976, tried to imitate these tactics, but as with Heath in 1970, lack of planning meant that things sometimes went disastrously wrong—notably when a walkabout outside a supermarket generated pictures of 'hapless and protesting shoppers being crushed by cameramen and journalists'. Sometimes Thatcher too was shown surrounded not by real members of the public, but by her travelling media circus of journalists, sound-men, cameramen, and the like. As the campaign progressed, ITN, in particular, grew weary of stage-managed media events and began to make greater use of long shots to expose their intrinsic artificiality, but their resistance did little to stem the tide.[21]

The media circus was not the only barrier between politicians and public in 1979. On 30 March, Airey Neave, the Conservatives' front-bench spokesmen on Irish Affairs, was murdered by a car bomb within the precincts of the Houses of Parliament. Security was immediately increased for all major public figures, and this inevitably carried over into the General Election which began in earnest a week later. There was now a massive police presence around the party leaders whenever they appeared in public, and the leaders' itineraries were kept secret until the last minute, greatly reducing the scope for meaningful exchanges with the public. On one impromptu morning walkabout in his Barnsley constituency, Roy Mason, the Labour Minister for Northern Ireland, found the streets so deserted that he only managed to talk to his police escort. The police pressed hard for all public meetings to be ticket only, though both Callaghan and David Steel, the Liberal leader, still held a number that were open to all comers, albeit with tight security at the doors. But Thatcher's five big set-piece rallies were all ticket-only. The contrast with earlier elections was striking. In 1966 Harold Wilson had toured the country as Prime Minister with just two detectives in tow. Even more remarkably, in 1970 Edward Heath had been wholly unprotected when he tried to join the election night celebrations at Conservative Central Office—with the result that an embittered bystander took advantage of the mêlée in Smith Square to stub a cigarette out on his neck. In 1979 Callaghan's open meetings witnessed a good deal of persistent, ill-tempered heckling by protesters demanding 'Troops Out' of Ireland, but it was noticeable that the broadcasters again chose to play this down in their coverage; either editing it out completely, or else showing Callaghan getting the upper hand over his unruly critics. Whether their aim was to ensure that the two leaders received broadly comparable coverage, or simply to avoid giving publicity to Irish republicanism in the wake of Neave's murder, is unclear.[22]

In 1979 Thatcher and Callaghan had been well-matched rivals—with her highly polished media campaign largely cancelled out by his natural gifts as an avuncular television personality and consummate platform performer (although it was already clear that Labour had gone backwards in media terms since Wilson's retirement). But Labour's media failings were obvious at the next election, in 1983. Thatcher was still a divisive political figure, but she went into the campaign buoyed by the Falklands factor, which gave her leadership a new status even amongst her fiercest critics. By contrast, the Labour party had suffered years of division since 1979, including the defection of many leading right-wing figures to form the Social Democratic Party—now fighting in tandem with David Steel's Liberal Party as the 'SDP/Liberal Alliance'. From the outset Labour fought a disorganized campaign which appeared almost wilfully to ignore the needs of the mass media. Michael Foot, the party's leader since 1980 and a one-time firebrand of the Labour Left, seemed like a figure from a lost age. Twelve years older than Thatcher, Foot was one of the last great platform orators in British politics, having moulded his style very much in the image of his great political hero Nye Bevan. In the 1950s Foot had been something of a TV celebrity, thanks mainly to his regular appearances on TV panel programmes such as ITV's *Free Speech*, but by the 1980s he was widely seen as a televisual disaster—unkempt, fidgety, and above all, unable to deliver the punchy political sound bite required in an age of media-led politics. Thatcher, by contrast, continued to pay close attention to questions of presentation. Unlike Heath in 1970, once in power she retained her carefully assembled team of media and publicity professionals and continued to listen to their advice about managing the mass media. In 1983 she again concentrated mainly on morning press conferences and carefully planned photo-opportunities, giving only six set-piece speeches, each an all-ticket affair carefully honed to meet the needs of television broadcasters. Thatcher's photo-opportunities and walkabouts were held at short notice to minimize disruption, mostly in Conservative heartlands where party organizers could rely on enthusiastic crowds and few (if any) vocal opponents. With Labour locked in a desperate battle to avoid being pushed into third place by the SDP/Liberal Alliance, there was no need to pull out all the stops; why not take the message to what Thatcher termed 'our own people', and in the process ensure that television would receive only warm, up-beat images of the Conservative campaign? In fact, as in 1979, such photo-opportunities generally offered only the most minimal interaction with real voters, but this time the media did little to expose the artifice of the whole business. Many talked darkly of media and politicians being in league to hoodwink the electors, creating a mutually convenient 'virtual' campaign of media events designed for passive consumption by viewers.[23]

Television wars since 1987

In 1983 Foot and his campaign team had, if anything, turned the clock back. His lively platform speeches paid less attention to the demands of television than any Labour leader since Attlee. Contrary to party mythology, this was not primarily Foot's fault—Wilson's media-savvy kitchen cabinet had never been accepted by the Transport House machine, and in both 1979 and 1983 the apparatchiks seized the chance to reclaim campaigning 'for the party'—with disastrous consequences. But Foot's old-style oratorical displays were a problem: broadcasters struggled to find convenient, bite-sized passages for splicing into news bulletins. Worse, on a number of occasions Foot omitted to deliver the specially scripted section that had been trailed to journalists as that evening's main news story. Such charming eccentricity was not to be seen again in British electioneering. In 1987 Thatcher and the Conservatives faced a much more professional Labour opposition, though with a leader, Neil Kinnock, whom many felt still lacked the key skills (such as brevity, gravitas, and hair) deemed necessary in the television age. Like Thatcher, Kinnock held ticket-only rallies of the party faithful to whom he delivered speeches intended not to raise passions in the hall, but to come across well as 'sound bites' in people's living rooms. Though since Kinnock, like Foot, was a man steeped in the traditions of the Bevanite Left, his meetings could still display signs of the party's old revivalist spirit—not least in his exuberant entrances, when Kinnock could be seen 'shaking hands with well-wishers and punching the air' (a habit that would land him in a great deal of trouble five years later). Under the influence of PR experts and pollsters such as Peter Mandelson and Philip Gould, Labour began to match the Conservatives' slick, media-friendly style of campaigning, making full use of the leader's 'photo-opportunity' as a key means of influencing 'soft' news coverage. With security intensified in the wake of the IRA's bomb attack on the British Cabinet at Brighton, the stage-managed photo-shoot gained ground against the more informal walkabout, further reducing the scope for direct interaction between leaders and public. Again broadcasters were accused of being too passive in their transmission of these carefully constructed visuals—sacrificing their critical news values for the quick-fix of a good image. Channel 4, the new independent station, proved more questioning from the outset, and some felt that its jaundiced coverage of the parties' 'media events' had begun to influence the mainstream news bulletins by the later stages of the 1987 campaign. ITN apparently instructed its reporters to concentrate on asking the leaders 'the questions of the moment', because 'the picture-opportunities had been seen enough'.[24]

Indeed, relations between party managers and broadcasters became more openly adversarial from 1987 as the party's PR experts increasingly sought to influence every aspect of television coverage. Inside knowledge of the medium allowed party advisers to mount detailed, technically informed critiques of programme formats and editorial decisions. At the same time, they used their expertise to tighten up party communication strategies. Morning press conferences became more sensational as the parties sought to exploit the 'issue-a-day' mentality of many journalists to hijack television and press news coverage. In the 1970s party press conferences had been held at a civilized hour, usually between 9.30 and 11.30 a.m., but the advent of breakfast television in the early 1980s changed all that—though not immediately. In 1987 the parties clung to tradition, and commentators observed that 'the day's political agenda is now being set by breakfast television before a single press conference is held'. They also wryly noted how difficult it was to get old-guard politicians such as Roy Jenkins to rise at dawn for television appearances. But everything had changed by 1992, when the Liberal Democrats kicked things off at 7.15 a.m. and the last conference was over just after 9 a.m. Besides helping the parties to restore control over the news agenda, this early start also meant that party leaders could be out on the streets (or rather in the hospitals, schools, and factories) in time to get strong positive footage onto the 'soft' lunchtime news bulletins. It was a game that all sides played—though many of the most memorable coups were engineered by Labour in this period. In 1987 Labour ran the story of Mark Burgess, a young hole-in-the-heart patient who had had potentially life-saving treatment postponed because of health service shortages. The news impact of this well-planned exposé almost certainly encouraged Labour to venture further down this road in 1992—with much less happy consequences. This time Labour used an emotive party election broadcast, reinforced by its morning press conference, to tell the story of two girls suffering from a painful ear condition: one is treated quickly because her parents can afford to go private, while the other, called 'Mandy', is doomed to long months of pain because of NHS waiting lists. This time Labour lost control of its story—the media began a frenzied search for the real 'Mandy'—and so the 'war of Jennifer's ear' began. The broadcast itself had used the docudrama format, with all parts played by actors, but the media spotlight quickly fell on the case of Jennifer Bennett when it emerged that her father had briefed Labour about her plight, while her Conservative grandfather had in turned tipped off Conservative Central Office. From there things got very messy and the issue of NHS waiting lists took a back-seat to squabbles over campaign ethics and political 'whodunnits' concerning who had named Jennifer. The story ran for days, but not because Labour, or even the Conservative Party, was keen that it should; rather the print and broadcast media made the running, as though wreaking revenge on the parties for their aggressive attempts at news management. There was also evidence that broadcasters were increasingly willing to retaliate with media coups of their own. In 1987 Anne Diamond had 'ambushed' Denis Healey on breakfast television with persistent questions about his wife's private hip operation (the *Sun*'s headline story that day). By 1992 no news editor would have considered ignoring the furore over 'Jennifer's ear' or censoring scenes of John Major waylaid by hostile crowds as he took to his 'soapbox'. The gloves were off on all sides.[25]

British broadcasters felt politically vulnerable in the late 1980s, with ITV, and especially ITN, worried about the looming Broadcasting Act, and the BBC's licence fee apparently under near-constant review. Many commentators argued that anxieties about charter renewal encouraged broadcasting executives to favour low-key, essentially passive, election coverage, so as to avoid alienating the politicians who would ultimately decide their fate. However, this argument is too simplistic. For one thing, as we have seen, the retreat from agenda-setting had occurred much earlier. For another, as controversies such as Edna Healey's hip and Jennifer's ear demonstrated, a strong combative streak was beginning to run through broadcasters' election coverage by the late 1980s. The golden era of the 'pseudo-event' had already passed. When Thatcher attended the economic summit in Venice during the 1987 election, television news editors treated it for what it was—a well-crafted election PR exercise, not a neutral foreign policy story. Not only was the summit itself given less coverage than normal, but broadcasters made sure to give opposition politicians the chance to decry the whole event as a flagrant piece of electioneering by shuttle-diplomacy. In fact, though there were still complaints that broadcasters were too willing to offer the parties de facto free advertising by passively transmitting their media stunts, there were now also voices warning that British broadcasters were in danger of going down the American road of cynical, anti-political coverage where presenters sought to bond with disinterested viewers by disdaining the whole electoral process. This, most agreed, would be far worse than the tyranny of the so-called 'tot' or 'stopwatch', the strict arithmetic formula used to ensure each party gained fair coverage in news and current affairs programming, even if it meant turning to bland media stunts as 'fillers'. Tony Benn was a particularly fierce critic of disdainful media coverage. As early as 1983 he was railing against *Newsnight* for its gimmicky coverage, including one episode where a fake candidate was shown shaking hands with people and kissing babies—'just mocking the democratic process completely' he fumed. In 1987 broadcast news editors were openly acknowledging their obligation 'to open the viewers' eyes to the manipulation underlying the message', and by the early 1990s politicians were beginning to complain that more attention was being paid to the processes of campaigning than to substantive political issues.[26]

In fact 'disdainful' coverage remained a minority strain in British election broadcasting, easily overshadowed by rival traditions such as the four distinct styles of reporting identified in Blumler, Gurevitch, and Nossiter's ethnographic study of the BBC's *Nine O'Clock News* team during the 1983 election. These were the 'prudential' style (or 'keep your heads down'), the neutral 'reactive' style, the 'conventionally journalistic' style (with its hard-headed emphasis on newsworthy stories), and finally the 'analytical' style—with its strongly didactic public service ethos. The authors felt that in 1983 the 'conventionally journalistic' approach had been dominant, but perhaps the most important lesson we should draw from their research is the need to avoid making sweeping generalizations about the ethos of British broadcast journalism. If one programme could house so many strands of opinion, television journalism as a whole must have been even more diverse. Besides the *Nine O'Clock News*, the BBC also offered 'softer' lunchtime and early evening news bulletins and a whole raft of more specialist current affairs programmes for politicos. British politicians were well aware that different programmes attracted different audiences and required different styles of presentation. In the late 1970s all party leaders were quick to follow Margaret Thatcher's example by appearing on the easy-listening Jimmy Young show on BBC Radio 2, with its large audience of 'swing' C1 and C2 housewives, and on Radio 1 programmes such as *Newsbeat* and *Speakeasy*, which reached the illusive 18–24 voters. Of course the same politicians also appeared on *Newsnight* and other late-night current affairs programmes for the hard-core politicos—where they naturally adopted a rather different persona—but they never forgot where the votes lay.[27]

In 1987 Labour also adopted another telegenic aspect of Thatcherite campaigning: the glitzy political rally. Since 1979, the Conservatives had ended their campaign with an up-beat, star-studded jamboree at Wembley on the final Sunday of the campaign. Masterminded by Harvey Thomas, who had cut his teeth organizing mass meetings for the evangelist Billy Graham, these events were designed to generate strong images of mass enthusiasm more akin to an American party convention than a British political meeting. Television viewers were expected to see the party leader buoyed by ecstatic supporters, and endorsed by familiar household names from the world of show business. Labour had tried something similar way back in 1964, when Wilson's campaign had been kicked off with a glitzy, star-studded rally at Wembley's Empire Pool. The experiment had generated considerable criticism from those fearful of the dread influence of 'Americanization' and vulgar populism. It was not repeated until Kinnock's 1987 'Coming Up Roses' rally in Islington on the final Sunday of the campaign, a celebrity-studded 'family fun day' for party supporters and their children deliberately staged to run head-to-head with the Conservatives' 'family rally' at Wembley. Such rallies were not wholly un-political—there had to be a chance for the party leader to greet the crowd and deliver a few telling sound bites—but their main purpose was to generate positive images for television that would create the general impression of a party 'on the up'. It was all about mood enhancement, not political debate, let alone meaningful engagement with flesh-and-blood voters. Max Atkinson's influential research on political oratory had convinced strategists that live audiences still mattered because, like the studio audience for a TV sitcom, they could influence viewer response at home. Politicians needed to learn the rhetorical tricks, such as the use of antitheses and triads, to ensure that their intended sound bites generated applause in the right places, but they also needed to ensure that audiences could be relied upon to play their part, which meant ticket-only affairs confined to the party faithful. Kinnock admitted as much in 1992 when he acknowledged that since Callaghan's trouble with 'Troops Out' protesters in 1979, it had become impossible to hold open meetings because 'television makes an open door to people to demonstrate and disrupt'. In 1987 only the Alliance leaders, David Steel (Liberal) and David Owen (SDP), exposed themselves to the risks involved when television cameras were allowed to film old-style hustings before real voters. The Alliance held a series of un-ticketed question-and-answer sessions across the country starring 'the Two Davids', perhaps hoping to rekindle the spontaneous public interest that had characterized the birth of the SDP in the early 1980s. These 'Ask the Alliance' sessions had been pioneered in 1983 in an attempt to portray the novel idea of a dual leadership (then Steel and Jenkins) in a positive light. Unfortunately, the 'Two Davids' double-act did not always run smoothly—it was not a marriage made in heaven—and in any case the sessions came across poorly on television in comparison with the up-beat, enthusiastic rallies organized by Labour and the Conservatives. By the end of the first week Alliance strategists were planning to reduce the pair's joint appearances, amidst quips from Steel that they looked like 'tweedledum and tweedledee'.[28]

In 1992 Paddy Ashdown's Liberal Democrats, successor to the Alliance, made no attempt to recreate the open, informal style associated with the 'Two Davids' roadshow. They too now embraced the need for carefully choreographed all-ticket party rallies. It was perhaps all the more remarkable, therefore, that Conservative strategists should have decided that the best way to present John Major (who had succeeded Margaret Thatcher as Conservative party leader in 1990) would be through a series of informal 'Meet John Major' sessions relying on the question-and-answer format that had proved so disappointing for Heath in October 1974 and for the Alliance leaders a decade later. Perched casually on a bar-stool to field questions from small invited audiences, the intention appears to have been to build on Major's image as an ordinary man made good—the antithesis of the professional politician (strategists also hoped to echo Major's successful 'in the round' meetings with troops during the 1991 Gulf War). But the idea was badly misconceived, and broadcasters again reacted negatively. Not only were the sessions highly stage-managed affairs providing hardly a whiff of the old hustings, but unlike other contrived media events they also generated very dull television. Although the Conservatives had spent a 'fortune' on the set, there was none of the colour and excitement of the glitzy party rally, and none of the strong visuals associated with a well-planned photo-opportunity. Major's team were breaking the compact of mutual interest that bound broadcasters and politicians and were sure to be punished. The 'Meet John Major' sessions were dropped halfway through the campaign in favour of extra all-ticket rallies, and some aggressive, open-air oratory in which Major harangued passers-by, opponents, and camera crews in market squares across the country. Stood atop an old packing case, loud-speaker in hand, Major's self-consciously anachronistic gesture managed to inject life and energy into a tired Conservative campaign that many feared could be heading for defeat (Fig. 18). It was a high-risk strategy—Major was exposing himself to the sort of organized opposition few politicians had faced since Callaghan's battles with the 'Troops Out' protesters in 1979. Since every moment was bound to be captured on film, there was an inherent danger that Major would get the worst of these exchanges with members of the public, even if they did allow him to break through the protective bubble imposed by the security state (it should be remembered that this was before the first IRA cease-fire—Major's security advisers were far from happy with his 'soapbox' stunts).[29]

There must be a strong suspicion that like Home in 1964, Major was hoping that television pictures of raucous Labour opposition would help to alienate wavering voters in a tightly balanced election. After being forced to abandon a walkabout at Bolton by a hostile crowd of opponents, Major denounced 'the ugly, intolerant face of the Labour party—a mob, obscene gestures, ugly chants and a return of the political flying picket'. Senior Conservatives were said to be 'privately delighted by the Bolton mobbing'. When protesters tried to shout him down at Luton, Major warned his audience (and hence the viewers at home): 'Don't let the

Fig. 18. John Major on his soapbox at Luton, 1992 (PA photos)

people who take to the streets take your country' (apparently oblivious to the fact that he too had taken to the streets in an extraordinary departure from recent electioneering practice). At Chester, Major faced only 'some jokey heckling', leading Gyles Brandreth, the city's celebrity Conservative candidate to observe 'we could have done with more'. Kenneth Baker was not alone in believing that it was Major's 'unflappable' style and his bold gamble to repackage soapbox oratory for the television age that saved the day for the Conservatives in 1992. Others pointed the finger at John Smith for misjudging the need to neutralize Conservative scare tactics on tax, and at Neil Kinnock for his vacillations on electoral reform and for getting carried away by the euphoric atmosphere at Labour's massive rally for 10,000 in the Sheffield Arena just over a week before polling. Kinnock's triumphal entry through the ecstatic crowd, followed by his rock-star like cries of 'We're all right', subsequently came to symbolize Labour's hubris at a moment when victory appeared, fleetingly, to be within their grasp. Certainly, Kinnock's wild whoops came across poorly on television—unlike Major's battling efforts on his soapbox or his low-key speeches at party rallies adorned with a hi-tech set said to have cost Conservative Central Office £500,000. And of course how things came across on television really was all that mattered by the early 1990s.[30]

The 1992 election witnessed something of a backlash against the stage-managed political rally. Perhaps predictably, Labour's extravaganza at Sheffield was denounced as more akin to the excesses of a Nazi rally than to a traditional English political meeting—an exercise in mass manipulation not political discussion. Such criticisms had strong resonances in British political culture, and probably explain why all three parties recoiled from the mass rally after the controversies of 1992. But it was not just the fascistic (or, perhaps more fairly, 'Yankee') overtones of the party rally that worried commentators in 1992. Many also voiced a broader frustration that elaborately planned media events effectively excluded real voters from any meaningful engagement with the politicians who claimed the right to represent them. In the *Independent* Peter Jenkins attacked 'the unholy alliance between politicians and broadcasters' which underpinned mass media politics, ensuring that most of the time what the public saw was 'not politicians meeting the people but politicians meeting the media'. Writing in the *Guardian* a day later, Hugo Young was if anything even more scathing about the artificiality of modern electioneering methods. Lamenting the eclipse of old-fashioned, open election meetings in favour of 'clinically anaesthetised' party rallies, Young concluded that in the modern era of 24-hour media surveillance 'politicians do not want the public, ragged and random, near them'. Voters were acceptable as 'walk-on extras at the walkabouts', but not as inconvenient interrogators. From 'active participants in a dialogue nobody controls', the public had been relegated to 'passive receivers' of a pre-packaged media politics that was honed, above all, to woo the key target groups identified by scientific polling.[31]

As we have seen, the trends that Jenkins and Young were complaining about had been in process for decades, but there was clearly a strong sense that they had reached an end-point in 1992—that the long decline of active public involvement in British elections had reached its logical conclusion in a contest where leaders had been all but hermetically sealed from any risk of genuine exposure to criticism or debate. Even Major's soapbox altercations were perceived as, at heart, stunts for the camera, rather than serious attempts to take politics 'to the people'. How could they be anything else given the basic mathematics of media electioneering—perhaps ten or twenty thousand people heard Major speak live from his soapbox during the campaign, but millions saw him every night on the main evening news bulletins (BBC1 and ITN both averaged just over six million viewers for their flagship news bulletins during the campaign). However, we must not lose sight of the important point that, in his hour of need, Major turned to direct interaction with real voters to save his campaign, and hence his political career. The often incestuous embrace between broadcasters and political leaders had not wholly banished the public from electoral politics. On the contrary, both recognized that public involvement transformed the credibility, and hence the perceived legitimacy, of mediated politics. Perhaps the greatest lesson of 1992 was therefore that, at critical moments, the ethos of the old hustings could still cast a long shadow.

9

The Public Banished?

Why politicians need the public

In the early 1990s critics such as Peter Jenkins and Hugo Young focused on the world that had been lost by the rise of pre-packaged, media-friendly politics. Their nostalgia for a time when even party leaders had been forced to face forensic interrogation of their policies at open meetings was understandable. But it was perhaps unduly negative about the effects of television on the political process. The open meeting might have died, but the public interrogation of Britain's political masters had not died with it. Just as many of the traditions associated with the hustings were transferred to the election meeting after 1872, so in turn many of the traditions associated with the election meeting reappeared in new forms in Britain's late twentieth-century mediated politics. Perhaps most striking was the rise of the television interviewer to take over the mantle of the persistent heckler at open public meetings. From Robin Day and Robert MacKenzie through to the Dimblebys and Jeremy Paxman, British television has subjected politicians to gruelling cross-examinations that have few parallels in other western democracies—perhaps because Britain is also almost alone in never witnessing head-to-head, televised confrontations between its party leaders. Nonetheless, in the set-piece interview the public is still only represented virtually—and represented, at that, by someone who is as much part of the political elite as the politicians he or she interrogates, however much they may wish to deny this.[1]

However, the broadcast media also have the power to make politicians more directly accountable to the public, particularly since, as Major demonstrated in 1992, politicians continue to crave the perceived legitimacy of being seen to meet the public face-to-face. True, there may be little genuine political interaction in a frantic walkabout or a stage-managed factory visit, but even such fleeting brushes with the public hold real dangers for the politician under constant surveillance from the mass media. Politicians need to be seen mingling with 'the people', but they can never be sure that 'the people' will appear suitably grateful. Well-timed interventions can derail the politician's message at any moment—with potentially disastrous consequences. It is no accident that the two most memorable incidents during the otherwise crushingly dull 2001 General Election occurred when members of the public upset carefully choreographed media events. The eggs thrown at John Prescott by Craig Evans, an angry North Wales farm worker, and Prescott's instinctively pugilistic response, demonstrated that the irreverent, disorderly traditions of British public politics had not been wholly eradicated by the civilizing processes of modern life, but post-mistress Sharron Storer's passionate harangue of Tony Blair during his visit to a Birmingham hospital was very different. Here an 'ordinary' member of the public had her say about probably the greatest political issue of the day: the quality of health provision under a universal system funded through direct taxation. Moreover, she had her say, not before a few hundred fellow voters in a public hall, but before the massed ranks of the British media who naturally seized on this fleeting outburst of spontaneity and excitement for all it was worth. Unlike John Major's self-consciously anachronistic rediscovery of the soapbox during the 1992 General Election, Storer's intervention appeared fresh and unpremeditated. In an election where public interest in politics seemed at an all-time low, this incident reminded everyone that voters could still be irreverent and questioning; and that, thanks to the power of television, millions could watch them put a politician—even a Prime Minister—on the spot. In 2005, when Blair's political stock had fallen considerably, he appeared consciously to seek out opportunities to be grilled publicly by voters, albeit in the relative safety of the television studio rather than in the street. In the run-up to the campaign, Blair undertook a series of televised question-and-answer programmes for broadcasters such as Sky and Channel Five. The day after one particularly gruelling exchange with a mother angry at the Government's policies on special needs education, Blair told Labour MPs that, whatever the pitfalls, there was 'no substitute for face-to-face contact' with voters, and that participation in such programmes 'can be better ways to win support than formal TV interviews and simply being quoted in newspapers'. The so-called 'masochism strategy', first developed in early 2003 as a means of confronting public opposition in the run-up to the invasion of

Iraq, was relaunched as a central plank of modern electioneering (its rather portentous official title was Operation Matrix).[2]

As Blair recognized in 2005, broadcasting can give the public a formal platform from which to interrogate politicians. After the raucous studio encounters of the 1959 election, particularly Granada's *The Last Debate*, politicians had run scared of facing the public live on-air for many years. However, by the mid-1970s their embargo had collapsed and public participation through phone-ins and studio audiences gradually became as much a staple of Britain's mediated politics as the leaders' set-piece interview or the morning press conference. This chapter will examine the history of public participation in election broadcasting since the 1950s, asking where the public fits in the complicated and often fraught relationship between politicians and broadcasters. Broadcasters have sometimes talked in lofty terms about their mission to promote accessibility and accountability in British politics, but have they lived up to these ideals in practice? In short, has television really evolved to perform the democratic role once assigned to the public meeting, or have broadcasters more often simply been the willing accomplices of the party campaign managers? Finally, even when broadcasters have clearly resisted the party embrace, can we really say that they have done much to champion public involvement in the political process? If modern, mediated politics is about a tripartite relationship between producers, politicians, and public, has the public's role in that triangle been anything other than essentially passive, and, perhaps even more crucially, have broadcasters done enough to facilitate the interrogation of politicians by members of the public?

The history of public participation

As we saw in the previous chapter, the balance of power between politicians and broadcasters has been in constant flux since the late 1950s and the transmission of the first election news and current affairs programmes. Broadcasting in Britain had been highly regulated from the outset, with the BBC expected to avoid controversy and to deny air-time to what was loosely termed 'extremist' voices. The very fact that the voluntary moratorium on election news coverage, like the 14 Day rule restricting discussion of Parliamentary business, survived until the late 1950s underlines how conservative British broadcasting was in its formative years. When politicians reacted violently to some aspects of the election coverage in 1959, it was therefore all but inevitable that broadcasters would feel obliged to accept the parties' onerous restrictions. As we have seen, after 1959 the main parties insisted that further cooperation would be dependent on broadcasters accepting significant restrictions on their freedom to determine programme formats, personnel, and even subject matter. There can be little doubt that politicians remained in the ascendancy throughout the 1960s. After Barbara Castle and Selwyn Lloyd's mauling by a Granada studio audience on *The Last Debate*, live audiences were barred from election programmes for more than a decade. On programmes such as *Election Forum* and *Question Time* professional journalists, rather than voters, posed the questions; 'uneasy proxies for a public the parties refused to confront inside a studio', as the Nuffield researchers observed. Broadcasters were not happy with the situation. In 1966 Granada commissioned a programme exploring the origins behind the ban, and Selwyn Lloyd reluctantly agreed to participate to clear himself and his party of allegations of 'illiberalism' and of being the prime instigators of the ban on public participation.[3]

Despite the parties' tight controls, which were policed with remarkable cooperation across the political divide, politicians remained anxious that they were losing control of political debate to the broadcasters—particularly in their battles over 'agenda setting'. Convinced that broadcasters were de-termined to wrest control of campaigning from party strategists, the parties reasserted their strict rules on programme formats in the run-up to the 1970 General Election. In so doing they overturned the moderate liberalization of the late 1960s, which had seen politicians willingly participate in live audience broadcasts, particularly on regional 'magazine' programmes. For instance, in 1968 Anglia Television had launched a new regional current affairs programme *Probe*, which included a regular slot where local MPs faced questions from an invited audience. Much was done to reassure MPs that the programme would 'not be a free-for-all': the parties were allowed to help choose the audience, and all questions were to be approved in advance. It was a far cry from Granada's *Last Debate*, but it nonetheless represented the first chinks in the parties' united front against voter partici-pation. By 1969 BBC local radio stations were also adopting the format, with Radio Nottingham leading the way. But at the 1970 election, broad-casters' plans for radio phone-in programmes and for a series of innovative audience discussion programmes on BBC2 faced strong opposition from the parties. However, the precedent of programmes such as *Probe* helped ITV channels to make a few regional programmes bringing candidates together with panels of real voters, and Thames Television overcame strong Labour opposition to make *Hook-Up*, a programme in which voters put questions direct to politicians, albeit from a remote location. The restrictions on the public's involvement in electoral politics were finally beginning to crumble.[4]

Four years later the floodgates were opened. Radio phone-ins proliferated across the country, with both local and national stations experimenting with the format (the newly established independent local radio companies proved especially keen pioneers). *Election Call*, chaired by Robin Day on BBC Radio 4, proved a particular success. The programme attracted over a million listeners, and perhaps more importantly, enough questions that the party stooges were clearly swamped. In turn ITV companies increasingly insisted that voters should be involved in their regional election programmes, although they still sometimes found it impossible to get politicians to participate on this basis, or else had to succumb to party demands that they should be able to vet panels of supposedly 'ordinary voters'. There was also a proliferation of 'vox pop' programming, where voters were given the chance to respond to the campaign and to debate the issues as they saw them. Granada's *Let the People Speak* (the title says it all), was perhaps the most influential, and went on to enjoy a long life first as *Granada 500* and later as the *ITV500*. A randomly chosen panel of electors from ultra-marginal Preston was encouraged to quiz experts on the burning issues of the day. Having perfected the format during the February 1974 election, in October Granada pulled off a coup when it was agreed that the five hundred would come to London to interrogate the three party leaders. That the programme was made at all clearly demonstrated the changing mood of British broadcasting; indeed among media professionals attitudes had changed much earlier. The big difference in 1974 was that, unlike in 1970, the politicians were prepared to play ball. Gus MacDonald recalled that he went to considerable lengths to persuade politicians that it would be safe to take part in *Let the People Speak*, and his efforts were vindicated. The memories of *The Last Debate* rumpus in 1959 were laid to rest—the three party leaders were 'politely questioned and warmly applauded'. According to MacDonald, this 'finally persuaded nervous party managers that electors did not come to studios looking for partisan punch ups'.[5]

The big question, of course, is why the politicians relented in their opposition to live audiences and phone-in programmes. The danger of high–profile 'gaffes' was undiminished, and, after a decade of radical protest, there was little reason to think that the public would be more deferential towards politicians than they had been in the 1950s (though in truth they were, at least at first). Some have speculated that politicians simply felt unable to hold out against the new consensus in favour of popular participation that had emerged from the 1960s counter-culture, but to understand the shift we probably need to look at politicians' interactions with the public more broadly. Attendance at public meetings had fallen threefold since 1959, and whilst surgery work had increased to help fill the void, this was of little relevance to electioneering. Politicians embraced the walkabout and the mass canvass as alternative ways to reach voters, but these offered only the most fleeting and superficial forms of interaction. In this context, it seems plausible to suggest that politicians began to look more favourably on media-facilitated interactions with the public because it was no longer possible to argue that such exercises merely replicated the real business of electioneering in an artificial setting. True, even in regional programmes politicians were rarely brought face-to-face with their own constituents, but they were given the chance to be seen taking voters' concerns seriously—not something to be dismissed lightly by the mid-1970s. Indeed in November 1973, during the Hove by-election, Tim Sainsbury had introduced his own 'Dial Tim' phone-in service explicitly as an alternative to poorly attended public meetings. Broadcasters were pushing at an open door. Indeed, by the late 1970s Labour candidates were officially being told to say 'yes' to any phone-in opportunity, though they were also advised to 'notify the party faithful to ask helpful questions'. Public participation was all very well for broadcasters, but party organizers had to take a more pragmatic view: what mattered was good media exposure, everything else, including the chance to interact with real voters, was necessarily secondary.[6]

Broadcasters may also have had ulterior motives for pushing the cause of 'popular participation'. Belief in the need to increase public participation was real enough, but it may not be a coincidence that, after the bruising battles of 1966 and 1970, and the furore over *Yesterday's Men* in 1971, broadcasters were in retreat on the burning question of agenda-setting. True, they rejected Heath's claim that the only question before the voters in February 1974 was 'Who governs Britain?', but overall there was less willingness to bring buried issues to the fore. Perhaps broadcasters hoped that the public would do this for them through phone-ins and studio debates—and do it with considerably more legitimacy at that—but if so this still represented a significant tactical withdrawal. By the late 1970s many observers were convinced that broadcasters had retreated to a 'safe', largely reactive, mode of election coverage: agenda-setting was over. As we have seen, at its worst this meant passively transmitting pictures of leaders' walkabouts and photo-opportunities; at best, it meant running hard with whatever appeared to the be 'bull point' story of the day—perhaps the latest trade figures, a politician's 'gaffe', or a particularly choice bit of party mud-slinging.[7]

The rise of the 'pseudo-event' in the 1970s and 1980s allowed politicians to reassert control of the mass media without having to rely on cross-party compacts. The parties increasingly undertook their own private negotiations with the broadcasters on a programme-by-programme basis, always hopeful that they would secure some minor tactical advantage over their opponents. Politicians still exerted enormous pressure on broadcasters behind the scenes, but their control of the representation of politics through the mass media was nonetheless becoming inherently unstable. During the 1979 election, the public gained an insight into the behind-the-scenes world of election broadcasting when news broke that an American television channel, NBC, had aired pictures of Prime Minister Callaghan angrily storming out of an interview because ITN's David Rose had persisted in asking questions that had not been agreed beforehand. The fact that ITN had honoured the convention that such footage should not be shown rather underlined the strong strain of deference that still ran through British broadcasting culture. These years witnessed an explosion of set-piece leaders' interviews, driven in part by the intense rivalry between the different ITV companies, but even the star interviewers gradually came to the conclusion that their gladiatorial encounters with Thatcher and her opponents shed all too little light on the election. Well-coached and well-briefed politicians increasingly found it relatively easy to seize control of the set-piece interview, transforming it from an idealized parliamentary exchange into what Robin Day acknowledged had become 'a series of statements planned for delivery irrespective of the question which had been put'. A pessimistic assessment subsequently confirmed by systematic analyses of interview transcripts, although Day went too far in predicting the death of the set-piece interview—it survives, albeit with diminished status, because skilfully devised questions cannot be evaded or wilfully misinterpreted with complete impunity.[8]

But if the growing influence of media advisers has helped politicians to neutralize the set-piece interview, the same techniques work much less well if the interrogator is an ordinary voter 'having their say'. On *Granada 500* in 1979, Callaghan fell into the trap of appearing to bully a young nurse critical of his Government's pay policy. Techniques that had stood him in good stead in set-piece interviews looked bad when they were turned on an underpaid health worker. Predictably the audience reacted sharply, with even the Labour supporters judging Callaghan's performance harshly. Similarly, in 1983 Thatcher breezed through all her set-piece interviews, but could not do the same when confronted by Mrs Diana Gould's persistent questions about the sinking of the *Belgrano* on the popular, early evening magazine programme *Nationwide* (which ran an election special called, fittingly, *On the Spot*). As these examples suggest, after the tentative experiments of 1974, the elections of 1979 and 1983 had witnessed a major extension of voter-participation programmes. In 1979 *Nationwide* had organized a series of regional 'nationwide debates' where party leaders were quizzed by invited audiences in a format said to have 'captured something of the hurly-burly of a political meeting'. By 1983, Robin Day's *Election Call* phone-in was being transmitted live on television as well as radio, while *Nationwide* had refined the phone-in format so that voters, including Mrs Gould, could interrogate party leaders live from regional studios. That year Day also chaired special editions of his popular audience participation programme *Question Time*, boasting that it 'revived the old hustings tradition of people face to face with the politicians'. Indeed Day subsequently argued that 'the 1983 election may be fairly described as the first real television election, if the volume and variety and vigour of election coverage is the test', whilst even television's staunchest critics acknowledged that the growth of voter participation provided a valuable corrective to the increasingly pre-packaged character of British politics. The *Guardian* felt that *On the Spot* represented 'the toughest test politicians have to face in the electronic election', not least because questioners tended to get 'a better share of the mike' than on other participation programmes, and appeared to be less overawed—perhaps because the remote live-feed helped to insulate them from politicians' well-developed 'people skills'.[9]

In 1987 the Conservatives sought to protect Thatcher from a repeat of the Diana Gould confrontation by getting party chairman Norman Tebbit to act as a stand-in on programmes such as *Granada 500* and *On the Spot*. But, when opinion polls briefly appeared to be turning against the Conservatives, taunts that the Prime Minister was 'frightened of facing the public' prompted a last-minute decision for her to appear on *Election Call, Channel 4 News*, and the BBC Radio 1 phone-in *On Line with Simon Bates*. It's clear that Thatcher recognized the special dangers of programmes involving public participation, observing in her autobiography that 'a well-briefed caller can expose gaps in a politician's understanding which most political opponents never could'. According to Martin Harrison, writing in the 1983 Nuffield study, such phone-ins and panel programmes created 'a democratic form that would be unimaginable in all but a handful of countries'. While four years later the *Guardian* celebrated Day's *Campaign Question Time* as the programme that came closest to capturing the spirit of the old hustings, and concluded 'it is the audience that makes the difference'. No wonder so many political commentators stressed the parallels with the traditional public meeting—but were they right?[10]

On the surface, there is a neat symmetry between the rise of public participation broadcasting and the final collapse of the public meeting, but the link between the two phenomena can only be speculative. Perhaps the decline of the meeting weakened party opposition to public participation, or perhaps the process worked in reverse. Hugo Young felt that phone-ins had helped to kill the meeting by persuading would-be hecklers to put their questions on air, where millions might hear them. More likely, politicians felt that troublesome meetings could finally be dispensed with now that public participation was underwritten by the broadcasters. Political organizers had been looking for a chance to drop the meeting for decades: now they had an alternative activity to occupy restless candidates determined to evangelize the electors as well as to organize them. Of course most candidates had no prospect of getting on to the main national phone-in programmes—either on radio or television—but local radio was a different matter. This grew massively during the 1970s and 1980s, led first by BBC expansion, and then by the burgeoning of commercial and community radio. Listener participation was at the heart of local radio from the outset, and it was only natural that the medium should embrace the election phone-in with gusto. Here candidates could be quizzed by local voters, but even then the analogy of the public meeting is not wholly accurate. For one thing, most local radio stations transmitted across dozens of separate parliamentary constituencies. A questioner *might* also be a constituent, but the odds were slim by contrast with the traditional local election meeting. From the politician's perspective the key point was rather that a good number of local constituents would be listening to his or her performance, and that many would be exactly the sort of constituent most difficult to reach by more traditional means, including the public meeting. Of course the corollary of this was that a politician's 'gaffe'—a flustered answer, a loss of cool, or a flagrant lie—would instantly be transmitted to more electors than the candidate was likely to meet face-to-face throughout a whole campaign; and if it was a big enough gaffe it could even go national. If the rewards were high, so were the risks. In this sense the local phone-in magnified the high-wire drama of the traditional election meeting—though not if the questioner was overawed by the experience of being 'on-air', as was often the case in the early days, nor if party workers got through the broadcasters' screening efforts and asked planted questions. Political parties tried to train their candidates in the required new media skills, but given the numbers involved they could only do so much. In the run-up to the 1992 election, Labour provided a weekend training course for its newly selected candidates, including courses in media skills and 'working with your local media'. It was a start, certainly, but hardly adequate preparation for handling the pressure of live phone-ins and studio interviews. In practice, even in winnable seats, candidates' 'training' was often left to local volunteers with no formal media experience—I know because I spent an evening a week with one such candidate in the long run-up to the 1992 election.[11]

By the 1990s, therefore, many of the most memorable moments of British electioneering were not just media moments (that was more or less inevitable given that for most electors the television election *was* the election), they were moments when the public crashed through the Westminster bubble to impose itself on the campaign. In the 1990s live audiences began to rediscover some of the raucousness that had seen them banned from the political stage three decades earlier. The *Granada 500* audience, in particular, gave all three party leaders a hard time in 1992. Neil Kinnock was all but shouted down for prevaricating on the question of Labour's attitude to proportional representation, John Major was hissed when he refused to apologize for the Poll Tax, and Paddy Ashdown was heckled and accused of 'blackmail' when he declared that the Liberal Democrats would insist on proportional representation as their condition for supporting either party in the event of a hung Parliament. Moreover, as in 1987, commentators agreed that the leaders were at greatest risk of being put on the spot, not in their set-piece interviews with broadcasting's heavyweights, but in spontaneous interactions with the public on programmes like *Election Call*.[12]

The 1990s also saw broadcasters beginning to appropriate some of the new tools of the professional campaign managers. In 1992 both the BBC and Channel 4 embraced 'people-metering' as a means of graphically representing voters' responses to the politicians' campaign messages. However, too often broadcasters fell into the trap of knowing cynicism—using the meters to demonstrate the hidden arts of political 'spin', rather than exploring more important questions about voter attitudes and the reception of political messages. *Question Time* was quick to use such devices to conduct instant polls of the studio audience, and there have also been initiatives involving selected panels of 'swing' voters, but the full potential of interactive technologies has not yet been explored. In theory they can enable vast numbers of voters to play an active role in shaping the election campaign. Whereas early experiments involved selected panels of voters being issued with specialist equipment, it is now possible to envisage formats that will be open to responses from the general public. Both the internet and digital television reached over half the population by 2005, but the most democratic communication technology by far is the mobile phone, and it is this that seems most likely to deliver real-time viewer interaction between politicians and public in the foreseeable future. Unusually, interactive technologies enable the inarticulate as well as the articulate to 'have their say'—although inevitably the range of what can be said with a keypad or hand-held dial is rather limited, leaving much to the interpretative skills of media professionals. The interaction they offer is also, by its nature, much less immediate and visceral than either traditional forms of face-to-face politics, or live phone-ins and audience participation programmes.[13]

Certainly Britain needs something to liven up the format of its mediated politics. By 1997 many observers felt that the media and party professionals had fought each other to a standstill: that the rules of the game had become so entrenched that each side was locked in a ritualized struggle to control the news agenda. With party efforts at news management intensified by the adoption of American 'instant rebuttal' techniques, broadcasters retaliated by paying even greater attention to the process of electioneering rather than to its substance. In part this was because media professionals believed that they had an obligation to demystify the activities of the 'sultans of spin', but, as Brian McNair observes, it was also because it is much harder to avoid charges of bias when commenting on policy issues. The result was not a happy one. In the *Guardian* Mark Lawson complained that election news bulletins seemed 'even more than usually dull, stilted and superficial'. An ethnographic study of BBC election news suggested that many television journalists shared these concerns. Crucially, they also believed that the only solution to the problem was to inject a stronger popular element into election coverage. The consequence was that, as in 1974 and 1983, the election of 1997 witnessed a further advance in both the extent and the importance of popular participation in British political broadcasting. But the principal impetus for change appears to have come from a desire to invigorate programming by upsetting the cosy 'Westminster village' relationship between journalists and politicians, rather than from any broader idealism about empowering voters. Significantly, 'people power' made fewest inroads into the flagship evening news bulletins, even though these were again greatly extended in length. Instead the usual cocktail of *Question Time, Election Call,* and *ITV500* was supplemented by popular input to *Breakfast News,* to the heavyweight *Newsnight,* and to a series of election specials such as *The People's Agenda, Power and the People,* and *Campaign Roadshow.* BBC producers had no intention of throwing open the airwaves in the manner of American-style 'shock jocks'—this was a decidedly muted populist revolution—but for all that it was still significant. With journalists and politicians locked in an increasingly sterile duel, 'real voters' were being mobilized as a means to restore credibility and freshness to political programming. As one BBC producer put it, 'with ordinary voters, politicians cannot slap them down ... It creates an edge for them.' Certainly there was plenty of edge when John Major pulled out of the *ITV500* at the last minute, asking his deputy, Michael Heseltine, to stand in for him. The studio audience responded with such anger that even Heseltine's charms were barely sufficient to gain a hearing. Heseltine entered to hissing and shouts of 'chicken' and 'shame', and found his answers frequently greeted with loud 'boos' from the audience. Ever the showman, Heseltine complained that the audience was 'obviously slanted against the Government', but in truth they were venting their anger at being stood up by a leader who appeared not to recognize how badly he needed to be seen 'facing the music' before real electors. According to the *Guardian* it was 'participation TV at its best': a classic example of 'the old-fashioned hustings transferred to a studio'.[14]

But we should not get carried away. For one thing, public participation in Britain has developed within a strongly paternalist vision of public service broadcasting. One consequence is that producers have never been prepared to relinquish control of how the public will interact with politicians. At the most basic level, most phone-in programmes retain a short time delay so that obscene, libellous, or inflammatory callers can be censored. But if this is simply responsible broadcasting, perhaps more controversially producers have also played an active role by vetting callers according to criteria such as 'newsworthiness', topicality, articulacy, and more recently, diversity. A study of the BBC's *Election Call* identified a clear 'media agenda' of issues flagged up for telephonists—callers who raised issues matching this agenda doubled their chance of getting on air. They also found a strong bias towards youth over age, but, perhaps surprisingly, little attempt to redress the gender imbalance among callers (between 70 and 74 per cent were male). In 1997, researchers felt that little had changed since Robin Day's first broadcasts almost a quarter-century earlier—perhaps callers now got a bit more of the air time, and had more chance to respond to politicians' answers, but as in 1974 the overall ethos was that such programmes represented 'a rather risky operation, best controlled by the strictest selection of appropriate callers'. Writing in 1998, Jonathan Freedland fumed at Britain's deferential political culture compared with the United States, citing as an example how it neutralized the phone-in format so that 'our programmes are called *Question Time* and *Any Questions*, implicitly inviting the public to put questions to those in authority rather than voice their own opinions'. However, arguably the greatest problem was not public deference, but rather the media paternalism which ensured that only 'appropriate' callers got on air, and that when they did so their role was to be 'newsworthy' and 'topical': that is, to conform to the media professionals' sense of what the public should care about. Intriguingly, in 2001 researchers at *Election Call* noted that callers were now asked to 'put their points' to politicians, rather than, as in 1997, to 'put questions'. Callers were also given more opportunity to interact with politicians, making supplementary points and commenting on the answer they had received. It was part of a wider revolution at the BBC epitomized by the popular news and sport station Radio 5 Live, launched in 1994, which pioneered a more demotic (and demonic) style of broadcasting that did much to shake up the paternalist spirit of BBC journalism. Texts, emails, and mobile phone calls were regularly fed into programming in real time, creating a more informal, interactive style of broadcasting. However, this approach has proved better at airing a range of disparate voices, than at bringing public and politicians directly into dialogue with one another. In consequence, whilst BBC journalism may be shedding its paternalist ethos, it is not obvious that its new-found populism will do much to enhance political accountability in Britain. On the contrary, at present all the signs are that broadcasters will be content to throw their programmes open to a multiplicity of voices in the name of pluralism and free expression. Laudable enough objectives in an age when the main parties appear locked in a relentless battle to align themselves with the all-important 'median voter', but ultimately less valuable than developing formats capable of obliging politicians to respond publicly to these same voices (and positively harmful if all it means is giving air time, and hence apparent legitimacy, to ill-informed rants about the political 'system').[15]

But the signs are not promising for the future of genuinely interactive political broadcasting. In 2001 *Election Call* was cut from an hour to forty-five minutes, and was moved from BBC1 to BBC2. In 2005, after more than thirty years, it lost its traditional morning slot, being shunted to the early afternoon, and ceased to be broadcast simultaneously on television at all. Worse, despite the 'masochism strategy', Blair passed up the chance to appear on the programme, leaving Jack Straw to fill his seat. Instead the 'vox pop' was the format of choice for broadcasters in 2005, with informal street interviews reinforced by programmes in which non-politicians were given the chance to outline the issues that *should* matter in the coming election, and the uncommitted decided how, and as often whether, to vote (*Newsnight*'s 'Student House' was especially effective). The main forum for serious political interaction was now the studio question-and-answer programme, with BBC1's *Question Time Leaders' Special* and ITV1's *Ask the Leader* occupying pride of place. Such programmes conform more easily to the rules of television than the phone-in, which has always appeared to be an awkward hybrid in its various translations from radio to television. However, studio audiences are often heavily weighted towards the politically engaged and the articulate, and in any case by definition tend to limit the scope for spontaneous interaction involving the wider public. The experiments with new interactive technologies may help here, but in the foreseeable future none is likely to be able to deliver a genuine two-way exchange as successfully as the traditional radio phone-in (or, for that matter, the old open public meeting).[16]

Worse, in 2005 the parties tried harder than ever to insulate their leaders from random encounters with the real public on the campaign trail. From Labour's perspective the excitement generated by Evans and Storer in 2001 had been a media disaster, though not because Blair or Prescott were damaged by these incidents—if anything the reverse was true. But what is often forgotten is that Storer and Evans struck on the day that Labour launched its election manifesto. Months of careful planning went out the window in a few minutes as the mass media worked themselves into a frenzy over the two incidents. As Alastair Campbell confided to his diary, 'All that work, and we will be lucky if most people see or read a bloody word of it, because one woman has a pop in front of the cameras' (he was writing before news of Prescott's fracas had come through). The result was that in 2005 chance encounters with the public were kept to an absolute minimum. According to Martin Harrison, 'apart from a few noises-off, he [Blair] moved in a strictly controlled invitation-only world'. Public engagements were more elaborately choreographed than ever, and there were stories that Labour was bussing crowds of photogenic party activists around the country to ensure a positive, and, above-all, a safe reception for their leader. From Campbell's account, Blair appears to have been genuinely shaken by the Storer incident—just as he was 'taken aback' by abuse from football fans at a Chelsea v. Manchester United game in 1997, even though Campbell had felt it to be 'pretty good-natured'. But like most modern politicians, Blair had never had to learn how to disarm the irreverent heckler. And so if, in 2005, the 'masochism strategy' demanded that Blair should be seen 'being beaten up by the public', Labour strategists made sure that it would happen on their terms—which meant in a television studio, with media professionals in charge to police the rules of exchange, not on the streets of Birmingham or North Wales.[17]

What is to be done?

We should be careful not to overstate the recent reaction against public participation in Britain's mediated politics. From Sharron Storer's im-promptu harangue, to Blair's masochistic studio grillings, broadcasters have made possible a series of high-profile public incursions into the campaign. But is this enough to refute the charge that, between them, media pro-fessionals and the parties' PR experts have taken politics away from the people, thereby fuelling a widespread sense of alienation from the political process? Disdainful coverage may remain a minority (if growing) taste, but the broadcast media's relentless focus on process rather than policy inevitably reinforces cynicism towards politics, even if its roots lie much deeper. Equally the tendency to present politics as another lifestyle or consumption choice, rather than as a civic duty, hardly helps, since it makes not voting appear to be the moral equivalent of not buying brand-label washing powder. But whatever their shortcomings, we need to recognize that broadcasters continue to play at least three vital roles that enhance our democratic culture. Firstly, they provide voters with unparalleled information about politics, and do so in a form which is both substantially unbiased and deliberately tailored to meet diverse tastes. Secondly, they provide almost the only arena in which members of the public can still gain direct access to politicians during an election—from the point of view of meaningful political interaction between politicians and public there really is no other show in town any more. Thirdly, through their 24-hour coverage of our political masters they provide members of the public with the chance to hijack the news agenda to advertise their grievances—as both Sharron Storer and Craig Evans demonstrated in 2001. However, we also need to recognize that here, as with 'people metering', or the vetting of studio audiences and phone-in callers, broadcasters play a powerful mediating role. Protesters will only be able to exploit Britain's 24/7 media culture if their interventions conform to the media professionals' sense of what is both 'newsworthy' and 'legitimate'. Otherwise their efforts will be ignored by the cameras, much as the lone drunk who invades the pitch at sporting events is now ignored.[18]

As Blair's 'masochism strategy' demonstrated in 2005, politicians are well aware of the political advantages to be gained from the media's ability to bring them face-to-face with real voters. Blair had always made good use of his strong 'people skills' during elections, and in 2005, with his credibility gravely weakened by Iraq, top-up fees, and the like, he threw himself on the public's mercy with unparalleled vigour. Philip Gould has acknowledged that this was 'a deliberate strategy to allow people to have their voices heard, and their frustrations vented'—the aim was 'Reconnection through direct televised contact with the electorate' (although Gould's use of 'allow' hints at a strong underlying elitism). By the time Blair appeared on *Question Time*, towards the close of the campaign, he appeared physically drained by the whole process. Evidently floored by a question about the disastrous impact of government targets on General Practitioners' appointment systems, he could only lamely offer to look into the matter after the programme. But this painful exchange was not the low point of the election for Blair; that was to come, not within the relatively safe confines of the television studio, but on the declaration platform in his Sedgefield constituency a few days later. Moreover, this was not a case of Blair choosing to be put on the spot in order to demonstrate his 'common touch', but rather a classic example of television providing a disgruntled voter with the chance to air his grievances to the nation at the Prime Minister's expense. But unlike Sharron Storer in 2001, Reg Keys did not hijack a photo-opportunity; rather he made use of the much older customs of the declaration to deliver a stinging indictment of the Prime Minister for his alleged indifference to the suffering caused by the war in Iraq. The impact of Keys's quiet anger was underscored not only by the fact that his own son had been killed in Iraq, but also by the fact that he had polled 4,252 votes in Blair's rock-solid County Durham constituency. The pictures of Blair standing motionless behind Keys, evidently trying to maintain an inscrutable expression, made for compelling viewing. If not exactly bringing the powerful to book, this moment underlined television's ability at least to humble those in power—neither political marketing, nor his legendary 'people skills', could turn that moment round for Blair.[19]

This example reminds us that, in many respects, political marketing should be understood as the parties' response to the increasingly difficult context within which political communication takes place in complex post-industrial societies. With the proliferation of channels and the diversification of leisure patterns, political communication is a much trickier business than in the 1960s, when parties could rely on monopoly terrestrial broadcasting and mass audiences to take their message into almost every home. Today's political marketeers would dearly love to have the voters corralled for them by the old duopoly of BBC1 and ITV, but instead they have to struggle to manage both the decentralized world of broadcast news, and an increasingly fragmented and illusive voting public. Far from seeking to banish the public from electoral politics, party strategists are constantly trying to devise new ways of harnessing the perceived legitimacy that engagement with the voting public can bring a politician—as long as the cameras are there to capture the moment for the viewing millions. True, they generally try to control this interaction as much as possible, to ensure that the images will be affirmative, or at the very least 'safe'—but as in the days of the old hustings, they also know that facing the public red in tooth and claw can bring great cachet to a politician. When Denis Healey was pictured jumping from the platform to quell fascist opposition at a Walthamstow by-election meeting in 1969, or when John Prescott threw a punch at his burly assailant in 2001, neither suffered for their hot-blooded reaction to violent opposition—on the contrary, in their different ways both were lionized. Similarly, in both 2001 and 2005, Tony Blair gained more from being seen patiently to hear out angry voters, than from countless well-rehearsed engagements and television interviews. The public still wants to see politicians brought down to its level, and elections remain one of the few moments when this routinely happens, despite all the restraints imposed by both the security state and party strategists.[20]

One might argue that it is easy to exaggerate the significance of phone-ins, studio grillings, and the occasional public confrontation between politicians and angry voters. Popular incursions into the electoral process may trip up politicians from time to time, but do such colourful incidents really have much long-term impact on the conduct of elections, let alone on the conduct of state policy—the real, if too often obscured, business of politics? In one sense, the very fact that we know so much about these incidents underscores the fundamental shift in broadcasters' approach to political coverage since the 1980s. Before then, high-minded broadcasters might struggle to keep important issues such as immigration and Europe before the public, but in covering election 'incidents' they generally went out of their way to show politicians in a favourable light. But by the late 1980s, 'incidents' had become the life-blood of television news, and politicians could be certain that any momentary slip, any awkward fracas, would receive maximum news exposure—aided, of course, by technical developments such as ENG and later the widespread dissemination of digital recording equipment. With the toughening of media attitudes towards fair usage, one could argue that we are witnessing the emergence of a new gladiatorial political battle to rival the struggle once played out between speaker and heckler at election meetings. But in its new form the ancient tussle between aspiring candidate and irreverent public is potentially played out before millions watching in their own homes, rather than before a few dozen political activists in a draughty public hall.

Media politics cannot be said to have banished the public from the campaign, but it remains far from clear whether Storer's ambush of a party leader, Blair's 'masochism strategy', or David Cameron's recent exchanges with internet bloggers, should be portrayed as representing the rediscovery of the activist spirit that once made elections such awkward occasions for British politicians. Unfortunately, it is also unclear whether British broadcasters possess sufficient commitment to public participation to ensure that, as new, more interactive mass media become available their potential as tools of democratic levelling will be fully realized. 'WebCameron', the Conservative leader's blog and podcast site launched in September 2006, represents an interesting initiative. Its format is less relentlessly one-way and top-down than most party websites, but it can hardly be said to have surrendered control of the political process. Indeed, when the Conservatives relaunched the site in May 2007 (as 'WebCameron Beta'), the more radical, interactive aspects of the site, such as the 'Ask David' feature, had been downgraded or axed, and many features became restricted to registered users. Inevitably, there is also a credibility gap to be overcome by any politician blogger—how do we know it's them? WebCameron was quick to post a podcast of Cameron up late at his desk, with his cocoa by his laptop, responding to bloggers' criticisms, but this merely served to highlight concerns about the disembodied, depersonalized nature of such political interactions (Fig. 19). Potentially broadcasters could use their considerable public authority to plug this credibility gap—hosting political blogs and collating postings so that politicians might reasonably be expected to respond to some, if not all, respondents' contributions. But, as early experiments along these lines have demonstrated, the logistical difficulties involved in such undertakings are immense, while the quality of interaction possible still compares poorly with an MP's surgery or even a conventional phone-in programme.[21]

But if broadcasters possess the power to nurture potentially invigorating popular incursions into electoral politics, do they also possess the will? Politicians are unlikely to try again to block public participation, as they did in the 1960s, but unlike broadcasters they have no reason to demand increased public involvement either. True, politicians benefit from televised coverage of them meeting real voters, but they have no reason to seek more than the semblance of meaningful interaction: if they can be filmed surrounded by crowds of party workers standing in for the public, or appear on television programmes where the questions to be asked have been agreed in advance, then they will do so. They would be mad not to. In turn, broadcasters cannot be expected to facilitate the rebirth of a truly activist public just because it would be good for us and our

Fig. 19. Replying to bloggers, David Cameron podcast, 'WebCameron', 2006

democracy. Even public service broadcasters are first and foremost part of the entertainment business: they will only embrace more ambitious forms of public participation if these can generate strong programmes capable of delivering respectable viewing figures. But broadcasters have much to gain if the irreverent public comes to dominate dull photocalls and potentially stilted phone-in programmes and studio debates. Such encounters can breathe new life into overly managed, ritualized election campaigns which seem incapable of capturing the popular imagination. Broadcasters have the power to rekindle the spirit of the hustings, embedding its irreverent, egalitarian ethos securely in twenty-first century British political culture. We can but hope that they embrace this challenge wholeheartedly; that fear of abandoning professional control will not lead them to make do with diluted forms of popular participation. Further expansion of 'vox pop' coverage will not do. Political interaction must lie at the heart of a healthy democracy, and broadcasting is uniquely placed to help facilitate that interaction between public and politicians. Its challenge is to devise ways that this can be done that will capture the attention of more than just a few hard-bitten politicos. At the old hustings this was done with cabbage stalks and dead cats—we have moved on since then, thankfully, but theatre and entertainment must be at the heart of any repackaging of mediated politics if it is to connect—and connect it must.

In 2005, Ant and Dec's *Saturday Night Takeaway* captured 2.5 million voters from the recently relaunched *Dr Who* when Tony Blair appeared being interviewed at No. 10 by 'Little Ant and Dec', two irreverent and at times cringingly smutty 10-year-olds. It was hardly a high point of political broadcasting—quite the reverse—but it did demonstrate three valuable lessons about early twenty-first-century British political culture. First, that politics as entertainment can attract viewers in significant numbers; second, that British politicians will still put up with considerable public humiliation as the price of securing office; and third, that whilst Labour may once have destabilized class hierarchies, blurring distinctions between 'us' and 'them', such ambiguities have long since evaporated. Wilson, the brilliant Oxford economist might just about get away with presenting himself as a pipe-smoking man of the people in the 1960s, but New Labour's leaders are as manifestly part of an alien political elite as their mainly public school-educated Conservative opponents. They know it and we know it. Discussing the 'masochism strategy' in 2005, a close aide explained that 'Blair ... is groping after a genuine change in the nature of the governing elite and its relationship with the governed': a refreshingly frank acknowledgement of the gulf between leaders and led. According to the aide, for 'the Kilroy generation' (read Oprah or Springer if you are American), sparky studio encounters represent 'the modern equivalent of Gladstone doing his public meetings—it's what people are used to now. There is no real sense of deference any more.' Of course the old hustings had frequently offered politicians far from deferential encounters, but even so the aide had a point—crowds might shout and scream at Lloyd George or Harold Wilson, but it takes different skills to hold one's own with a powerful statesman in a one-to-one exchange, especially in the media spotlight. It probably is only in post-Thatcherite Britain that the mystique of 'Establishment' power has been sufficiently eroded for this sort of egalitarian exchange to be possible. Indeed, it is only since the 1990s that media paternalism has faded sufficiently for it even to be imaginable.

But whether future election coverage will be dominated by gruelling studio encounters between political leaders and irreverent voters, or by prepubescent boys making jokes about farting and knickers, will largely depend on the priorities of British broadcasters. On this vital question about the future of our democracy it is they, rather than the politicians, who are the masters now.[22]

Notes

INTRODUCTION

1. Churchill, *Great Contemporaries*, 17–19, and his 'Humours of electioneering', CHAR 8/301 fos. 16–24, at 23 (typescript for *Strand Magazine*, 1931).
2. Meisel, *Public Speech*, 223–74, esp. 264.
3. See especially, Joyce, *Work, Society and Politics*, 189–90, and his *Democratic Subjects*, and Cockerell, *Live from Number 10*.
4. Donner, *Crusade*, 70.
5. Markham, *Nineteenth-Century Parliamentary Elections*, 39; more generally, see O'Gorman, *Voters, Patrons and Parties*.
6. Dawson, 'Money'.
7. Donner, *Crusade*, 64.
8. Owen, 'MacDonald's parties', 7–9.
9. Tanner, 'Parliamentary electoral system'; Davis and Tanner, 'Borough franchise'; Turner, 'Labour vote'.
10. Brodie, *Politics of the Poor*, ch. 2; Davis, 'Enfranchisement of the urban poor'; also Blewett, 'Franchise in the United Kingdom'; Davis, 'Slums and the vote'.
11. Jephson, *The Platform*, 1: 132.
12. Lloyd, *Elections*, 50.
13. Saunders, *New Parliament*, 141–2; 'Tidlewink', *Electioneering*, 16.
14. Lloyd, *Elections*, 60.
15. 'Tidlewink', *Electioneering*, 16; Lloyd, *Elections*, 45, 60.
16. Montague, *Disenchantment*, 89.
17. Self (ed.), *Neville Chamberlain Diary Letters*, 2: 194 (to Hilda, 17 Nov. 1923), 250 (to Hilda, 5 Oct. 1924).
18. James (ed.), *Chips*, 461 (28 Oct. 1951).
19. Gaby Hinsliff, 'Forget the policies, what about you?' *Observer*, 6 Mar. 2005.

CHAPTER I

1. O'Gorman, *Voters, Patrons and Parties*, esp. 126–71; O'Gorman, 'Campaign rituals'; Brewer, 'Theater and counter-theater'; Vernon, *Politics and the People*, esp. 80–104.

2. Anon., 'Corrupt Practices Bill', *Edinburgh Magazine* (1883), 731; 'Newscuttings of Bristol Parliamentary Elections, 1761–1880' (1784), 28049, 26 (a–b), BRO; O'Gorman, *Voters, Patrons and Parties*, 135.

3. Vernon, *Politics and the People*, esp. 164–82, 295–30; O'Gorman, 'Campaign rituals'; GKL, 27595 'Men of Bradford' (original emphasis); Driver, *Tory Radical*, 194–202; Jephson, *The Platform*, 2: 286; Prest, *Age of Cobden*, 118; Gammage, *Chartist Movement*, 193–4, 284–5.

4. Anon., 'Corrupt practices', *Edinburgh Magazine* (1883), 731; GKL, 27607, 'Preserve Order Forsooth!' (10 Dec. 1832; original emphasis); Driver, *Tory Radical*, 199; Hill, *Toryism and the People*, 22–3.

5. 'Bristol Newscuttings' (1812, 1826, and 1830), 28049 (26) a–b, BRO; *The Oxford Magazine*, 1 (Dec. 1768), 226–9; Rudé, *Wilkes and Liberty*, 59–61, and 'Middlesex Electors'; Anon., *Wit of the Day*, 71, 97; O'Gorman, *Voters, Patrons and Parties*, 255–9; Bridges, *Victorian Recollections*, 150–1; Lynch, *Liberal Party in Rural England*, 82–3.

6. Salmon, *Electoral Reform at Work*, 88–90; Vernon, *Politics and the People*, 87–90; 'To the electors of Totnes and Bridgetown', 'Totnes Borough Election Material', 1579A/12, fo. 31 (27 June 1837), DRO, Exeter; Norris, 'John Stuart Mill,' 94–5. For dead cats see *Report from the Select Committee on Parliamentary and Municipal Elections (Hours of Polling)*, PP1878, XIII, Q1061 (Sheffield).

7. McCormack, *Independent Man*; McCormack (ed.), *Public Men*, introd.; *Northumberland County Election [1826]*, HS. 74 1613 (29), BL; Anon., *Essex County Election (1830)*, 4; *Wakefield Journal and Examiner*, 20 Nov. 1868; Anon., *Poll Book for the Borough of Whitehaven*, esp. 38–9, 53, 59.

8. GKL, 28290, 'West Riding Meeting' (25 June 1833), and GKL, 27711, 'Huddersfield Election, 1832'; Driver, *Tory Radical*, 185, 198, 239; Vernon, *Politics and the People*, 111; Pickering, 'Class without words', 154–62; Belchem and Epstein, 'Gentleman leader'; Epstein, 'Understanding the Cap of Liberty', 86–9 and 108–13. For eighteenth-century precedents, Brewer, 'Theater and counter-theater'.

9. *Wit of the Day*, 112–13 ('Female Influence') and 120 ('The Tol De Rol Lol') (original emphasis); also Lana, 'Women and Foxite strategy'; Lewis, '1784 and all that', 100–13; *Northumberland County Election 1826*, BL HS. 74 1613 (20), 'Breeches for Ever'; GKL, 27702, 'To the electors of the Borough of Leeds'; Gatrell, *City of Laughter*, chs. 14–15, 18; Hilton, *Age of Atonement*.

10. Brougham, *Life and Times*, 2: 62 (letter to Grey, 16 Oct. 1812); also Jephson, *The Platform*, 1: 270; Meisel, *Public Speech*, 226; Dixon, *Canning*, 163–4; Anon., *Impartial Collection of Addresses* (1812), 23, 36, 56, 85, 97, 116, and 128; Anon., *Speeches of Canning (1812)*, 23–7.

11. Eastwood, 'Contesting deference', 30–1; Brougham, *Life and Times*, 2: 62; Anon., *Speeches of Canning (1812)*, 5–7; Jephson, *The Platform*, 1: 236, 239;

Dixon, *Canning*, 164, 195; Anon., *Regular Account* [1802], 21, 23, 28, 44; Thorne (ed.), *History of Parliament, 1790–1820*, 2: 228–34.

12. Markham, *1820 at Hedon*, 9; Seymour, *Electoral Reform*, 92; O'Gorman, *Voters, Patrons and Parties*, 258–85; Lawson, *Substance of a Speech*, 4, 6–8, 11, 30–2; Lawson-Tancred, *Records*, 317–19, 334–67; Golby, 'Great electioneer', 209–10; Thorne, *History of Parliament, 1790–1820*, 2: 443–5, 450–2; 4: 394–5.

13. Lawson, *Substance of a Speech*, 6–7, 24–5, 32; William Green to Henry Pelham-Clinton, 3 May 1820 (Ne C 6632), and William Hirst to Henry Pelham-Clinton, 17 May 1826 (Ne C 6709/2), Newcastle (Clumber) Collection, University of Nottingham; O'Gorman, *Voters, Patrons and Parties*, 225–6, 234; Eastwood, 'Contesting deference', 31–2.

14. O'Gorman, *Voters, Patrons and Parties*, 106–12; Wilson, *Sense of the People*, 29–73; Bradley, *Religion, Revolution and English Radicalism*; Nicholas Rogers, *Whigs and Cities*; Sweet, 'Freemen and independence'; Eastwood, 'Contesting deference', 30–1, 38; Smith, 'Yorkshire elections', 86–8.

15. 'Bristol Newscuttings' (1830–1), 28049 (26) a–b, BRO; Phillips, *Great Reform Bill*, 297–9; Eastwood, 'Contesting deference', 33; Forrester, *Northamptonshire County Elections*, 131–47.

16. Seymour, *Electoral Reform*, 16–20; Moore, *Politics of Deference*; Davis, 'Deference and aristocracy'; Hilton, *Mad, Bad and Dangerous People*, 433–6; Gash, *Politics in the Age of Peel*; Hanham, *Elections and Party Management*; Prest, *Age of Cobden*, 17–22.

17. Seymour, *Electoral Reform*, 31–6, 88 n.; Salmon, *Electoral Reform at Work*, 4, 22–42, 200–6; Taylor, 'Interests, parties and the state', 56–61.

18. Markham, *Nineteenth-Century Elections*, 10–11, 36; Trollope, *Autobiography*, 264, 267, 299; Allison (ed.), *History of East Riding*, 6: 141–9; Pollard, *Trollope's Political Novels*, 5–13; Briggs, *Victorian People*, 109–13.

19. Briggs, *Victorian People*, 111; Gash, *Politics in the Age of Peel*, 105–53; Dickens, *Pickwick Papers*, 177–97; Albery, *Parliamentary History of Horsham*, 339–56; *Parliamentary and Municipal Elections (Hours of Polling)*, PP1878, XIII, cols. 1684, 2527–8; 'Bristol Newscuttings' (1874), 28049 (26) a–b, BRO; Tingay, *Anthony Trollope Politician*, 8–9; Richter, *Riotous Victorians*, 63–8; Richter, 'The role of mob riot'.

20. O'Gorman, 'Culture of elections', 22–4; O'Gorman, 'Campaign rituals', 113–15; Gwyn, *Democracy and Cost*, 47–8; Salmon, *Electoral Reform at Work*, 88–9; 'Bristol Newscuttings' (1837 and 1841), 28049 (26) a–b, BRO; Phillips, *Great Reform Bill*, 34–5.

21. Grego, *History of Parliamentary Elections*, 402.

22. Beales, 'Electorate before and after 1832'; Phillips and Wetherell, 'Reform and the rise of partisanship'; Phillips and Wetherell, 'Reform and political modernization'; Phillips, *Great Reform Bill*, 32–6, 299–301; Salmon, *Electoral Reform*

at Work, 9–10, 20–42; Prest, *Age of Cobden*, 26–32, 44–5, 80–102. For subtle accounts of the diverse forces behind partisanship after 1832 see Mohamed Adel Manai, 'Electoral politics in mid-nineteenth-century Lancashire' (University of Lancashire, Ph.D., 1991), esp. 63–6, 100–4, 180–93, and Taylor, 'Interests, parties and the state'.

23. Fisher, 'Issues and influence', and 'Limits of deference'; Jaggard, '1841 Election'; Prest, *Age of Cobden*, 80–102.

24. Seymour, *Electoral Reform*, 92; Sack, 'House of Lords'; Jaggard, 'Small town politics'; Phillips and Wetherell, 'Reform and political modernization', 421, 432; Hoppen, 'Grammars of electoral violence'; Hoppen, *Mid-Victorian Generation*, 257–70.

25. Jones, *Powers of the Press*, 21–3; Scott, *Reporter Anonymous*, 17; Parry, *Rise and Fall*, 27–34; Barker, *Newspapers*, esp. chs. 1 and 2.

26. Southall, 'Mobility', 109–13, 123–6.

27. Jephson, *The Platform*, 1: 31, 129, 198, 271, 451; Emden, *The People*, 82–3; Parry, *Rise and Fall*, 40–1; Meisel, *Public Speech*, 229–31; Jordan, 'Reports of Parliamentary debates'; Robson, *What did he say*, 1–8; Anderson, 'Hansard's hazards'.

28. Rogers, *Crowds, Culture, and Politics*, and 'Crowds and political festival', 234, 251–9; Tilly, *Popular Contention*; Saville, *1848*; Hilton, *Mad, Bad and Dangerous?* esp. chs. 9 and 10.

29. Jephson, *The Platform*, 1: 453; Meisel, *Public Speech*, 233–4; Steele, 'Gladstone and Palmerston', 118, 120, 133; Russell, *Collections and Recollections*, 161; Taylor, 'Palmerston and Radicalism', 176–9.

30. Steele, 'Gladstone and Palmerston', 118; *The Times*, 13 May and 20 Oct. 1864, 19 and 20 July 1865, 7 Apr. 1866; *Gladstone Diaries* (ed. Matthew), 6: 370–1 (18 July 1865); Biagini, *Liberty, Retrenchment and Reform*, 379–85; Joyce, *Visions of the People*, 48–55; Matthew, *Gladstone, 1809–1874*, 127, 129, 140–2; Vincent, *Formation of the Liberal Party*, 34.

31. Meisel, *Public Speech*, 237–8; Vernon, *Politics and the People*, 225–30; Victoria Barbary, 'Popular politics in Newcastle-upon-Tyne, 1850–c.1862' (University of Durham, MA thesis, 2003), 58–9; James, *MP for Dewsbury*, 78.

32. Millicent Fawcett to JM, 7 Oct. 1884, John Massie Letters, Add MSS 8988/55, CUL.

33. Lewis, 'British by-elections', 175; Swaddle, 'Coping with a mass electorate: A study in the evolution of constituency electioneering in Britain, with special emphasis on the periods which followed the Reform Acts of 1884 and 1918' (University of Oxford D.Phil., 1990), 109–10; *Gladstone Diaries* (ed. Matthew), 12: 349 (11 Dec. 1890); Bunn, *Practical Notes*, 13, 14.

34. Meisel, *Public Speech*, 242–3; Jephson, *The Platform*, 2: 363–4; Russell, *Collections and Recollections*, 169; Matthew, *Gladstone, 1875–1898*, 1–6, 14–26; Swaddle, 'Coping with a mass electorate', 108. Salisbury sat unopposed as Conservative MP for Stamford between 1853 and 1868.

CHAPTER 2

1. Seymour, *Electoral Reform*, 248–54, 272–9, 286, 533; Smith, *Second Reform Bill*, 236; Hoppen, 'Franchise and electoral politics', 215–16; Hall, McClelland, and Rendall, *Defining the Victorian Nation*, 1–8, 240–5; Davis and Tanner, 'Borough franchise', 308. Figures in the text have been rounded.

2. 'Bristol Newscuttings' (1868 by-election and 1868), 28049 (26) a–b, BRO; *Report from the Select Committee on Parliamentary and Municipal Elections* (Hartington Committee), PP1868-69, VIII, Q4407-11 (Robert Bush) and Q5673-81 (Herbert Thomas); *Bristol Election Petition, Minutes of Evidence & Proceedings*, PP1867-68, VIII, 21 ff.

3. 'Bristol Newscuttings' (1868 by-election and 1868), 28049 (26) a–b, BRO; *Hartington Committee*, 1868–69, Q4699 (Thomas Colborne), Q5680-1 (Thomas); *Bristol Election Petition*, 1868; Cook, *Free and Independent*, 86; Richter, *Riotous Victorians*, 64–5.

4. *Report from the Select Committee on Parliamentary and Municipal Elections* (Hartington Committee), Final Report, PP1870, VI, 138; Seymour, *Electoral Reform*, 429–32; Matthew, *Gladstone, 1809–1874*, 172. For a humorous contemporary attack on undue influence see, Summers, *M.P. for Puddlepoor*.

5. *Hartington Committee* (Final Report), 1870, 136–7, 142, 146, 151; *Hartington Committee*, 1868–69, 18, Q2428 (Staleybridge), Q3217 (Bright/Blackburn), Q3418 (Liverpool), Q3698 (Henry Davies), Q5843-9 (Alexander Russell); 'Bristol Newscuttings' (1870 by-election), 28049 (26) a–b, BRO; Hanham, *Elections and Party Management*, 96–9; *Bristol Election Petition Judgement, 1870*, PP1870, LVI, 179–82; for examples of Conservative open primaries see Battersea, http://iaindale.blogspot.com/2006/09/jane-ellison-wins-battersea-selection.html and St Ives, http://www.stivesconservatives.com/index.php?sectionid=3&pagenumber=46 (both 17 Mar. 2008).

6. *Hansard* (Parl. Debates), 3rd ser., ccix (Commons), 15 Feb. 1872, cols. 499–500 (Fielden); *Hartington Committee*, 1868–69, Q1543-5 (Leeds), Q1775 (Liverpool), Q2431-3 and Q3998-4002 (Staleybridge), Q2872-7 (Bradford), Q3699 (Cheltenham), Q5843-4 (Edinburgh); Williams, *Keeping the Peace*.

7. *Hartington Committee*, 1868–69, Q1199 (Warrington), Q1992 (Liverpool), Q3209-30 (Bradford), Q4057-71, 4089 (Gravesend), Q4713-18 (Newport); Vernon, *Politics and the People*, 157–8; 'Bristol Newscuttings' (1870 by-election), 28049 (26) a–b, BRO.

8. Seymour, *Electoral Reform*, 432–6; *Report from the Select Committee on the Corrupt Practices Prevention Act (1854)*, PP1860, X, Q696-700 (Edwin James MP); *Report from the Select Committee on Corrupt Practices Prevention and Election Petition Acts*, PP1875, VIII, Q1066 (Norwich); *Report from the Select Committee on Parliamentary and Municipal Elections*, PP1876, XII, Q49, 59, 231 (Manchester), Q347 (Leeds), Q602 (Liverpool), Q933 (Hackney); *Wolverhampton Chronicle*, 11 Feb. 1874; *Leeds Daily News*, 6 Feb. 1874; *Leeds*

Mercury, 6 Feb. 1874; O'Leary, *Corrupt Practices*, 88–111; *The Times*, 10 and 11 Feb. 1874.

9. Richter, 'Role of mob riot', 22, 25–6; Richter, *Riotous Victorians*, 65–9; O'Leary, *Corrupt Practices*, 121–2; Saunders, *New Parliament*, 230–5; *Parliamentary and Municipal Elections (Hours of Polling)*, PP1878, XIII, Q2520-2 (Manchester); Reid, 'Saint Monday revisited'.

10. See Vernon, *Politics and the People, passim*; Lawrence, 'Decline of popular politics?', and *Speaking for the People*, ch. 7; *Report on Corrupt Practices Act (1854)*, iii. On elite control see also Seymour, *Electoral Reform*, 433–4 and Ostrogorski, *Democracy and Parties, passim*.

11. Woodings, *Conduct and Management*, 116; Lloyd, *Elections*, 115–16; *Hours of Polling Report*, Q1107 (Sheffield); 'Bristol Newscuttings' (1874), 28049 (26) a–b, BRO; Fisher, 'Electoral abuses', 42–3; 'Tidlewink', *Electioneering*, 23; *Controverted Elections (Judgements)*, PP1893-94, LXX, 61–8 (Walsall); Richards, *Candidates' Guide*, 111–12.

12. Kathryn Rix, 'The party agent and English electoral culture, 1880–1906' (University of Cambridge, Ph.D. thesis, 2001) and ' "Go out into the highways" ', 209–31; Hedderwick, *Parliamentary Election Manual*, 175; Bunn, *Political Organization*, 24; 'Tidlewink', *Electioneering*, 15; Howes, *Twenty-Five Years*, esp. 208–67; Lawrence, *Speaking for the People*, 224–7, 264–7.

13. GKL, 27697 'Northern Division of Derbyshire'; Rouse, *Manual for Election Agents*, 21, 23–5, 28.

14. Vernon, *Politics and the People*, 225–30, 337; Belchem and Epstein, 'Gentleman leader', 186–90; *Hartington Committee*, 1868–69, Q2431–3, 3998–4002 (Staleybridge), Q2791, 2872–7 (Bradford), Q3450 (Liverpool); Anthony D. Taylor, 'Ernest Jones: His later career and the structure of Manchester politics, 1861–1869' (University of Birmingham, MA thesis, 1984), 56–8, 67, 70–2, 81; Miles Taylor, *Ernest Jones*, 243–8; Richter, *Riotous Victorians*, 35–50 (on Murphy).

15. Meisel, *Public Speech*, 259, 262; Scott, *Reporter Anonymous*, 77–8; *Gladstone Diaries* (ed. Matthew), 9: 461 (24 Nov. 1879), 465 (8 Dec. 1879); *Wolverhampton Chronicle*, 4 Feb. 1874; Lloyd, *Elections*, 32–5.

16. Meisel, *Public Speech*, 235, 259–60; Monypenny and Buckle, *Life of Disraeli*, 2: 526, 532–4; Ostrogorski, *Democracy and Parties*, 1: 385–6; Matthew, *Gladstone, 1875–1898*, 45.

17. Jephson, *The Platform*, 2: 400 (Hartington addressed 24 meetings to Gladstone's 15); *Gladstone Diaries* (ed. Matthew), 9: 461–6 (Midlothian, 1879), esp. 466 (11 Dec. 1879); Foot (ed.), *Midlothian Speeches, 1879*, introd.; Mathew, *Gladstone, 1875–1898*, 46, 48; Meisel, *Public Speech*, 245, 255–6, 262–6; Bentley, *Lord Salisbury's World*, 295–302.

18. Gardiner, *Prophets, Priests and Kings*, 105–6, 155–6; Chamberlain, *Down the Years*, 255–7, 262, 270–2; Matthew, *Gladstone, 1875–1898*, 48–9; Churchill, *My Early Life*, 372.

19. *Portsmouth Times*, 4 July 1895; Matthew, 'Rhetoric and politics'; *Gladstone Diaries* (ed. Matthew), 9: 223 (31 May 1877), 11: 201–2 (1 Sept. 1884); Monypenny and Buckle, *Life of Disraeli*, 2: 527; Scott, *Reporter Anonymous*, 77–8.

20. Clarke, *Lancashire and the New Liberalism*, 130–1; Rowe, *Practical Manual*, 62; Richards, *Candidates' Guide*, 44, 46–7, 120–8; 'Newspaper cuttings, 1904–1910', 4629/1/4/4, Bridgeman Papers, Shropshire Archives; Jephson, *The Platform*, 2: 432; Woodings, *Conduct and Management*, 12; Lloyd, *Elections*, 31.

21. Richards, *Candidates' Guide*, 45–6; Howarth, 'Liberal revival', 95; Lloyd, *Elections*, 19–21, 30; Bunn, *Practical Notes*, 11–13; Houston and Valdar, *Modern Electioneering Practice*, 91, 94–6.

22. Woodings, *Conduct and Management*, 164–5; Lloyd, *Elections*, 20–3; Richards, *Candidates' Guide*, 131; Rowe, *Practical Manual*, 61; O'Leary, *Corrupt Practices*, 121.

23. Rowe, *Practical Manual*, 63; Arbuthnot (ed.), *Primrose League Guide*, 187–9; Pugh, *Tories and the People*; Reynolds, Woolley, and Woolley, *Seems So!*, 3–12; *Hartington Committee*, 1868–69, Q3385 (Liverpool).

24. J- C-, *Election Squibs*, 15–16 ('On Mr Allsopp's late visit to Bromsgrove'); Howes, *Twenty-Five Years*, 25; Hurst, 'Liberal versus Liberal', 707; *Oswestry and Border Counties Advertiser*, 17 July 1895; *Loughborough Examiner*, 25 July 1895. In this and following paragraphs I draw mainly on the findings of the Economic and Social Research Council funded project, 'Electing John Bull: The Changing Face of British Elections, 1895–1935' (ESRC RES-000-22-0345).

25. Rowe, *Practical Manual*, 60; Howes, *Twenty-Five Years*, 302–3; Richards, *Candidates' Guide*, 46; Lloyd, *Elections*, 24.

26. *The Times*, 14 Oct. 1884, 6a; Lawrence, *Speaking for the People*, 184–8 and 'Transformation of public politics', 188–94.

27. Lloyd, *Elections*, 22; Lowell, *Government of England*, 2: 65; Matthew, *Gladstone, 1875–1898*, 390; Pocock, *Machiavellian Moment*; Collini, *Public Moralists*, 193–4; Jephson, *The Platform*, 2: 406–7; James Thompson, 'The idea of "public opinion" in Britain, 1870–1914' (University of Cambridge Ph.D. thesis, 2000).

28. Seymour, *Electoral Reform*, 4–5, 518, 523–5; Gorst, 'Elections of the future', *Fortnightly Review* (1883), 698; *Seventeenth Annual Conference Report of the National Union of Conservative and Constitutional Associations*, 'The Condition of the Conservative Party in the Midland Counties', 2. On the Act itself see O'Leary, *Corrupt Practices*, 159–78; Swaddle, 'Coping', 64–8; and Rix, 'Elimination?'

29. Tholfsen, 'Origins of Birmingham caucus'; Griffiths, 'Caucus and the Liberal party'; Hanham, *Elections and Party Management*, 125–54; *Hartington Committee*, 1868–69, Q3385 (Liverpool); Waller, *Democracy and Sectarianism*, 16–18;

Seventeenth Annual Conference Report of the National Union of Conservative and Constitutional Associations, Debate on the Corrupt Practices Act, 4.

30. Asquith, *Election Guide;* Gorst, *Election Manual,* also Mattinson and Macaskie, *Law Relating to Corrupt Practices*; Anon., 'Corrupt Practices Bill', 728; Rowe, *Practical Manual,* 1; O'Leary, *Corrupt Practices,* 208; Richter, *Riotous Victorians,* 66–7; Lawrence, *Speaking for the People,* 183–4.

31. Seymour, *Electoral Reform,* 392, *contra* Ostrogorski, *Democracy and Parties,* 1: 472–82; O'Leary, *Elimination,* 208, 229–33; Hanham, *Elections and Party Management,* 273–6, 281–3; Rix, 'Elimination?'; Hedderwick, *Parliamentary Manual,* 35.

32. Seymour, *Electoral Reform,* 496, 504, 509–10, 514–16; Lowell, *Government of England,* 1: 199; Dunbabin, 'Single-member constituencies'; Swaddle, 'Coping', 60–4; Birrell, *Things Past Redress,* 102; Cornford, 'Transformation of Conservatism'; Coetzee, 'Villa Toryism'; Roberts, ' "Villa Toryism" '; Windscheffel, *Popular Conservatism.*

33. Seymour, *Electoral Reform,* 460–71, 488, 533; Howarth, 'Liberal revival', 95–6; Swaddle, 'Coping', 108; Oswestry Conservative and Unionist Association Minute Book, 1876–1887, Annual Report, 31 Oct. 1884, Oswestry Public Library, Shropshire; Joseph Chamberlain to William Bridgeman, 29 July 1904, 4629/1/1904/10, Bridgeman Papers; 'Tidlewink', *Electioneering,* 15; Lloyd, *Elections,* 16, 64; Bunn, *Instructions to Sub-Agents,* 14; Woodings, *Conduct and Management,* 114; Rowe, *Practical Manual,* 53. On the persistence of rituals in the countryside see, Lynch, *Liberal Party in Rural England,* 80–8, and on the radicalization of rural politics see Readman, *Land and Nation.*

CHAPTER 3

1. O'Leary, *Corrupt Practices,* 233; Matthew, 'Rhetoric and politics', esp. 39, 49, 54; also Matthew, McKibbin, and Kay, 'Franchise factor', esp. 743, 748–9.

2. Birrell, *Things Past,* 150; Lawrence, *Speaking for the People,* 223–4; Russell, *Liberal Landslide,* 126–7; 'The War's Result' (LPD. P23), Coll. Misc. 0519/51, BLPES—the poster also quoted charges of 'semi slavery' from the *Morning Leader*; Thompson, ' "Pictorial lies"?', 177–8; Ward, *Red Flag and Union Jack,* 66–8.

3. Lloyd, 'Uncontested seats', 263. Analysis of the January 1910 election is based on the Economic and Social Research Council funded project, 'Electing John Bull: The Changing Face of British Elections, 1895–1935' (ESRC RES-000-22-0345); see also Blewett, *Peers, Parties and People,* 103–29.

4. Lloyd, *Elections,* 32–5; Finn, *Outdoor Meeting,* 2; Bentley, *Salisbury's World,* 295, 299–302; Green, *Crisis of Conservatism,* 125–9; Lawrence, 'Class and gender', and 'Contesting the male polity', 215–16; Gilbert, *Churchill,* IV, *Companion* 1: 430 (29 Nov. 1918), 438 (13 Dec. 1918).

5. *The Times*, 24 June, 27 Sept. 1907, 6 June 1908; Churchill, *My Early Life*, 372; Clementine Churchill to WSC, n.d. (8 Nov. 1922), CHAR 1/158 fos. 54–9 on hiring 'Sergeant Thompson etc.'; Taylor, *Jix*, 48–9, 63–4; Churchill, 'Humours of electioneering', CHAR 8/301, fos. 16–24, Churchill Papers, CAC.

6. Birrell, *Things Past*, 151; Lloyd, *Elections*, 44–5; 'Tidlewink', *Electioneering*, 15; Clementine Churchill to WSC, n.d. (8 Nov. 1922), CHAR 1/158 fo. 56, Churchill Papers, CAC; Gilbert, *Churchill*, IV, 885; Churchill, 'Humours of Electioneering'. Also Bunn, *Political Organisation*, 24 (on the popularity of professional working-men speakers).

7. Peddie, *Outline History of Printing*, 29–32; Swaddle, 'Coping', 101–3, 126–31; Rix, 'Party agent', 274 91; Lawrence, *Speaking for the People*, 206–8; Ramsden, *Age of Balfour*, 232; Cockett, 'Party, publicity and media', 547; Hedderwick, *Parliamentary Manual*, 177–8; Richards, *Candidates' Guide*, 44; *Liberal Agent*, Apr. 1910, 179–80. On local leafleting strategy see Manchester Liberal Federation, Executive Committee Minutes, 1909–1918, 3 Feb. 1910 (Central Office Election Report), M283/1/3/3, Manchester Archives; Swaddle, 'Coping', 127; 'Amery Election Material, 1923': 'To Shopkeepers', AMEL, 4/11, Leo Amery Papers, Churchill Archives.

8. This paragraph draws extensively on Thompson, ' "Pictorial lies"?' See also Swaddle, 'Coping', 106–7, 115; Blewett, *Peers, Parties and People*, 332; Fisher, 'Electoral abuses', 43; Rowe, *Practical Manual*, 53, 57; Hedderwick, *Parliamentary Manual*, 177; Lloyd, *Elections*, 28, 64, 94; Labour Representation Committee, Hodgson to MacDonald, 26 Jan. 1906 (LRC, 30/106), Labour History Archive, Manchester; *Liberal Agent*, Jan. 1912, 161, 164; July 1912, 29; Oct. 1914, 115; Apr. 1915, 214; North-West Manchester Liberal Association Minutes, 9 Oct. 1911, M283/4/1/1, Manchester Archives; Woodings, *Conduct and Management*, 113–15.

9. John Johnson Collection, 'Elections', Box 3 (Belloc), and 'Cartoons', Box 5 (*Daily Chronicle*), Bodleian, Oxford; Blewett, *Peers, Parties and People*, 330–3; Swaddle, 'Coping', 114–16; Amery, *My Political Life*, 1: 331; Trentmann, 'National identity', 233–7.

10. 'Amery Election material, 1906–11': 'The case against the Government', 'The Old Age Pensions Lie', and 'Election Address, January 1910', AMEL 4/5, Leo Amery Papers, Churchill Archives; 'Bridgeman Political Diary 1906–18', 50 (Jan. 1910), 4629/1/2/1, and 'Newspaper Cuttings, 1915–1923' (though includes 1910 election leaflets), 4629/1/4/7, Bridgeman Papers, Shropshire Archives; *Handbook for Unionist Canvassers: General Election 1910* (Imperial Tariff Committee, Birmingham, 1910), 9–10; 'What price to-day?', Tariff Reform League poster, Coll. Misc. 0519/88, BLPES, London (see also 'Found out', 0519/7 and 'Chinese Labour', 519/60 for examples of other populist Conservative posters); Pugh, 'Working-class experience'.

11. Lloyd, *Elections*, 35; Swaddle, 'Coping', 109–10; Arbuthnot, *Primrose League Guide*, 178–81; Richards, *Candidates' Guide*, 135; Bateman Collection, Bristol

ILP Minute Books, Dec. 1906–July 1912, Executive committee, 1 Sept. 1909, DM 1532/Q1/1, Bristol University Library Special Collections.

12. Matthew, *Gladstone, 1875–1898*, 58, 363; Jalland, *Women, Marriage and Politics*, 199–201, 204–7; Martin, *Lady Randolph Churchill*, 1: 184–7. The subtle art of female canvassing was a perennial subject of comment, see Disraeli, *Year at Hartlebury*, 127–29, 146–52; also *Illustrated London News*, 10 July 1886, 49 ('A Lady Canvasser'), and 20 Jan. 1906, 81 ('Sirens of the Canvass').

13. Jalland, *Women*, 204–10; Linda E. Walker, 'The women's movement in England in the late nineteenth and early twentieth centuries' (University of Manchester Ph.D., 1984), 22–7, and 'Party political women'; Cowman, *'Mrs Brown is a Man'*, 42–3; Richards, *Candidates' Guide*, 129–36; Lloyd, *Elections*, 19; Lawrence, 'Contesting the male polity'.

14. The ideas in this paragraph are explored at length in Lawrence, 'Contesting the male polity'; see also Pankhurst, *My Own Story*, esp. 48.

15. Jalland, *Women*, 207–9; Lloyd, *Elections*, 138–9; *Illustrated London News*, 20 Jan. 1906, 81; ESRC project, 'Electing John Bull: The Changing Face of British Elections, 1895–1935'.

16. William Bridgeman Correspondence, 1904, letters: 10 (Chamberlain, 29 July); 17 (Jenkins, 3 Aug.) and 21 (Chamberlain, 8 Dec.), 4629/1/1904, Bridgeman Papers, Shropshire Archives; cutting from *The Outlook* (1913), Morrison-Bell Papers (2128), DRO, Exeter; Bunn, *Political Organization*, 20–2. On women in Conservative auxiliary organizations after 1900 see David Thackeray, 'British popular Conservatism and the radical Right, *c.*1910–1924' (University of Cambridge Ph.D. thesis, in progress).

17. Trentmann, 'Bread, milk and democracy', 129–30, and 'National identity', 234–7; Arbuthnot, *Primrose League Guide*, 189; William Bridgeman Correspondence, 1904, letter 21 (Chamberlain, 8 Dec.), 4629/1/1904, Bridgeman Papers, Shropshire Archives; Fisher, 'Electoral abuses', 35; Brodie, *Politics of the Poor*, 121–5; Pugh, *March of the Women*, 58–9, 78–83, 110–19.

18. Bunn, *Instructions to Sub-Agents*, 6; Birrell, *Things Past*, 178; Lloyd, *Elections*, 23; Dorothy Buxton letter (1910), Morrison-Bell Papers, 2128, DRO, Exeter.

19. Bridgeman Correspondence, 1900: 4329/1/1900/22, Bridgeman Papers, Shropshire Archives; Lloyd, *Elections*, 21–3; *Report of the Departmental Committee on the Duties of the Police with Respect to the Preservation of Order at Public Meetings*, 2 vols., PP1909, Cd. 4673 and Cd. 4674, XXXVI, I: 95, 97–8; II: *passim*; Helmore, *Corrupt and Illegal Practices*, 86, 98; Reeves, *Round About a Pound*.

20. Wallas, *Human Nature in Politics*, 103, 107–9, 127, 229–30; Wiener, *Between Two Worlds*; Qualter, *Graham Wallas*, 88–102; Clarke, *Liberals and Social Democrats*, 134–45; Swaddle, 'Coping', 111–12; Masterman, *The Condition of England*, 94–102, esp. 99, 101. See also Wallas's collection of material from the 1901, 1904, and 1907 LCC elections in Coll. Misc. 0840, BLPES, London.

21. Masterman, *Condition*, 96–8; Hobson, *Psychology of Jingoism*; Blewett, *Peers, Parties and People*, 110–11; ESRC project, 'Electing John Bull: The Changing Face of British Elections, 1895–1935'.

22. Grego, *History of Parliamentary Elections*, 402; Wright, *Life of Colonel Burnaby*, 163–4; Lawrence, *Speaking for the People*, 189–90; Howes, *Twenty-Five Years*, 208–83, esp. 252, 266–7.

23. 'Transcript of speech to Newton Abbott Constitutional Club' (*c.*1958) and 'Mid-Devon By-Election, Jan. 1908' (cuttings), Morrison-Bell Papers, DRO, Exeter; 'Five-Year Diary', MOR/3/2 (18 Jan. 1908), [Arthur] Morrison-Bell Papers, Parliamentary Archives; *The Times*, 20 Jan. 1908; *Women's Franchise*, 23 Jan. 1908; Pankhurst, *My Own Story*, 90–3.

24. 'Transcript' and miscellaneous cuttings: *Mayfair*, 14 Dec. 1911, *The Outlook*, 8 Nov. 1913, *Totnes Unionist*, Feb. 1926, Morrison-Bell Papers, DRO, Exeter; Lawrence, 'Contesting the male polity'; Bingham, *Gender, Modernity and the Press*, 111; Bearman, 'Suffragette violence'; J. S. Ainsworth to JM, 31 Dec. 1910, John Massie Letters, CUL, describing the conspiracy of silence surrounding a brutal suffragette attack on Birrell in Whitehall.

25. Fisher, 'Electoral abuses', 34, 36–7, 42–3; Rix, 'Elimination?', *passim*; Rowe, *Practical Manual*, 10–11; Richards, *Candidates' Guide*, 58; Hedderwick, *Parliamentary Manual*, 35–7; *Nottingham East Petition Judgment*, PP1911 vol. LXI, 467–77; Gwyn, *Cost of Politics*, 56–60, 67–8, 77, 90–2; Lloyd, *Elections*, 56–8; Clarke, *Lancashire and the New Liberalism*, 138–9, 198–219; Swaddle, 'Coping', 77–80, 90–3; 'Memo. on subscriptions' (1911), and GL to Buck, 28 Oct. 1913, GLLD 18/3, George Lloyd Papers, Churchill Archives.

26. Fisher, 'Electoral abuses', 39; Lloyd to Buck, 21 Oct. 1911, and 28 May 1913, Buck to Lloyd, 10 June 1913, GLLD 18/3 and Lloyd to Beaman, 19 Feb. 1912, GLLD 18/1, George Lloyd Papers, Churchill Archives; Bentley, 'Gladstonian Liberals', 179, 185; Nicholas, *To the Hustings*, 291–305; Belloc, *Mr Clutterbuck's Election*, 105–6, 110, 157–8, 242; Dawson, 'Moncy'; Morris, *Parliamentary Franchise*, 172.

27. Clarke, *Lancashire and the New Liberalism*, 200–1, 234–45; John Johnson Collection, 'Elections', Box 3, Bodleian, Oxford; Lawrence, *Speaking for the People*, 257–63, and 'Labour myths', 344–51; Owen, 'MacDonald's parties'.

CHAPTER 4

1. Taylor, *English History*, 235; Lawrence, 'Transformation of public politics', *passim*.

2. Stannage, *Baldwin Thwarts*, 178; Bowden, 'New consumerism', 246; James Adams to Baldwin, 9 Nov. 1935, and A. R. Fysh to Baldwin, 1 Nov. 1935 (original emphasis), vol. 39, Baldwin Papers, CUL; Ramsden, 'Baldwin and film', 130–1; Williamson, *Stanley Baldwin*, 83–5; Self (ed.), *Austen Chamberlain Diary Letters*, 258 (to Ida, 19 Oct. 1924); Stuart (ed.), *Reith Diaries*, 90 (11/12,

15, 16/17 Oct. 1924); Rowe, 'Broadcasting and 1929'; Matheson, *Broadcasting*, 99–101; Scott, *Reporter Anonymous*, 172–4; Scannell and Cardiff, *Social History of Broadcasting*, chs. 2–3.

3. Grant, *Propaganda*, esp. ch. 2; Cockett, 'Party, publicity and the media', 559–63; *Illustrated London News*, 4 May 1929, 764; Pronay, 'British news-reels', 412, and 'Newsreels: the illusion', 109–13; Gilbert, *Churchill*, V, *Companion* I: 1471 (Clementine to WSC, 6 May 1929); 1931 newsreels at http://www.screenonline.org.uk/film/id/1192584/index.html (MacDonald), and 10 id/1192614/index.html (Baldwin) (British Film Institute, visited 9 Aug. 2007); Williamson, *Stanley Baldwin*, 154–65; Ramsden, 'Baldwin and film', 127–30, 133–6; Hollins, 'Conservative Party and film'; Swaddle, 'Coping', 156–7; J. M. Harwill to SB, 11 Nov. 1935, vol. 39, Baldwin Papers, CUL; Taylor, 'Speaking to democracy', 81–3.

4. Mass Observation, *Report on the Press*, File Report 126 (Harvester Microfiche), Section 3: 1, 13–17, Section 4: 2; BBC [Jennings and Gill], *Broadcasting in Everyday Life*, 15; Laura DuMond Beers, ' "Selling Socialism": Labour, Democracy and the Mass Media, 1900–1939' (Harvard University Ph.D. thesis, 2007), 20–3.

5. Wadsworth, 'Newspaper circulations', 27–8; Lewis, 'British by-elections', 177; McKibbin, *Classes and Cultures*, 505; Rhodes, *Loaded Hour*, 44–5, 48–62, 83; Gliddon, 'Provincial newspapers'; Dawson, 'Provincial press'; Lee, *Origins of Popular Press*; Hampton, *Visions of the Press*, chs. 3 and 4 and 'Rethinking the "New Journalism" '.

6. Wadsworth, 'Newspaper circulations', 26–8, 35; Koss, *Rise and Fall*, chs. 23–4; Beers, ' "Selling Socialism" ', 23–35; Scott, *Reporter Anonymous*, 153–7, 180; Ball, *Baldwin*, esp. ch. 7; Williamson, *Stanley Baldwin*, 79–83, 231–5; Peele, 'St George's'; H. Pratt to Baldwin, 20 Nov. 1935, vol. 39, Baldwin Papers, CUL; Cockett, *Twilight of Truth*, and 'Party, publicity and the media'; Lawrence, 'Transformation of public politics', 198–9.

7. Lloyd, *Elections*, 24; Emden, *People and Constitution*, 84; Meisel, *Public Speech*, 227; Matthew, 'Rhetoric and politics'; Labour, *Conduct of Elections*, 1931, 2; Cambray, *Game of Politics*, 172; Rowe, 'Broadcasting', 119.

8. For a measure of the growing reliability of private cars for electioneering, compare Sir Arthur Clive Morrison-Bell's pre- and post-war 'Five-Year Diaries', MOR/3/2–5, Morrison-Bell Papers, Parliamentary Archives; Lewis, 'British by-elections', 175; Houston and Valdar, *Modern Electioneering*, 92; Muir, *How Britain is Governed*, 313–14; Cambray, *Game of Politics*, 172.

9. Finn, *Outdoor Meeting*, 120–5; Labour, *Conduct of Elections*, 1931, 2–3; Cockett, 'Party, publicity and the media', 557, 561; Principal Agent to J. C. C. Davidson, 12 Oct. 1928, vol. 36, Baldwin Papers, CUL.

10. Muir, *How Britain is Governed*, 314; Finn, *Outdoor Meeting*, 2–4, 106, 119–28; Gray, *Confessions of a Candidate*, 85–6; Labour, *Conduct of Elections*, 1931, 50–1; *Labour Organiser* [LO], Oct. 1935, 191–2; McHenry, *Labour Party in*

Transition, 198; Houston and Valdar, *Modern Electioneering,* 21–2, 95–9, 103–4; Cambray, *Game of Politics,* 172–5. For a brilliant discussion of the difficulties Labour politicians often faced bridging the relatively small social gap between themselves and their supporters, see Owen, 'MacDonald's parties'.

11. *Bristol Times and Mirror,* 15 Nov. 1922; Finn, *Outdoor Meeting,* 120; *The Times,* 29 and 30 Nov. 1923, 2 June 1925, 24 June 1927; Williamson and Baldwin (eds.), *Baldwin Papers,* 150–1 (SB to Joan Davidson, 30 July 1924), and 171–2 (SB to Joan Davidson, 4 June 1925); James (ed.), *Davidson's Memoirs,* 303; Ramsden, 'Baldwin and film', 128; W. H. Armitt to SL, 5 Apr. 1929, SELO 6/18, Selwyn Lloyd Papers, Churchill Archives; Self (ed.), *Neville Chamberlain Diary Letters,* 3: 135 (to Hilda, 27 Apr. 1929); Swaddle, 'Coping', 184–5.

12. Ramsden, 'Baldwin and film', 133; 'Diary of a Campaign Visit to the West Country', SELO 6/2, Selwyn Lloyd Papers, Churchill Archives; Houston and Valdar, *Modern Electioneering,* 14, 22; Cambray, *Game of Politics,* 172–3; Self (ed.), *Neville Chamberlain Diary Letters,* 2: 252 (to Ida, 11 Oct. 1924); Macmillan, *Winds of Change,* 143–4; Labour, *Conduct of Elections,* 1931, 2.

13. Houston and Valdar, *Modern Electioneering,* 136; Manchester Liberal Federation, EC Minutes, 3 Feb. 1910, M283/1/3/3, Manchester Archives; Lloyd, *Elections,* 16; Edwin Parker to H. E. Rogers, 14 Oct. 1931, Bristol East Labour Party Records, 40488/E/1/1, BRO; Lawrence and Good, 'Electing John Bull' (ESRC RES-000–22-0345).

14. Seager, *Parliamentary Elections,* 47; Morris, *Parliamentary Franchise,* 167–8, 173; Macmillan, *Winds of Change,* 143; Chesterton, *Oswald Mosley,* 105; Lawrence and Good, 'Electing John Bull' (ESRC RES-000-22-0345).

15. Dawson, 'Money', 375–6; Seager, *Parliamentary Elections,* v, 43–58; Metropolitan Conservative Agents' Association Minutes, 'On Questions of Election Procedure' (*c.*March 1919), CCA-3, BLPES, London; Swaddle, 'Coping', 137–9; Houston and Valdar, *Modern Electioneering,* 36; Cambray, *Game of Politics,* 29, 155–6.

16. Swaddle, 'Coping', 152–6, 176–7; Labour Party, *Conduct of Elections,* 1931, 3; James (ed.), *Davidson's Memoirs,* 297–8, 302–3, 317; Butler and Butler, *Political Facts,* 241; Cockett, 'Party, publicity and the media', 556–7; Ramsden, *Age of Balfour,* 219–23, 231–2, Macmillan, *Winds of Change,* 244; Cambray, *Game of Politics,* 155–7, 162–3, 178–9.

17. Labour Party, *Conduct of Elections,* 1931, 7; Gray, *Confessions of a Candidate,* 19–21; Houston and Valdar, *Modern Electioneering,* 13–14, 127, 108–10, 178–80; Cambray, *Game of Politics,* 8, 171–2, 182.

18. Cambray, *Game of Politics,* 22–3, 25–7; 'Political Diary, 1918–1935', 85–7 ('1923 Election'), 4629/1/2/2, Bridgeman Papers, Shropshire Archives; Williamson (ed.), *Bridgeman Diaries,* 172 (5 Dec. 1923); Ramsden (ed.), *Real Old Tory Politics,* 211 (12 Dec. 1923); Ferris and Bar-Joseph, 'Getting Marlowe', 115–16; Bennett, 'Zinoviev letter'; Ramsden, *Age of Balfour,* 200, 203–6,

232; James (ed.), *Davidson's Memoirs*, 300–1; *Illustrated London News*, 25 May 1929, 898.

19. Houston and Valdar, *Modern Electioneering*, 178–82; Anon., *Taint in Politics*, 241; *LO*, Oct. 1922, 18 and Dec. 1922, 2, Nov. 1923, 8, June 1924, 13–14; Labour, *Conduct of Elections*, 1931, 2; Cambray, *Game of Politics*, 123; Croft, *Conduct*, 3; McCarthy, 'Parties, voluntary associations'; *The Times*, 24 Nov. 1934 and 1 Nov. 1935 ('England and Peace'); Self (ed.), *Neville Chamberlain Diary Letters*, 4: 159 (to Hilda, 9/10 Nov. 1935).

20. Cambray, *Game of Politics*, 25–7, 77–85, 129–30; Houston and Valdar, *Modern Electioneering*, 18, 179; *The Times*, 22 May 1929, 26 Oct. and 2 Nov. 1931; *LO*, Dec. 1931, 230 (agent's letter); Thorpe, *General Election 1931*, 250–3; Self (ed.), *Neville Chamberlain Diary Letters*, 3: 287 (to Hilda, 24 Oct. 1931); Morgan, 'Election of 1935', 122; McHenry, *Labour in Transition*, 186; Stannage, *Baldwin Thwarts*, 147; Self (ed.), *Neville Chamberlain Diary Letters*, 4: 159 (to Hilda, 9/10 Nov. 1935).

21. *CAJ*, Nov. 1919, 1, Apr. 1923, 83; Houston and Valdar, *Modern Electioneering*, 20, 114–16, 127; Cambray, *Game of Politics*, 8, 30, 182; Gray, *Confessions of a Candidate*, 36–8, 47, 55, 79; *LO*, Apr. 1928, 69 ('Reaching the Million').

22. Cambray, *Game of Politics*, 176–7; Conservative pamphlets and leaflets: 'Mr Snowden's bombshell' (1931/114), 'Mr Snowden's startling exposure!' (1931/115), 'The truth at last!' (1931/116), 'Bolshevism run mad!' (1931/117), Harvester microfiche (though none *explicitly* uses the Post Office scare); *LO*, Oct. 1922, 1, 6–7, Oct. 1923, 4–7, 20; Jan. 1924, 1; Sept. 1924, 14–15; Nov. 1928, 215; Dec. 1931, 204–5; Sept. 1935, 173–4; Dec. 1935, 216–17; McHenry, *Labour in Transition*, 100, 199; Beers, ' "Selling Socialism" ', chs. 5 and 7; James (ed.), *Davidson's Memoirs*, 301; Lewis, 'British by-elections', 177; Boothby, *Boothby*, 205; *CAJ*, April 1947, 55–7.

23. Steel-Maitland to Baldwin, 24 May 1929, vol. 36, Baldwin Papers, CUL; Cockett, 'Party, publicity and media', 550–6; Williamson, *Bridgeman Diaries*, 219 (Bridgeman to Baldwin, 31 May 1929); Ball, *Baldwin*, 39–40; Williamson, ' "Safety First" ', 405–6; Maurice Petherick to Baldwin, 2 June 1929, vol. 37, Baldwin Papers, CUL; *LO*, Nov. 1931, 201–5, Dec. 1931, 223–5 and 232–3 (agent's letter); Swaddle, 'Coping', 147–8; Beers, ' "Selling Socialism" ', ch. 9.

24. Gray, *Confessions of a Candidate*, 47; Fenby, *Other Oxford*, 140, 143; Macmillan, *Winds of Change*, 162–3; Croft, *Conduct*, 40; Cambray, *Game of Politics*, 9; Hogg, *Sparrow's Flight*, 207.

25. Jarvis, 'Conservatism and class'; Webb, 'Stratified Electioneering', *LO*, Nov. 1922, 6; McHenry, *Labour in Transition*, 99; Wring, *Politics of Marketing*, 38–42; Swaddle, 'Coping', 149–50; Beers, ' "Selling Socialism" ', 61–8; Labour, *Conduct of Elections*, 1931, 3, 7, 38; Croft, *Conduct*, 3, 8–9.

26. Lawrence, 'Forging a peaceable kingdom'; Gilbert, *Churchill*, IV, *Companion I*: 429 (20 Nov. 1918); Self (ed.), *Austen Chamberlain Diary Letters*, 207 (21 Nov. 1922), 337 (6 June 1929); Clementine Churchill to WSC, n.d.

(8 Nov. 1922), CHAR 1/158 fos. 54–9, Churchill Archives; Gilbert, *Churchill*, IV, 875–87; Brodie, *Politics of the Poor*, ch. 2; Davis, 'Enfranchisement of the urban poor'; Morris, *Parliamentary Franchise*, 137, 157; Montague, *Disenchantment*, 198–9; Williamson, *Stanley Baldwin*, 145–50. See also Berthezène, 'Creating Conservative Fabians'.

27. Barker (ed.), *MacDonald's Political Writings*, 222; *LO*, Apr. 1921, 14; *CAJ*, Oct. 1923, 222, 225; *Morning Post*, 23 Oct. 1924; *Daily Telegraph*, 24 Oct. 1924; *Daily Herald*, 23, 24, 25, 29 Oct. 1924. See Lawrence, 'Transformation of public politics', *passim*, for an elaboration of this argument.

28. Dawson, 'Liberalism in Devon and Cornwall', 425–37; *South Wales Weekly Argus*, 8 Dec. 1923; *Westminster Gazette*, 29 Oct. 1924; Lawrence and Good, 'Electing John Bull' (ESRC RES-000-22-0345); Self (ed.), *Neville Chamberlain Diary Letters*, 3: 286 (to Hilda, 24 Oct. 1931); Worley, 'Call to action'; Thorpe, *General Election 1931*, 191–2; Marquand, *Ramsay MacDonald*, 669.

29. Morris, *Parliamentary Franchise*, 206; Montague, *Disenchantment*, 209; Ball (ed.), *Headlam Diaries, 1923–1935*, 173–4 (13 and 21 May 1929); Bridgeman to Baldwin, 24 May 1929, vol. 36, Baldwin Papers, CUL; Macmillan, *Winds of Change*, 246, 280; Davies and Morley, *County Borough Elections*, 3: 639–41 (on turnout); Morgan, 'General Election 1935', 122–3; Tilby, 'Election and after', 706. On the 'unusual lack of excitement' see Self (ed.), *Neville Chamberlain Diary Letters*, 4: 158 (to Hilda, 9/10 Nov. 1935), also Stuart (ed.), *Reith Diaries*, 122–3 (1, 5 Nov. 1935).

30. Houston and Valdar, *Modern Electioneering*, 145; Lawrence and Good, 'Electing John Bull' (ESRC RES-000-22-0345); Lawrence, 'Transformation of public politics', 207–8; *Scotsman*, 3 Dec. 1923; *Daily News*, 23 Oct. 1924; Marion Phillips, 'Organising the Women Electors', *LO*, Apr. 1922, 20–1; Eleanor Rathbone, 'Changes in public life'; Self (ed.), *Neville Chamberlain Diary Letters*, 1: 298 (to Ida, 1 Dec. 1918), 301 (to Ida, 14 Dec. 1918); *Sunday Graphic* cutting (26 May 1929), and MacDonald to Baldwin, June 1929, vol. 38, Baldwin Papers, CUL; Jarvis, 'Mrs Maggs', 136–7, 140; Self (ed.), *Austen Chamberlain Diary Letters*, 337 (6 June 1929).

31. Thackeray 'British popular Conservatism'; James (ed.), *Davidson's Memoirs*, 266–7; Self (ed.), *Neville Chamberlain Diary Letters*, 2: 129 (11 Nov. 1922), 198 (2 Dec. 1923), 246 (20 Sept. 1924), 248 (27 Sept. 1924); Gilbert, *Churchill*, V, *Companion* I: 212 (6 Oct. 1924); Amery, *My Political Life*, 2: 245, 285, 501; St George's Conservative Association Minutes, 12 and 20 July 1921, 9 Oct. 1922, 487/8, Westminster Public Library; Tanner, 'Gender, civic culture and politics', 170–93; Jarvis, 'Mrs Maggs', 144–5; Savage, 'Urban politics'; on Labour and women see the forthcoming work of Laura Beers (Newnham College, Cambridge).

32. *Durham County Advertiser*, 8, 15 Nov. 1935; *Worksop Guardian*, 8 Nov. 1935 (Malcolm MacDonald at Bassetlaw); Self (ed.), *Austen Chamberlain Diary Letters*, 201 (to Ida, 18 Nov. 1922); Lawrence, 'Fascist violence', 238–67, and 'Why

Olympia mattered', 263–72; Self (ed.), *Neville Chamberlain Diary Letters*, 2: 246 (20 Sept. 1924), 248–9 (27 Sept 1924); *[Wednesbury] Midland Advertiser*, 25 May 1929; *CAJ*, Oct. 1923, 221–5; Donner, *Crusade*, 71–3; Lewis, 'British by-elections', 176. See also Lawrence, 'Transformation of public politics', 200, 208, 211, although here the emphasis is mainly on the politicians' part in change.

33. Croft, *Conduct*, 3; McKibbin, *Classes and Cultures*, 84–98; Richards, *Castles on the Ground*; Durant, *Watling*, chs. 1–2; Olechnowicz, *Working-Class Housing*, chs. 4–6; Light, *Forever England*; McCarthy, 'Parties, voluntary associations'; Priestley, *English Journey*, 405; Self (ed.), *Neville Chamberlain Diary Letters*, 4: 159 (to Hilda, 9/10 Nov. 1935).

CHAPTER 5

1. Pimlott (ed.), *Diary of Hugh Dalton*, 356 (July 1945); Dalton, *Fateful Years*, 463; Morrison, *Herbert Morrison*, 236.
2. *LO*, Nov. 1945, 13.
3. Cited in Fielding, Thompson, and Tiratsoo, *'England Arise!'*, 176.
4. Williams (ed.), *Diary of Hugh Gaitskell*, 5 (6 Aug. 1945); *Yorkshire Post*, 27 July 1945; Williams, *Hugh Gaitskell*, 74.
5. Macmillan, *Tides of Fortune*, 31–2; Ball (ed.), *Headlam Diaries, 1935–1951*, 464 (22 June 1945); also McCallum and Readman, *Election of 1945*, 154.
6. *CAJ*, Oct. 1945, 54; Boyd-Carpenter, *Way of Life*, 74; Nicolson (ed.), *Harold Nicolson Diaries*, 318–19 (HN to Vita, 19 June 1945); McCallum and Readman, *Election of 1945*, 151–5 and 167 (Glasgow); Mitchell, *Election '45*, 60–1 (Beaverbrook at West Fulham); *Daily Mirror*, 30 June 1945, arguing that fascists were trying to foment disorder to discredit Labour.
7. Jenkins, *Life at the Centre*, 56; Amery, *Approach March*, 434–45; Churchill, *His Father's Son*, 109–12, 121–2. Also Wigg, *George Wigg*, 113 (Dudley); Howell, *Made in Birmingham*, 47–8 (West Birmingham); and all of the contributions to Mitchell, *Election '45*, esp. ch. 3 ('Fighting the good fight').
8. Boyd-Carpenter, *Way of Life*, 73; *LO*, Aug. 1945, 11; Amery, *Approach March*, 439; *Lancashire Daily Post*, 26 June 1945; *Yorkshire Post*, 27 June 1945; Bevins, *Greasy Pole*, 15; Nicholas, *Election of 1950*, 235.
9. Nicholas, *Election of 1950*, 128; Briggs, *History of Broadcasting*, 4: 627.
10. Amery, *Approach March*, 440; *Lancashire Daily Post*, 28 June 1945; *Yorkshire Post*, 27 and 28 June 1945; Colville, *Fringes of Power*, 609; Gilbert, *Churchill*, VIII: 50–4; *The Times*, 4 July 1945, 4, 8; *Manchester Guardian*, 3, 4, and 5 July 1945.
11. Harris, *Attlee*, 258; Mikardo, *Back-Bencher*, 85; *Daily Herald*, 11, 21, and 29 June 1945; *LO*, Aug. 1945, 8.
12. For instance, *LO*, June 1945, 8. Also McCallum and Readman, *Election of 1945*, 133.

13. McKibbin, *Classes and Cultures*, 419; Nicholas, *Election of 1950*, 129, Briggs, *History of Broadcasting*, 4: 627, 646, 668; Nicholas, 'Construction of a national identity'.

14. *CAJ*, Apr. 1949, 87; Labour, *Conduct of Elections*, 1931, 32.

15. McCallum and Readman, *Election of 1945*, 151; Gallup (ed.), *Gallup International*, 1: 112–13; Mass Observation File Reports, MO 2257 (1945), 'Youth and the election', 3, MO 2261 (1945), 'The new voters and the old', 3, and MO 2265 (1945), 'General Election' (1945), 4; Catterall (ed.), *Macmillan Diaries*, 109 (20 Oct. 1951).

16. Birch and Campbell, 'Voting behaviour' (Stretford, 1950), 205; Rallings and Thrasher (eds.), *Electoral Facts*, 106 (table 4.02).

17. Ball, 'Local Conservatism', 291; Ramsden, *Age of Churchill*, 110–12; Pelling, *Short History*, 176; *LO*, Jan. 1979, 19.

18. Ball (ed.), *Headlam Diaries, 1935–1951*, 618–20 (11, 13, and 22 Feb. 1950); Booth, *British Hustings*, 249; Amery, *Approach March*, 446; Bristol South-East Labour Party Records, 'Report of General Election Campaign, 1950', 40488/E/1/1, BRO; Chrimes (ed.), *Glasgow, 1950*, 83, 99; Milne and Mackenzie, *Straight Fight*, 141; Macmillan, *Tides of Fortune*, 312. See also, *South Devon Times*, 24 Feb. 1950.

19. Butler, *Election of 1955*, 147; Milne and Mackenzie, *Marginal Seat*, 14–19. See also, Benney, Gray, and Pear, *How People Vote*, 46–9; Blondel, 'Party in Reading', 115–16; Fielding *et al.*, 'England Arise!', 185–7; Fielding, 'Don't know'.

20. Nicholas, *Election of 1950*, 241; Butler, *Election of 1951*, 140–1, Butler, *Election of 1955*, 110; *The Times*, 25 May 1951; Bristol South East Labour Party, 'Report of General Election Campaign, 1950', BRO.

21. Nicholas, *Election of 1950*, 1–18; Pollock *et al.*, *British Election, 1950*, 20–1; Butler, *Election of 1951*, 140–1; *LO*, Apr. 1951, 64–5, Nov.–Dec. 1951, 218–19, and Feb. 1965, 35 (rural fly-posting at North Fylde); Milne and MacKenzie, *Straight Fight*, 68 and 74; Chrimes (ed.), *Glasgow, 1950*, 108–9 and 142; Benney *et al.*, *How People Vote*, 80; Butler, *Elections Since 1945*, 101; Conservative Central Office, 'General Election Memorandum No. 4' (1966), point 75, SELO 6/192, Selwyn Lloyd Papers, Churchill Archives; Kampfner, *Robin Cook*, 23.

22. Nicholas, *Election of 1950*, 242; Chrimes (ed.), *Glasgow, 1950*, 110.

23. Comparing *LO*, June 1945, 8 with ibid., Feb. 1950, 16.

24. Harris, *Attlee*, 490; Chrimes (ed.), *Glasgow, 1950*, 96–100; *Glasgow Herald*, 10, 14, 15, 16, 18 Feb. 1950; Nicholas, *Election of 1950*, 236–9; Butler, *Election of 1951*, 167; Butler and Rose, *Election of 1959*, 136; Williams (ed.), *Diary of Hugh Gaitskell*, 292–3 (16 Nov. 1951) and 447 (14–23 Feb. 1956); and Mitchell, *Election '45*, 78 (on how Evan Durbin hated the 'tomfoolery' of election parades). On suspicion of Bevan's emotional style see, Francis, 'Politics of restraint'.

25. Benney *et al.*, *How People Vote*, 155–6; Milne and MacKenzie, *Straight Fight*, 88; Mass Observation, *Voter's Choice*, 4–5. At Newcastle-under-Lyme in 1959 researchers found 9 per cent of electors had attended an election meeting, Bealey, Blondel, and McCann, *Constituency Politics*, 190.
26. Butler, *Election of 1951*, 141; Milne and MacKenzie, *Straight Fight*, 88; *News Chronicle, Behind the Gallup Poll*, 6; Whitelaw, *Whitelaw Memoirs*, 35–6; Pollock *et al.*, *British Election, 1950*, 4; Lord Woolton to Selwyn Lloyd, 15 Feb. 1950, SELO 4/23, Selwyn Lloyd Papers, Churchill Archives. Also Rawlinson, *Price too High*, 41–2, 46–7.
27. *News Chronicle, Behind the Gallup Poll*, 25; Benn, *Years of Hope*, 156 (15 Oct. 1951); Chrimes (ed.) *Glasgow, 1950*, 85, 99.
28. Gilbert, *Churchill*, VIII: 645.

CHAPTER 6

1. Butler, *Elections since 1945*, 2–3.
2. Macmillan, *Tides of Fortune*, 314; Williams (ed.), *Diary of Gaitskell*, 291 (16 Nov. 1951); Butler, *Election of 1955*, 109; Bochel and Denver, 'Scottish local newspapers'.
3. For instance, *News Chronicle, Behind the Gallup Poll*, 21; Mass Observation, *Voters' Choice*, 4–6, 11–13; Milne and Mackenzie, 'Floating vote', 65–8; Benney and Geiss, 'Social class' (Greenwich), 325; Birch and Campbell, 'Lancashire constituency', 200; Labour, *Interim Report on Organisation* (1955), 12–13; Birch, *Small-Town Politics*, 99; Benney *et al.*, *How People Vote*, 156.
4. See Benney and Geiss, 'Social class', 316–17; Birch and Campbell, 'Lancashire constituency', 201–2; Campbell, Donnison, and Potter, 'Voting behaviour' (Droylsden), 57–65; Stacey, *Tradition and Change*, 41–9; Rose and McAllister, *Voters Begin to Choose*.
5. For instance, Miller, 'Social class and party', and 'Class, region and strata'. More recent work exploring neighbourhood effects includes Johnston, *Geography of English Politics*; Johnston and Pattie, *Voters in their Place*, esp. chs. 3–4; Harrop, Heath, and Openshaw, 'Neighbourhood influence'.
6. Green, 'Conservative Party and the electorate', and his *Ideologies of Conservatism*, 187; Benney *et al.*, *How People Vote*, 91–2; *LO*, Feb. 1955, 23–4, Jan. 1959, 4; *CAJ*, Sept. 1955, 198 (Bolton), Dec. 1957, 280 (Ipswich), Feb. 1958, 37 (Garston); Labour, *Interim Report on Organisation*, 12–13.
7. Butler, *Election of 1951*, 142–3; *News Chronicle, Behind the Gallup Poll*, 25; Butler, *Election of 1955*, 111; Butler and Rose, *Election of 1959*, 140; Milne and Mackenzie, *Straight Fight*, 70; Benney *et al.*, *How People Vote*, 90. The debate about the efficacy of canvassing continued to rage through the 1960s; for contrasting views see Holt and Turner, *Political Parties in Action*, 226–38, and Rose, *Influencing Voters*, 153.

8. Heath, *Course of My Life*, 134; Baker, *Turbulent Years*, 23; *LO*, Sept. 1959, 170–4, Aug. 1964, 150–2; Labour, *Interim Report on Organisation*, 14; Mikardo, *Back-Bencher*, 111–13.

9. *News Chronicle, Behind the Gallup Poll*, 22; Crewe, Fox, and Day, *British Electorate 1963–1992*, 47 (table 2.1); Craig, *Electoral Facts*, 37 and 43; Särlvik and Crewe, *Decade of Dealignment*, 333–6; Rose and McAllister, *Voters Begin to Choose*.

10. *News Chronicle, Behind the Gallup Poll*, 25; Butler, *Election of 1955*, 47. In 1951 82 per cent of voters heard at least one radio broadcast, but only 12 per cent had seen a television broadcast.

11. Butler, *Election of 1955*, 94; Catterall (ed.), *Macmillan Diaries*, 431 (22 May 1955); Pimlott (ed.), *Diary of Hugh Dalton*, 671 (26 May 1955); *News Chronicle, General Election* (1955), 14; Gallup, *Gallup International*, I: 348; Morgan (ed.), *Backbench Crossman*, 418 (19 Apr. 1955).

12. Briggs, *History of Broadcasting*, 4: 683, 686; Pimlott (ed.), *Diary of Hugh Dalton*, 671; Milne and Mackenzie, *Marginal Seat*, 102; Butler, *Election of 1955*, 47–64; Miall, *Inside the BBC*, 138. There were also three televised party broadcasts before the formal dissolution of Parliament.

13. Macmillan, *Tides of Fortune*, 591, 602–3; Butler, *Election of 1955*, 58–62; Briggs, *History of Broadcasting*, 4: 680–2; Goldie, *Facing the Nation*, 142, 173, 205–6; Rosenbaum, *Soapbox to Soundbite*, 102–3; *LO*, June/July 1955, 108–9; Ramsden, *Age of Churchill*, 228 and 280 (Eden's 1951 broadcast had also been considered a triumph).

14. *CAJ*, Oct. 1955, 233, Mar. 1959, 48; Chrimes (ed.), *Glasgow, 1950*, 85; Butler, *Election of 1955*, 109, 125–7, 137, 149–50; Milne and Mackenzie, *Marginal Seat*, 102, 107.

15. Butler and Rose, *Election of 1959*, 136–7; Bealey *et al.*, *Constituency Politics*, 190; *News Chronicle*, 29 Sept. 1959; Day, *Grand Inquisitor*, 121–3; *Hereford Times*, 25 Sept. and 2 Oct. 1959.

16. Nabarro, *Nab 1*, 88–93, 246–8, and *Exploits*, 256–63; Ramsden, *Age of Churchill*, 278; Harris, *Attlee*, 533; Benn, *Years of Hope*, 313 (22 Sept. 1959) and 314 (3 Oct. 1959); *News Chronicle*, 7 Oct. 1959.

17. Briggs, *History of Broadcasting*, 4: 676; Benn, *Years of Hope*, 182 (June 1955); James (ed.), *Chips Diaries*, 440 (29 Jan. 1950) and 461 (28 Oct. 1951); Catterall (ed.), *Macmillan Diaries*, 104 (30 Sept. 1951), 108 (13 Oct. 1951), and 430–1 (20 May 1955); Williams (ed.), *Diary of Gaitskell*, 166 (21 Mar. 1950), 291 (16 Nov. 1951).

18. Butler, *Election of 1951*, 141; *LO*, Feb. 1955, 23–4 and Jan. 1959, 3–4.

19. Benney *et al.*, *How People Vote*, 85 and 155; Butler, *Election of 1951*, 213; Butler, *Election of 1955*, 112 and 125; Benn, *Years of Hope*, 313 (22 Sept. 1959); *CAJ*, Oct. 1947, 227–8, May 1955, 123–6, Jan. 1957, 4–6; also Milne and Mackenzie, *Straight Fight*, 70.

20. McCallum and Readman, *Election of 1945*, 171 (Edinburgh); Labour, *Conduct of Elections*, 1977, 70; *CAJ*, Oct. 1946, 92 (Barnet), May 1956, 125–6

(Gainsborough); Butler, *Election of 1951*, 182 ('Midland borough'); Nicholas, *Election of 1950*, 240 (Wavertree and Dorset); Healey, *Time of My Life*, 132; Chrimes (ed.), *Glasgow, 1950*, 109–10.

21. *LO*, June 1950, 10–11; Butler, *Election of 1955*, 126–7; Mitchell, *Election '45*, 62 (Barkston Ash).

22. Benney *et al.*, *How People Vote*, 84–5; Holt and Turner, *Political Parties in Action*, 74, 152, 162–3; Deakin (ed.), *Colour and the British Electorate*, 25 (Brixton) and 47 (Southall); *Kidderminster Times*, 9 Oct. 1959 (on the innovation of a candidates' panel organized by the United Christian Council); also *Rochdale Observer*, 29 Jan. 1958; *CAJ*, Feb. 1957, 42–5 and Sept. 1957, 199–200; Benn, *Out of the Wilderness*, 98 (13 Mar. 1964).

23. Jenkins, *Life at the Centre*, 301, 365–6; *CAJ*, Dec. 1957, 279; Benn, *Years of Hope*, 383; Benn, *Out of the Wilderness*, 50 (15 Aug. 1963); *Bristol Evening Post*, 16 Aug. 1963; Mitchell, *Election '45*, 66 (for an earlier example of bus queue canvassing).

24. For a detailed study in this mould see Norton and Wood, *Back from Westminster*, esp. chs. 1 and 3. See also Munroe, 'Member of Parliament', 577–87; Marsh, 'Representational changes'.

25. *Guardian*, 10 June 1987 (on Newens); *LO*, Dec. 1945, 7–8 (Binns's piece was titled 'Look after your people!'); Butler, *Election of 1955*, 144–5; Benney *et al.*, *How People Vote*, 65; Jenkins, *Life at the Centre*, 79–81; Benn, *Years of Hope*, 182 (June 1955); Earl Attlee, 'The role of the Member of Parliament', *Fabian Journal*, Nov. 1958, 5–8; Bevins, *Greasy Pole*, 21, 152. Also Healey, *Time of My Life*, 142; Nabarro, *Nab 1*, 89, 223; *CAJ*, Jan. 1951, 400–2 ('Going to the people!'); Deakin (ed.), *Colour and the British Electorate*, 27 (on the impact of Lipton's weekly surgeries at Brixton); Walker, *Staying Power*, 26–7.

26. Jay, *Change and Fortune*, 267.

27. Rosenbaum, *Soapbox to Soundbite*, 94–7; Nabarro, *Nab 1*, 3 (he was commending Christopher Soames for knowing better); *CAJ*, Aug. 1951, 613–15; Benn, *Years of Hope*, 314 (24 Sept. 1959).

28. Milne and Mackenzie, *Straight Fight*, 87; Milne and Mackenzie, *Marginal Seat*, 101 (this excludes voters who claimed to have 'glanced' at the literature); Benney *et al.*, *How People Vote*, 155–6; *CAJ*, Sept. 1957, 197. As with attendance at meetings, the Gallup post-poll survey suggested a somewhat higher level of voter engagement than that found in constituency studies. In 1959 it suggested that 62 per cent of voters had read candidates' election addresses, Gallup (ed.), *Gallup International*, 1: 542.

29. *News Chronicle, Behind the Gallup Poll*, 21; Cockett, 'Party, publicity and the media', 567; Rose, *Influencing Voters*, 38–44; Pearson and Turner, *Persuasion Industry*, 113, 237; Rosenbaum, *Soapbox to Soundbite*, 6–8, 27–8; Butler, *Elections Since 1945*, 101–2; Butler and Rose, *Election of 1959*, 281.

30. Gallup (ed.), *Gallup International*, 1: 496, 498, 508, 513, 519, 528; Craig, *Electoral Facts*, 103; *LO*, Oct./Nov. 1959, 185.

31. Miall, *Inside the BBC*, 236; Day, *Grand Inquisitor*, 1–6, 80–3, 104–5; Day, *But With Respect*, 20–35; Jones, 'Pitiless probing eye'; Goldie, *Facing the Nation*, 193, 197–8; Briggs, *History of Broadcasting*, 5: 239–49; Ramsden, *Winds of Change*, 36; *Rochdale Observer*, 1, 5, and 8 Feb. 1958; *Rochdale Times*, 7 Feb. 1958; Cockerell, *Live from Number 10*, 58–63. On Macmillan's 'make-over' for television in 1958 see Horne, *Macmillan*, 2: 145.

32. *CAJ*, Dec. 1957, 280–1 and Mar. 1958, 66–7; Morgan (ed.), *Backbench Crossman*, 778 (15 Sept. 1959), 780 (24 Sept. 1959); Butler and Rose, *Election of 1959*, 52–3, 59–60, 135; Rosenbaum, *Soapbox to Soundbite*, 115–16; Butler, *Elections since 1945*, 96.

33. Butler and Rose, *Election of 1959*, 54, 78, 96, 136–8, 173–85; Gallup (ed.), *Gallup International*, 1: 542; Trenaman and McQuail, *Television and the Political Image*, 81, 103; Bealey *et al.*, *Constituency Politics*, 190; Morgan (ed.), *Backbench Crossman*, 785 (5 Oct. 1959); Nabarro, *Nab 1*, 91; *LO*, Oct./Nov. 1959, 191; Holt and Turner, *Political Parties in Action*, 145–7.

34. *The Times*, 17 and 30 Sept. 1959; Butler and Rose, *Election of 1959*, 54, 84–90, 136–8; *Hereford Citizen and Bulletin*, 9 Oct. 1959; Gallup (ed.), *Gallup International*, 1: 542; Trenaman and McQuail, *Television and the Political Image*, 70–1.

35. Butler and Rose, *Election of 1959*, 77–84, 93; *The Times*, 8, 10, 15 Sept. 1959; *Manchester Guardian*, 1 Oct. 1959; Trenaman and McQuail, *Television and the Political Image*, 69–71, 81, 90; Cockerell, *Live from Number 10*, 68–74; T. E. Hewat (Granada TV) to Selwyn Lloyd, 7 Oct. 1959, SELO 2/16, Selwyn Lloyd Papers, Churchill Archives.

CHAPTER 7

1. Butler, *Election of 1955*, 143; Butler and King, *Election of 1964*, 156–8, 167–70; Butler and King, *Election of 1966*, 191.

2. Butler and Kavanagh, *Election of February 1974*, 201; Blumler, 'Mass media roles', 133; Butler and Kavanagh, *Election of February 1979*, 293; Butler, *Elections since 1945*, 111.

3. *CAJ*, Feb. 1955, 26–7, 37; *LO*, July 1979, 15; Briggs, *History of Broadcasting*, 5: 873 n.; Gaber, 'Debate on Section 93', 222–6; Denver and Hands, *Modern Constituency Electioneering*, 184–96.

4. Rhodes, *Loaded Hour*; Denver and Hands, *Modern Constituency Electioneering*, 163–84, 200–3; Deakin (ed.), *Colour and the British Electorate*, 90–1, 102; Butler and King, *Election of 1966*, 195; Butler and King, *Election of 1964*, 220, 273; A. James to J. Bray, 27 Mar. 1962, Acc. 610, fo. 717, Bray Papers, Churchill Archives; Crossman, *Diaries*, 3: 932 (30 May 1970). For the survival of verbatim reporting into the 1970s in some Scottish seats see Bochel and Denver, 'Scottish local newspapers', 17–18.

5. Rose, *Influencing Voters*, 73–4, 167; Labour, *Interim Report on Party Organisation*, esp. 6–14; Black, *Political Culture*, ch. 7, esp. 157, 182–5; J. Bray to George Brown, 10 June 1962, Acc. 610, fo. 717, Bray Papers, Churchill Archives; *LO*, Apr. 1964, 70–2 (Len Williams, 'Planning for Victory'); Wring, *Politics of Marketing*, 67–70. For an emphasis on 'image' as the main departure in 1964 see, Fielding, 'Rethinking 1964'.

6. Blumler and McQuail, *Television in Politics*, 33–4 (Pudsey and Leeds West); Alderman, *British Elections*, 50; Benney *et al.*, *How People Vote*, 157–8, and also Mass Observation, *Voters' Choice*, 6; *Gallup Political Index*, Report 163 (Feb. 1974), 250; Miller *et al.*, *How Voters Change*, 156, 160; Butler and Kavanagh, *Election of February 1974*, 201–2; Kavanagh, 'United Kingdom', 82; Labour, *Interim Report on Party Organisation*, 12, 23–5. On the failure of mutual aid see Butler and King, *Election of 1964*, 273 (Swansea); Holt and Turner, *Political Parties in Action*, 139; Crossman, *Diaries*, 3: 41 (8 June 1970—Black Country).

7. Butler and Kavanagh, *Election of February 1974*, 220, 223; Kavanagh, 'United Kingdom', 82; Butler, *Elections since 1945*, 101, 112; *LO*, Jan. 1979, 19; Butler and Butler, *British Political Facts*, 132, 147; Ball, 'Local Conservatism', 291; Gallup (ed.), *Gallup International*, 1: 764; Butler and Pinto-Duschinsky, *Election of 1970*, 316; Butler and Kavanagh, *Election of 1979*, 294; Butler and Kavanagh, *Election of 1983*, 249; Denver, *Elections and Voting*, 116; Butler and Kavanagh, *Election of 1987*, 215.

8. Butler and King, *Election of 1964*, 222; Butler and King, *Election of 1966*, 191; Penniman (ed.), *Britain at the Polls 1974*, 74, 87–8; *CAJ*, July 1964, 21, Dec. 1964, 6–7, Apr. 1974, 6–7, Nov. 1974, 11; Pinto-Duschinsky, *British Political Finance*, 27, 314–15; Butler, *Elections Since 1945*, 101; Alderman, *British Elections*, 49; *LO*, July 1974, 8, Dec. 1974, 11; Rennard, *Winning By-Elections*; Richards, *How to Win*, 156–60.

9. Kavanagh, 'United Kingdom', 74; Kavanagh, *Election Campaigning*, 12–13; Rose, *Influencing Voters*, 58, 74–85, 130, 155–8; Butler and Pinto-Duschinsky, *Election of 1970*, 189–93, 318; Blumler and McQuail, *Television in Politics*, 17, 184–7; *CAJ*, July 1970, 3, Apr. 1974, 3; *LO*, Jan. 1974, 2; Blumler *et al.*, *Challenge*, 44; Butler and Kavanagh, *Election of February 1974*, 131–8; Rosenbaum, *Soapbox to Soundbite*, 30–1; Butler and Butler, *British Political Facts*, 254. For scepticism about 'late swing' see Hurd, *End to Promises*, 21, 25, and Ramsden, *Winds of Change*, 315–17. On voter volatility and voters' increasing tendency to decide during the campaign see Rose and McAllister, *Voters Begin to Choose*; Särlvik and Crewe, *Decade of Dealignment*, and Denver, *Elections and Voting*, 75–7.

10. Kavanagh, 'United Kingdom', 74; Rosenbaum, *Soapbox to Soundbite*, 28–37; Butler and Kavanagh, *Election of 1979*, 195, 295; Bell, 'Conservative advertising', 12–14; Butler and Kavanagh, *Election of 1983*, 267; Tebbit, *Upwardly Mobile*, 205, 264; Butler, *Elections since 1945*, 78–80; Miller, *How Voters Change*, 142;

Butler and Kavanagh, *Election of 1987*, 107–12, 118, 250–1; Powell, 'Labour's advertising', 37.

11. Rose, *Influencing voters*, 23, 151, 187, 194–5, 278; Fisher, 'Campaign finance'; http://www.opsi.gov.uk/ACTS/acts2000/20000041.htm, also http://www.opsi.gov.uk/ACTS/acts1998/19980048.htm—the Registration of Political Parties Act, 1998 first introduced the legal obligation for political parties to be formally registered by the state (visited 24 July 2007).

12. Tebbit, *Upwardly Mobile*, 85–7, 133, 139; *West Essex Gazette and Guardian* (Epping and Ongar edn.), 5, 12 June 1970; *LO*, Sept.–Oct. 1964, 179, Mar. 1974, 7; *CAJ*, Jan. 1974, 5; Stevenson, *Third Party Politics*, 53–7; *The Times*, 2 Nov. 1973; *Brighton Evening Argus*, 2 and 9 Nov. 1973; *Brighton and Hove Gazette*, 27 Oct., 10 Nov. 1973; K. Weetch to D. Foot, 24 June 1974, DGFT 3/7, Dingle Foot Papers, Churchill Archives.

13. *LO*, Nov.–Dec. 1964, 205, Jan. 1965, 15–16, March 1966, 55, June–July 1966, 94, Feb. 1970, 23, July–Oct. 1970, 138, July 1979, 13; Holt and Turner, *Political Parties in Action*, 165, 169; Benn, *Against the Tide*, 108 (22 Feb. 1974); Castle, *Castle Diaries*, 32 (3 Mar. 1974); Benn, *End of an Era*, 288, 290, 334–6 (22 May, 2 June 1983, 16 Jan., 3–14 Feb. 1984).

14. Butler and King, *Election of 1966*, 196; Prior, *Balance of Power*, 40; *LO*, May 1978, 22; Crossman, *Diaries*, 3: 947 (17 June 1970). For earlier versions of the technique see Labour, *Conduct of Elections*, 1931, 32.

15. *CAJ*, Feb. 1966, 7, Nov. 1974, 11; *LO*, Nov. 1970, 199, May 1974, 4.

16. Pinto-Duschinsky, 'Conservative campaign', 101–2; Butler and King, *Election of 1966*, 192–3; *CAJ*, Nov. 1964, 4, Dec. 1964, 6, Mar. 1970, 10, Nov. 1974, 11; Butler and Kavanagh, *Election of February 1974*, 224; Holt and Turner, *Political Parties in Action*, 157–8; Benn, *Out of the Wilderness*, 136–7 (1 Sept. 1964).

17. *LO*, Dec. 1974, 10; Butler and Kavanagh, *Election of 1987*, 212–16, 229; Butler and Kavanagh, *Election of 1992*, 223; Powell, 'Labour advertising', 80–1; Denver and Hands, *Modern Constituency Electioneering*, 51, 82–8; Scammel, *Designer Politics*, 133, 145; *The Times*, 6, 10 Apr. 2005 (visited 23 July 2007); *Guardian*, 3 Mar. and 10 May 2005; www.business-strategies.co.uk/Content.asp?ArticleID=566 (Experian's Mosaic, visited 13 July 2005); also Andy McQue, 'High-tech. campaigning targets key voters', at http://management.silicon.com/government/0,39024852,39129879,00.htm (visited 13 July 2005); Kavanagh and Butler, *Election of 2005*, 39–40, 55, 170–3, 176–8; Fisher *et al.*, 'Constituency campaigning in 2005'; Ashcroft, *Smell the Coffee*.

18. Cook, 'Labour campaign'; Canzini, 'Conservative campaign'.

19. Butler and King, *Election of 1964*, 224, 249–50.

20. Butler and King, *Election of 1964*, 224, 281; Butler and Pinto-Duschinsky, *Election of 1970*, 315–16; *LO*, June–July 1966, 95; Bray to Jim Griffiths, Shirley Williams, and Philip Noel-Baker (Apr. 1962), Acc. 610, fo. 717, Bray Papers, Churchill Archives; Deakin (ed.), *Colour and the British Electorate*, 25; Ramsden, *Winds of Change*, 221; Blumler and McQuail, *Television in Politics*, 33–4; Butler

and King, *Election of 1966*, 248; Holt and Turner, *Political Parties in Action*, 143–7.

21. Butler and King, *Election of 1964*, 222; Holt and Turner, *Political Parties in Action*, 147; Butler and King, *Election of 1966*, 198, 220; Butler and Pinto-Duschinsky, *Election of 1970*, 315–16.

22. Butler and Pinto-Duschinsky, *Election of 1970*, 315–16; Crossman, *Diaries*, 2: 532 (23 Oct. 1967); *Guardian*, 10 June 1987 (Newens); *CAJ*, Nov. 1964, 2; Butler and King, *Election of 1964*, 221, 259; Butler and Kavanagh, *Election of October 1974*, 225; Butler and Kavanagh, *Election of 1979*, 295.

23. Butler and Pinto-Duschinsky, *Election of 1970*, 147, 209; Crossman, *Diaries*, 1: 483 (27 Mar. 1966); *LO*, Nov.–Dec. 1964, 208–9, July–Aug. 1970, 130–2.

24. Benn, *Out of the Wilderness*, 50–3 (15–20 Aug. 1963), 154 (14 Oct. 1964), 399 (1 Apr. 1966); Bristol South-East Labour Party Records, Edwin Parker to H. E. Rogers, 14 Oct. 1931, and 'Report of General Election Campaign, 1950', 40488/E/1/1, BRO; Benn, *Against the Tide*, 107–8 (14 Feb. 1974); Castle, *Castle Diaries*, 31; Pinto-Duschinsky, 'Conservative campaign', 89; Mitchell, 'Local campaign', 40.

25. Butler and Kavanagh, *Election of 1979*, 296; Butler and Kavanagh, *Election of 1983*, 170; Jenkins, *Life at the Centre*, 366.

26. Jenkins, *Life at the Centre*, 537–9, 541–2, 561–3; Benn, *End of an Era*, 335 (13 Feb. 1984), and 508 (4 June 1987); for politicians' speaking tours see http://www.celebrityproductions.org.uk (visited 14 Sept. 2005); *Cambridge Evening News*, 27 Apr. 2005; http://news.bbc.co.uk/1/hi/uk_politics/vote_2005/frontpage/4488429.stm (visited 14 Sept. 2005); Kavanagh and Butler, *General Election of 2005*, 73.

27. *Guardian*, 10 June 1987 ('Old style hustings are alive and well'); Butler and Kavanagh, *Election of 1983*, 158, 252; Rawlinson, *A Price too High*, 107; Atkinson, 'Live oratory'; Butler and Kavanagh, *Election of 1992*, 240–1; Howe, *Conflict of Loyalty*, 296.

28. Nabarro, *Exploits*, 261; Williams, *Inside Number 10*, 85; Butler and King, *Election of 1966*, 239; Dowse, 'M.P. and his surgery', tables 2 and 10; Walker, *Staying Power*, 26–7; *LO*, Sept. 1966, 145; Barker and Rush, *Member of Parliament*, 181–4; Marsh, 'Representational changes'; Cain, Ferejohn, and Fiorina, *Personal Vote*, 112.

29. Dinnage, 'Parliamentary advice bureau', 392–3; Munroe, 'MP as representative'; Benn, *Out of the Wilderness*, 143 (18 Sept. 1964); Richard Clark (Anglia TV) to Dingle Foot, 14 Aug. 1968 and Foot's undated reply, DGFT 3/5, Dingle Foot Papers, Churchill Archives; *CAJ*, Apr. 1974, 18.

30. Hampton, *Democracy and Community*, 96–7; Williams, 'Two notes'; Cain *et al.*, *Personal Vote*, 167–94; Norton and Wood, 'Constituency service'; Barker and Rush, *Member of Parliament*, 177–8; Clark, *Into Politics*, 69 (12 Aug. 1975), 70 (13 Sept. 1975), 102–3 (11 Aug. 1977), 264 (7 Nov. 1981); Clark, *Diaries*, 110 (9 May 1985), 193 (8 Jan. 1988); King, *Oona King Diaries*, esp. 125–7

(16 Apr. 1999), 165–7 (21 Jan. 2001); Brandreth, *Breaking the Code*, 500–1 (Jeremy Hanley, 2 May 1997).

31. Clark, *Into Politics* (30 July 1982), but also 89 (10 Nov. 1976) where he *is* criticized after complaints that he is not answering correspondence; Munroe, 'MP as representative', 583; Morrell, *Electors of Bristol*, 6–7; Benn, *Out of the Wilderness*, 97 (29 Feb. 1964); Dinnage, 'Parliamentary advice bureau', 393; *LO*, Oct. 1966, 173; Barker and Rush, *Member of Parliament*, 174; Norton and Wood, 'Constituency service', 198; Norton and Wood, *Back From Westminster*, 43–6. For an extreme example of the modern MP's mission creep see the *Oona King Diaries, passim*.

32. Denver and Hands, *Modern Constituency*, 181–4; Bochel and Denver, 'Scottish local newspapers', 16–18, 29; *LO*, Mar. 1964, 45–6, Oct. 1966, 166–7, 172, Dec. 1966, 206–7, May 1970, 92–3, June 1970, 105, May 1974, 7; Holt and Turner, *Political Parties in Action*, 114–16; Clark, *Diaries [1983–1991]*, 113 (11 May 1985); also Clark, *Into Politics*, 107 (4 Dec. 1977), 359 (29 Sept. 1982).

33. Clark, *Into Politics*, 42–3 (22 Feb. 1974), 54–5 (28 Sept. 1974), also 128–30 (29 Mar.–15 Apr. 1979); Brandreth, *Breaking the Code*, 73 (18 Mar. 1992), 489 (9 Apr. 1997); Clark, *Diaries [1983–1991]*, 109 (24 Apr. 1985), 120 (4 Sept. 1985) 149 (18 Nov. 1986), 211 (27 Apr. 1988), 339 (19 Sept. 1990).

34. Rawlinson, *Price too High*, 251–2; 'Walkabout guidelines' (memo), Box 48, Kinnock Papers, Churchill Archives; Kavanagh and Butler, *Election of 2005*, 71, 106, 174, 181.

CHAPTER 8

1. Cultural pessimists include Blumler and Gurevitch, *Crisis of Public Communication*; Hart, *Seducing America*; Bourdieu, *On Television and Journalism*; Lloyd, *What the Media*; and the more nihilistic, Baudrillard, *In the Shadow*. Optimists include, McNair, *Journalism and Democracy*; Street, *Mass Media*; Born, 'Digitising democracy'.

2. Cockerell, *Live from Number 10*, 88–9; Howard and West, *Making of the Prime Minister*, 41–2, 182; Pearson and Turner, *Persuasion Industry*, 261; West, 'Campaign journal', *Encounter*, 135 (1964), 14–19; Butler and King, *Election of 1964*, 156; Briggs, *History of Broadcasting*, 5: 438–49; Blumler and McQuail, *Television in Politics*, 36–40; Day, *Grand Inquisitor*, 181–2; Benn, *Out of the Wilderness*, 144 (20 Sept. 1964).

3. Butler and King, *Election of 1964*, 158, 161; Briggs, *History of Broadcasting*, 5: 442–3, 554–5; Day, *Grand Inquisitor*, 181–3; Butler and King, *Election of 1966*, 127–8; Cockerell, *Live from Number 10*, 125–7; Alderman, *British Elections*, 127, 132; Butler and Pinto-Duschinsky, *Election of 1970*, 208, 210; Blumler and McQuail, *Television in Politics*, 41 n.; Crossman, *Diaries*, 3: 942 (9 June 1970).

4. HMSO, *Annual Abstract of Statistics, 1971* (tables 72 and 268); Briggs, *History of Broadcasting*, 5: 876–8, 891, 983–5; Butler and Pinto-Duschinsky, *Election*

of 1970, 201, 226–7; Butler and Kavanagh, *Election of February 1974*, 80, 147 156–8, 167–9; Penniman, *Britain at the Polls, 1974*, 140–3; Gallup, *Gallup International*, 1: 742; Butler and Kavanagh, *Election of October 1974*, 140–1; *The Times*, 19 Feb. 1974; Blumler *et al.*, *Challenge of Broadcasting*, 40–2, 46–7; Even, 'Television broadcasting'; Nossiter *et al.*, 'Old values', 87 (quoting a MORI poll).

5. Even, 'Television broadcasting', 17–28; Butler and Kavanagh, *Election of 1983*, 157–8; Blumler *et al.*, *Challenge of Broadcasting*, 46; Crewe and Harrop (eds.), *Political Communications, 1987*, 148, 159–60, 172; Swanson and Mancini, *Politics, Media and Democracy*, introd. and chs. by Nimmo, Blumler *et al.*, and Swanson and Mancini; Pippa Norris *et al.*, *On Message*, 10–11, 23–34, 86, 94; Norris, *Electoral Change since 1945*, 196, 209; Scammel and Harrop, 'The press disarmed'; viewing figures from http://www.barb.co.uk/index1.cfm?flag=home (visited 13 Sept. 2005).

6. Butler and King, *Election of 1964*, 167–8; *The Times*, 9 Oct. 1964; *LO*, Nov.– Dec. 1964, 203–5, 214; Howard and West, *Making of the Prime Minister*, 121, 194–5, 204, 222–3; Home, *Way the Wind Blows*, 214–15; *CAJ*, Dec. 1964, 22; Butler and King, *Election of 1966*, 107, 129; Crossman, *Diaries*, 1: 479–81 (17 Mar. 1966); Cockerell, *Live from Number 10*, 127–8.

7. Butler and King, *Election of 1964*, 170; Home, *Wind Blows*, 214–15; Ramsden, *Winds of Change*, 227; Howard and West, *Making of the Prime Minister*, 188 n., 194–5; *The Times*, 9, 10, 12, 23 Oct. 1964; Holt and Turner, *Political Parties in Action*, 148–52.

8. Butler and King, *Election of 1966*, 107; http://news.bbc.co.uk/go/pr/fr/-/2/hi/ uk_news/poltiics/vote_2005/frontpage/4477901.stm and http://politics.guardian.co.uk/election/story/0,15803,1469601,00.html (both visited 26 Apr. 2005); *The Times*, 9, 10 Oct. 1964.

9. Blumler and McQuail, *Television in Politics*, 233–57; Butler and King, *Election of 1966*, 107; Howard and West, *Making of the Prime Minister*, 188 n.; Hurd, *End to Promises*, 15; Crossman, *Diaries*, 1: 480–1 (17 Mar. 1966).

10. Crossman, *Diaries*, 1: 486, (27 Mar. 1966); Butler and King, *Election of 1966*, 108–10; Butler and Kavanagh, *Election of February 1974*, 150, 154; Ramsden, *Winds of Change*, 378–80; Seymour-Ure, *Political Impact*, 99–136 ('Enoch Powell's earthquake'); Jones, *Sultans of Spin*, 4–8 (on Powell); Benn, *Office Without Power*, 287 (3 June 1970), 289 (8 June 1970), 291 (11 June 1970), and Benn, *End of an Era*, 289 (25 May 1983), where an ITN crew remove microphones as he speaks at one Bristol meeting.

11. Blumler, 'Producers' attitudes'; Butler and King, *Election of 1966*, 131–2, 146–7, 187–9; Seymour-Ure, *Political Impact*, 213–14, 219, 224–5; Cockerell, *Live from Number 10*, 125–30; Alderman, *British Elections*, 129–33.

12. Butler and Pinto-Duschinsky, *Election of 1970*, 144–6, 153, 163; *LO*, July– Aug. 1970, 138; Falkender, *Downing Street*, 50; Ramsden, *Winds of Change*, 308–10; John Lindsey to Alec Todd, 27 Oct. 1975 (Memo: On 'History of

Broadcasting Committee'), THCR, 2/6/1/201, Thatcher Papers, Churchill Archives; Hurd, *End to Promises*, 15–23; Prior, *Balance of Power*, 58.

13. Hurd, *End to Promises*, 16–18; Ramsden, *Winds of Change*, 310; Prior, *Balance of Power*, 59; Butler and Pinto-Duschinsky, *Election of 1970*, 145–6, 153; Williams, *Inside Number 10*, 337–41; Falkender, *Downing Street*, 51–66; Cockerell, *Live from Number 10*, 196–9.

14. Briggs, *History of Broadcasting*, V: 879; Williams, *Inside Number 10*, 343; Butler and Pinto-Duschinsky, *Election of 1970*, 152, 209; *LO*, July–Aug. 1970, 142.

15. Benn, *Against the Tide*, 7 (21 Feb. 1973), 107 (12 Feb. 1974), 108–9 (22 Feb. 1974); Falkender, *Downing Street*, 51–67; 'Report on February 1974 campaign tours', THCR, 2/7/1/55, Thatcher Papers, Churchill Archives; Butler and Kavanagh, *Election of February 1974*, 81–2; Penniman, *Britain at the Polls, 1974*, 80; Rosenbaum, *Soapbox to Soundbite*, 130–1; Donoughue, *Prime Minister*, 41; Donoughue, *Downing Street Diary*, 30 (21 Feb. 1974), 197 (23 Sept. 1974).

16. Cockerell, *Live from Number 10*, 176–80.

17. *LO*, Dec. 1974, 9; Penniman, *Britain at the Polls, 1974*, 210, 215–17, 220–1; Butler and Kavanagh, *Election of October 1974*, 224–5; Rosenbaum, *Soapbox to Soundbite*, 137; 'General Election October 1974: Mr Heath's tours', THCR, 2/7/1/55, Thatcher Papers, Churchill Archives.

18. Boaden, 'Tours', THCR, 2/7/1/55, Report on 'Possible special interest activities' and 'Election planning meeting, 15 Dec. 1978', 70, both in THCR 2/7/1/27, Michael Dobbs to Richard Ryder, 18 Jan. 1979, THCR 2/7/1/57, 'Daily tours schedules', 18 Apr. 1979 (Eastern and East Midlands), THCR 2/7/1/60, Thatcher Papers, Churchill Archives; *Guardian*, 19 Apr. 1979.

19. 'Election planning meetings, 15 Dec. 1978', 79, 82, THCR 2/7/1/27; David Boddy to Tom Hooson, 11 Mar. 1977, THCR, 2/6/1/201; 'Some guidelines on the media in a General Election', and A. J. B. Rowe, 'The General Election', both THCR 2/7/1/32; Gordon Reece Memo, 4 Dec. 1978, THCR, 2/6/1/202; Notes of 'Campaign tours' meeting, 21 Jan. 1977, THCR, 2/7/1/55, Thatcher Papers, Churchill Archives; Thatcher, *Path to Power*, 449–54.

20. 'Some guidelines', THCR 2/7/1/32, 'General guidelines on leader's tours', THCR 2/7/1/55, Thatcher Papers, Churchill Archives; Butler and Kavanagh, *Election of 1979*, 172, 202–6, 292; Livingstone, 'Conservative campaign', 143–5; Rosenbaum, *Soapbox to Soundbite*, 96–8.

21. Butler and Kavanagh, *Election of 1979*, 206, 229; Harrison, 'Television news', 73–4, 76.

22. Penniman, *Britain at the Polls, 1979*, 131–3; Butler and Kavanagh, *Election of 1979*, 165, 186, 212; Williams, *Inside Number 10*, 96; Hurd, *End to Promises*, 25; *Daily Telegraph*, 1 May 1979, 36.

23. Butler and Kavanagh, *Election of 1983*, 91–3, 159, 165, 251; Rosenbaum, *Soapbox to Soundbite*, 98, 133; Morgan, *Michael Foot*, 143, 426–7, 431; Wring,

Politics of Marketing, 76–80; *The Times*, 20 May 1983, 4, 27 May 1983, 5; Even, 'Television broadcasting'; and Blumler *et al.*, 'Setting the agenda'.

24. Donoughue, *Prime Minister*, 186; Donoughue, *Downing Street Diary*, 25 (17 Feb. 1974), 207 (2 Oct. 1974); Carroll, 'Alliance's campaign', 87 (a Callaghan speech-writer in 1979); Gould, *Unfinished Revolution*, 45; Delaney, 'Labour's advertising campaign', 27–31, 33; Atkinson, 'Live oratory', 38–55; Kellner, 'Labour campaign', 75–6; Butler and Kavanagh, *Election of 1987*, 90–4, 141–2; *Guardian*, 28 May 1987.

25. Rosenbaum, *Soapbox to Soundbite*, 66–8, 118–19; Crewe and Harrop, *Political Communications, 1987*, 149, 154, 157, 166; Butler and Kavanagh, *Election of 1987*, 112, 145–6, 149; Butler and Kavanagh, *Election of 1992*, 122–3; *The Times*, 27 May 1987, 16; *Guardian*, 20 May 1983, 10 June 1987, 26, 28 Mar. 1992; Wring, *Politics of Marketing*, 83–117; Lees-Marshment, *Political Marketing*, ch. 4. For the gloves off: Jones, *Soundbites and Spin Doctors* and *Sultans of Spin*; Campbell and Stott (eds.), *Blair Years*.

26. Crisell, *Introductory History*, 227–9; Crewe and Harrop, *Political Communications, 1987*, 148, 164; *Guardian*, 8 June 1987; Benn, *End of an Era*, 291 (4 June 1983); Rentoul *et al.*, 'People-metering', 109–10.

27. Blumler *et al.*, 'Setting the agenda', 114–18; Semetko *et al.*, *Formation of Campaign Agendas*; Butler and Kavanagh, *Election of 1979*, 213–18; Richard Ryder, 'Memo on coming broadcasting engagements, 4 Aug. 1977', THCR 2/6/1/16, and Gordon Reece, 'Memo on election broadcasting engagements, April 1979', THCR 2/7/1/32, Thatcher Papers, Churchill Archives.

28. Rosenbaum, *Soapbox to Soundbite*, 131–5; Cockerell, *Live from Number 10*, 103; Benn, *Out of the Wilderness*, 140 (12 Sept. 1964); Butler and Kavanagh, *Election of 1987*, 115–17, 137–8; 148; *The Times*, 14 Sept. 1964, 4, 15, 25 May 1983, 5, 25, 27 May 1987, 21 Mar. 1992, 6; *Guardian*, 25 May, 8 June 1987; Atkinson, 'Live oratory', and *Our Masters' Voices*; Carroll, 'Alliance's campaign'; Axford and Madgwick, 'Indecent exposure?'

29. Butler and Kavanagh, *Election of 1992*, 102, 124–6, 130, 167–8, 260; *Independent*, 16 Mar. 1992, 1; *The Times*, 14 Mar. 1992; Brandreth, *Breaking the Code*, 75–6 (31 Mar. 1992); Major, *Autobiography*, 289–90, 297–8.

30. Butler and Kavanagh, *Election of 1992*, 114, 124–6; *The Times*, 14, 21, 23 Mar. 1992; *Guardian*, 31 March 1992; Major, *Autobiography*, 289–90; Brandreth, *Breaking the Code*, 76 (31 Mar. 1992); Baker, *Turbulent Years*, 469; Rosenbaum, *Soapbox to Soundbite*, 135–7; Kavanagh, *Election Campaigning*, 204; Radice, *Diaries 1980–2001*, 268 (1 Apr. 1992).

31. Peter Jenkins, 'Unholy alliance that switches off the voters', *Independent*, 24 Mar. 1992; Hugo Young, 'Politics without people', *Guardian*, 25 Mar. 1992; also *Independent*, 18 Mar. 1992 ('Chancellor campaign sketch'); Nossiter *et al.*, 'Old values', 86.

CHAPTER 9

1. Jones, 'Pitiless probing eye', 66–90; Coleman (ed.), *Televised Election Debates*, 7, 17–18, 104–21; McNair, *Journalism and Democracy*, 85–92; Born, *Uncertain Vision*, 414.

2. For Evans see *Guardian*, 18 May 2001, and *Rhyl Journal*, 23 May 2001; for Storer, see http://news.bbc.co.uk/vote2001/hi/english/newsid_1334000/1334131.stm (visited 14 Sept. 2005), and *Birmingham Mail*, 17 May 2001; for the first 'masochism strategy' see *The Times*, 3 May 2003 (Peter Stothard's Blair diary, 10 Mar. 2003), and *Guardian*, 26 Apr. and 25 June 2003; for 2005 http://news.bbc.co.uk/1/hi/uk_politics/4272741.stm (visited 14 Sept. 2005), *The Times*, 17 Feb. 2005; *Observer*, 6 Mar. 2005. See also Kavanagh and Butler, *Election of 2005*, 57, 61, 95–6; Geddes and Tonge (eds.), *Britain Decides, 2005*, 2, 35–6, 209–10, 212; Wring *et al.* (eds.), *Political Communications, 2005*, 10.

3. Butler and King, *Election of 1964*, 158, 161, 164; Butler and King, *Election of 1966*, 127; Briggs, *History of Broadcasting*, 5: 442–3, 554–5; Selwyn Lloyd to Edward du Cann, 22 Mar. 1966, SELO 6/192, Selwyn Lloyd Papers, Churchill Archives.

4. Butler and Pinto-Duschinsky, *Election of 1970*, 203; Alderman, *British Elections*, 127; Richard Clark (Anglia TV) to Dingle Foot, 14 Aug. 1968, DGFT 3/5, Dingle Foot papers, Churchill Archives; Coleman, *Election Call*, 2–5.

5. Briggs, *History of Broadcasting*, 5: 982; Chignell, 'London Broadcasting Company'; Butler and Kavanagh, *Election of February 1974*, 155–8; Day, *Grand Inquisitor*, 184–5; Penniman, *Britain at the Polls, 1974*, 145–8; Alderman, *British Elections*, 130–1; MacDonald, 'Election 500', 125–6; Self, '*Granada 500*', 78, 80.

6. Penniman, *Britain at the Polls, 1974*, 147; *CAJ*, Jan. 1974, 5; *Brighton Evening Argus*, 3 and 7 Nov. 1973; *LO*, May 1978, 20.

7. Ramsden, *Winds of Change*, 378–80; Blumler *et al.*, *Challenge of Broadcasting*, *passim*; Gurevitch and Blumler, 'Construction of election news'. For Blumler's somewhat less pessimistic account of February 1974 see, Penniman, *Britain at the Polls, 1974*, esp. 135–6, 143.

8. Butler and Kavanagh, *Election of 1979*, 207–8; *Daily Telegraph*, 4 May 1979, 1; Crewe and Harrop, *Political Communications, 1983*, 128; Day, *Grand Inquisitor*, 245–6, 250; Day, *But with Respect*, 208–9, 230; Harris, 'Evasive action', 91–4; Jones, 'Pitiless probing eye', 83–5; McNair, *Journalism and Democracy*, 92–6, 104.

9. Butler and Kavanagh, *Election of 1979*, 213–14, 217; *Daily Telegraph*, 1 May 1979, 13; Self, '*Granada 500*', 81–3, and 109–10; Cockerell, *Live from Number 10*, 250, 282–3; Butler and Kavanagh, *Election of 1983*, 167–9; Day, *Grand Inquisitor*, 202–6, 245–6, 273–7; Benn, *End of an Era*, 288 (19 May 1983); *Guardian*, 17 May 1983, 2, 27 May 1983, 2.

10. Tyler, *Campaign!*, 139, 212–24, 233; Butler and Kavanagh, *Election of 1987*, 150 (140,000 voters phoned *Election Call* in 1987); Cockerell, *Live from Number 10*, 321–2, 328; Thatcher, *Path to Power*, 449; Butler and Kavanagh, *Election of 1983*, 167–9; *Guardian*, 30 May 1987, 4, 2 June 1987, 8, 5 June 1987, 4.

11. *Guardian*, 25 Mar. 1992; General Election Training Task Force, 'Report of training to date' (1991?), KNNK Box 49, Kinnock Papers, Churchill Archives.

12. *Guardian*, 7 Apr. 1992, 9; Butler and Kavanagh, *Election of 1992*, 172–3.

13. Rentoul *et al.*, 'People-metering'; Clark, 'Worm that turned'; Born, 'Digitising democracy'; Coleman, *Televised Election Debates*, 21; Coleman and Ward (eds.), *Spinning the Web*, 6, 12, 22.

14. McNair, *Journalism and Democracy*, 74–5, 136–8; *Guardian*, 22 Apr. 1997, 18, 29 Apr. 1997, 18; Blumler and Gurevitch, 'Change in the air', esp. 190; Butler and Kavanagh, *Election of 1997*, 148–9.

15. Coleman, *Election Call*, 2–5, 23; Coleman and Ross, *Spaces Between*, 4–6, 10; Freedland, *Bring Home the Revolution*, 25; Born, *Uncertain Vision*, 401–3, 408, 421–5; Hart, *Seducing America*, 16, 22, 75, 158–9; Walker and Jones, *Invisible Political Actors*, 1–2 (on BBC).

16. Coleman and Ross, *Spaces Between*, 4, 9, 33; Harrison, 'On Air', 107–9; Denver and Wring, 'Election unspun?', 209–13; Boulton, 'Reconnecting with viewers', 206–7.

17. Campbell and Stott, *Blair Years*, 157 (22 Feb. 1997), 529–30 (16 May 2001); Harrison, 'On Air', 106, 110; Kavanagh and Butler, *Election of 2005*, 71, 174, 180–1; *Guardian*, 26 Apr. and 25 June 2003 (on 'beating up'); *The Times*, 24 May 2005 ('Dirty tricksters work their magic' on a Channel 4 *Dispatches* exposé).

18. Hart, *Seducing America*, 157; Billig, 'Politics as appearance'; Street, *Mass Media*, ch. 9; Norris, *Virtuous Circle*; Lloyd and Seaton (eds.), *What Can be Done?*, 4–6.

19. See Gould, 'Labour's political strategy', 21; http://news.bbc.co.uk/1/hi/uk_politics/vote_2005/frontpage/4494597.stm; and http://news.bbc.co.uk/1/hi/uk_politics/vote_2005/frontpage/4506283.stm, which includes a video of Keys's speech (both visited 14 Sept. 2005).

20. *The Times*, 25, 26 Mar. 1969; Healey, *Time of My Life*, 297, where Healey acknowledges that 'the incident did wonders for my image'.

21. http://www.webcameron.org.uk/, and http://www.webcameron.org.uk/page.php?pseudo=videos&phb_off=96# (last visited 10 July 2007); Gibson and Ward (eds.), *Reinvigorating Democracy?*; Ward, Gibson, and Lusoli, 'Online participation'; Coleman and Ward, *Spinning the Web*, 5–8, 12, 21, 33–5; Oates, Owen, and Gibson (eds.), *Internet and Politics*; Coleman and Normann, *New Media*.

22. *Guardian*, 30 Mar., 4 Apr., 21 May 2005; *Independent on Sunday*, 3 Apr. 2005; Gaby Hinsliff, 'Forget the policies, what about you?', *Observer*, 6 Mar. 2005.

Bibliography

PRIMARY SOURCES

Manuscripts

Baldwin Papers, CUL, Cambridge.

Bateman Collection (Bristol Independent Labour Party), Bristol University Library Special Collections.

Bray Papers (BRAY) CAC, Cambridge.

Bridgeman Papers, Shropshire Archives, Shrewsbury.

Bristol East/South-East Labour Party Records, Bristol Record Office.

Churchill Papers (CHAR), CAC, Cambridge.

Dingle Foot Papers (DGFT) CAC, Cambridge.

George Lloyd Papers (GLLD), CAC, Cambridge.

John Massie Letters, c.1870–1928, Add. MSS 8988/55, CUL, Cambridge.

Kinnock Papers (KNNK) CAC, Cambridge.

Labour Representation Committee correspondence, Labour History Archive and Study Centre, Manchester.

Leo Amery Papers (AMEL), CAC, Cambridge.

Manchester Liberal Federation, Executive Committee Minutes, 1909–1918, Manchester Archives.

Metropolitan Conservative Agents' Association Minutes, Clapham Conservative Association collection (CCA-3), BLPES, London.

Morrison-Bell Papers (2128), Devon Record Office, Exeter.

Morrison-Bell Papers, Five-Year Diaries (MOR/3), Parliamentary Archives, London.

Newcastle (Clumber) Collection (Ne C), University of Nottingham Manuscripts and Special Collections.

North-West Manchester Liberal Association Minutes, Manchester Archives.

Oswestry Conservative and Unionist Association, minute book 1876–1887 (F33.3), Oswestry Public Library, Shropshire.

St George's Conservative Association Minutes (487/8), Westminster Public Library, London.

Selwyn Lloyd Papers (SELO), CAC, Cambridge.

Thatcher Papers (THCR), CAC, Cambridge.

Official Publications

Bristol Election Petition, Minutes of Evidence & Proceedings, PP1867–68, VIII, 21.

Bristol Election Petition Judgement, 1870, PP1870, LVI, 179.

Controverted Elections (Judgements), PP1893–94, LXX.

Hansard (Parliamentary Debates).

HMSO, *Annual Abstract of Statistics, 1971* (London, 1971).

Nottingham East Petition Judgment, PP1911, LXI, 467 ff.

Report from the Select Committee on the Corrupt Practices Prevention Act (1854), PP1860, X.

Report from the Select Committee on the Corrupt Practices Prevention and Election Petition Acts, PP1875, VIII.

Report from the Select Committee on Parliamentary and Municipal Elections (Hartington Committee), PP1868–69, VIII.

Report from the Select Committee on Parliamentary and Municipal Elections (Hartington Committee), Final Report, PP1870, VI.

Report from the Select Committee on Parliamentary and Municipal Elections (Ballot Act), PP1876, XII.

Report from the Select Committee on Parliamentary and Municipal Elections (Hours of Polling), PP1878, XIII.

Report of the Departmental Committee on the Duties of the Police with Respect to the Preservation of Order at Public Meetings, 2 vols., PP1909, Cd. 4673 & 4674, XXXVI. http://www.opsi.gov.uk/ACTS

Other Published Primary

Anon., *The Wit of the Day, or the Humours of Westminster* (election squibs, 1784) (anon., London, 1784), Houghton Library Broadsides, Harvard University.

Anon., *A Regular Account of the Electioneering Paper War Between Generals Gascoyne & Tarleton, Mr Chalmer and Mr Birch* (Castle Street Booksellers, Liverpool, 1802).

Anon., *An Impartial Collection of Addresses, Songs, Squibs &c* (Timothy Herring, Liverpool, 1812).

Anon., *The Speeches, &c of the Right Honourable George Canning Delivered on Public Occasions During the Election at Liverpool* (T. Kaye, Liverpool, 1812).

Anon., *Essex County Election, Report of the Speeches Delivered at the Hustings* (Meggy & Chalk, Chelmsford, 1830).

Anon., *The Poll Book of the Election of a Representative in Parliament for the Borough of Whitehaven* (R. Gibson, Whitehaven, 1832).

Anon. [Joseph McCabe], *The Taint in Politics: A Study in the Evolution of Parliamentary Corruption* (Grant Richards, London, 1920).

ARBUTHNOT, G. A. (ed.), *The Primrose League Election Guide* (Eveleigh Nash, London, 1914).

ASQUITH, H. H., *An Election Guide: Rules for the Conduct and Management of Elections in England and Wales Under the Corrupt Practices Act, 1883* (Liberal Central Association, London, 1884).

BARKER, BERNARD (ed.), *Ramsay MacDonald's Political Writings* (Allen Lane, London, 1972).

BELLOC, HILAIRE, *Mr Clutterbuck's Election* (Eveleigh Nash, London, 1908).

British Film Institute, film archive at http://www.screenonline.org.uk/film/

BUNN, E. NICHOLAS, *Instructions to Sub-Agents, Canvassers and Voluntary Workers in a Contested Election* (private, London, 1905).

——— *Political Organization: Practical Notes and Suggestions* (private, London, 1905).

——— *Practical Notes on the Management and Work of a County Parliamentary Election* (private, London, 1905).

CAMBRAY, PHILIP G., *The Game of Politics: A Study of the Principles of British Political Strategy* (John Murray, London, 1932).

CHESTERTON, A. K., *Oswald Mosley: Portrait of a Leader* (London, n.d. [1937]).

Conservative Party/National Union, Pamphlets and Leaflets series, Harvester microfiche.

CROFT, HAROLD, *Conduct of Parliamentary Elections* (Labour Party, London, 1945).

DICKENS, CHARLES, *The Pickwick Papers* (1837: Clarendon Press, Oxford, 1986).

DISRAELI, BENJAMIN, and DISRAELI, SARAH (Cherry and Fair Star), *A Year at Hartlebury or The Election* (1834: John Murray, London, 1983).

FINN, J. F., *The Outdoor Meeting: How to Organise, Conduct and Speak at it* (Chapman & Halls, London, 1930).

FISHER, W. J., 'Electoral abuses', *Independent Review*, ix, 31 (Apr. 1906), 34–44.

FOOT, M. R. D. (ed.), *Midlothian Speeches, 1879: W. E. Gladstone* (Leicester University Press, Leicester, 1971).

Goldsmiths'-Kress Library of Economic Literature (GKL), Baker Business Library, Harvard University (microfilm edition).

GORST, J. E., *An Election Manual Containing the Parliamentary Elections (Corrupt and Illegal Practices) Act, 1883. With Notes* (Chapman & Hall, London, 1883).

HEDDERWICK, T. C. H., *Parliamentary Election Manual* (Stevens, London, 1892).

HOBSON, J. A., *Psychology of Jingoism* (Richards, London, 1901).

HOUSTON, HENRY JAMES, and VALDAR, LIONEL, *Modern Electioneering Practice* (Charles Knight, London, n.d. [1922]).

Imperial Tariff Committee, *A Handbook for Unionist Canvassers: General Election 1910* (Imperial Tariff Committee, Birmingham, 1910).

J- C- [John Cotton], *Election Squibs, Ballads and Broadsides with Other Impromptu Verses* (J. L. Allday, Birmingham, n.d. [1887?]).

John Johnson Collection, 'Cartoons' and 'Elections' series, Bodleian Library, Oxford.

Labour Party, *Conduct of Elections: A Practical Guide to the Organisation and Management of Parliamentary and Local Elections* (Labour Party, London, 1931).

Labour Party, *Interim Report of the Sub-Committee on Party Organisation* (Labour Party, London, 1955).

Labour Party, *Conduct of Parliamentary Elections* (Labour Party, London, 1977).

LAWSON, M., *The Substance of a Speech Delivered at the Boroughbridge Election Previous to the Poll*, 2nd edn. (E. & J. Goode, Cambridge, 1818).

LLOYD, J. SEYMOUR, *Elections and How to Fight them*, 2nd edn. (Vacher, London, 1909).

London County Council Election, 1907 [Wallas], Coll. Misc. 0840, BLPES, London.

Mass Observation, File Reports, Harvester microfiche.

MASTERMAN, C. F. G., *The Condition of England* (1909: Methuen, London, 1960).

MATTINSON, MILES WALKER, and MACASKIE, STUART CUNNINGHAM, *The Law Relating to Corrupt Practices at Elections and the Practice of Election Petitions* (Waterlow, London, 1883).

MONTAGUE, C. E., *Disenchantment* (1922: Phoenix Library edn., London, 1929).

'Newscuttings of Bristol Parliamentary Elections, 1761–1880' (BRO, 28049, (26) a–b), Bristol Record Office.

Northumberland County Election (1826), *A Collection of Election Addresses, Hand-Bills and Offprints from the* Newcastle Chronicle (HS. 74 1613 (1–81)), BL, London.

'Political and Tariff Reform Posters, *c.*1892–1910', Coll. Misc. 0519, BLPES, London.

PRIESTLEY, J. B., *English Journey* (Heinemann/Gollancz, London, 1934).

REEVES, M. S., *Round About a Pound a Week*, (G. Bell, London, 1913).

RENNARD, CHRIS, *Winning By-elections* (Association of Liberal Councillors, Activists' Guide no. 8, n.d. [1985?]).

REYNOLDS, STEPHEN, WOOLLEY, BOB, and WOOLLEY, TOM, *Seems So! A Working-Class View of Politics* (Macmillan, London, 1911).

RICHARDS, H. C., *The Candidates' and Agents' Guide in Contested Elections*, 4th edn. (Jordon, London, 1904).

RICHARDS, PAUL, *How to Win an Election*, 2nd edn. (Politico's, London, 2004).

ROUSE, ROLLA, *A Manual for Election Agents, Candidates and Others…* (Edmund Spettigue, London, 1841).

ROWE, W. H., *A Practical Manual on the Conduct and Management of Parliamentary Elections for the Use of Conservative Candidates and Elections Agents* (Conservative Central Office, London, 1890).

SEAGER, J. RENWICK, *Parliamentary Elections under the Reform Act, 1918, as Amended by Later Legislation*, 2nd edn. (P. S. King, London, 1921).

Seventeenth Annual Conference Report of the National Union of Conservative and Constitutional Associations (1883), Harvester microfilm.

SUMMERS, KNIGHT, *M.P. for Puddlepoor; or the Borough Election: A Farce in One Act* (Thomas Hailes Lacy, London, 1869).

'Tidlewink', *Electioneering* (Simpkin, London, 1895).

'Totnes Borough—Election Material', 1579A/12, Devon Record Office, Exeter.

WALLAS, GRAHAM, *Human Nature in Politics* (Archibald Constable, London, 1908).

WOODINGS, WILLIAM, *The Conduct and Management of Parliamentary Elections: A Practical Manual*, 4th edn. (Liberal Publication Department, London, 1900).

Newspapers and Journals

Birmingham Mail
Blackwood's Edinburgh Magazine
Brighton and Hove Gazette
Brighton Evening Argus
Bristol Evening Post
Bristol Times and Mirror
Cambridge Evening News
Conservative Agents' Journal (CAJ)
Daily Herald
Daily Mirror
Daily News
Daily Telegraph
Durham County Advertiser
Fabian Journal
Gallup Political Index
Glasgow Herald
Hereford Citizen and Bulletin
Hereford Times
Illustrated London News
Independent
Independent on Sunday
Kidderminster Times
Labour Organiser (LO)
Lancashire Daily Post
Leeds Daily News
Leeds Mercury
Liberal Agent
Loughborough Examiner
Manchester Guardian/Guardian
Morning Post
News Chronicle
Observer
Oswestry and Border Counties Advertiser
Oxford Magazine
Portsmouth Times
Rhyl Journal
Rochdale Observer
Rochdale Times
Scotsman
South Devon Times
South Wales Weekly Argus
The Times

Wakefield Journal and Examiner
Wednesbury Midland Advertiser
West Essex Gazette and Guardian
Westminster Gazette
Wolverhampton Chronicle
Women's Franchise
Worksop Guardian
Yorkshire Post

Published Letters and Diaries

BALL, STUART (ed.), *Parliament and Politics in the Age of Baldwin and MacDonald: The Headlam Diaries, 1923–1935* (Historians' Press, London, 1992).

——(ed.), *Parliament and Politics in the Age of Churchill and Attlee: The Headlam Diaries, 1935–1951*, Camden 5th Ser., vol. 14 (Cambridge University Press/Royal Historical Society, London, 1999).

BENN, TONY, *Out of the Wilderness: Diaries, 1963–67* (Hutchinson, London, 1987).

——*Office Without Power: Diaries, 1968–72* (Hutchinson, London, 1988).

——*Against the Tide: Diaries, 1973–76* (Arrow, London, 1990).

——*The End of an Era: Diaries, 1980–1990* (Hutchinson, London, 1992).

——*Years of Hope: Diaries, Letters and Papers, 1940–1962*, ed. Ruth Winstone (Hutchinson, London, 1994).

BRANDRETH, GYLES, *Breaking the Code: Westminster Diaries May 1990–May 1997* (Weidenfeld & Nicolson, London, 1999).

CAMPBELL, ALASTAIR, and STOTT, RICHARD (eds.), *The Blair Years: Extracts from the Alastair Campbell Diaries* (Hutchinson, London, 2007).

CASTLE, BARBARA, *The Castle Diaries, 1974–76* (Weidenfeld & Nicolson, London, 1980).

CATTERALL, PETER (ed.), *The Macmillan Diaries: The Cabinet Years, 1950–1957* (Macmillan, Basingstoke, 2003).

CLARK, ALAN, *Diaries* [vol. 2: 1983–1991] (Weidenfeld & Nicholson, London, 1993).

——*Diaries: Into Politics, 1972–1982* (Phoenix, London, 2001).

COLVILLE, JOHN, *The Fringes of Power: Downing Street Diaries, 1939–1955* (Hodder & Stoughton, London, 1985).

CROSSMAN, RICHARD, *The Diaries of a Cabinet Minister*, vol. 1: *Minister of Housing, 1964–1966* (Hamish Hamilton & Jonathan Cape, London, 1975).

——*The Diaries of a Cabinet Minister*, vol. 2: *Lord President of the Council and Leader of the House of Commons, 1966–68* (Hamish Hamilton & Jonathan Cape, London, 1976).

——*The Diaries of a Cabinet Minister*, vol. 3: *Secretary of State for Social Services, 1968–70* (Hamish Hamilton & Jonathan Cape, London, 1977).

DONOUGHUE, BERNARD, *Downing Street Diary: With Harold Wilson in No. 10* (Jonathan Cape, London, 2005).

GILBERT, MARTIN, *Winston S. Churchill—Companion* (documents), 5 vols. (Heinemann, London, 1967–82).

Gladstone Diaries, The, ed. M. R. D. Foot and H. C. G. Matthew, 14 vols. (Clarendon Press, Oxford, 1978–94).

JAMES, ROBERT RHODES (ed.), *Chips: The Diaries of Sir Henry Channon* (Weidenfeld & Nicolson, London, 1967).

——(ed.), *Memoirs of a Conservative: J.C.C. Davidson's Memoirs and Papers, 1910–37* (Weidenfeld & Nicolson, London, 1969).

KING, OONA, *The Oona King Diaries: House Music* (Bloomsbury, London, 2007).

LAWSON-TANCRED, Sir THOMAS, *Records of a Yorkshire Manor* (Edward Arnold, London, 1937).

MORGAN, JANET (ed.), *The Backbench Diaries of Richard Crossman* (Hamish Hamilton & Jonathan Cape, London, 1981).

NICOLSON, NIGEL (ed.), *The Harold Nicolson Diaries, 1907–1963* (Weidenfeld & Nicolson, London, 2004).

PIMLOTT, BEN (ed.), *The Political Diary of Hugh Dalton, 1918–40, 1945–60* (Jonathan Cape/LSE, London, 1986).

RADICE, GILES, *Diaries 1980–2001: From Political Disaster to Election Triumph* (Weidenfeld & Nicolson, London, 2004).

RAMSDEN, JOHN (ed.), *Real Old Tory Politics: The Political Diaries of Sir Robert Sanders, Lord Bayford, 1910–35* (Historians' Press, London, 1984).

SELF, ROBERT C. (ed.), *The Austen Chamberlain Diary Letters: The Correspondence of Sir Austen Chamberlain with his Sisters Hilda and Ida, 1916–1937*, Camden 5th Ser., vol. 5 (Cambridge University Press/Royal Historical Society, Cambridge 1995).

——(ed.), *The Neville Chamberlain Diary Letters*, vol. 1: *The Making of a Politician, 1915–20* (Ashgate, Aldershot, 2000).

——(ed.), *The Neville Chamberlain Diary Letters*, vol. 2: *The Reform Years, 1921–27* (Ashgate, Aldershot, 2000).

——(ed.), *The Neville Chamberlain Diary Letters*, vol. 3: *The Heir Apparent, 1928–1933* (Ashgate, Aldershot, 2002).

——(ed.), *The Neville Chamberlain Diary Letters*, vol. 4: *The Downing Street Years, 1934–1940* (Ashgate, Aldershot, 2005).

STUART, CHARLES (ed.), *The Reith Diaries* (Collins, London, 1975).

WILLIAMS, PHILIP M. (ed.), *The Diary of Hugh Gaitskell, 1945–1956* (Jonathan Cape, London, 1983).

WILLIAMSON, PHILIP (ed.), *The Modernisation of Conservative Politics: The Diaries and Letters of William Bridgeman, 1904–1935* (Historians' Press, London, 1988).

——and BALDWIN, EDWARD (eds.), *Baldwin Papers: A Conservative Statesman, 1908–1947* (Cambridge University Press, Cambridge, 2004).

Memoirs

AMERY, JULIAN, *Approach March: A Venture in Biography* (Hutchinson, London, 1973).

AMERY, L. S., *My Political Life, Volume One: England Before the Storm* (Hutchinson, London, 1953).

_____ *My Political Life, Volume Two: War and Peace* (Hutchinson, London, 1953).

BAKER, KENNETH, *The Turbulent Years: My Life in Politics* (Faber & Faber, London, 1993).

BEVINS, REGINALD, *The Greasy Pole: A Personal Account of the Realities of British Politics* (Hodder & Stoughton, London, 1965).

BIRRELL, AUGUSTINE, *Things Past Redress* (Faber & Faber, London, 1937).

BOOTHBY, ROBERT [Baron Boothby], *Boothby: Recollections of a Rebel* (Hutchinson, London, 1978).

BOYD-CARPENTER, JOHN, *Way of Life: The Memoirs of John Boyd-Carpenter* (Sidgwick & Jackson, London, 1980).

BRIDGES, J. A., *Victorian Recollections* (G. Bell, London, 1919).

BROUGHAM, HENRY, *The Life and Times of Henry Brougham, by Himself*, 3 vols. (William Blackwood, Edinburgh, 1871).

CHAMBERLAIN, AUSTEN, *Down the Years* (Cassell, London, 1935).

CHURCHILL, WINSTON S., *My Early Life: A Roving Commission* (Thornton Butterworth, London, 1930).

_____ *Great Contemporaries* (Thornton Butterworth, London, 1937).

DALTON, HUGH, *The Fateful Years: Memoirs, 1931–1945* (Muller, London, 1957).

DAY, ROBIN, *Grand Inquisitor: Memoirs of Sir Robin Day* (Weidenfeld & Nicolson, London, 1989).

_____ *... But With Respect: Memorable Television Interviews with Statesmen and Parliamentarians* (Weidenfeld & Nicolson, London, 1993).

DONNER, PATRICK, *Crusade: A Life against the Calamitous Twentieth Century* (Sherwood Press, London, 1984).

DONOUGHUE, BERNARD, *Prime Minister: The Conduct of Policy under Harold Wilson and James Callaghan* (Jonathan Cape, London, 1987).

FALKENDER, MARCIA, *Downing Street in Perspective* (Weidenfeld & Nicolson, London, 1983).

GAMMAGE, ROBERT GEORGE, *History of the Chartist Movement, 1837–1854*, 2nd edn. (Browne & Browne, Newcastle, 1894).

GOULD, PHILIP, *The Unfinished Revolution: How the Modernisers Saved the Labour Party* (1998: Abacus, London, 1999).

GRAY, FRANK, *The Confessions of a Candidate* (Martin Hopkinson, London, 1925).

HEALEY, DENIS, *The Time of My Life* (Joseph, London, 1989).

HEATH, EDWARD, *The Course of My Life: My Autobiography* (Hodder & Stoughton, London, 1998).

HOGG, QUINTIN [Lord Hailsham], *A Sparrow's Flight: The Memoirs of Lord Hailsham of St Marylebone* (Collins, London, 1990).

HOME, ALEC DOUGLAS- [Lord Home], *The Way the Wind Blows: An Autobiography* (Collins, London, 1976).

HOWE, GEOFFREY, *Conflict of Loyalty* (1994: Pan Books, London, 1995).

HOWES, JOSEPH, *Twenty-Five Years Fight with the Tories* (the author, Morecambe, 1907).

HOWELL, DENIS, *Made in Birmingham: The Memoirs of Denis Howell* (MacDonald Queen Anne, London, 1990).

HURD, DOUGLAS, *An End to Promises* (Collins, London, 1979).

JAY, DOUGLAS, *Change and Fortune: A Political Record* (Hutchinson, London, 1980).

JENKINS, ROY, *A Life at the Centre* (Macmillan, London, 1991).

MACMILLAN, HAROLD, *Winds of Change, 1914–1939* (Macmillan, London, 1966) _____ *Tides of Fortune, 1945–1955* (Macmillan, London, 1969).

MAJOR, JOHN, *The Autobiography* (Harper Collins, London, 1999).

MIKARDO, IAN, *Back-Bencher* (Weidenfeld & Nicolson, London, 1988).

MORRISON, HERBERT [Lord Morrison of Lambeth], *Herbert Morrison: An Autobiography* (Odhams Press, London, 1960).

NABARRO, GERALD, *Nab 1: Portrait of a Politician* (Robert Maxwell, Oxford, 1969). _____ *Exploits of a Politician* (Arthur Baker, London, 1973).

PANKHURST, EMMELINE, *My Own Story* (Hearst's International, New York, 1914).

PRIOR, JIM, *A Balance of Power* (Hamish Hamilton, London, 1986).

RAWLINSON, PETER, *A Price too High: An Autobiography* (Weidenfeld & Nicolson, London, 1989).

RUSSELL, G. W. E. *Collections and Recollections by One Who has Kept a Diary* (Smith Elder, London, 1898).

TEBBIT, NORMAN, *Upwardly Mobile* (Weidenfeld & Nicolson, 1988).

THATCHER, MARGARET, *The Path to Power* (Harper Collins, London, 1995).

TROLLOPE, ANTHONY, *An Autobiography* (1883: Williams & Norgate, London, 1946).

WALKER, PETER, *Staying Power: An Autobiography* (Bloomsbury, London, 1992).

WHITELAW, WILLIAM, *The Whitelaw Memoirs* (Aurum Press, London, 1989).

WIGG, GEORGE [Lord Wigg], *George Wigg* (Michael Joseph, London, 1972).

WILLIAMS, MARCIA, *Inside Number 10* (Weidenfeld & Nicolson, London, 1972).

Reference

BUTLER, DAVID, and BUTLER, GARETH, *British Political Facts, 1900–1994*, 7th edn. (Macmillan, London, 1994).

COOK, CHRIS, and RAMSDEN, JOHN (eds.), *By-Elections in British Politics* (Macmillan, London, 1973).

CRAIG, F. W. S., *British Electoral Facts, 1832–1987*, 5th edn. (Gower, Aldershot, 1989).

CRAIG, F. W. S., *British Parliamentary Election Results*, 5 vols. (Parliamentary Research Services, Chichester, 1974–89).

—— *Chronology of British Parliamentary By-Elections, 1833–1987* (Parliamentary Research Services, Chichester, 1987).

CREWE, IVOR, FOX, ANTHONY, and DAY, NEIL, *The British Electorate 1963–1992: A Compendium of Data from the British Election Studies* (Cambridge University Press, Cambridge, 1995).

DAVIES, SAM, and MORLEY, BOB, *County Borough Elections in England and Wales, 1919–1938: A Comparative Analysis*, vols. 1–3 (Ashgate, Aldershot, 1999–2006).

GALLUP, GEORGE H. (ed.), *The Gallup International Public Opinion Polls: Great Britain, 1937–1975*, 2 vols. (Random House, New York, 1976).

RALLINGS, COLIN, and THRASHER, MICHAEL (eds.), *British Electoral Facts, 1832–1999* (Ashgate, Aldershot, 2000).

SECONDARY SOURCES

Contemporary Political

Anon. [A. D. R. W. Cochrane-Baillie], 'The Corrupt Practices Bill', *Blackwood's Edinburgh Magazine*, 134 (Dec. 1883), 728–39.

ASHCROFT, MICHAEL A., *Smell the Coffee: A Wake-up Call for the Conservative Party* (the author, London, 2005).

ATKINSON, MAX, 'The 1983 election and the demise of live oratory', in Crewe and Harrop (eds.), *Political Communications, 1983*.

ATTLEE, CLEMENT [Earl Attlee], 'The role of the Member of Parliament', *Fabian Journal* (Nov. 1958), 5–8.

AXFORD, BARRIE, and MADGWICK, PETER, 'Indecent exposure? Three-party politics in television news during the 1987 General Election', in Crewe and Harrop (eds.), *Political Communications, 1987*.

BARKER, ANTHONY, and RUSH, MICHAEL, *The Member of Parliament and his Information* (George Allen & Unwin, London, 1970).

BBC [Jennings and Gill], *Broadcasting in Everyday Life: A Survey of the Social Effects of the Coming of Broadcasting* (BBC, London, 1939).

BEALEY, FRANK, BLONDEL J., and McCANN, W. P. *Constituency Politics: A Study of Newcastle-under-Lyme* (Faber & Faber, London, 1965).

BELL, TIM, 'The Conservative advertising campaign', in Worcester and Harrop, *Political Communications, 1979*.

BENNEY, MARK, and GEISS, PHYLLIS, 'Social class and politics in Greenwich', *British Journal of Sociology*, 1, 4 (1950), 310–27.

—— GRAY, A. P., and PEAR, R. H., *How People Vote: A Study of Electoral Behaviour in Greenwich* (Routledge & Kegan Paul, London, 1958).

BILLIG, MICHAEL, 'Politics as an appearance and reality show: the hermeneutics of suspicion', in Wring *et al.* (eds.), *Political Communications, 2005*.

BIRCH, A. H., *Small-Town Politics: A Study of Political Life in Glossop* (Oxford University Press, Oxford, 1959).

——— and CAMPBELL, PETER, 'Voting Behaviour in a Lancashire Constituency' (Stretford, 1950), *British Journal of Sociology*, 1, 3 (1950), 197–208.

BLONDEL, JEAN, 'The Conservative Association and the Labour Party in Reading', *Political Studies*, 6 (1958), 101–19.

BLUMLER, JAY G., 'Producers' attitudes towards television coverage of an election campaign: a case study', in Paul Halmos (ed.), *The Sociology of Mass Media Communications*, Sociological Review Monograph, 13 (Keele University Press, Keele, 1969).

——— 'Mass media roles and reactions in the February election', in Penniman (ed.), *Britain at the Polls, 1974.*

——— and GUREVITCH, MICHAEL, 'Change in the air: campaign journalism at the BBC, 1997', in Crewe *et al.* (eds.), *Political Communications, 1997.*

——— and MCQUAIL, DENIS, *Television in Politics: Its Uses and Influence* (Faber & Faber, London, 1968).

——— *et al.*, *The Challenge of Election Broadcasting* (Leeds University Press, Leeds, 1978).

——— GUREVITCH, MICHAEL, and NOSSITER, T. J. 'Setting the television news agenda: campaign observation at the BBC', in Crewe and Harrop (eds.), *Political Communications, 1983.*

BOCHEL, J. M., and DENVER, D. T., 'Political communication: Scottish local newspapers and the General Election of February 1974', *Scottish Journal of Sociology*, 2 (1977), 11–30.

BOULTON, ADAM, 'Reconnecting with the viewers: Sky News' election coverage', in Wring *et al.* (eds.), *Political Communications, 2005.*

BUTLER, D. E., *The British General Election of 1951* (Macmillan, London, 1952).

——— *The British General Election of 1955* (Macmillan, London, 1955).

——— and ROSE, RICHARD, *The British General Election of 1959* (Macmillan, London, 1960).

——— and KING, ANTHONY, *The British General Election of 1964* (Macmillan, London, 1965).

——— and ——— *The British General Election of 1966* (Macmillan, London, 1966).

——— and PINTO-DUSCHINSKY, MICHAEL, *The British General Election of 1970* (Macmillan, London, 1971).

——— and KAVANAGH, DENNIS, *The British General Election of February 1974* (Macmillan, London, 1974).

——— and ——— *The British General Election of October 1974* (Macmillan, London, 1975).

——— and ——— *The British General Election of 1979* (Macmillan, London, 1980).

——— and ——— *The British General Election of 1983* (Macmillan, London, 1984).

——— and ——— *The British General Election of 1987* (Macmillan, Basingstoke, 1988).

——— and ——— *The British General Election of 1992* (Macmillan, Basingstoke, 1992).

BUTLER, D. E., and KAVANAGH, DENNIS, *The British General Election of 1997* (Macmillan, Basingstoke, 1997).

—— and —— *The British General Election of 2001* (Palgrave, London, 2002).

CAIN, BRUCE, FEREJOHN, JOHN, and FIORINA, MORRIS, *The Personal Vote: Constituency Service and Electoral Independence* (Harvard University Press, Cambridge, Mass., 1987).

CAMPBELL, PETER, DONNISON, DAVID, and POTTER, ALLEN, 'Voting behaviour in Droylsden in October, 1951', *Manchester School of Economic and Social Studies*, 20 (1952), 57–65.

CANZINI, DAVID, 'The Conservative Campaign', in Wring *et al.* (eds.), *Political Communications*, 2005.

CARROLL, ROGER, 'The Alliance's non-advertising campaign', in Crewe and Harrop (eds.), *Political Communications, 1987*.

CHRIMES, S. B. (ed.), *The General Election in Glasgow February, 1950* (Jackson, Glasgow, 1950).

CLARK, HELEN, 'The worm that turned: New Zealand's 1996 General Election and the televised "worm" debates', in Coleman (ed.), *Televised Election Debates*.

COLEMAN, STEPHEN, *Election Call: A Democratic Public Forum?* (Hansard Society, London, 1999).

—— and NORMANN, EMILIE, *New Media and Social Inclusion* (Hansard Society, London, 2000).

—— and ROSS, KAREN, *The Public, Politics and the Spaces Between:* Election Call *and Democratic Accountability* (Hansard Society, London, 2002).

—— and WARD, STEPHEN (eds.), *Spinning the Web: Online Campaigning in the 2005 General Election* (Hansard Society/ESRC, London, 2005).

COOK, GREG, 'The Labour Campaign', in Wring *et al.* (eds.), *Political Communications, 2005*.

CREWE, IVOR, and HARROP, MARTIN (eds.), *Political Communications: The General Election Campaign of 1983* (Cambridge University Press, Cambridge, 1986).

—— and —— (eds.), *Political Communications: The General Election Campaign of 1987* (Cambridge University Press, Cambridge, 1989).

—— and GOSSCHALK, BRIAN (eds.), *Political Communications: The General Election Campaign of 1992* (Cambridge University Press, Cambridge, 1995).

—— —— and BARTLE, JOHN (eds.), *Political Communications: Why Labour Won the General Election of 1997* (Frank Cass, London, 1998).

DEAKIN, NICHOLAS (ed.), *Colour and the British Electorate, 1964: Six Case Studies* (Pall Mall Press, London, 1965).

DELANEY, TIM, 'Labour's advertising campaign', in Worcester and Harrrop, *Political Communications, 1979*.

DENVER, DAVID, and HANDS, GORDON, *Modern Constituency Electioneering: Local Campaigning in the 1992 General Election* (Frank Cass, London, 1997).

—— and WRING, DOMINIC, 'Election unspun? Mediation of the campaign', in Geddes and Tonge (eds.), *Britain Decides, 2005*.

DINNAGE, ROSEMARY, 'Parliamentary advice bureau', *New Society*, 19 (24 Feb. 1972), 392–3.

DOWSE, ROBERT E., 'The M.P. and his surgery', *Political Studies*, 11 (1963), 333–41.

DURANT, RUTH, *Watling: A Survey of Social Life on a New Housing Estate* (P. S. King, London, 1939).

EVEN, MAYA, 'Television broadcasting of post-war elections and the case of 1983', in Crewe and Harrop (eds.), *Political Communications, 1983*.

FISHER, JUSTIN, 'Campaign finance', in Geddes and Tonge (eds.), *Britain Decides, 2005*.

—— *et al.*, 'Constituency campaigning in 2005: ever more centralization?', in Wring *et al.* (eds.), *Political Communications, 2005*.

GABER, IVOR, 'Debate on Section 93 of the Representation of the People Act: the case against', in Crewe *et al.* (eds.), *Political Communications, 1997*.

GARDINER, A. G., *Prophets, Priests and Kings* (Alston Rivers, London, 1908).

GEDDES, ANDREW, and TONGE, JONATHAN (eds.), *Britain Decides: The UK General Election 2005* (Palgrave, Basingstoke, 2005).

GORST, J. E., 'Elections of the future', *Fortnightly Review*, xxxiv (1883), 690–9.

GOULD, PHILIP, 'Labour's political strategy', in Wring *et al.* (eds.), *Political Communications, 2005*.

GREGO, JOSEPH, *A History of Parliamentary Elections and Electioneering in the Old Days* (Chatto & Windus, London, 1886).

GUREVITCH, MICHAEL, and BLUMLER, JAY G., 'The construction of election news: an observation study at the BBC', in James S. Ettema and D. Charles Whitney (eds.), *Individuals in Mass Media Organizations: Creativity and Consent* (SAGE, Beverly Hills, 1982).

HAMPTON, WILLIAM, *Democracy and Community: A Study of Politics in Sheffield* (Oxford University Press, London, 1970).

HARRISON, MARTIN, 'Television news coverage of the 1979 General Election', in Worcester and Harrop (eds.), *Political Communications, 1979*.

—— 'On Air', in Kavanagh and Butler, *Election of 2005*.

HOLT, ROBERT T., and TURNER, JOHN E., *Political Parties in Action: The Battle for Baron's Court* (The Free Press, New York, 1968).

HOWARD, ANTHONY, and WEST, RICHARD, *The Making of the Prime Minister* (Jonathan Cape, London, 1965).

JONES, NICHOLAS, *Soundbites and Spin Doctors: How Politicians Manipulate the Media and Vice Versa* (Cassell, London, 1995).

—— *Sultans of Spin: The Media and the New Labour Government* (1999: Orion, London, 2000).

KAVANAGH, DENNIS, and BUTLER, DAVID, *The British General Election of 2005* (Palgrave, Basingstoke, 2005).

KELLNER, PETER, 'The Labour campaign', in Ranney (ed.), *Britain at the Polls 1983*.

LIVINGSTONE, WILLIAM S., 'The Conservative campaign', in Penniman (ed.), *Britain at the Polls, 1979*.

LOWELL, A. L., *The Government of England*, 2 vols. (Macmillan, London, 1908).

McCALLUM, R. B., and READMAN, ALISON, *The British General Election of 1945* (Oxford University Press, Oxford, 1947).

MacDONALD, GUS, 'Election 500', in Crewe and Harrop (eds.), *Political Communications, 1983*.

McHENRY, DEAN E., *The Labour Party in Transition, 1931–1938* (Routledge, London, 1938).

MARSH, JAMES W., 'Representational changes: the constituency MP', in Philip Norton (ed.), *Parliament in the 1980s* (Basil Blackwell, Oxford, 1985).

MASS OBSERVATION, *The Voters' Choice: A Special Report by Mass Observation* (Art & Technics, London, 1950).

MATHESON, HILDA, *Broadcasting* (Thornton Butterworth, London, 1933).

MILNE, R. S., and MACKENZIE, H. C., *Straight Fight: A Study of Voting Behaviour in the Constituency of Bristol North East at the General Election of 1951* (Hansard Society, London, 1954).

—— and —— 'The Floating vote', *Political Studies*, 3 (1955), 65–8.

—— and —— *Marginal Seat: A Study of Voting Behaviour in the Constituency of Bristol North East at the General Election of 1955* (Hansard Society, London, 1958).

MITCHELL, AUSTIN, 'The local campaign in 1977–9', in Worcester and Harrop (eds.), *Political Communications, 1979*.

MORGAN, WILLIAM THOMAS, 'The British General Election of 1935', *South Atlantic Quarterly* 37, 2 (1938), 108–31.

MORRELL, FRANCES, *From the Electors of Bristol*, Spokesman Pamphlet No. 57 (Spokesman Press, Nottingham, 1977).

MUIR, J. RAMSAY, *How Britain is Governed: A Critical Analysis of Modern Developments in the British System of Government* (Constable, London, 1930).

MUNROE, RONALD, 'The Member of Parliament as representative: the view from the constituency', *Political Studies*, 25 (1977), 577–87.

News Chronicle [Henry W. Durant and W. Gregory], *Behind the Gallup Poll, With a Detailed Analysis of the 1951 General Election* (H. Clarke, London, n.d. [1951]).

News Chronicle, The General Election: Who Will Win? What the Gallup Poll Shows (H. Clark & Son, London, 1955).

NICHOLAS, H. G., *The British General Election of 1950* (Macmillan, London, 1951).

NOSSITER, T. J., *et al.*, 'Old values versus news values: the British 1992 General Election campaign on television', in Crewe and Gosschalk (eds.), *Political Communications, 1992*.

PEARSON, JOHN, and TURNER, GRAHAM, *The Persuasion Industry* (Eyre & Spottiswoode, London, 1965).

PENNIMAN, HOWARD R. (ed.), *Britain at the Polls: The Parliamentary Elections of 1974* (American Enterprise Institute, Washington, DC, 1975).

—— (ed.), *Britain at the Polls, 1979: A Study of the General Election* (American Enterprise Institute, Washington, DC, 1981).

PINTO-DUSCHINSKY, MICHAEL, 'The Conservative campaign: new techniques versus old', in Penniman (ed.), *Britain at the Polls, 1974.*

POLLOCK, JAMES K., LAING, LIONEL H., ELDERSVELD, SAMUEL J., JENKIN, THOMAS P., and SCAMMON, RICHARD M., *British Election Studies, 1950* (Geo. Wahr, Ann Arbor, 1951).

POWELL, CHRIS, 'The role of Labour's advertising in the 1997 General Election', in Crewe *et al.* (eds.), *Political Communications, 1997.*

RANNEY, AUSTIN (ed.), *Britain at the Polls 1983: A Study of the General Election* (American Enterprise Institute/Duke University Press, Durham, NC, 1985).

RATHBONE, ELEANOR, 'Changes in public life', in Ray Strachey (ed.), *Our Freedom and its Results: by Five Women* (Hogarth Press, London, 1936).

RENTOUL, J., *et al.*, 'People-metering: scientific research or clapometer?' in Crewe and Gosschalk (eds.), *Political Communications, 1992.*

RICHARDS, J. M., *The Castles on the Ground* (Architectural Press, London, 1946).

ROSE, RICHARD, *Influencing Voters: A Study of Campaign Rationality* (Faber & Faber, London, 1967).

SAUNDERS, WILLIAM, *The New Parliament, 1880* (Cassell, Peter, Galpin, London, n.d. [1880]).

SCAMMEL, MARGARET, and HARROP, MARTIN, 'The press disarmed', in Butler and Kavanagh, *The British General Election of 2001.*

SELF, BOB, 'The *Granada 500*: a continuing experiment in TV General Election coverage', in Worcester and Harrop (eds.), *Political Communications, 1979.*

SEMETKO, HOLLI, *et al.*, *The Formation of Campaign Agendas: A Comparative Analysis of Party and Media Roles in Recent American and British Elections* (Lawrence Erlbaum Associates, Hillsdale, NJ, 1991).

STACEY, MARGARET, *Tradition and Change: A Study of Banbury* (Oxford University Press, Oxford, 1960).

TILBY, A. WYATT, 'The Election and after', *Nineteenth Century and After*, CXVIII (Dec. 1935), 705–17.

TRENAMAN, JOSEPH, and MCQUAIL, DENIS, *Television and the Political Image: A Study of the Impact of Television on the 1959 General Election* (Methuen, London, 1961).

TYLER, RODNEY, *Campaign! The Selling of the Prime Minister* (Grafton Books, London, 1987).

WALLAS, GRAHAM, *Human Nature in Politics* (Archibald Constable, London, 1908).

WEST, RICHARD, 'Campaign journal', *Encounter*, 135 (Dec. 1964), 14–19.

WILLIAMS, PHILIP M., 'Two notes on the British electoral system: The M.P.'s personal vote', *Parliamentary Affairs*, 20 (1966–7), 24–30.

WORCESTER, ROBERT, M., and HARROP, MARTIN (eds.), *Political Communications: The General Election of 1979* (Geo. Allen & Unwin, London, 1982).

WRIGHT, THOMAS, *The Life of Colonel Fred Burnaby* (Everett, London, 1908).

WRING, DOMINIC, GREEN, JANE, MORTIMORE, ROGER, and ATKINSON, SIMON (eds.), *Political Communications: The General Election Campaign of 2005* (Palgrave, Basingstoke, 2007).

Other Published

ALBERY, WILLIAM, *A Parliamentary History of the Ancient Borough of Horsham, 1295–1885* (Longmans Green, London, 1927).

ALDERMAN, GEOFFREY, *British Elections: Myth and Reality* (B. T. Batsford, London, 1978).

ALLISON, K. J. (ed.), *A History of the County of York East Riding: Volume 6, The Borough and Liberties of Beverley* (Oxford University Press/IHR, Oxford, 1989).

ANDERSON, OLIVE, 'Hansard's hazards: an illustration from recent interpretations of married women's property law and the 1857 Divorce Act', *English Historical Review*, 112 (1997), 1202–15.

ATKINSON, MAX, *Our Masters' Voices: The Language and Body Language of Politics* (Methuen, London, 1984).

BALL, STUART, *Baldwin and the Conservative Party: The Crisis of 1929–1931* (Yale, New Haven, 1988).

—— 'Local Conservatism and the evolution of the party organization', in Anthony Seldon and Stuart Ball (eds.), *Conservative Century: The Conservative Party Since 1900* (Oxford University Press, Oxford, 1994).

BARKER, HANNAH, *Newspapers, Politics and English Society, 1695–1855* (Longman, Harlow, 2000).

BAUDRILLARD, JEAN, *In the Shadow of the Silent Majorities ... and Other Essays*, trans. Paul Foss, John Johnston, and Paul Patton (Semiotext(e), New York, 1983).

BEALES, DEREK, 'The electorate before and after 1832: the right to vote, and the opportunity', *Parliamentary History*, 11 (1992), 139–50.

BEARMAN, C. J., 'An examination of suffragette violence', *English Historical Review*, 120 (2005), 365–97.

BELCHEM, JOHN, and EPSTEIN, JAMES, 'The nineteenth-century gentleman leader revisited', *Social History*, 22, 2 (1997), 174–93.

BENNETT, GILL, ' "A most extraordinary and mysterious business": The Zinoviev letter of 1924', *Foreign & Commonwealth Office History Notes*, 14 (1999).

BENTLEY, MICHAEL, 'Gladstonian Liberals and provincial notables: Whitby politics, 1868–1880', *Historical Research*, 64 (1991), 172–85.

—— *Lord Salisbury's World: Conservative Environments in Late-Victorian Britain* (Cambridge University Press, Cambridge, 2001).

BERTHEZÈNE, CLARISSE, 'Creating Conservative Fabians: The Conservative party, political education and the founding of Ashridge College', *Past & Present*, 182 (2004), 211–40.

BIAGINI, EUGENIO, *Liberty, Retrenchment and Reform: Popular Liberalism in the Age of Gladstone, 1860–1880* (Cambridge University Press, Cambridge, 1992).

BINGHAM, ADRIAN, *Gender, Modernity and the Popular Press in Inter-War Britain* (Clarendon, Oxford, 2004).

BLACK, LAWRENCE, *The Political Culture of the Left in Affluent Britain, 1951–64* (Palgrave, Basingstoke, 2003).

BLEWETT, NEAL, 'The franchise in the United Kingdom, 1885–1918', *Past & Present*, 32 (1965), 27–56.

_____ *The Peers, the Parties and the People: The General Elections of 1910* (Macmillan, London, 1972).

BLUMLER, JAY G., and GUREVITCH, MICHAEL, *The Crisis of Public Communication* (Routledge, London, 1995).

BOOTH, A. H., *British Hustings, 1924–1950* (Frederick Muller, London, 1956).

BORN, GEORGINA, *Uncertain Vision: Birt, Dyke and the Reinvention of the BBC* (Secker & Warburg, London, 2004).

_____ 'Digitising democracy', in Lloyd and Seaton (eds.), *What Can be Done?*.

BOURDIEU, PIERRE, *On Television and Journalism*, trans. P. P. Ferguson (Pluto Press, London, 1998).

BOWDEN, SUE, 'The new consumerism', in Paul Johnson (ed.), *20th Century Britain: Economic, Social and Cultural Change* (Longman, Harlow, 1994).

BRADLEY, JAMES E., *Religion, Revolution and English Radicalism: Nonconformity in Eighteenth-Century Politics and Society* (Cambridge University Press, Cambridge, 1990).

BREWER, JOHN, 'Theater and counter-theater in Georgian politics: the mock elections at Garrat', *Radical History Review*, 22 (1979–80), 7–40.

BRIGGS, ASA, *Victorian People* (1954: Pelican, London, 1965).

_____ *The History of Broadcasting in the United Kingdom*, 5 vols. (Oxford University Press, Oxford, 1961–95).

BRODIE, MARC, *The Politics of the Poor: The East End of London, 1885–1914* (Clarendon Press, Oxford, 2004).

BUTLER, DAVID, *British General Elections since 1945* (Basil Blackwell, Oxford, 1989).

CHIGNELL, HUGH, 'The London Broadcasting Company (LBC) and Independent Radio News (IRN) Archive', *Twentieth-Century British History*, 18 (2007), 514–25.

CHURCHILL, WINSTON S. [jnr.], *His Father's Son: The Life of Randolph Churchill* (Weidenfeld & Nicolson, London, 1996).

CLARKE, PETER, *Lancashire and the New Liberalism* (Cambridge University Press, Cambridge, 1971).

_____ *Liberals and Social Democrats* (Cambridge University Press, Cambridge, 1978).

COCKERELL, MICHAEL, *Live from Number 10: The Inside Story of Prime Ministers and Television* (Faber & Faber, London, 1988).

COCKETT, RICHARD, *Twilight of Truth: Chamberlain, Appeasement and the Manipulation of the Press* (Weidenfeld & Nicolson, London, 1989).

_____ 'The Party, publicity and the media', in Anthony Seldon and Stuart Ball (eds.), *Conservative Century: The Conservative Party since 1900* (Oxford University Press, Oxford, 1994).

COETZEE, FRANS, 'Villa Toryism reconsidered: Conservatism and suburban sensibilities in late-Victorian Croydon', *Parliamentary History*, 16 (1997), 29–47.

COLEMAN, STEPHEN (ed.), *Televised Election Debates: International Perspectives* (Macmillan/Hansard Society, Basingstoke, 2000).

COLLINI, STEFAN, *Public Moralists: Political Thought and Intellectual Life in Britain, 1850–1930* (Clarendon Press, Oxford, 1991).

COOK, HARTLEY KEMBALL, *The Free and Independent: The Trials, Temptations and Triumphs of the Parliamentary Elector* (George Allen & Unwin, London, 1949).

CORNFORD, JAMES, 'The transformation of Conservatism in the late nineteenth century', *Victorian Studies*, 7 (1963), 35–66.

COWMAN, KRISTA, *'Mrs Brown is a Man and a Brother!': Women in Merseyside's Political Organisations, 1890–1920* (Liverpool University Press, Liverpool, 2004).

CRISELL, ANDREW, *An Introductory History of British Broadcasting* (Routledge, London, 1997).

DAVIS, JOHN, 'Slums and the vote, 1867–1890', *Historical Research*, 64 (1991), 375–88.

—— 'The enfranchisement of the urban poor in late-Victorian Britain', in Peter Ghosh and Lawrence Goldman (eds.), *Politics and Culture in Victorian Britain: Essays in Memory of Colin Matthew* (Oxford University Press, Oxford, 2006).

—— and TANNER, DUNCAN, 'The borough franchise after 1867', *Historical Research*, 69 (1996), 306–27.

DAVIS, RICHARD W., 'Deference and aristocracy in the time of the Great Reform Act', *American Historical Review*, 81 (1976), 532–9.

DAWSON, MICHAEL, 'Money and the real impact of the fourth Reform Act', *Historical Journal*, 35 (1992), 369–81.

—— 'Liberalism in Devon and Cornwall, 1910–1931: "the old-time religion"', *Historical Journal*, 38 (1995), 425–37.

—— 'Party politics and the provincial press in early twentieth-century England: the case of the South-West', *Twentieth-Century British History*, 9 (1998), 201–18.

DENVER, DAVID, *Elections and Voting Behaviour in Britain*, 2nd edn. (Harvester Wheatsheaf, Hemel Hempstead, 1994).

DIXON, PETER, *Canning: Politician and Statesman* (Weidenfeld & Nicolson, London, 1976).

DRIVER, CECIL, *Tory Radical: The Life of Richard Oastler* (Oxford University Press, New York, 1946).

DUNBABIN, JOHN P. D., 'Some implications of the 1885 British shift towards single-member constituencies: a note', *English Historical Review*, 109 (1994), 89–100.

EASTWOOD, DAVID, 'Contesting the politics of deference, 1820–60', in Lawrence and Taylor (eds.), *Party, State and Society*.

EMDEN, CECIL S., *The People and the Constitution: Being a History of the Development of the People's Influence in British Government* (Clarendon Press, Oxford, 1933).

EPSTEIN, JAMES, 'Understanding the Cap of Liberty: symbolic practice and social conflict in early nineteenth-century England', *Past & Present* 122 (1989), 75–118.

FENBY, CHARLES, *The Other Oxford: The Life and Times of Frank Gray and his Father* (Lund Humphries, London, 1970).

FERRIS, JOHN, and BAR-JOSEPH, URI, 'Getting Marlowe to hold his tongue: the Conservative party, the intelligence services and the Zinoviev letter', *Intelligence and National Security*, 8 (1993), 100–37.

FIELDING, STEVEN, ' "Don't know and don't care": popular political attitudes in Labour's Britain, 1945–51', in Nick Tiratsoo (ed.), *The Attlee Years* (Pinter, London, 1991).

——— 'Rethinking Labour's 1964 campaign', *Contemporary British History*, 21 (2007), 309–24.

——— THOMPSON, PETER, and TIRATSOO, NICK, *'England Arise!': The Labour Party and Popular Politics in 1940s Britain* (Manchester University Press, Manchester, 1995).

FISHER, J. R., 'Issues and influence: two by-elections in south Nottinghamshire in the mid nineteenth century', *Historical Journal*, 24 (1981), 155–65.

——— 'The limits of deference: agricultural communities in a mid-nineteenth century election campaign', *Journal of British Studies*, 21 (1981), 90–105.

FORRESTER, ERIC G., *Northamptonshire County Elections and Electioneering, 1695–1832* (Oxford University Press, London, 1941).

FRANCIS, MARTIN, 'The Labour Party: modernisation and the politics of restraint', in Becky Conekin, Franck Mort, and Chris Waters (eds.), *Moments of Modernity: Reconstructing Britain, 1945–1964* (Rivers Oram, London, 1999), 114–33.

FREEDLAND, JONATHAN, *Bring Home the Revolution: How Britain Can Live the American Dream* (Fourth Estate, London, 1998).

GAMMAGE, ROBERT GEORGE, *History of the Chartist Movement, 1837–1854*, 2nd edn. (Browne & Browne, Newcastle, 1894).

GASH, NORMAN, *Politics in the Age of Peel: A Study in the Technique of Parliamentary Representation, 1830–1850* (Longmans, London, 1953).

GATRELL, VIC, *City of Laughter: Sex and Satire in Eighteenth-Century London* (Walker, New York, 2007).

GIBSON, RACHEL, and WARD, STEPHEN (eds.), *Reinvigorating Democracy? British Politics and the Internet* (Ashgate, Aldershot, 2000).

GILBERT, MARTIN, *Winston S. Churchill*, 8 vols. (Heinemann, London, 1966–88).

GLIDDON, PAUL, 'The political importance of provincial newspapers, 1903–1945: the Rowntrees and the Liberal press', *Twentieth-Century British History*, 14 (2003), 24–42.

GOLBY, JOHN, 'A great electioneer and his motives: the Fourth Duke of Newcastle', *Historical Journal*, 8 (1965), 201–18.

GOLDIE, GRACE WYNDHAM, *Facing the Nation: Television and Politics, 1936–1976* (Bodley Head, London, 1977).

GRANT, MARIEL, *Propaganda and the Role of the State in Inter-War Britain* (Clarendon Press, Oxford, 1994).

GREEN, E. H. H., *The Crisis of Conservatism: The Politics, Economics and Ideology of the British Conservative Party, 1880–1914* (Routledge, London, 1995).

—— 'The Conservative Party, the state and the electorate', in Lawrence and Taylor (eds.), *Party, State and Society*.

—— *Ideologies of Conservatism: Conservative Political Ideas in the Twentieth Century* (Oxford University Press, Oxford, 2002).

GRIFFITHS, P. C., 'The Caucus and the Liberal party in 1886', *History*, 61 (1976), 183–97.

GWYN, WILLIAM B., *Democracy and the Cost of Politics in Britain* (Athlone Press, London, 1962).

HALL, CATHERINE, McCLELLAND, KEITH, and RENDALL, JANE, *Defining the Victorian Nation: Class, Race, Gender and the Reform Act of 1867* (Cambridge University Press, Cambridge, 2000).

HAMPTON, MARK, *Visions of the Press in Britain, 1850–1950* (University of Illinois Press, Urbana, 2004).

—— 'Rethinking the "New Journalism", 1850s–1930s', *Journal of British Studies*, 43 (2004), 278–90.

HANHAM, H. J., *Elections and Party Management: Politics in the Time of Disraeli and Gladstone* (Longmans, London, 1959).

HARRIS, KENNETH, *Attlee* (Weidenfeld & Nicolson, London, 1982).

HARRIS, SANDRA, 'Evasive action: how politicians respond to questions in political interviews', in Paddy Scannell (ed.), *Broadcast Talk* (SAGE, London, 1991).

HARROP, MARTIN, HEATH, ANTHONY, and OPENSHAW, STAN, 'Does neighbourhood influence voting behaviour—and why?', in Ivor Crewe *et al.* (eds.), *British Elections and Parties Yearbook, 1991* (Harvester Wheatsheaf, Hemel Hempstead, 1992).

HART, RODERICK P., *Seducing America: How Television Charms the Modern Voter* (Oxford University Press, New York, 1994).

HELMORE, L. M., *Corrupt and Illegal Practices: A General Survey and a Case Study of an Election Petition* (Routledge, London, 1967).

HILL, R. L., *Toryism and the People, 1832–1846* (Constable, London, 1929).

HILTON, BOYD, *The Age of Atonement: The Influence of Evangelicalism on Social and Economic Thought, 1785–1865* (Clarendon, Oxford, 1988).

—— *A Mad, Bad and Dangerous People? England, 1783–1846* (Oxford University Press, Oxford, 2006).

HOLLINS, T. J., 'The Conservative Party and film propaganda between the wars', *English Historical Review*, 96 (1981), 359–69.

HOPPEN, K. THEODORE, 'The franchise and electoral politics in England and Ireland, 1832–1885', *History*, 70 (1985), 202–17.

—— 'Grammars of electoral violence in nineteenth-century England and Ireland', *English Historical Review*, 109 (1994), 597–620.

—— *The Mid-Victorian Generation, 1846–1886* (Oxford University Press, Oxford, 1998).

HORNE, ALISTAIR, *Macmillan, 1957–1986: The Official Biography*, vol. II (Macmillan, London, 1989).

HOWARTH, JANET, 'The Liberal revival in Northamptonshire, 1880–1895: a case study in late nineteenth-century elections', *Historical Journal*, 12 (1969), 78–118.

HURST, MICHAEL, 'Liberal versus Liberal: the general election of 1874 in Bradford and Sheffield', *Historical Journal*, 15 (1972), 669–713.

JAGGARD, EDWIN, 'The 1841 British General Election: a reconsideration', *Australian Journal of Politics and History*, 30, 1 (1984), 99–114.

—— 'Small town politics in mid-Victorian Britain', *History*, 89, 293 (2004), 3–29.

JALLAND, PAT, *Women, Marriage and Politics, 1860–1914* (Oxford University Press, Oxford, 1986).

JAMES, CHRISTOPHER J., *MP for Dewsbury: One Hundred Years of Parliamentary Representation* (the author, Brighouse, 1970).

JARVIS, DAVID, 'Mrs Maggs and Betty: the Conservative appeal to women voters in the 1920s', *Twentieth-Century British History*, 5 (1994), 129–52.

—— 'British Conservatism and class politics in the 1920s', *English Historical Review*, 111 (1996), 59–84.

JEPHSON, HENRY, *The Platform: Its Rise and Progress*, 2 vols. (Macmillan, London, 1892).

JOHNSTON, R. J., *The Geography of English Politics: The 1983 General Election* (Croom Helm, London, 1985).

—— and PATTIE, CHARLES, *Putting Voters in their Place: Geography and Elections in Great Britain* (Oxford University Press, Oxford, 2006).

JONES, ALED, *Powers of the Press: Newspapers, Power and the Public in Nineteenth-Century England* (Scolar, Aldershot, 1996).

JONES, BILL, 'The pitiless probing eye: politicians and the broadcast political interview', *Parliamentary Affairs*, 46 (1993), 66–90.

JORDAN, H. DONALDSON, 'The reports of Parliamentary debates, 1803–1908', *Economica*, xi (1931), 437–49.

JOYCE, PATRICK, *Work, Society and Politics: The Culture of the Factory in later Victorian England* (Harvester, Brighton, 1980).

—— *Visions of the People: Industrial England and the Question of Class, 1840–1914* (Cambridge University Press, Cambridge, 1991).

—— *Democratic Subjects: The Self and the Social in Nineteenth-Century England* (Cambridge University Press, Cambridge, 1994).

KAMPFNER, JOHN, *Robin Cook* (revised edn., Phoenix, London, 1999).

KAVANAGH, DENNIS, 'The United Kingdom', in David Butler and Austin Ranney (eds.), *Electioneering: A Comparative Study of Continuity and Change* (Clarendon Press, Oxford, 1992).

—— *Election Campaigning: The New Marketing of Politics* (Blackwell, Oxford, 1995).

KOSS, STEPHEN, *The Rise and Fall of the Political Press in Britain* (Fontana, London, 1990).

LANA, RENATA, 'Women and Foxite strategy in the Westminster election of 1784', *Eighteenth-Century Life*, 26 (2002), 46–69.

LAWRENCE, JON, 'Class and gender in the making of urban Toryism, 1880–1914', *English Historical Review*, 108 (1993), 629–52.

—— 'The decline of popular politics?', *Parliamentary History*, 13 (1994), 333–7.

—— *Speaking for the People: Party, Language and Popular Politics in England, 1867–1914* (Cambridge University Press, Cambridge, 1998).

—— 'Labour—the myths it has lived by', in Duncan Tanner, Pat Thane, and Nick Tiratsoo (eds.), *Labour's First Century* (Cambridge University Press, Cambridge, 2000), 341–66.

—— 'Contesting the male polity: the suffragettes and the politics of disruption in Edwardian Britain', in Amanda Vickery (ed.), *Women, Privilege and Power: British Politics, 1750 to the Present* (Stanford University Press, Stanford, Calif., 2001).

—— 'Fascist violence and the politics of public order in inter-war Britain: the Olympia debate revisited', *Historical Research*, 76, 192 (2003), 238–67.

—— 'Forging a peaceable kingdom: war, violence and fear of brutalization in post First World War Britain', *Journal of Modern History*, 75 (2003), 557–89.

—— 'Why Olympia mattered', *Historical Research*, 78, 200 (2005), 263–72.

—— 'The transformation of British public politics after the First World War', *Past & Present*, 190 (2006), 185–216.

—— and TAYLOR, MILES (eds.), *Party, State and Society: Electoral Behaviour in Britain since 1820* (Scolar Press, Aldershot, 1997).

LEE, ALAN J., *The Origins of the Popular Press in England, 1855–1914* (Croom Helm, London, 1976).

LEES-MARSHMENT, JENNIFER, *Political Marketing and British Political Parties: The Party's Just Begun* (Manchester University Press, Manchester, 2001).

LEWIS, EDWARD G., 'British by-elections as a reflection of public opinion', *University of California Publications in Political Science*, 1 (1943–5), 147–241.

LEWIS, JUDITH S., '1784 and all that: Aristocratic women and electoral politics', in Amanda Vickery (ed.), *Women, Privilege and Power: British Politics, 1750 to the Present* (Stanford University Press, Stanford, Calif., 2001).

LIGHT, ALISON, *Forever England: Femininity, Literature and Conservatism Between the Wars* (Routledge, London, 1991).

LLOYD, JOHN, *What the Media are Doing to Our Politics* (Constable, London, 2004).

—— and SEATON, JEAN (eds.), *What Can be Done? Making the Media and Politics Better* (Blackwell/*Political Quarterly*, Oxford, 2006).

LLOYD, TREVOR, 'Uncontested seats in British general elections, 1852–1910', *Historical Journal*, 8 (1965), 260–5.

LYNCH, PATRICIA, *The Liberal Party in Rural England, 1885–1910: Radicalism and Community* (Oxford University Press, Oxford, 2003).

MCCARTHY, HELEN, 'Parties, voluntary associations and democratic politics in interwar Britain', *Historical Journal* 50, 4 (2007), 891–912.

McCORMACK, MATTHEW, *The Independent Man: Citizenship and Gender Politics in Georgian England*, Gender in History series (Manchester University Press, Manchester, 2005).

—— (ed.), *Public Men: Masculinity and Politics in Modern Britain* (Palgrave, Basingstoke, 2007).

McKIBBIN, ROSS, *Classes and Cultures: England, 1918–1951* (Oxford University Press, Oxford, 1998).

McNAIR, BRIAN, *Journalism and Democracy: An Evaluation of the Political Public Space* (Routledge, London, 2000).

MARKHAM, JOHN, *The 1820 Parliamentary Election at Hedon: A Study of Electioneering in a Yorkshire Borough before the Passing of the Reform Act* (the author, Beverley, n.d. [1971]).

—— *Nineteenth-Century Parliamentary Elections in East Yorkshire* (East Yorkshire Local History Society Series, no. 37, Beverley, 1982).

MARQUAND, DAVID, *Ramsay MacDonald* (Jonathan Cape, London, 1977).

MARTIN, RALPH G., *Lady Randolph Churchill: A Biography*, 2 vols. (Sphere Books, London, 1974).

MATTHEW, H. C. G., *Gladstone, 1809–1874* (Oxford University Press, Oxford, 1986).

—— 'Rhetoric and politics in Great Britain, 1860–1950', in P. J. Waller (ed.), *Politics and Social Change in Modern Britain: Essays Presented to A. F. Thompson* (Harvester, Brighton, 1987).

—— *Gladstone, 1875–1898* (Clarendon Press, Oxford, 1995).

—— McKIBBIN, R. I., and KAY, J. A., 'The franchise factor in the rise of the Labour Party', *English Historical Review*, 91 (1976), 723–52.

MEISEL, JOSEPH S., *Public Speech and the Culture of Public Life in the Age of Gladstone* (Columbia University Press, New York, 2001).

MIALL, LEONARD, *Inside the BBC: British Broadcasting Characters* (Weidenfeld & Nicolson, London, 1994).

MILLER, W. L., 'Social class and party choice in England: a new analysis', *British Journal of Political Science*, 8 (1978), 257–84.

—— 'Class, region and strata at the British General Election of 1979', *Parliamentary Affairs*, 32 (1979), 376–82.

—— et al., *How Voters Change: The 1987 British General Election in Perspective* (Clarendon Press, Oxford, 1990).

MITCHELL, AUSTIN, *Election '45: Reflections on the Revolution in Britain* (Fabian Society/Bellew, London, 1995)

MONYPENNY, WILLIAM FLAVELLE, and BUCKLE, GEORGE EARLE, *The Life of Benjamin Disraeli, Earl of Beaconsfield*, 2nd edn., 2 vols. (John Murray, London, 1929).

MOORE, D. C., *The Politics of Deference: A Study of the Mid-Nineteenth-Century English Political System* (Harvester, Hassocks, 1976).

MORGAN, KENNETH O., *Michael Foot: A Life* (Harper, London, 2007).

MORRIS, HOMER LAWRENCE, *Parliamentary Franchise Reform in England from 1885 to 1918*, Studies in History, Economics and Public Law (Columbia University Press, New York, 1921).

NICHOLAS, H. G., *To the Hustings: Election Scenes from English Fiction* (Cassell, London, 1956).

NICHOLAS, SIÂN, 'The construction of a national identity: Stanley Baldwin, "Englishness" and the mass media in inter-war Britain', in Martin Francis and Ina Zweiniger-Bargielowska (eds.), *The Conservatives and British Society, 1880–1990* (University of Wales Press, Cardiff, 1996).

NORRIS, PIPPA, 'John Stuart Mill versus bigotry, bribery and beer', *Corruption and Reform*, 1 (1986), 79–100.

_____ *Electoral Change since 1945*, Making Contemporary Britain series (Blackwell, Oxford, 1997).

_____ *A Virtuous Circle: Political Communications in Post-Industrial Democracies* (Cambridge University Press, Cambridge, 2000).

_____ et al., *On Message: Communicating the Campaign* (SAGE, London, 1999).

NORTON, PHILIP, and WOOD, DAVID, 'Constituency service by Members of Parliament: does it contribute to a personal vote?', *Parliamentary Affairs*, 43 (1990), 196–208.

_____ and _____ *Back From Westminster: British Members of Parliament and their Constituents* (University of Kentucky Press, Lexington, 1993).

OATES, SARAH, OWEN, DIANA, and GIBSON, RACHEL K. (eds.), *The Internet and Politics: Citizens, Voters and Activists* (Routledge, London, 2006).

O'GORMAN, FRANK, *Voters, Patrons and Parties: The Unreformed Electorate of Hanoverian England, 1734–1832* (Clarendon Press, Oxford, 1989).

_____ 'Campaign rituals and ceremonies: the social meaning of elections in England, 1780–1860', *Past & Present*, 135 (1992), 79–115.

_____ 'The culture of elections in England: from the Glorious Revolution to the First World War, 1688–1914', in Eduardo Posado-Carbó (ed.), *Elections Before Democracy: The History of Elections in Europe and Latin America* (Macmillan, Basingstoke, 1996).

O'LEARY, CORNELIUS, *The Elimination of Corrupt Practices in British Elections, 1868–1911* (Oxford University Press, Oxford, 1962).

OLECHNOWICZ, ANDRZEJ, *Working-Class Housing in England between the Wars: The Becontree Estate* (Clarendon Press, Oxford, 1997).

OSTROGORSKI, M., *Democracy and the Organization of Political Parties*, 2 vols. (Macmillan, London, 1902).

OWEN, NICHOLAS, 'MacDonald's parties: the Labour Party and the "aristocratic embrace", 1922–31', *Twentieth-Century British History*, 18 (2007), 1–53.

PARRY, JONATHAN, *The Rise and Fall of Liberal Government in Victorian Britain* (Yale University Press, New Haven, 1993).

PEDDIE, ROBERT ALEXANDER, *An Outline of the History of Printing to which is Added the History of Printing in Colours* (Grafton, London, 1917).

PEELE, GILLIAN, 'St George's and the Empire crusade', in Chris Cook and John Ramsden (eds.), *By-elections in British Politics* (Macmillan, London, 1973), 79–108.

PELLING, HENRY, *A Short History of the Labour Party*, 6th edn. (Macmillan, London, 1978).

PHILLIPS, JOHN A., *The Great Reform Bill in the Boroughs: English Electoral Behaviour, 1818–1841* (Clarendon Press, Oxford, 1992).

——and WETHERELL, CHARLES, 'The Great Reform Act of 1832 and the rise of partisanship', *Journal of Modern History*, 63 (1991), 621–46.

——and —— 'The Great Reform Act of 1832 and the political modernization of England', *American Historical Review*, 100 (1995), 411–36.

PICKERING, PAUL, 'Class without words: symbolic communication in the Chartist movement', *Past & Present* 112 (1986), 144–62.

PINTO-DUSCHINSKY, MICHAEL, *British Political Finance, 1930–1980* (American Enterprise Institute, Washington, DC, 1981).

POCOCK, J. G. A., *The Machiavellian Moment: Florentine Political Thought and the Atlantic Republican Tradition* (Princeton University Press, Princeton, 1975).

POLLARD, ARTHUR, *Trollope's Political Novels* (Hull Printers, Hull, 1968).

PREST, JOHN, *Politics in the Age of Cobden* (Macmillan, London, 1977).

PRONAY, NICHOLAS, 'British newsreels in the 1930s, 1: audience and producers', *History*, 56, 188 (1971), 411–18.

—— 'The newsreels: the illusion of actuality', in Paul Smith (ed.), *The Historian and Film* (Cambridge University Press, Cambridge, 1976), 95–119.

PUGH, MARTIN, *The Tories and the People, 1880–1935* (Blackwell, Oxford, 1985).

—— *The March of the Women: A Revisionist Account of the Campaign for Women's Suffrage, 1866–1914* (Oxford University Press, Oxford, 2000).

—— 'Working-class experience and state social welfare, 1908–1914: old age pensions reconsidered', *Historical Journal*, 45 (2002), 775–96.

QUALTER, TERENCE H., *Graham Wallas and the Great Society* (Macmillan, London, 1980).

RAMSDEN, JOHN, *The Age of Balfour and Baldwin, 1902–1940* (Longman, London, 1978).

—— 'Baldwin and film', in Nicholas Pronay and D. W. Spring (eds.), *Propaganda, Politics and Film, 1918–45* (Macmillan, London, 1982).

—— *The Age of Churchill and Eden, 1940–1957* (Longman, Harlow, 1995).

—— *The Winds of Change: Macmillan to Heath, 1957–1975* (Longman, London, 1996).

READMAN, PAUL, *Land and Nation in England: Patriotism, National Identity and the Politics of Land, 1880–1914* (RHS/Boydell & Brewer, Woodbridge, 2008).

REID, DOUGLAS A., 'Weddings, weekdays, work and leisure in urban England 1791–1911: the decline of Saint Monday revisited', *Past & Present*, 153 (1996), 135–63.

RHODES, PETER, *The Loaded Hour: A History of the* Express & Star (S.P.A., Hanley Swan, Worcs., 1992).

RICHTER, DONALD C., 'The role of mob riot in Victorian elections, 1865–1885', *Victorian Studies*, 15 (1971), 19–28.

——— *Riotous Victorians* (Athens, Ohio, 1981).

RIX, KATHRYN, ' "Go out into the highways and the hedges": the diary of Michael Sykes, Conservative political lecturer, 1895 and 1907–8', *Parliamentary History*, 20 (2001), 209–31.

——— 'The elimination of corrupt practices in British elections? Reassessing the impact of the 1883 Corrupt Practices Act', *English Historical Review*, CXXIII (2008), 65–97.

ROBERTS, MATTHEW, ' "Villa Toryism" and popular Conservatism in Leeds, 1885–1902', *Historical Journal*, 49 (2006), 217–46.

ROBSON, JOHN M., *What did he say? Editing Nineteenth-Century Speeches from Hansard and the Newspapers*, F. E. L. Prestley Lecture Series (University of Lethbridge Press, Alberta, 1988).

ROGERS, NICHOLAS, *Whigs and Cities: Popular Politics in the Age of Walpole and Pitt* (Oxford University Press, Oxford, 1989).

——— *Crowds, Culture, and Politics in Georgian Britain* (Clarendon Press, Oxford, 1998).

——— 'Crowds and political festival in Georgian England', in Tim Harris (ed.), *The Politics of the Excluded, c.1500–1850* (Palgrave, Basingstoke, 2001).

ROSE, RICHARD, and MCALLISTER, IAN, *Voters Begin to Choose: From Closed-Class to Open Elections in Britain* (SAGE, London, 1986).

ROSENBAUM, MARTIN, *From Soapbox to Soundbite: Party Political Campaigning in Britain since 1945* (Macmillan, Basingstoke, 1997).

ROWE, E. A., 'Broadcasting and the 1929 General Election', *Renaissance and Modern Studies*, 12 (1968), 108–19.

RUDÉ, GEORGE, 'The Middlesex Electors of 1768–1769', *English Historical Review*, 75 (1960), 601–17.

——— *Wilkes and Liberty: A Social Study of 1763 to 1774* (Oxford University Press, Oxford, 1962).

RUSSELL, A. K., *Liberal Landslide: The General Election of 1906* (David & Charles, Newton Abbott, 1973).

SACK, JAMES A., 'The House of Lords and parliamentary patronage, 1802–1832', *Historical Journal*, 23 (1980), 913–37.

SALMON, PHILIP, *Electoral Reform at Work: Local Politics and National Parties, 1832–1841* (RHS/Boydell Press, Woodbridge, 2002).

SÄRLVIK, BO, and CREWE, IVOR, *Decade of Dealignment: The Conservative Victory of 1979 and Electoral Trends in the 1970s* (Cambridge University Press, Cambridge, 1983).

SAVAGE, MIKE, 'Urban politics and the rise of the Labour party, 1919–39', in Lynn Jamieson and Helen Corr (eds.), *State, Private Life and Political Change* (Macmillan, Basingstoke, 1990).

SAVILLE, JOHN, *1848: The British State and the Chartist Movement* (Cambridge University Press, Cambridge, 1987).

SCAMMEL, MARGARET, *Designer Politics: How Elections are Won* (Macmillan, Basingstoke, 1995).

SCANNELL, PADDY, and CARDIFF, DAVID, *A Social History of Broadcasting: Volume One, 1922–1939: Serving the Nation* (Blackwell, Oxford, 1991).

SCOTT, GEORGE, *Reporter Anonymous: The Story of the Press Association* (Hutchinson, London, 1968).

SEYMOUR, CHARLES, *Electoral Reform in England and Wales: The Development and Operation of the Parliamentary Franchise, 1832–1885* (David & Charles, Newton Abbot, 1970).

SEYMOUR-URE, COLIN, *The Political Impact of Mass Media* (Constable, London, 1974).

SMITH, E. A., 'The Yorkshire elections of 1806 and 1807: a study in electoral management', *Northern History*, 2 (1967), 62–90.

SMITH, F. B., *The Making of the Second Reform Bill* (Cambridge University Press, Cambridge, 1966).

SOUTHALL, HUMPHREY, 'Mobility, the artisan community and popular politics in early nineteenth-century England', in Gerry Kearns and Charles W. J. Withers, *Urbanising Britain: Essays on Class and Community in the Nineteenth Century* (Cambridge University Press, Cambridge, 1991).

STANNAGE, TOM, *Baldwin Thwarts the Opposition* (Croom Helm, London, 1980).

STEELE, DAVID, 'Gladstone and Palmerston, 1855–65', in Peter J. Jagger (ed.), *Gladstone, Politics and Religion: A Collection of Founder's Day Lectures Delivered at St Deiniol's Library, Hawarden, 1967–83* (Macmillan, London, 1985).

STEVENSON, JOHN, *Third Party Politics since 1945: Liberals, Alliance and Liberal Democrats* (Blackwell, Oxford, 1993).

STREET, JOHN, *Mass Media, Politics and Democracy* (Palgrave, Basingstoke, 2001).

SWANSON, DAVID L., and MANCINI, PAOLO, *Politics, Media and Modern Democracy: An International Study of Innovations in Electoral Campaigning and their Consequences* (Praeger, Westport, Conn., 1996).

SWEET, ROSEMARY, 'Freemen and independence in English borough politics, c.1770–1830', *Past & Present*, 161 (1998), 84–115.

TANNER, DUNCAN, 'The parliamentary electoral system, the "fourth" Reform Act and the rise of Labour in England and Wales', *Bulletin of the Institute of Historical Research*, 56 (1983), 205–19.

—— 'Gender, civic culture and politics in South Wales: explaining Labour municipal policy, 1918–39', in Matthew Worley (ed.), *Labour's Grass Roots: Essays on the Activities and Experiences of Local Labour Parties and Members, 1918–1945*, Studies in Labour History (Ashgate, Aldershot, 2005).

TAYLOR, A. J. P., *English History, 1914–1945* (Oxford University Press, Oxford, 1965).

TAYLOR, ANDREW, 'Speaking to democracy: The Conservative Party and mass opinion from the 1920s to the 1930s', in Stuart Ball and Ian Holliday (eds.), *Mass Conservatism: The Conservatives and the Public since the 1880s* (Frank Cass, London, 2002).

TAYLOR, ANTHONY, 'Palmerston and Radicalism, 1847–1865', *Journal of British Studies*, 33 (1994), 157–79.

TAYLOR, H. A., *Jix: Viscount Brentford* (Stanley Paul, London, 1933).

TAYLOR, MILES, 'Interests, parties and the state: the urban electorate in England, c. 1820–72', in Lawrence and Taylor (eds.), *Party, State and Society*.

—— *Ernest Jones, Chartism, and the Romance of Politics, 1819–1869* (Oxford University Press, Oxford, 2003).

THOLFSEN, T. R., 'The origins of the Birmingham caucus', *Historical Journal*, 2 (1959), 161–84.

THOMPSON, JAMES, ' "Pictorial lies"?—Posters and politics in Britain, c. 1880–1914', *Past & Present*, 197 (2007), 177–210.

THORNE, R. G. (ed.), *The History of Parliament: The House of Commons, 1790–1820*, 5 vols. (Secker & Warburg, London, 1986).

THORPE, ANDREW, *The British General Election of 1931* (Clarendon, Oxford, 1991).

TILLY, CHARLES, *Popular Contention in Great Britain, 1758–1834* (Harvard University Press, Cambridge, Mass., 1995).

TINGAY, LANCE O., *Anthony Trollope Politician: His Parliamentary Candidature at Beverley, 1868* (Silverbridge Press, London, 1988).

TRENTMANN, FRANK, 'Bread, milk and democracy: consumption and citizenship in twentieth-century Britain', in Martin Daunton and Matthew Hilton (eds.), *The Politics of Consumption: Material Culture and Citizenship in Europe and America* (Berg, Oxford and New York, 2001).

—— 'National identity and consumer politics: free trade and tariff reform', in Donald Winch and Patrick K. O'Brien (eds.), *The Political Economy of British Historical Experience* (British Academy/Oxford University Press, Oxford, 2002).

TURNER, JOHN, 'The Labour vote and the franchise after 1918', in Peter Denley and Deian Hopkin (eds.), *History and Computing* (Manchester University Press, Manchester, 1987), 136–43.

VERNON, JAMES, *Politics and the People: A Study in English Political Culture, c.1815–1867* (Cambridge University Press, Cambridge, 1993).

VINCENT, JOHN, *The Formation of the British Liberal Party, 1857–68* (1966: Pelican edn., London, 1972).

WADSWORTH, A. P., 'Newspaper circulations, 1800–1954', *Transactions of the Manchester Statistical Society* (1954–5), 1–41.

WALKER, DAVID, and JONES, NICHOLAS, *Invisible Political Actors: The Press as Agents of Anti-Politics* (New Politics Network, London, 2004).

WALKER, LINDA E., 'Party political women: a comparative study of Liberal women and the Primrose League, 1890–1914', in Jane Rendall (ed.), *Equal or Different: Women's Politics, 1800–1914* (Blackwell, Oxford, 1987).

WALLER, P. J., *Democracy and Sectarianism: A Political and Social History of Liverpool, 1868–1939* (Liverpool University Press, Liverpool, 1981).

WARD, PAUL, *Red Flag and Union Jack, Englishness, Patriotism and the British Left, 1881–1924* (RHS/Boydell & Brewer, Woodbridge, 1998).

WARD, STEPHEN, GIBSON, RACHEL, and LUSOLI, WAINER, 'Online participation and mobilisation in Britain: hype, hope and reality', *Parliamentary Affairs*, 56 (2003), 652–68.

WIENER, MARTIN J., *Between Two Worlds: The Political Thought of Graham Wallas* (Clarendon Press, Oxford, 1971).

WILLIAMS, DAVID, *Keeping The Peace: The Police and Public Order* (Hutchinson, London, 1967).

WILLIAMS, PHILIP M., *Hugh Gaitskell: A Political Biography* (Jonathan Cape, London, 1979).

WILLIAMSON, PHILIP, ' "Safety First": Baldwin, the Conservative party, and the 1929 General Election', *Historical Journal*, 25 (1982), 385–409.

_____ *Stanley Baldwin: Conservative Leadership and National Values* (Cambridge University Press, Cambridge, 1999).

WILSON, KATHLEEN, *The Sense of the People: Politics, Culture and Imperialism in England, 1715–1785* (Cambridge University Press, Cambridge, 1995).

WINDSCHEFFEL, ALEX, *Popular Conservatism in Imperial London, 1868–1906* (RHS/Boydell Press, Woodbridge, 2007).

WORLEY, MATTHEW, 'A call to action: New Party candidates and the 1931 General Election', *Parliamentary History*, 27, 2 (2008), 236–55.

WRING, DOMINIC, *The Politics of Marketing the Labour Party* (Palgrave Macmillan, Basingstoke, 2005).

Unpublished Secondary

BARBARY, VICTORIA, 'Popular politics in Newcastle-upon-Tyne, 1850–c.1862' (University of Durham, MA thesis, 2003).

BEERS, LAURA DUMOND, ' "Selling Socialism": Labour, Democracy and the Mass Media, 1900–1939' (Harvard University, Ph.D. thesis, 2007).

LAWRENCE, JON, and GOOD, KIT, 'Electing John Bull: The changing face of British elections, 1895–1935' (ESRC RES-000-22-0345) [end of award report].

MANAI, MOHAMED ADEL, 'Electoral politics in mid-nineteenth-century Lancashire' (University of Lancashire, Ph.D. thesis, 1991).

RIX, KATHRYN, 'The party agent and English electoral culture, 1880–1906' (University of Cambridge, Ph.D. thesis, 2001).

SWADDLE, K. M. O., 'Coping with a mass electorate: A study in the evolution of constituency electioneering in Britain, with special emphasis on the periods which followed the Reform Acts of 1884 and 1918' (University of Oxford, D.Phil. thesis, 1990).

TAYLOR, ANTHONY D., 'Ernest Jones: His later career and the structure of Manchester politics, 1861–1869' (University of Birmingham, MA thesis, 1984).

THACKERAY, DAVID, 'British popular Conservatism and the radical Right, c.1910–1924' (University of Cambridge, Ph.D. thesis, in progress).

THOMPSON, JAMES, 'The idea of "public opinion" in Britain, 1870–1914' (University of Cambridge, Ph.D. thesis, 2000).

WALKER, LINDA E., 'The women's movement in England in the late nineteenth and early twentieth centuries' (University of Manchester, Ph.D. thesis, 1984).

Index